PHILOSOPHIC CONFLICTS IN AMERICAN EDUCATION, 1893–2000

Related Titles of Interest

Current Issues and Trends in Education
Jerry Aldridge & Renitta Goldman
ISBN: 0-321-07978-7

*The Way Schools Work: A Sociological
  Analysis of Education,* Third Edition
Kathleen Bennett de Marrais & Margaret LeCompte
ISBN: 0-8013-1956-0

*How to Develop a Professional Portfolio:
  A Manual for Teachers,* Third Edition
Dorothy M. Campbell, Pamela Bondi Cignetti,
  Beverly J. Melenyzer, Diane H. Nettles, &
  Richard M. Wyman
ISBN: 0-205-39341-1

*Researching Teaching: Exploring Teacher
  Development through Reflexive Inquiry*
Ardra L. Cole & J. Gary Knowles
ISBN: 0-205-18076-0

*Developing a Professional Teaching Portfolio:
  A Guide for Educators*
Patricia Costantino & Marie De Lorenzo
ISBN: 0-205-32955-1

*The Moral Stake in Education: Contested
  Premises and Practices*
Joan F. Goodman & Howard Lesnick
ISBN: 0-321-02340-4

Historical Documents in American Education
Tony W. Johnson & Ronald Reed
ISBN: 0-8013-3314-8

*The Digital Teaching Portfolio Handbook:
  A How-To Guide for Educators*
Clare R. Kilbane & Natalie B. Milman
ISBN: 0-205-34345-7

*Education in a Global Society:
  A Comparative Perspective*
Kas Mazurek, Margret A. Winzer, &
  Czeslaw Majorek
ISBN: 0-205-26752-1

*Life in Schools: An Introduction to Critical
  Pedagogy in the Foundations of Education,*
  Fourth Edition
Peter McLaren
ISBN: 0-205-35118-2

*Teaching and Schooling in America:
  Pre- and Post-September 11*
Allan Ornstein
ISBN: 0-205-36711-9

*Teaching, Learning and Schooling:
  A 21st Century Perspective*
Eugene F. Provenzo, Jr.
ISBN: 0-205-28970-3

Philosophical Documents in Education
Ronald Reed & Tony W. Johnson
ISBN: 0-8013-3316-4

*American Schools, American Teachers:
  Issues and Perspectives*
David Schuman
ISBN: 0-321-05399-0

*Teaching Convictions: Critical Ethical
  Issues and Education*
Patrick Slattery & Dana Rapp
ISBN: 0-321-05401-6

For further information on these and other related titles, contact:

College Division
ALLYN AND BACON
75 Arlington Street, Suite 300
Boston, MA 02116
www.ablongman.com

PHILOSOPHIC CONFLICTS IN AMERICAN EDUCATION, 1893–2000

JOSEPH WATRAS

University of Dayton

Boston   New York   San Francisco
Mexico City   Montreal   Toronto   London   Madrid   Munich   Paris
Hong Kong   Singapore   Tokyo   Cape Town   Sydney

Executive Editor and Publisher: *Stephen D. Dragin*
Senior Editorial Assistant: *Barbara Strickland*
Marketing Manager: *Tara Whorf*
Production Editor: *Michelle Limoges*
Editorial Production Service: *Holly Crawford*
Compositor: *Peggy Cabot, Cabot Computer Services*
Composition and Prepress Buyer: *Linda Cox*
Manufacturing Buyer: *Andrew Turso*
Cover Designer: *Kristina Mose-Libon*

For related titles and support materials, visit our online catalog at www.ablongman.com.

Library of Congress Cataloging-in-Publication Data

Watras, Joseph.
    Philosophic conflicts in American education, 1893–2000 / Joseph Watras.
       p.   cm.
    Includes bibliographic references and index.
    ISBN 0-205-38621-0
       1. Education—United States—History—20th century.   2. Education—
    Philosophy.   I. Title.

 LA209.W38   2004
 370'.1'0973—dc21

                                                                2003054859

Printed in the United States of America

10   9   8   7   6   5   4   3   2   1   08   07   06   05   04   03

CONTENTS

CHAPTER TWELVE

PREFACE

While many commentators portray the debates about educational reform as a struggle for the American curriculum, this text demonstrates that the apparently competing groups had a great deal in common. As particular problems emerged during different historical periods, educators reacted to these circumstances. Because they faced similar conditions, theorists with different interests came to adopt surprisingly similar perspectives. Two examples illustrate this point.

First, after World War I, many Americans expressed the hope that the growth of industries and the development of science would improve society. Not surprisingly, educators adopted such views. As a result, even when educators disagreed about their approaches to subject matter or the ways to prepare children for the lives they would lead, they used similar concepts of efficiency and sought empirical evidence to justify their claims. Most important, they looked to the concept of democracy to offer ways to blend the nineteenth-century ideas of individualism with the interrelations forced on people as they forged an urban nation. To them, this meant that schools should meet the students' needs in ways that enabled them to occupy places in society from which they could contribute to the common good.

Second, during the Civil Rights movement, people worried about the growth of large corporations and the tendency of the conformist society to ignore the rights of many minority group members. Following the ideals expressed by Martin Luther King, Jr., many educators thought about the ways the schools could affirm the rights of the different people who lived in the United States. As a result, advocates for several different groups of students argued that local schools ignored the rights of their constituents. They asked the federal government to adopt legislation to force local school districts to adopt particular curriculum practices. At other times, they sought wide-scale political action to force school teachers and administrators to do what the educators thought was necessary to affirm the rights of the students.

This point is important. Although some curriculum theories differed from other ideas, the theorists tended to follow patterns of thought particular to the period of time in which they lived and worked. As a result, the ways that these educators thought about schools offered similar benefits and produced similar problems.

Although the educators who worked in the first half of the twentieth century disagreed among themselves, they sought to use the concept of democracy to blend ideas of individualism with understandings of cooperation required by an age of growing industrialism and urbanization. For example, some educators sought to find ways to teach children the skills they would need to become contributing adults. Other educators sought to allow children the freedom to pursue their own aims and to satisfy their own desires. Although these represented distinct sets of ideas, they shared the views that children had to learn to work together to contribute to the common good. Both sets of ideas tended to make social harmony more important than individual freedoms.

The educators who worked during the Civil Rights movement took the opposite tack. They sought ways to affirm the students' rights. These educators urged schools to offer appropriate educations to children with disabilities or they campaigned to provide children with limited English proficiency the right to learn the language and culture of their families. In these actions, they thought less about social harmony and more about individual fulfillment.

These tendencies are equally dangerous. On the one hand, as the educators concerned with the common good would point out, individuals cannot achieve their potentials outside of the complex web of opportunities and responsibilities that society provides. On the other hand, as educators concerned with the rights of certain constituencies would add, society cannot advance unless unique individuals preserve their particular ideas from which they can offer alternatives to the general direction of events or inventions.

Recognizing this dilemma, this book asks readers to think about the ways apparently different educational theories share similar benefits and face similar problems. Instead of trying to show readers that any particular approach to curriculum is correct, the text encourages readers to recognize the patterns of thought that educators used, to identify the ways that practical school programs developed from particular ideas, and to use those understandings to find ways to increase the benefits offered by any program and to reduce the dangers posed by those same programs.

This book does not ask readers to understand particular approaches to instruction as a way out of educational confusion. Instead of depending on the mastery of some method, the text is based on the view that whatever solutions are possible will come from the understandings people develop among themselves.

To many critics, a hope that is predicated on the diffusion of intelligence among the citizenry will appear to be impractical. These critics may believe that problems are pressing and they cannot delay in offering answers. Worse, to them, traditional efforts to enlighten people cannot reduce the incidence of intolerance, inhumanity, or wars. Instead, larger and more aggressive methods of educational or social change are needed.

To such a charge, there is no answer except to urge the rebirth of what classical authors called the "tragic sense." This is the realization that human labors are flawed and cannot succeed. Nonetheless, in a tragic spirit, people persist in the directions that enable them to fulfill themselves. At all times, of course, they have to beware of excessive pride that would cause them to continue efforts to the point where they cause harm.

This book may improve the art and science of teaching if readers accept the faith in intelligence and the warning against excessive zeal that the book expresses. The different chapters describe the combinations of ideas and experiences that different educators tried to use to improve schools and to better society. At all times, though, warnings appear that suggest the ways these efforts failed. Such warnings do not emerge to inspire pessimism, though. They do not mean that nothing will work. Instead, such warnings are intended to encourage readers to think more deeply about what they want schools to do. It is this type of thinking that enables people to fulfill their own humane ambitions.

At this point, it is appropriate to acknowledge the assistance of many people. The first group should be the publishers and editors who took a manuscript and turned it into a book. I would especially like to express my gratitude to Steve Dragin, my editor at Allyn and Bacon, for his constant support. The second group should be the many librarians whose constant and careful work enables scholars to learn and grow. The third group includes the authors whose books and articles appear in the works cited. Almost every paragraph in this text contains a citation. Without these references, this book could not exist. The fourth group includes the members of learned societies who regularly attend annual meetings and offer invaluable assistance to the authors who read papers. Although the chapters of this book did not appear as articles in journals, some of the ideas that later became chapters were read as papers to participants of several conferences. The attendees offered many helpful suggestions. These conferences included meetings of the Ohio Valley Philosophy of Education Society, the Midwest History of Education Society, the Society for the Study of Curriculum History, the Southern History of Education Society, the History of Education Society, and the American Educational Studies Association. Finally, several individuals read the manuscript in its entirety and offered many helpful comments. I am grateful to the following reviewers: Myra J. Baughman, Pacific Lutheran University; Deron R. Boyles, Georgia State University; and Joseph Newman, University of South Alabama. To all these people, many thanks are due.

ACRONYMS

ACE   American Council on Education
AFT   American Federation of Teachers
AHA   American Historical Association
AIBS   American Institute of Biological Sciences
AIR   American Institutes for Research
ASCD   Association of Supervision and Curriculum Development
BSCS   Biological Sciences Curriculum Study
CAHSC   Committee on the Articulation of High School and College
CCC   Civilian Conservation Corps
CEC   Council for Exceptional Children
CEEB   College Entrance Examination Board
CRSE   Commission on the Reorganization of Secondary Education
EPC   Educational Policies Commission
ESEA   Elementary and Secondary Education Act of 1965
ESL   English as a Second Language
HEW   U.S. Department of Health, Education, and Welfare
IDEA   Individuals with Disabilities Education Act
MACOS   Man: A Course of Study
METCO   Metropolitan Council for Educational Opportunity
NAC   National American Committee
NAEP   National Assessment of Educational Progress
NCEE   National Commission on Excellence in Education
NCTE   National Council of Teachers of English
NDEA   National Defense Education Act of 1958
NEA   National Education Association
NSF   National Science Foundation
NSPIE   National Society for Promotion of Industrial Education
NSSE   National Society for the Study of Education
OCR   U.S. Office of Civil Rights
PARC   Pennsylvania Association for Retarded Children
PEA   Progressive Education Association
PSSC   Physical Science Study Committee
SCLC   Southern Christian Leadership Conference
SMSG   School Mathematics Study Group
UICSM   University of Illinois Committee on School Mathematics

PROLOGUE

This book describes the ideas that educational reformers expressed during the twentieth century. As each chapter indicates, a set of major educational issues arose during particular periods of time, and groups of educators suggested different reforms to solve those problems. Despite their disagreements, these educators shared certain assumptions. As a result, the reforms they suggested contained similar aspects and similar problems.

A major shift in educational thinking took place in the 1960s. From 1918 to 1960, the distinct groups of educators sought the best ways for students to learn skills that would be personally rewarding and that would enhance social harmony. The different options included such innovations as relating academic skills to everyday life, vocational education, or providing what was called child-centered education. They shared the common assumption that education should enhance the democratic ideal. After 1963, educators tended to see themselves as advocates seeking to affirm the rights of children to appropriate education. Sharing this common approach, these educators sought to force schools to offer appropriate education to children with disabilities, children with linguistic differences, and children who are gay or lesbian.

Although many of these alternatives were well constructed, they suffered from limitations that arose from the unavoidable contradiction between individual desires and social needs. The educators who sought to enhance social harmony believed that they could overcome the dilemma if they thought more about the meaning of democracy. Unfortunately, as the later chapters will explain, these educators tended to err on the side of social requirements. In a similar manner, the educators who acted as advocates for the rights of particular students offered limited views of wider social issues. They tended to err on the side of individual desires.

Many authors have pointed out that educators tend to fall into groups. For example, philosophers of education have written many texts describing the different sets of ideas that different groups of educators held. In 1939, John S. Brubacher published his book, *Modern Philosophies of Education*. Complaining that most texts at the time set forth the ideas of one person, Brubacher sought to acquaint students with a wide variety of different philosophies. Thus, he demonstrated how different philosophers of education held to different questions in metaphysics, epistemology, and psychology (Brubacher, *Modern* viii–ix).

In 1942, Brubacher served as the chair of the yearbook committee of the National Society for the Study of Education (NSSE). In this capacity, he gathered essays written by spokespeople of different philosophical perspectives about education. Thus, for example, the yearbook contained a chapter from William Heard Kilpatrick on experimentalism, a chapter from Frederick Breed on realism, and a chapter from Herman H. Horne on idealism (NSSE, *Philosophies* vi, ix).

The view that philosophies of education could best be presented as competing or distinct schools of thought became so popular that Brubacher repeated the yearbook in 1955 with a different set of authors and somewhat different perspectives. At the same time, other authors borrowed the system of organization, and textbooks in philosophy of education presented what came to be called different "isms" for prospective teachers to learn.

In 1972, the pattern among philosophy of education texts changed, at least to some extent, when the NSSE presented another yearbook devoted to the philosophy of education entitled *Philosophical Redirection of Educational Research.* As in the previous volumes, different philosophers of education wrote the different chapters. This time, however, they did not seek to explain systemic philosophical positions or to build prescriptive theories. Instead, the different philosophers of education analyzed the meanings of educational concepts on the grounds that such work could advance research and guide practice (NSSE, *Redirection* 1).

Several philosophers of education argued that the NSSE volume on philosophical redirection did not show how completely the field had moved away from what they called "systems of philosophy." To demonstrate how philosophers of education used rigorous methods to attack a broad array of educational issues, the NSSE published in 1981 the yearbook entitled *Philosophy and Education.* The authors selected the title to show how philosophers of education were penetrating into a variety of areas. Again, different philosophers of education wrote the individual chapters to illustrate how they did philosophy (NSSE, *Philosophy* 1–4).

Although the editors of *Philosophy and Education* contended that they did not want to denigrate the idea that philosophy of education could refer to systematic conceptions of education, this seems to have happened. At least, the NSSE did not publish another yearbook devoted strictly to philosophy of education although philosophers wrote articles for volumes on other topics.

As philosophers turned away from describing competing philosophic perspectives, historians began to argue that the record of educational changes was the result of conflicts among groups of educators and academic scholars. For example, in 1986, Herbert M. Kliebard argued that, from 1893 to 1958, a series of battles took place among four different groups that he called the humanists, the developmentalists, the social efficiency educators, and the social meliorists. Entitling his book *The Struggle for the American Curriculum,* Kliebard asserted that no one group gained ascendancy, but that each group won partial victories. As a result, he claimed that American schools did not hold to a single clear purpose but, at different times, the curriculum reflected the different and contradictory goals of each of these groups (Kliebard 23–25, 230).

Although some historians disagreed with parts of this view of educational change, they presented different versions of the same theme. For example, in a recent text, *The Failed Promise of the American High School*, David Angus and Jeffrey Mirel contended that, during the twentieth century, schools of education developed within universities, and the professional educators who had been trained in those institutions sought to wrest control of the school curriculum from college presidents and liberal arts faculty. According to Angus and Mirel, these professional educators shared many ideas that set them apart from the liberal arts faculty and that continue to influence the thinking of contemporary educators. These ideas were as follows: Academic training in high schools was irrelevant to the lives of many young children;

the high school curriculum should be expanded; and the professional educators had to design new courses to meet the needs of the students and of the society (Angus and Mirel 10–13).

In a similar manner, Diane Ravitch complained that, as school enrollments increased in the early twentieth century, educators who sought alternative curriculums for noncollege bound students split from those scholars who favored the academic subjects. The result was an increasing stratification of the schools so that children of immigrants, of racial minorities, and of low-income families lost the chance to enjoy academic training. She noted that some scholars, such as William Torrey Harris, William Chandler Bagley, and Isaac Kandel, criticized these reforms, but she contended that contemporary historians denigrate these critics and thereby aid the movement against the academic subjects (Ravitch, *Left Back* 14–16).

The weakness of books that describe differences or conflicts among groups of educators is that the authors cannot easily acknowledge the assumptions that the different educators shared. When they do recognize similarities, they do so to show how a group garnered strength to face its opposition.

This is the problem that this book, *Philosophic Conflicts in American Education, 1893–2000,* seeks to correct. In the chapters that follow, the reader will not find arguments aimed at discrediting the views of other contemporary authors. This text acknowledges that different groups of educators existed and that the members of the groups disagreed with the members of other groups and with each other. This book argues, however, that these competing groups of educators shared assumptions about the nature of education and the ways that schools should serve the students and the community. This book will not contend that educators shared the same notions throughout the twentieth century; instead, it will explore two major shifts in the conceptions that educators shared as time passed.

In 1894, W. T. Harris represented idealistic educators as he sought to retain the view that academic subjects had to be isolated from practical concerns. He met considerable resistance from Herbartian educators who claimed that teachers had to integrate the academic subjects with the experiences children had outside school. This represented the first shift from a nineteenth-century idealistic view to a more practical realistic conception. Thus, from 1894 until 1963, the members of different groups, such as liberal and conservative educators, asserted that teachers should tie lessons to practical affairs in ways that met the students' needs and served to improve society. Although these educators disagreed about the way schools could meet students' needs, the different approaches they recommended seemed to reinforce wider social changes more than they reflected desires to protect individual freedoms. The second shift in the assumptions that educators shared took place in the middle of the century. In 1963, following the March on Washington and the subsequent U.S. Civil Rights legislation, educators and politicians argued that school personnel must affirm students' and parents' rights. Although these educators chose to advance the interests of different groups, the reforms they suggested seemed to exaggerate the needs of particular students at the expense of the wider society.

To explain how educators came to share the idea that schools should meet students' needs, the first chapter describes the report of the Committee of Fifteen and the defense that William Torrey Harris made of teaching academic studies. Harris held a view of education that differed radically from his younger contemporaries who called themselves Herbartians. According to Harris, children had to learn the abstract academic studies separate from each other and apart from practical affairs. Arguing that the type of thinking used in acquiring these abilities differed from each other, Harris asserted that the only way children could integrate and apply those understandings was for them to move, through an activity of their own souls, to a higher and different type of thinking. On the other hand, the Herbartians argued that the processes of learning were seamless. They contended that teachers could utilize children's interests, begin lessons with everyday events, and help children recognize the ways that different academic subjects reinforced each other and enabled people to solve everyday problems. Harris was the last important, secular educational leader to contend that academic courses precipitated children's spiritual development. Most educators who supported the academic subjects took views similar to those of the Herbartians. They claimed that the academic subjects could be tailored to meet the individual needs that children brought to schools in ways that advanced the democratic ethos.

The importance of the differences between Harris and his contemporaries is illustrated in Chapter Two. The campaign for compulsory education seemed to encourage educators to determine the value of any study by considering its future, practical usefulness. Although some educators wanted to preserve academic training as an important part of school, they rejected the idealistic notions of Harris. These educators claimed that vocational training restricted the chances of students to develop the necessary skills to think independently, but they had difficulty determining the point at which vocational training became excessive.

To some extent, Chapter Three moves outside schools by considering three parts of the Americanization movement. These extend from the efforts of such liberal, progressive individuals as Jane Addams to the vitriolic campaigns of political Americanizers. The fact that the Americanization movement did not decline until the U.S. Congress restricted immigration indicates that educators could not easily determine when efforts to help children adapt to society became hurtful.

Chapter Four describes the National Educational Association's Commission on the Reorganization of Secondary Education (CRSE). By proposing that the model of the comprehensive high school should become the standard in the United States, the CRSE set the stage for future reforms. At the same time, two models of curriculum development—scientific curriculum making and the project method—became popular. Although the advocates of each perspective differed from each other, these three reforms seemed to lean in the direction of helping students adjust to society.

Chapters Five and Six consider different aspects of educational reforms during the Great Depression. Chapter Five describes the American Historical Association's Commission on the Social Studies, the Civilian Conservation Corps, and the New Deal's effort to revitalize arts and crafts of Native Americans and Hispanic Americans in New Mexico. Chapter Six describes the Progressive Education Association's Eight-Year Study. Although each of these reforms differed from each other, they shared the view that traditional academic activities should be tied to the daily activities of students. As a result, they tended to lead students to conform to the wider society.

Chapters Seven and Eight discuss two contradictory reforms sponsored by the federal government during the Cold War. The first is James Conant's effort to reinforce the comprehensive high school. The second is the effort of mathematicians and scientists to develop new curriculums in math, biology, physics, and social studies. Although the different programs followed distinct plans to advance democracy in society, they shared the view that schools were the places where students could acquire the skills and the understandings necessary for adult life. As a result, the schools seemed to help children adjust to the social settings in which they lived.

The book takes a turn with Chapter Nine. In the 1960s, the efforts of lawyers, politicians, and educators to establish the right of African Americans to an equal education and the related efforts to offer an appropriate education to children from low-income families set the model for the reforms that followed. Since the federal government offered billions of dollars to achieve these ends, advocates for other types of children tried to establish the right to appropriate educations for their constituents. The result was that, from this point on, educators imitated the legal and political tactics of the NAACP and the SCLC. These reformers saw themselves as advocates struggling to force local schools to affirm students' rights to an appropriate education.

Chapter Ten shows how advocates for children with disabilities and children with linguistic differences followed legal and political campaigns to establish the rights of these children to appropriate educations. An important part of this chapter is the description of the differences this form of thinking caused among special educators and bilingual educators. Before 1963, most educators tried to blend concern for the democratic ethos with efforts to meet students' needs. In the two cases described in this chapter, educators either did not concern themselves with an understanding of democracy or they thought about wider social questions in superficial manners.

If Chapter Ten covers liberal educators, Chapter Eleven considers the work of conservative educators in affirming the rights of parents to seek effective schools for their children. Chapter Twelve describes the work of critical pedagogues, feminists, and advocates for gay and lesbian youth as they sought to provide the rights of their constituents to form supportive communities. The common thread among these chapters is that the reformers based their efforts on some attempt to affirm the rights of some limited group of people. These efforts differed from earlier efforts to meet students' needs in that they seemed to pursue a more pluralistic society that allowed every person to live according to his or her own wishes.

Thus, during the first half of the twentieth century, progressive educators sought to meet student needs in ways that advanced the democratic ethos. On the other hand, educators who wanted to affirm students' or parents' rights pursued a pluralistic vision. Although these views share similar values such as tolerance and respect for persons, they seem to lead to different results. Democracy seems to invite social harmony and personal growth at the expense of ethnic traditions. On the other hand, pluralism appears to emphasize ethnic traditions and personal choice at the expense of social harmony.

Each perspective carried endemic difficulties because the relation between the individual and the society is contradictory. The individual cannot flourish outside society, but the society has to direct the efforts of its citizens into socially constructive channels. Although some educational reforms were better than others, there was not a steady line of progress through the twentieth century. Instead of solving the problems derived from one set of assumptions, educators exchanged those difficulties for another set of problems. For example, in the 1940s, philosophers of education complained that teachers disguised their authoritarianism by saying the students needed to learn the subject matter that the teachers had decided was essential for social progress. In the 1980s, advocates for children with disabilities succeeded in having the federal government require school districts to design educations that were appropriate for each child's special needs. The IEPs, as the plans were called, removed the problem of forcing all children to learn the same things, but they raised new questions of how schools could meet broader social concerns because the model defined a good education as correcting certain individual deficiencies.

Since the different chapters provide descriptions of the convoluted paths that curriculum theorists took in seeking to make schools better, the book is organized chronologically. Each chapter provides descriptions of the major educational issues of a period. Within each chapter, there are criticisms of the approaches that the educators took. Most important, the chapters are tied together by explanations of the appropriate reforms that the different educators shared during different eras, the benefits that these reforms offered, and the problems the reformers faced because of weaknesses in the assumptions they shared.

In order to evaluate the educational issues of a period, the text has to cover more than conflicting philosophic ideas. It has to examine the effects of contradictory slogans. Unfortunately, this may appear to violate the implications of the title because philosophers of education tend to concentrate their efforts on serious, intelligently conceived conceptions of education, and they tend to disregard slogans. In fairness, though, philosophers of education acknowledge that slogans can become sources of philosophic concern. For example, Israel Scheffler believed that slogans serve as rallying symbols expressing the key ideas and attitudes shared by members of a movement. He noted that these slogans are not definitions in that they do not clarify ideas. Instead, slogans foster a common spirit, attract adherents, and offer reassurance to veterans. Despite warning that slogans cannot be taken as accurate descriptions of educational perspectives, Scheffler added that members come to believe the slogans as doctrines when they repeat them continually and the slogans take on the force of a doctrine. At this point, Scheffler concluded, scholars and philosophers should examine the slogans seriously and criticize them as they would educational definitions (Scheffler 36–37).

The hope that lies behind *Philosophic Conflicts in American Education* is that readers can think about educational slogans to develop a better understanding of the problems that beset any one seeking to define the aims and means of education. This is a reasonable method of thinking. For example, in *Experience and Education*, John Dewey noted that progressive educators had a simple slogan in their view that children should learn from experience, but he complained that the progressive educators did not have a thorough understanding of what that slogan meant. Therefore, in his essay, Dewey criticized the commonsense approaches educators took and explained what aims and procedures should appear within an education based on learning by experience.

This text will not imitate Dewey in offering a better understanding of what should be the aims and the methods of education. In fact, there may not be any best way to think about the aims of education. That is, all reform efforts seem to fall prey to the unavoidable and contradictory relationship that exists between individuals and the society within which they live. Given this fact, the best thing educators can do is to think deeply about the approach they wish to take and try to minimize the problems that will inevitably result. This book should help by providing the framework for a discussion of a wide range of proposals and counterproposals to meet a limited number of problems. When the readers have finished this account of educational reform, they should be able to recognize the similarities among reform efforts and the patterns they followed. They should also be able to recognize the dangers that exist within any theoretical justification of any plan for educational reform. With these understandings, readers may be able to control the difficulties that will accompany the policies they wish to advance.

PART I

FROM HUMANIST STUDIES TO THE PRACTICAL CURRICULUM, 1893–1918

The first chapter, "From Separate Studies to an Integrated Curriculum," describes the transition from the idealistic views of educators such as W. T. Harris to the more realistic and practical views of the Herbartians. According to Harris, children had to learn the abstract academic studies separate from each other and apart from practical affairs. Harris wanted to keep the studies separate because they called for different types of thinking. While Harris wanted children to integrate their understanding of academic subjects and practical affairs, he thought such integration required a type of knowing teachers could not convey. According to Harris, the children acquired this higher and different type of thinking through an activity of their own souls. On the other hand, the Herbartians argued that students could learn academic skills and moral views by beginning with practical affairs. The Herbartian view that academic and practical affairs were similar became the popular perspective in the twentieth century. As this perspective spread, educators who favored the liberal arts came to change their views as practical subjects invaded the curriculum.

Chapter Two, "Introducing the Practical Curriculum," describes how the campaign for compulsory education encouraged educators to adopt the Herbartian view and evaluate subjects by the usefulness those subjects would offer in the future. Thus, educators offered manual training as a means to provide a set of general skills that complemented academic skills. Ironically, by 1906, educators argued that manual training was as abstract as academic teaching and that the curriculum should offer students opportunities to select vocational preparation. In 1917, the federal government created the Smith-Hughes Act and began to support vocational education programs to meet the economic and military defense needs of the country. The difference between manual training and vocational preparation was the extent to which the training was tailored to the work the children would do as adults. Thus, most educators supported either more or less direct vocational training depending on the ways that they assessed the needs of the children and the needs of the society.

CHAPTER ONE

FROM SEPARATE STUDIES TO AN INTEGRATED CURRICULUM, 1893–1918

An educational historian, Herbert Kliebard, contends that two reports that appeared in the 1890s brought issues of curriculum reform to national attention. These reports were those of the National Education Association's (NEA's) Committee of Ten and Committee of Fifteen. While Kliebard acknowledges that concerns about curriculum occupied American citizens before those reports appeared, he argues that the reports set the main lines of curriculum change and caused four different interest groups to take on recognizable features. In his book, Kliebard describes the ways that those different groups battled for the next sixty-five years over the correctness of the various reforms they advocated (Kliebard xvi–xvii).

Building on Kliebard's observation, David Angus and Jeffrey Mirel begin their history of the secondary school curriculum with a discussion of the report of the Committee of Ten. They agree with Kliebard that this report was the single most important educational document written during the nineteenth century. They agree that this report signaled the beginning of controversies among different groups of scholars and educators over the direction of curriculum reform. Angus and Mirel consider the report to be the first and only back to basics movement led by professional educators, and they claim that the report set off a protracted struggle for control of the curriculum among different groups of professional educators who had been trained in recently developed schools of education in universities. They disagree with Kliebard, however, in arguing that these groups of professional educators shared a desire to meet students' and society's needs. According to Angus and Mirel, college presidents and liberal arts faculty continued to support the academic subjects (Angus and Mirel 8–16).

Kliebard, Angus, and Mirel may overstate the case when they contend that the reports of the NEA Committees of Ten and Fifteen set off debates about the direction of curriculum reform. Controversies had existed for many years, but the criticisms that educators directed at the ideas of William Torrey Harris, then U.S. Commissioner of Education, signaled the end of the nineteenth-century tendency to justify curriculum reforms on transcendent grounds. During the nineteenth century, educators appealed to some common view of religion or to the nature of children's souls. In the twentieth century, the debates focused on practical concerns that could be verified by observation or measurement in some way.

During his long career, Harris repeated explanations of educational problems through ideas found in the works of Georg Wilhelm Friedrich Hegel. Born in 1835, Harris was nearing the end of his career when he appeared before an NEA conference in 1895 to defend the report of the Committee of Fifteen. (He died in 1909.) In the report of the Committee of Fifteen, Harris used Hegel's philosophical orientation to retain concern for the spiritual development of children without committing the public schools to any sort of religious training. Harris argued that the academic subjects acquainted children with physical nature and with human nature in ways that enabled them to meet the demands of the institutions of family, civil society, the state, and the church. Thus, the subjects did not serve utilitarian goals but furthered broad, traditional goals of human fulfillment. Harris contended that lessons had to be planned in ways that allowed children to form a worldview or Weltanschauung that provided insights into the nature of the world and of human beings because such perceptions transcended personal experience.

By expressing concern for spiritual development through the academic subjects, Harris showed his affinity for the ideas that had fueled the common school movement. From 1830 to 1860, educators such as Horace Mann and Calvin Stowe had argued that schools could enhance the spiritual and moral development of children if they adopted some universal Christian aspects and avoided denominational affiliations. For example, Mann and Stow urged teachers to have children read the Bible in the common schools because they thought that this activity could enhance all religious faiths, encourage spiritual growth, and teach morality.

Although Harris sympathized with the ideas of the common school movement, he did not want public schools to be seats of religious instruction. Consequently, in making his arguments, Harris ignored religion and followed Hegel in asserting that things at one level could and should contradict each other because the effort to resolve these contradictions led people to develop new perceptions of a higher level. Thus, the relations within families differed from and, to some extent, contradicted the relationships found in states. In a similar way, Harris thought that work contradicted play. According to Harris, these areas of life should remain distinct, just as he believed that school subjects should remain distinct. When people became aware of these contradictory influences in the human institutions and in school subjects, Harris believed, they developed higher understandings or faculties (Harris, *Psychologic* ix–x).

When Harris thought about school subjects, he found the same pattern of different logical levels. For example, Harris argued that children did not move smoothly from discerning objects to using words to describe those objects. Harris believed that the type of thinking required at the lower level of discerning objects was different from that found at the higher level of describing objects. To move up, the child had to make a synthesis of his or her impressions in order to form ideas. Harris called this movement from one level to another self-activity because no one could do it for the child. In fact, when teachers stayed at one level, such as exposing the child to different sensations, in an effort to help the child gather enough sensations to form ideas, the child's development might never proceed beyond gathering impressions.

On the other hand, the critics who attacked Harris disagreed that intellectual and moral growth took place as a result of mental functions that teachers could not manipulate. Instead, the critics looked for practical explanations to help children develop the moral sensibilities and the skills they believed to be appropriate for adult life. They argued that children were interested in learning skills that would help them in life outside school and that teachers could plan lessons based on this principle so the children could express their personal desires in ways that fulfilled social requirements.

After the turn of the century, many people continued to agree with Harris that the liberal arts were important. Few people, however, contended that some subject matters were valuable because they enhanced the human qualities of the person who learned them. An exception was Jacques Maritain, a Catholic theologian, who stated a view similar to that of Harris. In 1943, Maritain argued that the act of knowing was an essential human ability and that it was distinct from any skills needed to do any sort of trade or craft. As a result, when Maritain recommended for all students a curriculum fitted to what he called the dignity of human beings, it began with such courses as mathematics, literature, natural science, history, and fine arts. When all the students had mastered these liberal arts courses, Maritain allowed them to separate and pursue some form of vocational or professional training (Maritain 55–57, 66–67).

In general, though, most supporters of the liberal arts dropped Harris's views and argued that those academic lessons improved students' abilities to function in twentieth-century society. Unfortunately, by claiming that abstract classical subjects had a practical benefit, those supporters found their points difficult to defend. For example, Angus and Mirel may be correct in stating that college presidents retained their faith that all high school students should study the liberal arts. Some of those college presidents, such as Charles W. Eliot, however, had to relinquish their faith in the liberal arts for all students when critics attacked that perspective.

How did Harris think elementary schools could help students become more fully human?

Harris made one of the clearest statements of the way academic subjects could enhance a person's human qualities on 18 February 1895 when the Committee of Fifteen presented its final report to the NEA in Cleveland, Ohio. According to the editors of the *Educational Review,* the meeting signaled a new and intensely serious approach to the development of educational theory because the different speakers offered remarks of high intellectual content to which the audience listened attentively and everything proceeded in a dignified manner.

The report was divided into three parts: the training of teachers, correlation of studies, and organization of city school systems. Harris was responsible for the report of the subcommittee concerned with the correlation of different subjects, and his report dominated the meeting. Explaining that his subcommittee selected five subjects to be central to elementary education, Harris offered an unusual definition of correlation. At the time, correlation was considered some form of integration of the subject matters. Harris claimed his subcommittee thought of it as the ways that literature, grammar, mathematics, geography, and history correlated pupils with their spiritual and natural environment (NEA, *Committee of Fifteen* 42–44).

In his report to the NEA, Harris had carefully separated and ordered the academic subjects so they would develop different mental functions in children's minds. Harris held language to be primary because it made social organization possible, and he believed that reading and writing were the means by which students acquired all other knowledge. As a result, he felt that reading, writing, and spelling should make up the first four years of schooling. To him, these skills required considerable effort because he thought that words had a twofold character: They addressed the senses of hearing or sight, and they called on ideas that children already had. As a result, Harris did not think that students acquired language when they experienced things. He believed that language represented a form of what he called "self-activity." That is, the children learned words when they had already formed general impressions of many things and could apply names to the common natures they found in the objects (NEA, *Committee of Fifteen* 44–45).

Harris was careful to point out that the study of language consisted of the distinct areas of literature and grammar. Literature offered an aesthetic and an ethical nature from which the children could develop insights into human nature. On the other hand, grammar developed logical thinking. To illustrate the distinct nature of these areas, Harris complained that teachers who concentrated on the grammatical construction of the sentences as students read literature destroyed the ethical content of the stories (NEA, *Committee of Fifteen* 47–51).

Mathematics was the next most important subject area for Harris because it enabled human beings to count things and thereby to control nature. Applying the same idea of distinct levels of thought, Harris complained that teachers who taught arithmetic by having students memorize addition and multiplication tables and who moved into solving problems with fractions and decimals could impede the children's ability to learn such higher forms as algebra that involved what Harris called the transformation of functions. To avoid this possibility, Harris urged teachers not to spend excessive time on learning the mechanical aspects of arithmetic (NEA, *Committee of Fifteen* 52–58).

In the study of geography, Harris wanted the students to learn the material habitat of human beings and the ways this environment influenced them. Thus, Harris wanted the first phase of the study of geography to be the study of the obstacles that separate human beings and how people overcame them through industry and commerce. For Harris, the study of geography should expand from things close to the children and lead them to study things that are more remote and important for their own sakes. Thus, he urged that industry and commerce form the center of the studies. This would lead to studies of the differences among climates, soils, and productions. In addition, Harris thought that geography could show how people striving to overcome the environment created different occupations, and this could lead to studies of differences of race and religion. At this point, Harris argued, the students could approach topics such as the way continents were formed, mountains were built, winds were created, and rain was distributed. From these studies, Harris thought the students would proceed to a study of cities and how they grew. Thus, geography should show how physical conditions led to differences among societies and how industry and commerce rendered those differences of use to the whole world (NEA, *Committee of Fifteen* 58–61).

History was the last important field of study. Since history described the institutions that human beings created, it recorded the career of nations in a manner similar to the way that biography described the career of an individual. This corporate self made rational development possible, Harris argued. Without states, human beings lived in poverty, war, and wretchedness. With governments, they enjoyed justice, peace, and security. Thus, for Harris, history should show more than citizenship. It should develop the ideas of political evolution to forms of government better adapted to permit individual freedom and participation of all citizens in the activities of government. Through a study of history, the children should learn the true nature of freedom, which Harris defined as the freedom through just laws enforced by a strong government (NEA, *Committee of Fifteen* 62–65).

One year after delivering his part of the report of the Committee of Fifteen, Harris read a paper to the National Education Association to explain the assumptions on which he had based the report. His view was that children in elementary schools should grasp fundamentals of the culture in which they lived. These include reading and writing, use of figures, and understanding maps. In secondary schools and colleges, students can learn the science to preserve the culture, and in postgraduate schools they take on specific vocational training and learn the theory and art of some profession. Harris believed that if the students at the elementary level were to learn about the culture, the five main subject areas of literature, grammar, arithmetic, geography, and history had to be presented in a symmetrical and coordinated fashion. That is, the students had to see that each study called on different methods of observation and distinct trains of thought. The problem with integrating the subject matters around some topic of interest to the children was that this practice blurred the distinctions among the subject matters (Harris, "Co-ordinate Studies" 323–325).

Why did other educators criticize Harris's views?

When Harris died in 1908, there was no one of similar stature who could or would defend the idea that the nature of intellectual pursuits differed from those of practical activities. One of Harris's recent biographers, William Reese, contends that, in the early years of the twentieth century, educators repudiated virtually everything Harris advocated. According to Reese, Harris had little influence beyond his lifetime because he did not teach at a university and failed to write a major text that kept his message alive (Reese 155).

While Harris did not teach at a university where he could shape graduate students to act as disciples, Harris did write extensively, and his book entitled *Psychologic Foundations of Education* counts as a major text although present-day readers may find the title and the book's organization to be awkward. A more likely explanation for Harris's fall from popularity is that during the last years of his life, educators discarded his notion that the academic subjects constituted a realm that was separate and distinct from practical activities. Instead, educators preferred the idea that they could create some sort of seamless transition from practical activities to the academic subjects and back again. Although some religious educators retained the view that intellectual pursuits differed from those of practical activities, with few exceptions, these people did not align themselves with Harris or Hegel's ideas because Harris sought to separate religious training from academic education.

To the modern reader, Harris may appear foolish because he defended most of his ideas with psychological explanations that came from philosophical beliefs rather than from experiments. During the nineteenth century, though, this was a common way of thinking. As a result, his critics depended as much on different psychological bases, and they focused their attention on philosophical theories that rivaled those of Harris. This came out when these educators complained about Harris's report because they aimed their criticisms at the ways that Harris had misconstrued words such as "correlation" that many educators had made central to their theories. They did not offer experimental evidence to contradict his views.

The rival philosophical view and the importance of concepts such as correlation came from the educator and philosopher Johann Friedrich Herbart, who developed his theories in Germany from 1805 until 1833. In the United States, several school people, such as Francis W. Parker, found inspiration in Herbart's words and used them with other theories to find new ways to offer the traditional subject matters to children. In 1894, Parker published his *Talks on Pedagogics*. Parker did hold to any theoretical orientation. He had worked with teachers in

Boston, New York, and Chicago, and these talks came from those efforts. In his book, he claimed that what he called the doctrine of concentration, another of Herbart's concepts, was the proper direction for educational reform. Parker called concentration the science of education. By this, he meant that teachers should try to unify the curriculum, and he offered ways to organize the curriculum around the subject, geography. For example, children could learn to work with numbers while measuring continents. According to Parker, all the academic subjects should merge into the study of life and this would be a study of God (*Talks* v, 42–46).

When Parker commented on the report of the Committee of Fifteen, he asked the committee to revise its report. Although he knew the committee members had read the works of Herbart and his followers, he could not find Herbart's ideas in the report. Yet, Parker believed the idea of the correlation of studies that Herbart stressed to be a most important guide to teachers (Parker, "Dissent" 105–106).

A second group of educators were more zealously committed to Herbart's ideas than was Parker. These critics included Charles De Garmo and Charles and Frank McMurry who had studied in Germany and believed that Herbart's model of teaching offered a theoretical foundation that could be combined with organized practical materials. According to Harold Dunkel, Americans found Herbart's work attractive because Herbart had tried to introduce realism into German philosophical thinking against the then current domination of the idealism advanced by the more renowned philosopher, Hegel. To honor the source of their ideas, De Garmo and the McMurrys organized the Herbart Society for the Scientific Study of Teaching in 1895. They recruited several prominent educators, such as Nicholas Murray Butler and John Dewey, to join them (Dunkel 120–123, 130).

When Charles McMurry complained about Harris's report, he stressed the importance that Herbartians placed on correlation. According to McMurry, the idea Harris expressed in the report of the Committee of Fifteen was not correlation but coordination of distinct and independent branches of study with equal rank in a way that introduced the child to the world. The problem that McMurry found in this form of coordination was that it encouraged teachers to ignore the interconnections that existed among studies. McMurry believed that students had to recognize this correlation and hold it in their minds (McMurry, *Elements* 165–166).

To illustrate their complaints about the use of the word *correlation,* De Garmo wrote that the Herbartians thought about correlation as making the student aware of interesting and valuable cross-relations existing among different studies. For the Herbartians, the aim of correlation was a more direct series of connections that appealed to students' interests, enhanced their understandings, enlarged their outlooks on life, and improved their conduct by deepening their insights. Thus, De Garmo claimed that "instruction in the studies of the public school must be made to reveal to the pupil the moral order of the world; and not only must it furnish this moral insight, but it must so touch the heart that a permanent right disposition toward all men, both in their individual and in their organized capacity, may result" (De Garmo, "Introductory" 7–8).

De Garmo noted that there were several ways by which Herbartians sought to correlate elementary school studies. One was to use literature such as the story of Robinson Crusoe. De Garmo argued that this model failed to fit the child for the complex society into which he or she would live. Another method Herbartians followed was to use nature or science studies to organize history, literature, mathematics, and geography. De Garmo did not approve of these approaches because he believed that they weakened the cultural studies. Finally, De Garmo noted some Herbartians sought to correlate different aspects of the same area. Thus, instead of teaching physical, political, and economic geography as if they were separate subjects, teachers blended these in ways that enabled students to understand industry, commerce, and politics. De Garmo hoped that this could be a first step toward discovering ways of integrating the subject areas without weakening their integrity (De Garmo, "Introductory" 9–26).

In short, the Herbartians held as a tenet of their faith that they could construct the curriculum so that one thing could lead into another with the subjects overlapping or intertwining. They seemed convinced that the distinct levels of thought that Harris described were actually different experiences, each connected to the other. For example, De Garmo claimed that Herbart offered teachers a way to examine all problems of instruction, school government, and moral training from the standpoint of actual experience. The path that Herbart created was simple: Teachers should recognize the children's previous experiences; they must impart information so that the students could assimilate it by relating it to previous knowledge; and they must lead the students to acquire new understandings (De Garmo, *Herbart* 33–34).

Care is needed here. De Garmo did not want teachers to place excessive stress on developing children's sense perception by having them concentrate on what were called "object lessons." The method of object lessons had become popular during the nineteenth century because its proponents claimed that sense observations provided the foundation of knowledge. These organized series of lessons could begin at home and move to the school. Parents could arrange different types of materials of different colors, and the children could learn to identify the colors. In schools, teachers could help the children identify the characteristics of everyday objects and move into more complicated lessons on forms and shapes. Throughout these lessons, the teachers asked questions about the objects to develop and to test the children's abilities to distinguish the qualities found in the objects (Clifton 15–35, 47–53).

De Garmo thought the object lessons were inferior to Herbart's system because they ignored the complex phenomenon Herbart called "apperception." The concept was that every perception stimulated ideas already in the mind, and this combination of sensation and recall brought up more ideas that were similar and repressed memories that were contrary. According to De Garmo, in this combination of sense perception and memory, the new experience fused with older ones and became assimilated or apperceived. This differed from the object lessons because the connected experiences could lead to moral insights about the world (De Garmo, *Herbart* 8, 34).

Although teachers of object lessons asked students to compare the Lord to a father, they seemed to have more difficulty leading the children to see the moral connections among everyday activities. On the other hand, in lessons about bread, the Herbartian activities might include some form of experiences with planting, reaping, threshing, grinding, baking, eating, digesting, and gaining new strength for labor.

To De Garmo, the Herbartian instruction was not only superior, but also appealing to parents and to students. He thought that the parents liked it because they wanted their children to have training in activities related to modern life, and the students liked the lessons because the activities appealed to their interests (De Garmo, *Herbart* 25–26).

How did the doctrine of appealing to students' interests illustrate the conflicting views of curriculum?

According to De Garmo, the children had to be interested in what they learned in order for the lessons to develop into ideals of conduct. Thus, for the Herbartians, interest was more than a means to secure the children's attention. They hoped that, by presenting the proper amount of interest at the right time in the best manner, they could incite an interest that would abide within the students after the knowledge had faded from their minds (De Garmo, *Herbart* 57–60).

De Garmo thought two kinds of interests concerned teachers. The first type included interests that were related to knowledge, such as the pleasure the students felt when learning something new. Since these interests changed as the novelty faded, a more lasting type of intellectual interest was what De Garmo called the speculative interest. This was the pleasure that came from searching for the reason behind things or events. Another intellectual interest was what De Garmo called the aesthetic interest. Unrelated to cause, it was the pleasure that a person derived when contemplating an ideal such as the pleasure that came from recognizing the character of Moses when looking at Michelangelo's statue of him (De Garmo, *Herbart* 60–63).

For the Herbartians, the second type of interest was the pleasure that arose from association with other people. A simple form of this category was the joy that came from cooperating with other people to achieve an end. De Garmo pointed out that children felt this when they learned that mothers, fathers, sisters, and brothers engaged in different tasks to keep the family's household running. The joy of cooperation in small groups extended into the social interest, De Garmo added. This was the pleasure the students felt when they learned about their country's growth and expansion. Studies such as literature, civics, and commercial geography fed these interests. The ultimate social interest came from religion. Herbartians believed schools could appeal to this religious interest by using historical studies showing that the successes and failures of humankind involved more than human power (De Garmo, *Herbart* 63–66).

On the other hand, Harris argued that the Herbartians offered illogical and contradictory explanations for organizing things around the students' interests. Harris claimed that the Herbartian theories became illogical because Herbart reduced everything to the same substance. That is, Harris described Herbart as believing people engaged in acts because they desired something. From these acts, they formed collections of mental pictures, and these images interpenetrated or mingled with each other. Herbart gave a name, "apperceptive mass," to this jumble of concepts in children's minds, and he considered this mass to be what some people called the "children's will" or intellect. Thus, Harris complained that Herbart denied that people had some internal mechanism given to them by God that could be called the will or the intellect. Instead, Herbart postulated that an endless number of desires and deeds had created a body of impressions in each child's mind, and these impressions worked together in ways that made it appear there was an independent will or intellect. This explanation did not satisfy Harris who contended that Herbart defined the intellect by explaining what it did. Intellect could not exist, Harris argued, unless there was something within people that caused them to integrate their experiences into some meaningful pattern. This was what he called "self-activity" (Harris, "Herbart's Doctrine" 71–73, 76–77).

According to Harris, the Herbartians contradicted themselves when they tried to build a system of moral training on this doctrine of interest without holding to a concept of a soul or an intellect capable of self-activity. The problem that Harris found appeared in what Herbart called the "formal steps of instruction." The first of these formal steps was to have the pupils absorb themselves in a subject. After a period of single-minded absorption, the students entered another formal step wherein they recoiled from the specialization and spread their attention through related general human interests. At the same time, though, Herbart wanted to relate all the subjects to some central core, such as a reading of Homer's *Odyssey*. Harris contended that when the teachers tied subjects to some central core, the students never experienced the initial step of clarity because the lessons disguised what was peculiar to the different branches of study by relating the subjects to the central core. Thus, Harris called this process "conglomeration" instead of concentration (Harris, "Herbart's Doctrine" 78–80).

In making his complaints about the doctrine of interest, Harris restated the central difference between his view and that of the Herbartians. He complained that the Herbartian sequences of activities were overly simple. For example, in the lesson about bread that included experiences with planting, reaping, threshing, grinding, baking, eating, digesting, and gaining new strength for labor, Harris claimed teachers should provide the higher view of the relativity of all things. That is, each thing had been derived from something else. The bread was different from what it was when it was grain, and it had a destiny beyond its present state, when it would become the source of a person's strength. Harris argued that the Herbartians presented new objects in ways that could be explained by previous experiences instead of offering profound and important philosophical thoughts. In order to go beyond these simple chains of experiences, the Herbartian teachers had to believe the children had souls with the ability and freedom to determine themselves (Harris, "Herbart's Doctrine" 71–73).

In 1896, Frank McMurry defended the doctrine of interest against Harris's assertion that the Herbartians concerned themselves with children's interest because they did not believe in a transcendent will or intellect that had the power of self-activity. On the one hand, McMurry claimed that Herbartians thought the question of the existence of the will did not belong in discussions of teaching. It was a problem for metaphysics. The daily experience of teachers showed that interest awoke children's desires and influenced their wills. If children's wills were independent of their desires or interests, as he understood Harris to imply, McMurry added that teachers could not influence children to perform their duties. McMurry noted that most people thought a teacher could influence children to be moral, and McMurry thought that teachers could do this because children would return again and again to whatever they loved, add new information to material learned earlier, and recognize new or different aspects of the subject. This did not mean the lessons should be easy. It meant that children would approach their work as if it were play. Nor did it mean the children would never learn to fulfill painful duties. For example, children took interest in the story of George Washington undergoing hardships at Valley Forge; they admired his moral qualities; and they began to feel they should be able to imitate Washington. McMurry did not think that involving the students' interests made the children selfish. He noted that a scientist making experiments to win a prize may act selfishly, yet students conducting studies to learn something about the world were not. McMurry thought the distinction was important because the students conducted their unselfish actions thoughtfully and, as a result, the insights gained stayed in their minds. Finally, McMurry dismissed the complaint that students would never learn to cope with drudgery if the lessons appealed to their interests. He asserted that students gained a momentum of working when they did things they understood. As a result, on approaching boring or routine tasks, they could perform those duties (McMurry, "Interest" 146, 148–155).

John Dewey cautioned that there was a danger in the Herbartian view. In February 1896, in a paper presented to the Herbart Society, Dewey warned against making interest an end of education. He thought that the best thing to do was to find those conditions that made something interesting and to use them to compel the interest to come forward. This meant that teachers should find children's impulses or habits, supply the proper environment, and thereby set those impulses to work in a fruitful and orderly way. While Dewey seemed to separate himself from the Herbartians, such as McMurry, by claiming that the children's interests were indications of other more important aims, Dewey did not accept Harris's view that children should pursue subject matters to form their intellects. Instead, Dewey defined the will as a name given to the intelligent adjustment of means to an end. Thus, he considered anything to be proper training of the will if it enabled students to develop independence, proper deliberation, and firmness in action (Dewey, "Interest in Relation" 33–34).

In May 1896, Harris complained that Dewey considered interest to be a function of self-expression but he rejected a spiritual basis for an understanding of interest. Harris claimed that people expressed themselves when they understood and conformed to what he called the "Divine will." Since this meant that interest was subordinate to goals that transcended experience, Harris thought educators should begin by searching for the rational purpose of civilization. He believed that this could be found in the various branches of knowledge. Teachers should find how they could express themselves by attaining these goals, and the teachers could study the pupils' interests in order to bring them into conformity with the highest goals. In short, Harris concluded, Dewey's paper could lead to more cooperation between school people and the Herbartians if everyone acknowledged that the higher question of which course of study would correlate the children with the civilization into which they were born was more important than how to the serve children's interests (Harris, "Professor Dewey" 487, 491–493).

On the other side, De Garmo enthused over Dewey's paper. He praised Dewey for showing that teachers could draw on children's interests and still teach them to be diligent. If children took interest in the aims of their work, they would apply themselves in achieving those ends. De Garmo claimed that Dewey had to make this truth obvious because teachers associated education with drill on reading, arithmetic, and grammar. Further, De Garmo acknowledged some truth to Harris's criticisms that Herbartians relied so much on interest in forming the will that they did not distinguish between good and bad interests. With these concessions, De Garmo hoped teachers would use the doctrine of interest as an angle from which to view other elements of education (De Garmo, "Present Status" 142–144).

How did educators want to reform secondary school programs?

In 1893, Harris was part of the NEA's Committee of Ten when it delivered its report describing the high school courses students should take to enter college. Unlike the later report of the Committee of Fifteen, Harris had little influence in writing the summary. As a result, when the academic specialists provided specific recommendations about the subject areas, some of these reports advocated methods of curriculum construction that contradicted Harris's ideas.

In its summary, the committee's report recommended that all secondary school students choose from four programs that concentrated on what would be called academic subjects. Three of the programs included either Latin or Greek, and one included only one foreign language. There were no courses in music, drawing, or elocution although many high schools found these to be popular offerings. The committee did not ignore these offerings because the members expected students to study these subjects in such areas as history, botany, or geography. No industrial or commercial courses appeared among the committee's recommendations, but the committee suggested that in one program, there was an option for algebra, which high schools could use for bookkeeping or commercial arithmetic. The committee members hoped that all schools would offer these four courses because "taught consecutively and thoroughly . . . , they would all be used for training the powers of observation, memory, expression, and reasoning" (NEA, *Committee of Ten* 52).

The chairperson of the Committee of Ten was Charles W. Eliot, president of Harvard University. Although Eliot asserted that the committee sought to coordinate the separate subjects in ways that illuminated the relationships among distinct bodies of knowledge, De Garmo pointed out that the report did not achieve such an end. In fact, De Garmo claimed that the Committee of Ten could not investigate ways to interrelate the subject areas because the committee members drafted their overall report from the work of nine independent conferences whose members were specialists in such areas as Latin, Greek, English, modern languages, and mathematics. Following such a system, each subject area maintained its independence and no one was in a position to construct what De Garmo called the "organic connections" among the various branches of knowledge. Nonetheless, De Garmo acknowledged that the Committee of Ten's report was an advance for the time because each subject area presented claims for the sequence of studies. As result, each branch of knowledge was coordinated into a rational pattern of treatment (De Garmo, *Herbart* 215–216).

Although De Garmo complained that the report of the Committee of Ten ignored how the subjects should correlate with each other, this was not true of the subject matter specialists appointed to the Madison Conference charged to make recommendations about the ways that history, civil government, and political economy should be taught in the high schools. These experts called for a curriculum that blended subjects and lessons that built on the students' interests.

In their separate report, the members of the Madison Conference resolved that history and its kindred subjects be taught in the last eight years of school. They complained that if the methods of teaching through drill and memory from textbooks continued to be used, they might prefer to omit history from school curriculums. They noted, though, that the subject could flourish when conducted by well-trained teachers who had a fondness for the subject. They cautioned against excessive use of textbooks and urged systems similar to one they called the "topical method." Used in German schools, this method allowed students to prepare individual reports about important historical figures, political issues, or historical changes. Teachers had to exercise care in allowing students to select the topics because they had to be manageable and appropriate. The topical method had several advantages, however, according to the Madison Conference. For example, the students could work independently, they could criticize each other's work, and they relieved the teacher of excessive preparation and grading. At the same time, the topical method allowed students to work with original sources, which the members of the Madison Conference claimed was much more exciting than reading a text. Further, by moving away from recitations, history teachers could relate their courses to those in other areas, such as English. Thus, unlike the previous generation of historians, these scholars in the Madison Conference did not urge the study of the ways that governmental institutions developed with the hope the students would feel more patriotic. Further, the Madison Conference report recommended that students pursue civil government by visiting city, state, or national governments and that study of political and economic geography accompany historical investigations (NEA, *Report of the Committee of Ten* 164–165, 194–197).

Instead of urging teachers to show the development of nations in ways that illustrated the evolution of freedom as Harris wanted, the report of the Madison Conference recommended that teachers concentrate on topics that were closer to the lives of their students. Since the topics allowed students to work on issues of interest to them and that correlated with the work in other subject areas, these ideas were closer to those of De Garmo than those of Harris. One reason why the members of the Madison Conference turned away from the traditional orientation of history was that the historians who participated in the conference sought to transform their discipline. Among the ten scholars who the Committee of Ten assigned to the Madison Conference were Woodrow Wilson, Albert Bushnell Hart, and James Harvey Robinson. Although Wilson and Hart retained their allegiances to history, they considered themselves political scientists because they sought to apply their work to support present-day policy reforms (Novick 69).

An illustration of the affection that these historians had for the topical method is the *Guide to the Study and Reading of American History* that Hart published in 1896 with coauthor Edward Channing. Revised in 1912 with Frederick Jackson Turner, the guide urged teachers to study less about the development of forms of government and more about the customs of people. In the guide, Hart and his coauthors listed appropriate books and topics, such as slavery in certain colonies, the students could investigate on their own (Channing, Hart, and Turner 6, 10–11, 24).

For his part, Robinson became famous for his calls for a new history. Robinson complained that the studies of the development of large state governments skipped from one gruesome battle to another imitating the way popular newspapers informed their readers about various but unrelated crimes. According to Robinson, the result was that historical writing had turned into lists of names of persons and places purporting to represent the great events in the world's history. But, Robinson added, these histories of kings and queens overlooked the ways that contemporary ways of thinking and acting developed and left readers unable to understand why such conventions as trial by jury or the study of the liberal arts appeared. As a result, people tended to follow these practices uncritically out of affection for tradition. Thus, he concluded that the new history should help people make sense of their world by availing itself of the discoveries of anthropologists, economists, psychologists, and sociologists (Robinson, *New History* 8–24).

Robinson found several supporters for his views. For example, Frederick Jackson Turner urged historians to look beyond institutions and constitutions to the social and economic history of the nation. But, at the same time, Robinson's ideas sparked controversies among historians. For example, when Robinson introduced intellectual history as a subject to Columbia University, the former chairperson of the history department, William M. Sloan, complained that Robinson and his colleagues ignored traditional history and established courses in such subjects as sociology and economics that competed with established departments. Most troubling to Sloan, Robinson was not expert in these areas. Thus, Robinson's critics made charges against him that were similar to those Harris made about the Herbartians: He blurred the distinctions among the subject areas, mingling the methods and information appropriate to each field (Novick 89).

Why did critics complain about the report of the Committee of Ten?

At first, the report of the Committee of Ten enjoyed a warm reception. In 1904, however, critics complained that the report ignored the interests and abilities of the students. Unfortunately, the chairperson of the report offered such a weak defense of the need for separate academic subjects for all students that he had to reverse his opinions.

According to Kliebard's account, the Committee of Ten based the recommendation of academic studies for all students on an antiquated and dangerous psychological principle called "mental discipline." Kliebard adds that this principle justified teaching techniques based on drill and repetition that made children dislike schools (Kliebard, *Struggle* 5–7).

Contrary to Kliebard's assertions, though, commentators at the time praised the Committee of Ten for rejecting the doctrine of mental discipline. Writing in 1894, Cecil Bancroft complimented the Committee of Ten for taking a broader outlook than the perspective offered by the theory of mental discipline. Although Bancroft noted that one paragraph in the report did use the terms common to mental or formal discipline, he added that the rest of the report contradicted this doctrine. Bancroft's comments illustrate the favorable reception the report of the Committee of Ten enjoyed. Most contemporary complaints about the committee's report turned on questions about the number of courses and reasonable class hours for the subjects. These were the grounds on which one member of the Committee of Ten, James H. Baker, dissented from the report. He complained that not all programs offered the same amount of history, literature, or music, and the report overlooked some areas of study that he believed would develop imagination, enhance deductive reasoning, and further the education of the will through ethical ideas (NEA, *Committee of Ten* 57–58).

In 1904, G. Stanley Hall raised an issue similar to those that De Garmo and his fellow Herbartians made against Harris. Hall condemned the Committee of Ten's report because it stressed academic subjects at the expense of vocational interests. In this regard, Hall found three flaws in the report. First, the report sought to teach the same subjects to every student in the same way and to the same extent disregarding the students' vocational interests and the differences in their abilities. Hall pointed out that European countries offered different types of schools for different types of pupils who could afford to spend different amounts of time in schools. Second, Hall noted that the committee held the view that all subjects are of equal value if taught well. This assertion overly promoted the importance of teaching methods and disregarded the many volumes of books and articles written to defend the value of certain courses. Third, Hall complained that the committee asserted that fitting students for college would also prepare them for life. Hall thought this might be true if success in life depended on passing a series of written exams such as one finds in college (Hall, *Adolescence* 510–514).

In 1905, the chairperson of the Committee of Ten, Charles W. Eliot, objected to Hall's contentions. First, Eliot claimed that the committee did not intend for all students to study the same courses for the same length of time. Rather, Eliot noted, the committee intended this principle to mean that there was a best way to begin and to pursue each course, there were topics within each course that students should cover, and experts in the fields should define these topics. Eliot disagreed with Hall's contention that many children could not finish an academic course; he claimed the number of children incapable of learning academics was smaller than Hall believed. According to Eliot, Hall thought teachers could determine who should go to college and who should leave for work. Eliot replied that this was not something teachers could do easily. Sometimes, the children who learned slowly continued for longer periods and understood more than those who grasped the material quickly. Thus, for Eliot, an early end of schooling was an evil to be avoided (Eliot, "Assumptions" 328–333).

Second, while Hall contended that the Committee of Ten reported that all subjects were of equal educational value if taught equally well, Eliot argued that such a statement did not appear in the report. Eliot noted that it might be inferred from the fact that the committee allowed choices among programs. Eliot added that the report's recommendations restricted the possible selections to ensure all students took excursions into languages, mathematics, history, and natural science. While the report noted that these courses could all be used for training the powers of observation, memory, and expression, Eliot claimed that the report made this contention to assure colleges that they could admit students confident they were well prepared no matter which of the four programs they had elected (Eliot, "Assumptions" 333–335).

Third, Eliot claimed that when Hall attributed to the Committee of Ten the assertion that preparing students for college is the same as fitting them for life, he misrepresented the report because these words did not appear in it. Eliot acknowledged these words could be assumed because the committee sought to form high school programs that would help students succeed in careers beyond school or college. The problem was that, at the time of the report, high schools did not properly organize or teach vocational programs. Realizing this weakness, Eliot and the members of the Committee of Ten decided to allow students to choose from one of four programs that prepared for college believing that these superior courses would prepare for life better than poorly organized vocational ones (Eliot, "Assumptions" 333–341).

Throughout his defense of the report of the Committee of Ten, Eliot noted that he had written several articles making pleas similar to those of Hall's. He believed that schools should pay more attention to the differences in the abilities of students. The report of the Committee of Ten, Eliot claimed, did not show he had changed his mind. The Committee of Ten sought uniformity in programs so children from different parts of the United States could use programs in their home cities to prepare for college in other places. Thus, the committee tried to select courses that would help students in later life and that the students could follow from the elementary through secondary schools. They envisioned that a course taken in one grade would illuminate the subject taken at a more advanced level. Eliot wrote that the members believed that such programs would enable students to develop more abilities, improve their characters, and make them better and happier citizens (Eliot, "Assumptions" 341–343).

Despite this protest, less than three years later, in 1908, at a meeting of the National Society for the Promotion of Industrial Education, Eliot argued that teachers had to sort the children and place each in the line where he or she could do the best work. Eliot took this view, he said, because the modern world had developed such a variety of occupations that a person could no longer approach almost any trade (Eliot, "Industrial Education" 13–14).

According to Kliebard, Eliot changed his mind between 1905 and 1908 because the movement to support industrial education had grown rapidly and threatened to take over all aspects of high school training. Kliebard contended that Eliot offered a compromise that would preserve some academic studies in secondary schools (Kliebard 106–107), but he overstated Eliot's affection for academic education. In his speech to the National Society for the Promotion of Industrial Education, Eliot began by noting that increasing numbers of children had to leave public schools before the age of fourteen. These children could not be served by ordinary high school or by former arrangements whereby employers allowed children to leave work for six to twelve hours per week. Eliot claimed that he supported strict vocational education in specifically designated trade schools for these children (Eliot, "Industrial Education" 9). This view was not new to Eliot. In his reply to Hall, Eliot defended the Committee of Ten's choice of academics over vocational training by claiming that academic courses were the best courses offered by high schools at the time. Although Eliot complained about Hall's wanting to separate children and send them into different vocational training tracks, Eliot acknowledged he had long held a similar view. Since he never claimed that the liberal arts were humanizing forces, he could write in 1908 that some students needed vocational training in high schools.

Could theorists forge a synthesis of the views of Harris and the Herbartians?

Until his death, Harris remained the stronger advocate for the academic courses, and he remained opposed to the Herbartians. For example, at a discussion at the 1898 annual meeting of the National Herbart Society, Harris stated that his desire to retain the separate nature of the subject areas such as literature, grammar, mathematics, and history came from his belief that they were correlated in a person's worldview. That is, he believed that each branch of study has a place in an overarching perception that becomes the source of genuine interest. Since Herbart had no such concept in his philosophy, his disciples had to follow the view that children's interests were important. When Harris's comments appeared in the society's yearbook of 1898, the editor added a note explaining that teachers could not use Harris's view about the relation of every branch of study to a person's worldview because a person did not achieve a worldview until late in life. The editor argued that the Herbartians' view was more useful to teachers because they held that interest was a principle that invigorated every hour of children's study. At the end of the discussion, Frank McMurry noted that Harris and the Herbartians remained opposed on the question of whether following children's interest was an aid to moral training. McMurry noted that Harris continued to believe children had transcendent wills containing a principle of self-activity from which they took moral knowledge. If the children's wills were independent of desires and interests, McMurry asked, how could a teacher influence them? In apparent frustration, McMurry asserted that the problem could not be solved; he declared that the two sides of the question remained apart (Wilkinson 111–115).

According to historians Wayne Urban and Jennings Wagoner the sides did not stay apart. They claimed that Dewey offered his essay "The Child and the Curriculum" as a synthesis combining the views of educators who wanted to stay with traditional subject matters, such as Harris, and those of reformers who wanted to build a curriculum by utilizing the interests of children, such as the Herbartians. Urban and Wagoner contended that Dewey used this pattern of argument to show how a new formulation of the problem blended the two poles (Urban and Wagoner 221–222).

If Dewey's synthesis combined Harris and the Herbartians, it was an unfair blending that showed how the realistic views of the Herbartians overshadowed the idealistic concerns Harris expressed. Dewey used a form of dialectical reasoning wherein he spelled out each side of the debate and then pulled elements from each side to create a new conception in a manner that imitated Harris. Yet the content of Dewey's synthesis fell on the side of the Herbartians because Dewey refused to separate a person's will or intellect from the person's body and define it as something transcendent awaiting self-perfection. Like Herbart, Dewey sought some way to reduce everything to the same substance.

In his essay, "The Child and the Curriculum," Dewey wrote about using subject matter to help children select and improve their present capacities and their present attitudes. While Dewey acknowledged that subject matter could stay separate in the mind of the specialist, he thought that children should consider subject matter as a tool to help them achieve their ends. Dewey offered the hope that, when teachers used subject matter to serve and guide the interests of the children, the two poles, respect for children's interests and the importance of subject matter, could enhance each other. While subject matter retained ultimate superiority as goals toward which the teacher would bend the children's activities and interests, Dewey presented subject matter as subservient to the children's interests in daily classroom activities.

The point is that Dewey's synthesis did not differ from what the Herbartians had been doing and to which Harris objected. Instead of using cultural objects, such as Homer's *Odyssey,* to capture children's interests, Dewey asked the teachers to build on the things children did in everyday life. Thus, Dewey argued that knowing and doing were aspects of the same process. For example, a person might stop doing something and think, but the action of thinking was a plan for future actions.

Dewey's synthesis ignored Harris's view that the important knowledge in life was not related to any form of doing but was an aid in understanding the development of the Divine Will. This was a form of understanding the way history progressed and societies formed, and it was not the type of knowledge that came from the same conditions that produced plans for action. To preserve these distinctions, Harris wanted to distinguish the work of the school from the work found in occupations. The five major subject areas introduced the children to the knowledge of intercommunication, Harris argued. Manual training, or doing, limited the attention of the students to what they could produce in a narrow sphere of activity. While manual training enabled the students to contribute to the well-being of humankind, Harris did not think it led to the understanding of the culture. Dewey disagreed. For him, children could begin with practical activities, which he called "active occupations," and their expanding interests could lead them into studies of intellectual disciplines. For example, after planting a garden, children might want to pursue studies of botany or chemistry to improve their work.

Incidentally, both Harris and Dewey's views were flawed. Harris postulated that the self-activity of children's intellect enabled children to move to a higher level of thinking. Unfortunately, he could not explain how children did it. Dewey thought that children could move to different types of thinking through forms of association as if the ways of thinking were linked in a sort of spiral staircase. Unfortunately, he could not show how active accomplishments turned into aesthetic appreciations.

Despite the fact that Harris could defend his views from important critics, his ideas faded quickly after he died. In 1911, Hall proclaimed that twenty-five years earlier education was based on what he called the "sonorous metaphysical platitudes" of Harris who, according to Hall, had acquired almost papal authority among educators. Hall expressed relief that the view of psychology had changed. In his popular talks, Hall asserted that what he called the "child study movement" enabled schools to fit the development of the child. Although Hall claimed that he started a science of education, in reality, his contribution was to extend the ideas of Harris's critics, the Herbartians, who wanted children to develop naturally. The Herbartians had claimed that psychology would show how children developed naturally. Hall changed the notion of psychology from a given system to a belief that scientific studies would uncover the developmental laws. Unfortunately, Hall thought he could conduct these scientific studies by distributing questionnaires to teachers, principals, and superintendents around the country asking them about such subjects as children's fears. Although this method appeared impersonal and objective, Hall received fragmentary, inconclusive information that he supplemented with personal reminisces. As a result, few psychologists built studies on his findings (Hall, *Educational Problems* iii–vii; Ross 103–124, 290–292).

It fell to Thorndike to use more sophisticated methods and thereby transform Hall's child study movement into educational psychology. Ironically, although Thorndike may have started educational psychology, he did not urge educators to follow his studies to change schools. Writing in 1912, Thorndike noted that, in some cases, educators could determine the changes that studying a subject would produce in students. More frequently, though, educators could consider what the effect of a subject might be on such things as the students' health, conduct, or interests. When he surveyed the offerings in most schools, he found that elementary schools required all students to study the same academic materials that included what he called the three Rs and some other things such as manual training, geography, history, and nature study. But he noted approvingly that high school course offerings in 1911 showed many more practical courses such as civics, mathematics, commercial subjects, and industrial arts although the same academic courses appeared as were found in 1891. Further, he predicted that elementary and high schools would increase the vocational subjects so that children would be better fitted to do their work in life rather than to recall useless and disconnected facts. In this same line, he praised educators for recognizing that schools could be social centers where adults attended lectures and concerts and the school grounds could provide space for children to plant gardens and engage in athletics (Ross 347–348; Thorndike 126–127, 267–273).

Thorndike congratulated educators for widening the aims of school so that they became the aims of education in the widest sense. This was to make all people want what was good and to get for everyone the goods that they deserved. He predicted these reforms would have ever expanding effects. He felt that parents could do better by their children, churches could do better by their neighborhoods, and governments could do better by their citizens (Thorndike 273–275).

In expressing these hopes, Thorndike could have added that the Herbartians shared the same aims and approved of a similar and equally practical curriculum. Although he did not mention the Herbartians, his comments illustrate that by 1911 Harris's ideas had become less viable among reformers. Instead, reformers agreed that the appropriate curriculum had to have a realistic justification and that it should meet some practical conception of students' needs and the society's needs. Thus, although educators may have disagreed on the extent to which practical concerns should dominate the curriculum, they seemed to agree that the schools should serve the students' needs and the society's needs. Further, although the social requirements could contradict the individual needs, educators, such as Thorndike, turned away from the justifications for a curriculum that depended on some understanding of the children's souls. They trusted that these problems could be resolved by thinking in practical and realistic terms.

Summary

In the 1890s, two educational reports set the main lines for the curriculum reforms that followed during the first half of the twentieth century. Basing their ideas on those of German idealists, supporters of the reports, such as W. T. Harris, offered philosophical justifications for students to concentrate on traditional academic subjects. Critics found these explanations to be overly abstract and impractical and, as a result, turned to simpler, more realistic alternatives. At the same time, academics such as historians turned their disciplines toward studies of the more contemporary and conventional concerns of most people. The result was that in a short time, philosophical idealism disappeared as an important source of educational reform. It was replaced by more realistic explanations of how schools should work. These changes made it easier for teachers to consider offering a variety of new courses, to introduce more vocational education, and to tailor instruction to match the everyday experiences of the children. By providing opportunities for critics to diffuse their ideas, these reports acted as catalysts for educational reform during the first half of the twentieth century. In a short time, most educational reformers asserted that the schools should meet the children's needs. They added that since the children's needs were related to their lives, teachers could determine what those needs were. They believed that the teacher should help the children learn to satisfy their desires in ways that solved the needs of the society.

CHAPTER TWO

INTRODUCING THE PRACTICAL CURRICULUM, 1893–1918

During the nineteenth century, many educators wanted schools to improve students' general abilities and moral outlooks. They avoided offering direct vocational education. During the twentieth century, people campaigned for state governments to enact legislation making education compulsory. They argued that schools would reduce the problems that resulted from the growth of cities and immigration because teachers would provide the guidance children lacked in the new industrialized settings. Part of the campaign for compulsory education was the hope that schools could prepare the children for the work they would do as adults in a manner similar to the ways children learned vocational skills on farms and in small towns.

Although many educators tried to resist the vocational education movement, they had difficulty determining the point at which vocational training became excessive. The problem was that these educators blurred the line between academic studies and vocational education that Harris had stoutly maintained. They did this in two related ways. First, they imitated the Herbartians by trying to show that practical concerns, such as baking bread, could lead to academic studies, such as geography. Second, they offered manual training, promising that exercises, such as filing a piece of metal, reinforced the skills of reasoning the students needed for their academic studies. While such approaches promised to make school lessons more interesting for the students and to please the parents who wanted their children to learn more about everyday life, they left twentieth-century educators without defenses against the encroachment of the vocational educational movement. Educators who favored intellectual training found themselves in agreement with the view that schools should offer some form of vocational education to those students whom it could benefit. But the qualification that the child should need the vocational training offered little protection for abstract studies because it seemed that every child could profit from some form of vocational training. Thus, people could not easily condemn the vocational education movement even when it exacerbated the differences among social classes, benefited the owners of factories more than the students, and took jobs away from adults.

What benefits did people see in education and why did they think state governments should require all children to attend schools?

After the Civil War, citizens in the United States tended to favor the state regulation of education. But schools remained tied to their local communities. In fact, David Tyack argued that, in the last half of the nineteenth century, as people moved into cities, they brought with them the model of the district school that they had created in rural areas. Under this model, prominent families in an area came together and controlled educational matters, such as school construction, teacher selection, and curriculum formation. Tyack pointed out that in the cities, the residents of each ward elected a school board. Since many neighborhoods were ethnically homogenous, the residents created ethnic public schools (Tyack 3–12).

In rural areas, district schools offered opportunities for children to learn basic academic skills that would help them as they worked on the farms. In the cities, though, children lacked the opportunities to work closely with adults as they had on the farms. As a result, people in the cities expected schools to take on larger responsibilities. In part at least, citizens expressed these increased expectations in their campaigns to enact compulsory education laws. According to Forest Chester Ensign, proponents argued that these laws would enable the children to develop skills with which they could protect their morals and support themselves. At the same time, proponents added that compulsory education would provide intelligent and useful citizens to the state (Ensign 233–234).

In keeping with the perspective of protecting the children, the Illinois legislature passed the state's first law for compulsory education in 1883 and entitled it "An act to secure to all children the benefit of an elementary education." But, in 1888, when the Chicago City schools failed to enforce this law, the Chicago Women's Club sent the school board a petition stating their belief that compulsory education could restore civil order. Complaining that there was an appalling increase in crime among youth, a large number of vagrant children, and many dangers associated with child labor, the Women's Club demanded that the board enforce the statute. The women received a reply that the board had the question under consideration (Abbott and Breckinridge 53–57).

As the example of the Women's Club illustrates, in Illinois, the drive for stronger truancy laws accompanied legislative efforts to restrict child labor. In 1892, the superintendent of Chicago schools complained that over 1,000 children between the ages of ten and fourteen had been excused from schools, given working certificates, and allowed to take jobs. The board of education appointed a committee to make recommendations. But this time, a member of Jane Addams's Hull House, Florence Kelley, urged Governor Altgeld to ask the Illinois Bureau of Labor Statistics to determine what number of young children worked in city factories instead of attending schools. Altgeld appointed Kelley as a special investigator for the commission. On the basis of Kelley's report listing the extensive dangers to the children's health and safety, the legislature strengthened the law (Abbott and Breckinridge 69–72).

The initial impetus for compulsory education came from organizations of laborers. For example, in 1881, the members of the American Federation of Labor (AFL) adopted a plank in their constitution urging that laws forbid the employment of children less than fourteen years of age. By 1887, the AFL urged that compulsory education laws include requirements that all children study government and Americanization. Working together, the AFL and organizations of philanthropists enlisted universities, started investigations, and published articles and books about the need for compulsory education. In 1912, the U.S. Department of Labor formed the Federal Children's Bureau, which advanced the campaign (Ensign 246–247).

By 1918, every state adopted and enforced laws forcing children to attend schools. Not surprisingly, school attendance figures jumped dramatically. For example, writing in 1921, Forest Chester Ensign noted that in 1870, about 46 percent of the children of school age in Connecticut attended schools. He found that, by 1910, the rate of attendance jumped to about 58 percent, but Ensign complained that this increase in school attendance did not reduce illiteracy. Instead, literacy rates remained about the same, and Ensign argued that most of the children in Connecticut who were illiterate were foreign born (Ensign 252–253).

Although Ensign complained that immigrant children remained out of school, some authors of the period noted that the movement for compulsory education had not focused on the needs of these children. For example, in 1917, writing about the enforcement of compulsory education laws in Chicago, Edith Abbott and Sophonisba P. Breckinridge noted that the compulsory education laws in Chicago had been devised in the 1890s to meet the needs of American-born children of American parents before the city faced the problem of assimilating non-English-speaking immigrants. By the 1910s, though, immigration posed sufficient problems that Abbott and Breckinridge argued that truancy laws should be strictly enforced to help reduce the poverty of the immigrants. Abbott and Breckinridge found that non-English-speaking immigrants in Chicago often chose not to send their children to school because they needed money for food and shelter. Abbott and Breckinridge argued that the lack of education increased the immigrants' difficulties because being unable to speak English and lacking important skills, they could never earn much money. The authors admitted, however, that there was no simple way to bring the children to school. Immigration authorities did not alert school officials when families with school-age children arrived. Furthermore, when school authorities discovered immigrant children who did not attend, they seemed unwilling to force the children to come to school (Abbott and Breckinridge 264–269, 273).

Some researchers of the period disagreed with the view of Ensign and of Abbott and Breckinridge that immigrants presented the difficult problems. For example, in 1907, the Russell Sage Foundation extended a grant to Leonard Ayres to determine how many children failed in public schools and to investigate the reasons why they did not succeed. Ayers began by looking at the records of one school in New York City. From this case, he expanded to look at records of fifteen schools in Manhattan, and finally he analyzed the records of the schools in most of the large cities in the United States. When Ayers considered the accomplishments of foreign-born children, he found them to be less likely to fall behind in their progress through the grades than native-born children. Furthermore, he argued that nationwide, there were more illiterates proportionately among white people of native-born parents than among white people with foreign-born parents (Ayers xiii–3, 6).

Ayers surveyed the different ways that schools accommodated the needs of the non-English-speaking children. He claimed that many officials treated unfairly the large numbers of non-English-speaking immigrant children who enrolled in schools. A common practice was to place these children in the lower grades no matter what accomplishments the children had achieved in their home country. The children lingered in these lower grades until their command of English improved, Ayers complained. The result was the children could not learn enough to qualify for a working certificate when they reached age fourteen, and the lower grades contained too many children of a variety of ages for teachers to offer effective instruction (Ayers 197).

Ayers believed foreign-born children could succeed with an academic curriculum if their teachers made some adjustments for them. Noting that most children of immigrants acquired the new language quickly, he urged school officials to help this process. He complimented officials in New York and Cincinnati who organized special classes to help the foreign-born children learn English and offered special preparation to non-English-speaking children of the fifth or sixth grade so they could enter seventh grade (Ayers 197).

Ayers noted that many educational reformers in his day claimed that schools had developed an excessive failure rate because new types of students had entered. These reformers argued that this failure rate illustrated the need for vocational training instead of academic education. To Ayers, this argument implied that high rates of failure were new to schools. Although he had difficulty determining the failure rate because most schools did not keep accurate records, he found that the rate had declined from 1895 when about 69 percent of the students fell behind their fellow students to 1906 when about 65 percent fell behind. While Ayers thought this showed that schools were improving, he admitted that the changes were small (Ayers 170–174).

What did people think were the needs of different children and how did they think that manual training could meet these needs?

Ayers took a conservative approach to reform and made suggestions to improve the efficiency of schools. For example, he recommended that school officials enforce compulsory attendance, thereby ensuring the children had opportunities to learn. Other educators called for more radical changes to the curriculum, such as offering manual training to the children of immigrants, to meet the problems of the growing city. For example, writing in 1892, Jacob A. Riis praised the Children's Aid Society for establishing industrial schools in areas of New York City that he called slums. At the time, Riis reported that the society conducted twenty-one industrial schools with a total of 5,139 students of whom about half had been born overseas. Although more than 10 percent of the students did not speak English, Riis claimed that they picked up the language by observing the daily activities in the schools (Riis 184–190).

The schools of the Children's Aid Society offered little instruction in industrial practices. According to Riis, in these schools, the mainstay of the educational plan was a hot, square meal. In addition to offering what was often the only meal the children had all day, the schools offered medical care to students who were ill. Although the schools lacked workshops or tools to offer much manual training, Riis noted the students grew gardens, cooked food, and learned to sew. He was particularly impressed with the fact that in the schools, the students learned citizenship by participating in elections to decide rules of school governance. In his typical exuberance, Riis applauded these industrial schools for combating habitual drunkenness and poverty among the immigrants (Riis 191, 197, 204, 205, 213).

Other commentators repeated Riis's claims about the value of manual training for the children of immigrants. For example, in 1898 in a collection of essays about the South End

House in Boston, Robert A. Woods argued that manual training had three benefits for the children who lived in what he called "tenement-house districts." First, this was a practical form of learning that had no direct application to a trade, but it developed manual dexterity and in this way could prepare boys for the physical labor they were likely to do as adults. Second, Woods contended that since children made things in manual training, it encouraged them to be creative, careful, and patient. Woods believed these tendencies would counter the destructive, irresponsible attitudes they developed on the streets and in the gangs. Finally, Woods claimed that the children developed self-respect in manual training because they succeeded in making things that were plainly visible and in which they could take pride (Woods 237–240).

Despite these pleas for manual training for immigrants, Marvin Lazerson argued that, during the 1890s, many educators asserted that city life threatened the traditional values of society and, therefore, every resident risked contamination. According to Lazerson, these educators recommended some form of manual or industrial training for all students, and they hesitated to claim that manual or industrial training had particular value for the children of the tenement districts. Lazerson believed that in this way the educators maintained the notion of a common school offering instruction applicable to all people rather than aiming lessons at specific groups of deprived people (Lazerson 111).

Lazerson's portrayal of teachers urging every student to pursue manual training is in keeping with the manual training movement. Most people, such as Riis and Woods, used the terms *industrial* and *manual training* without having a specific curriculum in mind. In fact, during the 1880s and 1890s, terms such as *manual training* and *industrial education* lacked any specific reference. Through the championship of Calvin M. Woodward, manual training took on specific meaning and became a popular movement (Coates 14–16).

Woodward's campaign began in 1873 when, as director of the poly-technical school at Washington University in St. Louis, he claimed that students had to engage in practical affairs to understand them and, therefore, learning from books should be augmented by practical experiences. He called for opportunities in such areas as shop work and drawing to teach children how to work with tools and how to make judgments. Thus, his view was similar to that of the Herbartians in that he believed practical activities could lead to more abstract understandings (Woodward, *Manual Training School* 255–258).

On the one hand, Woodward noted that schools had to offer some sort of vocational or practical training because large industries and unions had made it impossible for young men to become apprentices. But on the other hand, he disapproved of trade schools because these prepared children to work in specific vocations and offered training that was very narrow. The solution for Woodward was to abstract the mechanical processes in different trades and to arrange them in a systematic course of instruction. He believed that, when joined with academic studies, such instruction would offer breadth to the children's education and enable each student to learn specific trades later in life (Woodward, *Manual Training School* 272–276).

To offer examples of the types of exercises that he wanted the students to perform, he quoted a lesson in using the file developed at the Massachusetts Institute of Technology. In the exercise, the teacher gave each student a flat piece of cast iron with two round holes drilled through it. In addition, each student had six files and two try squares. The object of the lesson was for the students to learn to identify the use of each type of file, to apply them properly, and to use the tools in graded steps to make the piece of iron square, to make the round holes square, and to remove all file marks (Woodward, *Manual Training School* 280–282).

To outside observers, lessons such as filing a square of metal appeared fruitless, but to Woodward, they were valuable. He acknowledged that there was no commercial value to the articles the students produced, but he claimed the exercises offered students opportunities to acquire the correct techniques (Coates 64–65).

Woodward's strongest critic was William Torrey Harris. In fact, Woodward and Harris appeared together at conventions of national organizations presenting their different opinions. For example, in 1889, the National Educational Association invited Woodward and Harris to present papers explaining their positions to the annual meeting held in Tennessee that year. In that session, Woodward chose to describe four results of his manual training school. The first was that many elementary and high schools had adopted programs of manual training since his program opened in St. Louis. The second was that more students attended for longer periods of time when they could take practical courses than they did when all the instruction was academic. Third, graduates of high schools with manual training tended to go on to higher education. Woodward claimed the program enhanced the students' desire for learning because in the shop work students confronted concrete applications of the abstract ideas they learned in academic classes. He added that the shop work provided the opportunity for relief from reading, and the students could recognize the practical value of their studies (Woodward, "Results" 73–77). At the meeting in Tennessee, Harris claimed that manual training was a lower form of instruction than academic training. As a result, the skills acquired within such academic training as arithmetic included the lessons that Woodward thought were found in manual training. Harris acknowledged there was a valid place for manual training, but he thought it was not in schools. It was in apprenticeship programs (Harris, "Intellectual" 96–98).

As Chapter One describes, Harris's objection stemmed from his belief that, at certain points, the various parts of a whole had to remain distinct from each other. Once the parts established their identity, they could join as a whole unit at a later point. As Chapter One illustrates, Harris argued that children had to learn different subjects separately in order to understand the relationships that existed among them. In a similar manner, he contended that the different institutions in society had to remain distinct so that they could perform their unique functions to make the citizens complete human beings. For example, he thought that churches offered spiritual guidance, schools provided intellectual development, and shops and farms gave vocational instruction.

Woodward made three important counterarguments against Harris. First, he claimed that Harris misrepresented manual training. Woodward claimed that Harris presented the work students performed in the manual training exercises as endless repetition done in a mindless fashion. In fact, Woodward argued that in the shop, thoughtful, deliberative reasoning was the significant characteristic of the work students performed. Second, Woodward claimed that Harris made subjects such as mathematics, in which students learned to control objects, appear more inclusive than manual training, in which students learned particular skills such as building a box. According to Woodward, in making this objection, Harris confused the general with the particular. That is, in mathematics students solved particular problems about the cost of certain carpets, for example, to learn larger principles about determining the area of shapes. He claimed manual training worked at particular problems, making a box, for example, to learn the principles of construction. In both cases, the students did particular projects to learn general principles. Third, Woodward claimed Harris thought learning to read was the most important lesson taken from school because it enabled children to acquire the wisdom of authors from the past. Although Harris claimed that manual training did offer such opportunities, Woodward disagreed by claiming that manual training opened to students valuable human experiences that had not become parts of books (Woodward, "Results" 80–89).

Ten years after the exchange of papers in Tennessee, Harris repeated his objections to manual training. First, he contended that manual training repeated the lessons found in the academic subjects. For example, Woodward claimed that drawing would provide children opportunities to coordinate skills between their hands and their eyes. In contrast, Harris claimed the students did not need separate classes in drawing because children could develop coordination between their hands and their eyes as they pursued academic studies of plants and animals. Second, Harris argued that some of the supposed benefits of manual training were best learned outside schools. For example, Woodward claimed students learned skills needed to transform materials in such exercises as the lesson on using the file; Harris thought that learning such skills as the proper techniques in using a file should be acquired in workplaces where such lessons contributed directly to the students' vocations. As a result, although Harris acknowledged the importance of learning to handle materials, he thought manual training had no place in schools (Harris, *Psychologic* 333).

The arguments with Harris frustrated Woodward. Although other school districts adopted programs of manual training, Woodward had difficulty instituting some form of practical education in the St. Louis schools even though he served on the city school board. A part of the school district's resistance came from the fact that Harris had been superintendent of the schools in St. Louis and was later the U.S. Commissioner of Education (Troen 171).

Although manual training enjoyed a short period of popularity, it did not fade because of the criticisms that Harris made. The more significant opponents to Woodward's program were vocational educators who became strong enough that, by 1918, vocational programs replaced the more general training exercises that Woodward favored. More important, vocational educators ignored Harris's pleas that human beings were rational and required academic studies to understand their civilization and to fulfill their natures.

How did vocational educators decide what students needed and how did they want to meet those needs?

Advocates for vocational education advanced their courses by using the same argument that Woodward had used to advance manual training. That is, Woodward argued that manual training provided concrete experiences to supplement the literary, academic curriculum. In a similar manner, critics argued that manual training was abstract and should be supplemented with training for practical experiences or vocational education. For example, summarizing the testimony of witnesses to the Commission on Industrial and Technical Education, the commission's report noted that manual training was not popular among the general public even though a Massachusetts law in 1894 required cities of more than 20,000 inhabitants to include such training in high schools. In 1898, this requirement spread to elementary schools. According to the commission's report, the problem was that school people presented manual training as a cultural subject that served as a stimulus to other forms of intellectual effort. Concluding that manual training was separated from life in the same way that other school subjects were cut off from their connections in the world, the commission's report complained that schools did not offer children any opportunities to prepare for work (Massachusetts Commission on Industrial and Technical Education 14–18).

Thus, the factor that Woodward thought was the strength of manual training was the weakness according to the critics. Woodward had selected the name, "manual training," because his school did not teach any trade or profession. Instead, it gave a wide training in practical arts, in commercial fields, and in literary studies. Woodward claimed manual training offered the students opportunities to reinforce in the shop, the skills they learned in mathematics and literature classes. As far as the practical techniques were concerned, Woodward claimed the students learned only enough about a skill to understand what it was and how it related to other shop procedures. They did not become adept at any of particular trade (Coates 60–67).

Unfortunately for Woodward, manufacturers did not want to hire students who understood the relation of one skill to another. Several industrialists told the Commission on Industrial and Technical Education in 1906 that their factories needed people who could join the workforce as productive members. The commission's report agreed, adding that training in specific trades would benefit the children as well because training them could also enhance their physical, intellectual, and moral growth (Massachusetts Commission on Industrial and Technical Education 18–19).

Another irony appeared in the arguments about vocational education. In the last years of the nineteenth century, Harris argued that there should be two separate spheres of learning, and he used this argument to retain an exclusively academic curriculum in schools. Vocational educators gave the argument a different twist, however, and used it to justify the inclusion of vocational education along with academic programs. For example, writing in 1910, David Snedden, then Commissioner of Education for Massachusetts, claimed that students should learn cultural values in schools and they should acquire practical values through some experience that was similar to an apprenticeship. But, Snedden added that children could not find employment in large cities because the apprenticeship system no longer existed. As a result, he concluded that schools had to introduce vocational education to restore the balance between school and work that had previously existed in the society (Snedden, "The Problem" 4–18).

Since Snedden wanted vocational training to be practical, he warned that there would have to be a variety of different types of vocational education. Snedden thought this would include different types of training for industry and for agriculture and different arrangements to provide the instruction. For example, in addition to students taking classes in schools, he noted that people working on farms might want short courses on particular aspects of agricultural production, such as raising poultry, and people working in factories might want short courses on the use of particular tools. Snedden thought these classes should be offered on a short-term basis at times convenient to the adults (Snedden, "The Problem" 62–63).

Although Snedden had narrow views of vocational training, he claimed he did not want vocational education to replace academic instruction. Instead, he thought that various arrangements of vocational education would restore the avenues to success that once existed in society for some students and adults. He argued that communities, states, and the federal government should spend tax money on vocational education because it allowed people to work to their capacities and thereby improved the society. Consequently, Snedden argued, vocational education should stand apart from and supplement academic training (Snedden, "The Problem" 81–82).

Finally, vocational educators claimed that students should be able to choose some of the classes they wanted to study. Called the "elective principle," this idea had appeared in a limited form in the report of the Committee of Ten. Furthermore, it was an important factor in the development of the curriculum at Harvard, although classical scholars complained that students used the elective principle to select courses that would not challenge their abilities or they took a preponderance of courses in one area at the expense of developing other talents and abilities. In 1901–02, Paul H. Hanus, a professor at Harvard, surveyed about one thousand undergraduates to determine the bases by which they chose their courses. He found that they favored the system because it allowed them to select courses that prepared them for their future vocations and they could take work in areas that permanently interested them. In other cases, Hanus found the undergraduates praising the elective system because it allowed them to pursue courses they had not realized could be interesting (Hanus 287–306).

By the time that Hanus published the results of his study, he was an important voice in vocational education, and he repeatedly urged the adoption of vocational education on the grounds that schools offering exclusively academic training were undemocratic. Writing in 1913, he recommended that elementary schools should offer vocational training because it would meet the needs of the students and benefit the society. He asserted that most children left school after eighth grade and never attended high school. Yet, he believed some students could select vocational studies in high school and in college. As a result, to serve these students who lacked academic interests, he urged educators to add vocational courses, such as carpentry, plumbing, or millinery, in the seventh and eighth grades so that the students could choose some studies that they could pursue as a career. In this way, Hanus claimed the students could attain what he called self-realization and could offer public service as productive citizens (Hanus 201–208).

Claiming that vocational education would meet the needs of the students and the needs of the society, supporters sought to revitalize public schools. Although they agreed that students should take different courses including many vocational options depending on their needs, they disagreed how the vocational programs should be offered. In Massachusetts, the first Commission on Industrial and Technical Education recommended in 1906 that all elementary and secondary schools should include instruction in the elements of productive industry. It suggested that these classes should be part of elective programs in public high schools. But the report also recommended that the state establish a system of independent vocational schools apart from the locally controlled public schools. Thus, the commission wanted the state to support separate, independent programs of industrial training (Massachusetts Commission on Industrial and Technical Education 20–21).

Less than a year later, a second commission chaired by Hanus made the same recommendation, and the Massachusetts state legislature adopted a bill authorizing an administrative commission to develop a state system of industrial schools independent of the board of education. The bill would have created a dual system of education, but the policy failed quickly. By 1909, the vocational school commission had done so little to begin vocational schools that the legislature moved the commission into the Massachusetts State Board of Education (Hawkins, Prosser, and Wright 35–36).

A similar debate about the ways to offer vocational education took place after the Commercial Club of Chicago sent Edwin Cooley, the former superintendent of Chicago's public schools, to make a survey of European industrial education in 1909. On his return, Cooley recommended that the city establish a set of vocational schools entirely separate from the academic schools. The purpose of such separate training was to offer boys and girls between the ages of fourteen and sixteen an opportunity to earn an honest living. Cooley claimed these schools would reduce crime and disarm growing socialist sentiments among the laboring classes. After Cooley presented his report, the club began to lobby the state legislature for funds to create such systems. This effort failed because labor unions, teachers' organizations, and civic leaders opposed a completely separate system (Hogan 175–181).

In 1913, John Dewey argued against the idea of setting up separate vocational schools. Calling Cooley's idea an undemocratic proposal, Dewey claimed the idea had three inherent flaws. First, the independent school systems required duplication of administrative resources and costs. Second, separating vocational training from academic preparation would prevent teachers of academic subjects to use manual activities to revitalize the academic subjects. Finally, the proposal would harm students in the vocational schools who, unable to pursue academic studies, would be deprived of the opportunity to learn the historic, economic, and social influences of their trade. Thus, Dewey complained that bankers and manufacturers seemed to support the Cooley proposal to produce a class of workers who possessed particular narrow skills that they could exploit. They did not want to create schools that could infuse the students with character and intelligence (Dewey, "Some Dangers" 100–102).

Despite the controversies about separating academic schools from vocational institutions, vocational education advocates began an effective campaign to garner federal support. Although they did not pursue dual systems directly, they left that option open in their publicity efforts. In 1906, about 250 prominent businessmen and educators gathered to form the National Society for Promotion of Industrial Education (NSPIE). In the society's constitution, the members affirmed their affection for training students to become proficient in trades but expressed uncertainty about the way to best carry out such instruction. As a result, they sent out questionnaires purporting to sample the views of manufacturers and labor leaders. In addition to surveying public opinion about vocational education, the questionnaires also informed people about the NSPIE and its campaign. Among the respondents was then U.S. President Theodore Roosevelt who claimed that the country faced a shortage of skilled workers and that public schools contributed to prejudices among the students against manual labor. He expressed the wish that the new organization could make labor appear as dignified as the higher professions and thereby encourage more young people to enter such callings (Hawkins, Prosser, and Wright 68–71).

As part of its campaign, the NSPIE created state-level organizations to support the activities. As these organizations began campaigns in their own areas, the NSPIE drafted model legislation that supported vocational education, which they sent to members of the U.S. Congress. Although these bills failed, in 1914, U.S. President Woodrow Wilson appointed a Commission on National Aid to Vocational Education. Submitting its report in less than six months, the commission noted that the country needed vocational education for several reasons: to conserve natural resources, to utilize human labor effectively, to replace disappearing apprenticeships, to increase wage earning, to offset escalating costs of living, to provide wise investments, and to protect national prosperity. In addition, the report claimed that when students chose their vocational studies, schools acted more democratically. Also, such training prevented labor unrest because it opened avenues of advancement to the workers (Hawkins, Prosser, and Wright 81–82, 90–104).

The commission's report repeated the claim the members of the NSPIE made frequently that states could not provide vocational training by themselves. If local districts or state governments tried to offer vocational training, they would have to tax their citizens at excessive rates to meet the obligations. Further, the commission noted that the federal government had a long history of supporting vocational agricultural education through such devices as the land-grant colleges (Hawkins, Prosser, and Wright 105–106).

President Wilson urged Congress to accept the recommendation of the commission and set up a Federal Board for Vocational Education. In December 1915, Wilson argued that the federal government should stimulate industrial and vocational education so the country could be ready for military mobilization. One month later, Wilson repeated his pleas for federal support of vocational education contending that industrial preparedness was as important in a war as military preparedness. Finally, in December 1916, when Wilson repeated his pleas again, Congress responded by passing the National Vocational Education Act (Smith-Hughes Act). Within ten months, each of the then forty-eight states accepted the provisions of the Act (Hawkins, Prosser, and Wright 87–89).

According to officials and their critics, what was the effect of the National Vocational Education Act?

It is difficult to assess the effects of the Smith-Hughes Act. The programs that it established grew in popularity in a short time. But the enrollment figures were unreliable, and it appears the programs did not reach many students. The training probably did not help laborers earn more money, but studies never determined if this was true or false. One thing that the legislation prompted was to make educators think more about including vocational education in some form.

The Smith-Hughes Act promised that the federal government would pay for one-half of the expenses in providing vocational education in a state if the state government provided the other half. The federal money went for teachers' salaries and training. State governments had to provide and equip buildings. With the exception of teacher training institutions, the schools had to be below college level and the students, more than fourteen years old. They could offer agricultural subjects, trade or industrial instruction, and home economics preparation (Douglas 293–296).

The Smith-Hughes Act required that the federal government establish a Federal Board for Vocational Education. The duty of this board was to oversee the distribution of the funds. The members of the federal board claimed success because federal aid rose from about $2.6 million in 1918 to about $10.6 million in 1921. Over the same period, enrollment in federally aided vocational schools rose from about 150,000 students to over 320,000 (Hawkins, Prosser, and Wright 121–122).

Larry Cuban contended that the federal board enjoyed a high level of success. He noted that in a short period of time, every state passed enabling legislation to receive federal funds and submitted plans that complied with the law's requirements. Cuban credited this success to the fact that the first director of the board, Charles A. Prosser, had been secretary of the NSPIE before accepting this administrative position, many of Prosser's assistants belonged to the organization, and members of the board were associated with NSPIE. According to Cuban, this implied that the people who were conducting the program agreed with its aims and had placed supporters in various state organizations to help them (Cuban 68–69).

Despite the administrative achievements, an evaluation of the Smith-Hughes Act conducted in 1938 by the Advisory Committee on Education chaired by John Dale Russell raised doubts about the enrollment increases. According to Russell, a problem was that if a person attended one or two class sessions of an evening course, the federal board reported that person as one enrollment. Russell thought better figures came from records of full-time high school students. In these cases, Russell determined that, in 1920, the federal program assisted 3.1 percent of the total high school enrollment, and most of these were in vocational agriculture, not industrial or home economics training. Assuming that each high school student could take one federally funded vocational course during two high school years, Russell reasoned that the Smith-Hughes Act met about 15 percent of the potential demand in 1938. Russell added that supporters of the Smith-Hughes Act expected the legislation to help people who had left school. He found that in 1936, about 700,000 persons attended the part-time or evening programs while about 560,000 students took advantage of federally supported vocational classes while in school. Ironically, though out-of-school enrollments were greater, the efforts for students in school exhausted about one-half of the resources because the classes for out-of-school people were shorter (Russell 114–125).

Another problem was that the federal board evaluated only those things that improved the administration of the programs. For example, they knew how many centers there were and how many teachers the centers employed. Several studies described ways to improve the instruction through such methods as analyzing the components of the jobs the students had to learn and describing the skills involved in each step. Yet, no studies appeared about the effectiveness of vocational instruction. Most important for this chapter, researchers avoided questions of whether vocational education was more effective if taught in specialized forms or if it should appear in some more general forms (Russell 48–50, 112–113).

Surprisingly, researchers ignored the question of whether vocational training improved the wages of the students. Writing in 1921, Paul Howard Douglas complained there was little evidence about this possibility, but he found one study that compared the wages of 201 workers before they had vocational training to the wages they received after they left a trade school. This study determined that the education did not improve the workers' earning power, and Douglas doubted that vocational education could improve the wages of laborers because they would remain at the mercy of employers and the market conditions. He thought workers could better influence their wages through collective bargaining and trade unions (Douglas 308–310).

Despite the problems, researchers agreed that since the passage of the Smith-Hughes Act a surprisingly large number of educators had come to believe that vocational education programs were needed to meet the needs of the new groups of children who were entering the high schools. Several critics warned, however, that the vocational programs could serve the needs of industry while ignoring the needs of the children.

Many educators warned against separating vocational education from academic studies because they feared that strict vocational education would serve the needs of the factories and ignore the needs of the children. For example, in 1913, Helen Thompson Woolley, a member of the Child Labor Department in Cincinnati, warned against separating vocational education from the public schools and placing it in separate facilities guided by industrialists. After following the careers of thousands of children between the ages of fourteen and sixteen who had applied for working certificates to leave school, Woolley found that even the best labor laws in the country could not ensure the appropriate education of the children. She argued that industrialists could not concern themselves with the fullest development of the children. Above all, industrialists wanted efficient workers, and they could not reform their factories to suit the developing needs of the children. Thus, she recommended that, as long as possible, children should remain in schools and teachers should seek to train the children for citizenship, intelligence, and character (Woolley 232–233).

On the other hand, supporters of vocational education claimed that children from poor families had to leave school to support their families. For example, in 1912, Ernest L. Talbert conducted a study of 904 boys and girls living in the area of the University of Chicago settlement who had left school to work. Most of the children came from Russian and southeastern European families that had recently arrived in the United States. The bulk of these children left school between fourth and sixth grades to work in a variety of low-paying factory jobs, such as wrapping bars of soap, from which they could never rise. When Talbert compiled the reasons 330 children gave for leaving school at age fourteen, he found that 171 of the children claimed financial necessity. Another researcher in St. Louis asked 1,085 children why they left school, and she found that 202 used the same excuse. When Talbert asked why his responses were so different from those in St. Louis, he decided the despotism of the families differed. That is, he thought that in both cities, most of the families could easily live without the small amount of money the children contributed, but that, in his sample of newly arrived immigrants, the parents had no faith in the power of education to increase the earning power of children, and they held to traditions wherein the children had to contribute something to the family before they married (Talbert 396–407, 410–413).

Although Talbert noted the children did not leave school because of authentic financial necessity, he thought that schools should offer vocational training to meet these needs and keep the children in schools. He claimed the children could not appreciate the schools they had. At best, the children replied that school had been all right. Most of them could not see any value in the lessons, and their parents remained ignorant of the schools and the educational facilities available in the area where they lived. Since these people tended to obey laws requiring school attendance, Talbert recommended that the minimum age for leaving be raised to sixteen years of age. In addition, he thought schools should incorporate more laboratory and workshop opportunities to introduce training in the occupations available in the neighborhood. At the high school level, Talbert recommended separate trade schools. He claimed these would not be narrow because they would keep the children in school longer, teach the children to be better workers, and improve their incomes in later life (Talbert 407–410, 444–449).

Nonetheless, critics of separate vocational studies contended that trade schools would not meet children's needs. In 1917, Dewey delivered an address to the Public Education Association criticizing the tendency to separate academic from vocational education. He acknowledged that most elementary schools should incorporate some sorts of vocational education into their programs but he warned that, if educators removed the vocational component and placed it in separate trade schools, five evil tendencies would result. First, in efforts to clarify the differences between general and trade education, administrators would offer a narrow range of vocational skills in the trade schools to show they were preparing children for particular jobs. Second, this tendency would make people think that education should prepare for specific tasks rather than develop someone's general human capacities. Third, the trade education would neglect topics in history and civics that helped workers become intelligent citizens.

Fourth, the manner of teaching in the trade schools would become a form of drill and repletion to ensure the students became proficient in the needed skills. Finally, the program would conceive of guidance as a form of job placement rather than an opportunity to prepare students to render service to themselves and to their communities (Dewey, "Learning" 147–148).

When researchers evaluated the effects of the Smith-Hughes Act, they found that Dewey had predicted many of the problems. For example, while conducting a survey in 1921, Paul Howard Douglas found that thirty-one state boards included a vocational board of education within the state board of education. Although states had separate administrative bodies for vocational education, Douglas found that educators controlled those boards of vocational education. Nonetheless, as Dewey predicted, Douglas found that the training was aimed at improving the students' skills at the trades in which they worked rather than at providing an understanding of a wide range of trades or at other more general educational goals. Douglas accused the Federal Board for Vocational Education of causing this narrowness because the board had chosen to support supplementary training for work the students were already doing. This meant that much of the training took place in night schools or in continuation schools that offered part-time instruction after the children had left full-time schools (Douglas 301–305).

Other committees repeated Douglas's complaints. As already discussed, in 1938, John Dale Russell headed the Advisory Committee on Education, which complained that the administrators of the Smith-Hughes Act imposed the view that narrow training was preferred to general instruction. Russell added that the act did not require narrow vocational training, but Prosser and his colleagues supported training in particular skills for specific industries. More important, Russell found that the board refused to recognize any connections between academic training and vocational preparation. As a result, in some states, officials took money that should have gone to general education programs and spent it on vocational programs to obtain the matching federal dollars. Russell criticized this practice because it weakened elementary education programs that should have been the states' first priority. Furthermore, in some states, the state supervisor directed the vocational teachers while public school administrators supervised regular teachers. This separation of authority reinforced the idea of a dual system (Russell 126–130).

The narrow, practical nature of vocational education supported by the Smith-Hughes Act caused unions, such as the American Federation of Labor (AFL), to reverse its support. From 1910, the AFL supported vocational training in schools. The unions conducted campaigns, passed resolutions at their annual conventions, and appointed special committees on industrial education. These actions were in accord with the union's traditional support of education and the members' desires that schools be available for all children. Furthermore, the union supported vocational education because they feared the growth of private schools offering industrial training. The members reasoned that private schools would be more likely to cater to the desires of factory owners than would public authorities. By 1935, the members of the AFL changed their minds. In several states, the Smith-Hughes Act supported classes held in factories. The teacher was paid by the state, and the students received no pay. Yet, the work the students performed was the work that factory employees would normally provide. Thus, the vocational class took the place of adult laborers and did the work at no expense to the factory. While the teachers thought these offered opportunities to help the students gain the skills needed for employment, the union members complained that the program reduced the cost of training the workforce, took jobs away from employees, and ignored the educational development of the students. As a result of these abuses of the Smith-Hughes Act, the AFL considered resolutions to withdraw federally supported programs within private industrial plants and to change the existing legislation to support broader, more educational experiences (Russell 245–251).

Despite the negative report by Russell's committee and the complaints of the unions that vocational education served factory owners and ignored the needs of children, Congress continued to support vocational education as implemented by the Smith-Hughes Act. In 1938, Congress approved an allocation for the Smith-Hughes Act of about $14.5 million. This was unusual because it was during the Great Depression and President Franklin Roosevelt had suggested the amount be $4.5 million. Although Roosevelt signed the bill, he complained that Congress was not acting intelligently but was responding to demands from vocational teachers, supervisors, and administrators who would receive the money from the bill (Krug, Volume II 310–311).

How did vocational education influence educators' conception of guidance?

Before Congress approved the Smith-Hughes Act, educators had created vocational guidance plans. In 1909, the Boston school committee appointed a committee on vocational direction. In what became one of the first vocational guidance programs, the committee reported later that year that every high school had a vocational counselor and that all but one of the elementary schools had a counselor. The vocational committee held regular meetings with the counselors to discuss how to improve the schools. The committee selected three goals: to have parents and students think about their career aims, to try to place students in appropriate jobs when they finished school, and to keep in touch with the students after they left school. To facilitate their work, the committee and the counselors invited different speakers to come to the schools and explain different careers to the students. At the same time, the counselors began to keep vocational record cards that followed the children from elementary school through high school. These cards contained information about the students' interests, aptitudes, and vocational plans that counselors could draw upon while talking to the students (Bloomfield 25–43).

These early guidance programs were simplistic. The Smith-Hughes Act did not contain funds for guidance counseling, and Dewey objected that vocational guidance was one-sided. The problem was that the programs found in Boston made guidance into a form of job selection and placement. On the other hand, Dewey thought of guidance as an opportunity to prepare students to render service to themselves and to their communities in a much wider form. Dewey thought of guidance as the essential characteristic of all education. It was the way a young child came to share the meanings, values, and skills of the adult society. In primitive societies, children obtained this guidance when they participated in shared activities with the older members of the group. Dewey noted that industrial societies were too complicated for children to learn the activities of adults in such a casual manner. Therefore, schools codified and simplified the essential lessons. Unfortunately, Dewey thought it was ineffective to present this information to the children. Students had to participate in activities that had meaning to them, and the cooperation the students experienced as they worked together to accomplish a goal they shared provided the guidance. As the activities unfolded, the students developed more abilities and realized they could attain new goals (Dewey, *Democracy* 23–40).

Most high school teachers did not accept Dewey's view of occupations as essential activities for students, but they were aware that guidance leading only to vocational placement was one-sided. Thus, as educators began what they called a movement for vocational guidance, they tried to consider guidance as an effort to transform the society as well as a set of activities to change the student.

In 1918, the National Education Association convened a Commission on the Reorganization of Secondary Education (CRSE). Although Chapter Three of this book describes in more detail the efforts and the results of this commission, it is important to note here that the commission's members affirmed that vocational guidance was an essential function of the secondary school. As a result, the CRSE formed a committee on vocational guidance chaired by Frank Mitchell Leavitt in the first national attempt to define the requirements of vocational guidance. Leavitt's committee defined vocational guidance as a continual process to help students choose, plan for, enter upon, and make progress in an occupation. The committee's report noted that this meant high schools had to coordinate their offerings with the needs of industries and to offer guidance to the students after they left the schools (NEA, *Vocational* 9).

Leavitt's committee report noted that teachers had to develop plans to accommodate the needs of three different groups of students. One group included students who left school at fourteen years of age. For this group, the report recommended employment supervision. The aim of the counselor in these cases was to encourage the children to remain in their positions as long as possible, to help them gather as much benefit from their employment as possible, and in some cases to offer continuation classes so the students could proceed with their education as they worked (NEA, *Vocational* 12–13).

Included in the second category were students who remained in high school beyond the age of fourteen but did not attend college. The aim of a guidance program for these students was to offer vocational information through the schoolwork. For example, in academic courses, such as English, students could research and write about the different occupations open to them. Another option was for the school to offer special career information courses from which the students could earn credit toward graduation. In addition, the school should offer placement services that would function like employment agencies for the students (NEA, *Vocational* 12, 14–15).

The third group contained the students going on to college. For this group, the plan should provide information on the courses and electives that would best prepare them for their academic careers. This service could help all students, the report added, especially as schools added a range of different courses to meet the different needs of different students (NEA, *Vocational* 12–13, 15–16).

As the members of Leavitt's committee considered the different obligations the guidance counselors faced, they noted that a guidance plan had to work toward the progressive modification of economic conditions. This meant that students had to learn more than how to adjust to the demands of employers. Guidance counselors had to show students how to achieve cooperative solutions for community problems in ways that increased the welfare of most people. Although the report did not offer any details in the ways students could learn how to do this, it is reasonable to assume that the CRSE members thought that the students could learn these attitudes and skills in such classes as civics which another committee had developed (NEA, *Vocational* 23–24).

The committee on vocational guidance offered many suggestions of which Dewey might approve. The report called for counselors to use every available measure to determine the students' capacities, to visit students' homes in hopes they could learn about the students' backgrounds and involve the parents in the guidance plan, and to cooperate with such agencies as the Y.M.C.A. and the Camp Fire Girls that could facilitate the guidance process. Furthermore, the report called for counselors to receive extensive training in counseling and to have the time to perform the function for the students (NEA, *Vocational* 24–28).

In a passing reference, the report suggested that school districts should consider the benefits of junior high schools because teachers could use those grades to introduce students to vocational choices. In 1910, the Berkeley, California, schools adopted such a model under the direction of Frank Bunker. Writing about what he saw as the success of his innovation, Bunker claimed that by separating grades seven, eight, and nine into a junior high school, his teachers could ease the transition to high school, provide for closer supervision of the students during these difficult years, and reduce dropout rates. An important benefit that Bunker found was that the students could explore several career avenues during these junior high years. When the students went to high school, they could concentrate on the career preparation they had found most appealing while in junior high (Bunker 102–114, 137–148).

Despite the high goals that guidance counselors held for themselves, two problems plagued their efforts. The first problem was that the recommendations they gave were not always correct. For example, as already mentioned, counselors encouraged children who had left school to remain at their place of initial employment and improve their salaries by advancing within the company. A study conducted in Cincinnati in 1913 of 2,000 children between the ages of fourteen to sixteen who left school to work indicated that the children who changed their jobs and joined another company improved their salaries more than did children who remained with one company year after year (Woolley 226–227).

The second problem was that some school districts ignored the counselors' recommendations. For example, Harvey Kantor noted that in 1917, the Berkeley, California, schools began a vocational guidance program. Rather than hire and train guidance counselors, the administrators assigned to each high school teacher a group of twenty-five or thirty students to advise. Although most experts disapproved of such arrangements, school districts assigned teachers to counseling duty because the practice saved money. Kantor added that when schools did employ counselors, their job changed. By the late 1920s, counselors in California concentrated on administering achievement or intelligence tests, adjusting schedules, and maintaining student files. Thus, guidance shifted from enabling the student to enter the world of work to facilitating life within the school (Kantor 157–163).

What did John Dewey think vocational education did to society?

In 1916, before Congress passed the Smith-Hughes Act, Dewey offered an extensive evaluation of the social effects of vocational education in *Democracy and Education*. He gave five reasons why there was increased concern for vocational education. First, democratic communities hold manual labor in higher esteem than do aristocratic ones. Second, industrial occupations had become matters of worldwide concern and the problems of social readjustment focused on the relations of labor and capital. Third, industry no longer depended on craftspeople but on technological discoveries and organization. Fourth, the pursuit of knowledge was no longer literary but had become scientific. Finally, the advances in psychology implied that children should learn in ways that led them to understand how adults worked (Dewey, *Democracy* 313–315).

As a result of these positive factors, Dewey thought that vocational education could transform schools and society in desirable ways. He believed such a transformation would lead to each person working at something that fit his or her capacities, that improved the lives of other people, and that made clearer the connections among the people in the society. For Dewey, this meant that teachers should build the instruction around what he called "occupations" (Dewey, *Democracy* 310, 315–316).

Dewey gave the term *occupations* an unusual meaning. To some extent, he borrowed the idea from Woodward that children should learn about industrial progress, and he considered the activities children performed in manual training, such as gardening, cutting, folding, and weaving, as the beginnings of occupations. The two important differences were that Dewey wanted children to do things to satisfy some purpose they had and he wanted to include academic studies in the occupations. Centering the occupations on human beings' concerns for food, shelter, and clothing, Dewey expected the students to engage in them as avenues to explore the historical development of human society. For example, gardening became a way to learn about botany, chemistry, and animal life. From activities in these areas, the students went on to learn about geography, cultural differences, and human migrations. Thus, when the curriculum was made up of occupations, the students met Dewey's definition of education because they reconstructed human experience (Dewey, *Democracy* 80, 194–200).

Vocational education had a different orientation. When separated from general education, Dewey complained that it aimed at preparing students to work in industries and professions as they were organized. As a result, trade schools and academic high schools perpetuated the existing social order because trade schools taught the children of the lower social classes to work at jobs they disliked because they had to support themselves while academic schools catered to other people who controlled excessive wealth and could indulge their fancies in various diversions. In this way, Dewey complained that vocational education hardened dangerous social divisions instead of trying to show ways that people could restructure their society (Dewey, *Democracy* 316–317).

At best, Dewey offered anecdotes about students pursuing what he called "occupations" to illustrate the insights they gained. Other researchers confirmed Dewey's prediction that vocational studies exacerbated the differences among social classes. For example, in 1922, George Counts traced the relationships between students' enrollments in high schools and their parents' occupations. Counts included in his study over 17,000 students from four cities spread across the United States. The results were as Dewey predicted. More children of professionals came to high schools than did children of laborers. The children of laborers who did attend high schools tended to take vocational courses while the children of professionals tended to take academic courses that led to college. Moreover, Counts found that the students' intelligence did not influence this distinction. When Counts looked at the students' scores on IQ tests, he noted similar median scores for the students in all of the course tracks (Counts, *Selective* 5, 32–33, 48, 69–73, 87, 127–129).

Contemporary historians confirm Dewey's prediction that vocational educators would reinforce social class distinctions, as Dewey feared. In 1988, Marvin Lazerson surveyed the development of vocational education in Boston schools. He contended that during the early years of the twentieth century, vocational educators claimed that a democratic school had to offer students opportunities to study things that fit their abilities and their needs. Lazerson added that this view of fitting the school to the child turned into a type of predestination. The children of laborers were sent to classes to learn to labor. Equality of opportunity became an excuse to place the children into categories according to their social backgrounds and train them in occupations appropriate to their status (Lazerson 200–201).

The process that Lazerson described was almost irresistible. Once the public approved compulsory education, educators disagreed as to what form the schools should take. Although the traditional academic program remained popular, educators began to consider ways to introduce practical activities. Manual training was an early step in that direction. Its supporters thought they were supplementing the academic training rather than replacing it. But the two forms existed separately. As a result, educators who favored the academic curriculum could argue that students should wait until they left school to master the skills found in manual training. Many vocational educators took the notion that manual training complemented academic courses to argue that manual training was too abstract to offer practical advantages, such as job training. These vocational educators also believed that society had changed to such an extent that children could not find apprenticeships. Therefore, the children could not learn on the job. As a result, supporters of vocational education claimed that the new industrial society forced schools to provide some students the opportunities to master vocational skills. Using this argument, they persuaded Congress to support vocational education. Unfortunately, the training the government supported was a narrow form of skill acquisition.

Some educators complained that vocational education separated from general education distorted the schools' aim to fulfill deep-seated human needs. But since most educators sought to integrate practical and academic training in some form, they had difficulty knowing when vocational training became excessive. Vocational training was popular. When labor unions complained about the way industrialists used vocational training to reduce their training and production costs, the federal government ignored these complaints and continued to support narrow, job-related vocational training.

As vocational training grew in popularity, educators realized they had to help children make intelligent choices. As a result, they began offering guidance services. At first, these programs sought to place students in appropriate jobs. By 1918, though, educators came to recognize that guidance had to consider ways of transforming the society as well as discover techniques to direct the students.

In a short time, vocational education became an important force. The transition was important because the vocational educators wanted students to acquire specific skills that manufacturers could use. As a result, schools seemed to be advancing the interests of factory owners more than they helped children understand democracy. Yet, the transition had taken place because vocational educators used arguments to advance their programs that were similar to those used by educators who favored more general courses. For example, educators favoring manual training had argued that exercises in wood shop or sewing offered concrete applications of abstract academic skills. In a short time, vocational educators claimed that specific vocational training taught those same problem-solving skills.

The result was that educators could not easily defend the more general studies. Educators who disapproved of vocational training complained that such training denied children's needs to become intelligent and contributing citizens. Yet, there was no evidence that general education made students more informed citizens. Interestingly, educators who favored direct vocational training claimed it was necessary to meet the students' needs to gain remunerative employment. Although studies could not prove that vocational education enhanced students' earning power, there seemed to be no way to limit the slide toward vocational training.

Summary

As the twentieth century began, compulsory education laws and increased immigration brought new types of students to the schools. To meet the needs of these new students, teachers opened the curriculum to manual training. Proposed by Calvin M. Woodward as a means to train the students' eyes and the hands, manual training provided a set of general skills rather than direct vocational training. In this way, Woodward thought manual training supplemented W. T. Harris's ideas of the liberal arts. Woodward justified his views on practical grounds and ignored the idealistic considerations Harris employed. Thus, by 1906, vocational educators could claim that manual training was impractical because society had changed and students who left schools early could not find jobs in large cities. On the grounds that the curriculum should offer more choices including opportunities to select vocational preparation, the federal government created the Smith-Hughes Act in 1917 and began to support vocational education programs to meet the economic and military defense needs of the country. Although the Smith-Hughes Act suggested that vocational education could appear in ways the states chose to offer it, critics claimed that federal administrators made narrow interpretations and imposed patterns that separated vocational education from the wider general aims. The educators feared such narrow vocational education sought to fit children into the society and exacerbated social distinctions by offering skill training to the children of laborers while middle-class children studied academics. Since the educators thought that academic subjects could be related to everyday life, they could not easily indicate when vocational education became excessive. As a result, the tendency of educators to disregard the possibility that academic courses had intrinsic value caused problems.

PART II

CHANGING THE CURRICULUM TO SERVE DEMOCRATIC NEEDS, 1918–1929

In the period following World War I, educators sought to meet the needs of the immigrants and to diversify the course offerings in the high schools. The two chapters in this section consider these two topics. Chapter Three, Meeting the Needs of the Immigrants and of the Society, discusses three efforts to help immigrants adjust to their adopted country. Before the war began, progressive educators felt that immigrant children needed to learn the language and customs of their new country. This was the first effort. But some religious groups, such as European Jews and Catholics, objected to the effort to establish settlement houses and to place all children in public schools. As a result, believing they needed to preserve their ethnic identities, these groups established their own institutions. This was the second effort. During the war, public pressure to unify the country increased and led to the third effort, the Americanization movement. When supporters of this movement tried to eliminate private and religious schools, they encountered considerable controversy. In 1924, the U.S. Congress restricted immigration and conflicts about Americanization diminished. Since the movement to Americanize immigrants grew in hurtful directions, this may indicate that educators found it difficult to recognize when the drive for social harmony overextended itself.

Chapter Four, Balancing Individual and Social Needs, describes the effects of the NEA's Commission on the Reorganization of Secondary Education. Several historians claim that this commission established the model for the comprehensive high school that became an important American institution. At the same time, two important models of curriculum formation became popular. One was called "scientific curriculum making" and the other was named the "project method." These three efforts were related because advocates thought that they could reconcile the potential conflicts that existed between individual student needs and the wider social requirements by depending on the term *democracy*. The three models differed in the importance their supporters attached to academic studies, vocational preparation, and student interest or freedom. Despite the differences among them, they appeared to lean more in the direction of achieving social harmony than toward the route of satisfying the desires of individual students.

CHAPTER THREE

MEETING THE NEEDS OF THE IMMIGRANTS AND OF THE SOCIETY, 1916–1930

From World War I to the Great Depression, a movement to Americanize immigrants gathered strength, took different directions, and then declined in importance. The different methods included what might be called the liberal progressive model, the Jewish Zionist or the ethnic Catholic school approach, and the Americanization program initiated by the federal government. Although there was no doubt that educators had to help the immigrants adjust to their adopted country, some of these efforts, especially the Americanization program, reinforced bigotry and enforced enculturation. Since these harmful effects lasted until Congress restricted immigration, they may illustrate that educators could not easily find the point at which the need for social harmony began to harm individuals.

What was the liberal, progressive model of Americanization?

Before World War I, teachers grappled with ways to meet what they thought were the needs of the children of immigrant families. They set up special classes to help the children acquire English, adopted the manual training method on the grounds that this would teach the children industriousness, and turned to vocational training in order to meet the children's needs to earn money and support their families. In other enlightened efforts, liberal progressives such as Jane Addams and John Dewey sought to find in the definition of the term *democracy* a way to meet the needs of the immigrants and to enable these new citizens to strengthen the society.

Addams and other settlement house workers used a manner of thinking that was similar to that of the members of the industrial training movement to explain how they wanted to solve the problems of the cities. Vocational educators claimed that specific vocational training was necessary to accommodate the new urban conditions that prevented children from becoming apprentices and learning a trade. Agreeing that new urban conditions called for new measures to help people, Addams claimed that the settlement house movement was an experiment to bridge the gaps that existed between the groups that made up the city. When the wealthier social classes helped the less fortunate, they moved toward a democratic society, and this was the most valuable contribution that America made to the world. In this spirit, Addams claimed that the settlement house movement owed its existence to young people's desire to apply the ideal of democracy to life in the city by bringing together people from different social classes. As a result, Addams wanted settlement house members to view life in the city as organic and to find ways to enable each group or social class to contribute to the well-being of the other groups or classes (Addams, *Twenty* 41–42, 115–127).

When Addams began the Hull House in 1889, she and her colleagues selected a site in Chicago in the middle of Italian and Bohemian communities. To her surprise, not only did she find that the more established social classes in other parts of the city looked down on these newly arrived immigrants, but also she noticed that the children of the immigrants rejected their parents. For example, she was amazed to hear girls refuse to wear the beautiful clothing their mothers made for them by hand. The girls preferred cheap factory-made clothes available in local stores. To correct the disdain the children felt for their parents, Addams constructed a labor museum in which the children could discover that the simple tools the immigrant mothers used to spin thread were related to the huge machines in textile factories. She hoped these lessons would teach the children and observers Addams brought in from outside that industrial progress came from exchanges among peoples who spoke different languages and followed different religions (Addams, *Twenty* 172–177).

For Addams, the labor museum represented the spirit of the settlement house as a progressive, educative institution. The other measures that she and her colleagues undertook, such as a community kitchen to show mothers how to prepare the nutritious food cheaply available in Chicago, built on this same principle. The fundamental idea was that groups could share their best ideas, meet each other's needs, and, in the process, discover new ways of doing things that improved life for everyone.

In 1894, John Dewey moved to Chicago and began to work closely with Jane Addams. According to his daughter, Dewey's experiences sharpened his faith in democracy as the guiding force in education (Wirth 23–24). To test his ideas of democracy and education, Dewey conducted a laboratory school from 1896 to 1904 that seemed to be based on the ideas found in the labor museum. As noted in Chapter Two, Dewey thought of occupations as opportunities for children to trace the evolution of academic subjects. This aim was similar to Addams's hope that the exhibits in the labor museum would enable the children of immigrant families to trace the evolution of industrial techniques from those found in small European villages to the systems of mass production employed in large urban factories. In these ways, Dewey and Addams wanted children to recognize that methods of solving problems improved when people shared ideas and combined them to arrive at better alternatives for action. They believed that this way of thinking characterized what was best about democracies.

Throughout his career, Dewey attempted to reconcile opposing ideas and to arrive at better conceptions. While Dewey may have borrowed this method of thinking from those of Hegel or Harris described in Chapters One and Two, he applied the process in ways that he made distinctly his own. Using this pattern, in 1916, Dewey delivered an address to the National Educational Association (NEA) asking the members to extend the motto of the United States, "One from Many," into an educational ideal. Instead of trying to shape a narrow conception of Americanism, he advised educators to welcome the different cultures that appeared within the country, to extract from each people its special good, and to contribute that strength to the common fund of wisdom. He thought this was the way to deal with "hyphenism," such as German-American. He objected to the hyphenism in which a group retained certain cultural traits and rejected the blending (Dewey, "Nationalizing Education" 184–186).

Dewey delivered his speech to the NEA while the United States embarked on a program of military preparedness. Although his topic was nationalizing education, he repeated the progressive notion that the best way to make a nation was to combine the different ideas that people had and derive an improved system from the combination. He did not pursue the various administrative arrangements to improve local and state systems of schools because he thought that if educators grasped the correct ideal they would work out the arrangements. Yet, in his speech to the NEA, Dewey warned that some national leaders wanted to foster nationalism by pointing out the differences among various groups in the nation, urging them to drop any unique practices, and encouraging everyone to stand ready to fight those nations that threatened America. Dewey worried that these warnings against the differences among groups made people conform to some artificial standard and weakened the ideal of democracy (Dewey, "Nationalizing Education" 183–184).

Of course, Addams and Dewey did not speak for all the people who shared what might be called liberal, progressive perspectives. For example, an associate of Dewey's, Randolph Bourne, defended the hyphenated blending that Dewey rejected. Sharing Dewey's distaste for a bland homogeneous Americanism, Bourne claimed that states such as Wisconsin and Minnesota had reversed the usual ideal, and the result was a vibrant culture. In these states, Bourne believed the Scandinavian and German cultures adopted those parts of the Anglo-Saxon image that fit their ideas. They retained their central cultural nucleus, complete with foreign press, vernacular literature, and schools. Bourne pointed out that many other groups did the same in other places. From the centers of these cultural groups, gradations extended to a fringe where the cultural tendencies disappeared. It was the individuals in the fringe that Bourne thought destroyed society because they were the type of people who became materialistic, grasping Americans. The Bohemian who retained his cultural center and supported Bohemian schools represented to Bourne the best sort of American because he had faith that schools would improve society, and he blended that notion with his own cultural ideals (Bourne 278–280).

Liberal progressives such as Addams and Dewey thought that members of every group could best meet their needs and form a good society if they shared ideas and modified their cultural practices by adopting the most effective suggestions. Groups with strong cultural or religious orientations, however, avoided this model of Americanization. They believed the pluralistic model that Bourne offered best served the needs of their group and the requirements of a common society.

How did Jewish Zionists and ethnic Catholics construct their own ways to help immigrants?

The liberal progressives were not alone in their concern for the plight of immigrants. The immigrants themselves set up their own institutions to help themselves in the process. This was the second type of effort to enable immigrants to adjust to their new situations.

When Hull House first opened, Russian Jews did not attend, but in a short period of time, Jewish families began to take part in the concerts, educational opportunities, and recreational pursuits the settlement house offered. As a result, from 1896 until 1910, Eastern European Jews dominated some Hull House–sponsored clubs, such as those concerned with drama, literature, and social topics. At the same time, according to Rivka Shpak Lissak, anti-Semitism grew in Chicago, and Zionists, who doubted the religious leadership could meet the problems of life in the United States, became the leaders in several Jewish communities in Chicago. These Zionists urged the building of communal centers where Jewish youth could use libraries, gymnasiums, and music and lecture halls. Although these facilities were similar to those Hull House provided, the Jewish communal centers operated under Jewish direction. Lissak argued that the Zionists did not like the fact that members of Hull House did not recognize the Yiddish language or culture in the same way that they recognized the Italian or the Greek culture even while Addams and her colleagues felt sympathy for the Jewish people and their suffering under religious prejudice. Lissak added that, for American Jewish youth, these Jewish centers replaced Hull House. As a result, Jewish children stopped attending Hull House, and problems developed in the relations between the Zionist leaders and Addams (Lissak 80–81, 84–91, 113–117).

In a manner similar to that of Zionists, strongly religious Catholic leaders tended to think of Hull House as a threat to the religious beliefs of the immigrants rather than a source of aid for the immigrant families. For example, in 1892, two years after Addams opened Hull House, Catholic laypeople organized a Catholic settlement house similar to Hull House to enable Catholic families in need to avoid the danger of being drawn away from the church by well-meaning but non-Catholic philanthropists (Sanders 38, 68).

In part, this was due to the hostility Hull House members showed toward religious education. Hull House was in an area dominated by ethnic Catholic immigrants, yet many settlement workers opposed the practice of sending the children to Catholic parochial schools. Some of Addams's colleagues, such as Edith Abbott and Sophonisba P. Breckinridge, tried to prevent immigrant children from attending Catholic schools and, failing to eliminate the parochial schools, tried to prevent Catholic schools from teaching in the children's native language. Although these efforts failed, the Hull House supporters believed the children should spend their school time mastering English so they could survive in their adopted land (Lissak 49–53).

Writing a survey of compulsory education laws in Chicago, Abbott and Breckinridge observed that Catholic schools and some public schools tried to cater to the immigrants, but that these schools hampered the education of the immigrant children by offering instruction in the children's native language. According to the authors, this impeded the children's ability to learn English. As a result, Abbott and Breckinridge recommended two reforms: They wanted the Illinois legislature to mandate that the instruction be in English and that children had to speak English to obtain a certificate to work (Abbott and Breckinridge 279–280).

While Hull House workers glorified the public schools, Catholic priests in Chicago mounted their pulpits and portrayed the public schools as godless institutions that threatened the religious faith of children. Many Catholic adults accepted this view and considered the parish school a symbol of defiance against an established order that despised their faith. As the popular press criticized the inadequacy of Catholic schools, Catholic parishioners drew together in a common effort to improve their parish schools. As if in answer to critics' complaints, enrollments in the Catholic schools grew steadily (Sanders 36–37).

The priests won the battle for enrollments. Despite the efforts of the Hull House workers to remove Catholic ethnic schools, those schools gained in popularity. By 1900, more than 55 percent of the Catholic school children in Chicago attended officially ethnic parochial schools where instruction was in their native language. The percentages remained almost the same until about 1930. One further point should be made, though. In Chicago, priests threatened that children could not be confirmed unless they attended Catholic schools. No doubt this increased

Catholic school enrollments, but these may have been limited increases. Some Catholic children attended Catholic schools until they reached the age of their first communion. At that point, they withdrew from the Catholic schools and attended public schools (Sanders 35, 44–45; Talbert 399).

Ironically, some Catholic educators fought against public schools that offered instruction in the children's native language even though Catholic educators realized that ethnic Catholic schools attracted immigrant families. For example, in 1865, Germans in Chicago won the right to have instruction in elementary schools in German. In 1876, however, the school board voted to drop the teaching in German. Catholic educators supported this change on the grounds that any measure that weakened the attraction of public schools among immigrant families would help Catholic schools. In a similar fashion, in 1911, the Polish National Alliance, a secular organization, convinced the Chicago school board to introduce Polish language study in a Chicago high school. The Polish Roman Catholic Union argued against the reform because it would diminish the attractiveness of the Catholic schools (Sanders 42, 47).

Since Jane Addams realized that immigrant families favored schools that used the children's native language, she tried to find a substitute that she believed would be appropriate for public schools. In 1908, Addams delivered an address to the National Education Association urging public school teachers to temper their tendencies to separate the immigrant children from their families. Acknowledging that care and intelligence were required to blend the culture of the children's homes with the conceptions they learned in school, Addams believed that cultivated teachers could combine the charm and beauty of the immigrants' cultures into a worldwide perspective. Further, Addams urged the public school teachers to help the children understand the international development of industry. Finally, she recommended that the school recognize its obligation to change the families through the children. For example, by teaching the children how to test milk for cleanliness, the teachers could improve the health of the family members. Such changes required that teachers understand the life of the immigrant families, but she believed they would enable teachers to lead the immigrant children and their families to hold to a wider sense of community (Addams, "Public School" 100–102).

In order to understand the problems these groups faced in the early part of the twentieth century, it is essential to consider the complicated roles that ethnic Catholic schools played. Unfortunately, it is not always clear what they accomplished, who supported them, or why things unfolded as they did. According to one historian, James W. Sanders, the concept of the ethnic parish came from Europe where the Catholic Church required priests to offer the mass in Latin and to follow an identical rite. Other parts of the church life, such as confessions, sermons, or catechisms, took place in the language of the people. This worked because the church was organized, in large part, into geographic regions called dioceses. Usually, each diocese operated under the control of a bishop. The dioceses were broken into smaller units, parishes, and each parish had its church building administered by a priest. Under this system, churches in particular areas could follow the cultural traditions in architecture and in celebrations. In Europe, this system worked well because people in particular areas felt traditional ties, observed similar customs, and spoke the same language. In the United States, this system posed serious problems for Catholic bishops. For example, in 1906, in an area of less than one square mile in Chicago, there were nine different ethnic Catholic churches and each church had its own school. As would be expected, some schools were overfull while a neighboring facility was nearly empty. Yet, students could not transfer from overcrowded schools to underused facilities because the language of instruction differed (Sanders 43, 48).

Writing from a secular perspective, historian Daniel S. Buczek offered a different view. He claimed that the ethnic church and its affiliated parish school enhanced the assimilation of Polish-Americans into mainstream society. Conducting his research in Polish language newspapers in Milwaukee and Chicago published in the 1920s, Buczek found that Polish immigrants brought to the United States two related, traditional views of social organization. One was the belief that the father governed the activities of the family members. The other was the belief that the priest was Christ's representative on earth. Combined together, these views reinforced the belief in a structured, hierarchical social order for Polish immigrants and impeded the immigrant Polish priests and parishioners from accepting the democratic order in the United States. While the Irish Catholics who came to dominate the church hierarchy succeeded in separating church matters from secular political affairs, Polish priests and their parishioners could not accept such a separation. By the 1920s, many Polish priests had been born in the United States, and Polish parishes accepted members from other ethnic groups. Consequently, the priests had to use English and create hyphenated parishes and hyphenated schools. Thus, Buczek described three phases in the Americanization of the Polish parish. The first was the retention of the traditional forms. The second was the hyphenated version. And finally, there appeared American parishes. This gradual acculturation served the Polish community well, Buczek concluded. Parents did not have to resist the priest; the children did not have to choose between the priest and the family; and the families could remain intact. Had the Polish church adopted the model of instant conversion advocated by John Ireland, Buczek supposed, the feelings of dislocation among the parishioners would have been enormous, and there were no other resources for guidance in the Polish communities. The Polish intellectuals who published frequently in the Polish language papers did not offer any intelligent guidance to immigrants living in the United States. Their stories focused on the situation in Poland (Buczek 155–163).

While Buczek concluded that the ethnic parish enhanced assimilation, most immigrant Catholics adopted the ethnic parish model to protect against Americanization rather than to invite it into their midst. For example, some German Catholics advanced the slogan that language brought faith. In 1845, the Belgian provincial of the Redemptorists told his people that German priests had to serve German immigrants in the United States using the German language to protect the immigrants from what he called the pernicious influence of American morals and habits. Some years later, Bishop Joseph Neumann of Philadelphia repeated the same sentiment claiming that unless German priests spoke the German language to the German immigrants, the immigrants would drift away from the faith. Neumann acknowledged a transition to English could take place, but he thought it should be slow in coming (Barry 10–11).

German-American Catholics held to the belief that language brought faith to the extent that they joined with German Lutherans to defend what they thought of as their obligation to satisfy their children's need for instruction in their native language. But they based their defense on the assumption that parents had the right to choose the type of education for their children. In 1889, the Illinois legislature approved the so-called Edwards law that required that instruction be in English. At the same time, the Wisconsin legislature approved the so-called Bennett Law that had a similar effect. In both states, the Catholic and Lutheran coalition mounted such opposition that the incumbent Republican governors and the legislative representatives lost reelection campaigns and the new Democratic legislatures repealed the laws (Shanabruch 62–77).

Although the German-Americans strongly supported foreign language parishes and schools, Italians did not. According to Sanders, Italians distinguished themselves for their disinterest in their own churches and schools. In 1910, there were 45,000 native-born Italians in Chicago and another 28,000 people of Italian parentage in the city. In the Chicago diocese, there were ten Italian parishes but only one of these had a school. Sanders claimed that this is surprising because at that time in Chicago nearly every parish had a school (Sanders 67–69).

Another historian, JoEllen McNergney Vinyard, offered several explanations for the reluctance of Italian Catholics to support parochial schools. Studying changes in Catholic schools in Detroit, Vinyard noted that more than half the Italian men who moved to Detroit took such low-paying jobs outside the industrial workforce as day laborers or as self-employed peddlers that they could not afford to support Catholic schools. Further, she claimed that typically Italian men held nonchalant attitudes toward organized religion. While they observed the important religious sacraments, such as baptism and marriage, they left the typical rituals to their wives and children. Other Italian men were opposed to the Catholic Church because they blamed the pope for retarding the unification of Italy. But a larger reason may have been that Italians did not think of themselves as part of a unified nationality. They thought of themselves as Neapolitan or Genoese, or Piedmontese or Sicilian, and these groups tended to be small and sometimes dispersed. They would not attend a parish or school of another group or nationality because they felt out of place (Vinyard 159–172).

The attitude of the U.S. bishops demonstrated the complex nature of the issue of ethnic Catholic schools. In the United States, in 1884, the Third Plenary Council of Baltimore, Maryland, commanded the priest in every parish in the United States to open a school within two years. On the one hand, some prominent U.S. Catholic bishops, such as John Ireland, took this to mean that Catholic churches should be American and conduct services in English. On the other hand, many bishops believed that parishes should be organized in ways that united the members of each nationality. Whichever side a bishop took, though, the parish priests thought they were obliged to construct, organize, and administer elementary schools. Since ethnic groups and ethnic priests worked together, the churches in cities usually followed lines of nationality, and many of the schools became ethnic schools (Vinyard 90–95).

In such a divided process, bishops might have been unable to control the proliferation of ethnic parishes and schools even if they wanted to stop it. According to Jay P. Dolan, in the early twentieth century, bishops exhorted their followers to build schools, but the bishops could not direct what went on in those schools. Dolan cited the efforts of some urban bishops to hire school superintendents. He claimed that these positions held little authority because the local pastor was the supreme authority in the parish and the school. Dolan argued that the parish priest built the school, hired the teachers, and paid the bills. The result was that in cities, such as Chicago or New York, neighboring ethnic parishes had no connection to each other and, when the bishops hired diocesan superintendents, those individuals concentrated on influencing the Irish schools that taught in English. Thus, for example, in 1905, in New York, the Catholic school superintendent introduced the history of Ireland for the entire seventh and eighth grades in the diocese, but the religious women teaching in Polish Catholic schools in New York did not use these texts. They taught the children about Poland (Dolan 291).

The point is that ethnic Catholic parishes and schools served a variety of purposes. For some parishioners, they retarded assimilation. Progressives, such as Addams, thought this was true. Some historians think that the parishes and the schools facilitated assimilation. The bishops may have wanted to remove the ethnic parishes, but they recognized that those ethnic motivations led to the spread and the construction of parishes and schools. As a result, the views of the Catholic parishioners, the liberal progressives, and the Catholic bishops differed according to what the different groups considered to be the needs of the people and the best ways to meet social needs.

How did the Americanization movement change efforts to meet the needs of immigrants during World War I?

The threat of war created the third effort to meet the needs of the immigrants. This approach differed from the efforts of the liberal progressive educators and the Catholic educators. Called the Americanization movement, it was led by politicians and business people who sought to make foreign-born adults become loyal citizens who would support the war because they felt strong ties to their adopted home. This effort led to many abuses of power. Yet, some historians credit it with the development of longer lasting programs of adult education.

John F. McClymer, a historian who wrote about Americanization, claimed that Theodore Roosevelt was the first politician of national stature to use the phrase "100 percent American" and to campaign actively against what he called hyphenated Americans. Woodrow Wilson borrowed the sentiment and in 1916 he placed in the Democratic Party's platform statements condemning ethnic conspiracies to influence foreign policy. As a result of the war effort, many native-born Americans came to believe that anyone coming to live and work in the United States should become a loyal American (McClymer 25).

The Americanization movement owed much of its motivating force to a private, philanthropic organization, the National American Committee (NAC). In January 1916, the NAC held a conference in Philadelphia bringing together leaders of industry, education, and government to discuss the problems of the Americanization of immigrants. The aim of the conference was to determine the national needs and the ways the different parts of society could cooperate in meeting these needs (Hartmann 134–140).

The same year, Frances A. Kellor, vice-chair of the NAC, wrote her monograph, *Straight America: A Call to National Service* in which she defined Americanization as basic preparedness for national defense. Kellor claimed that the nation's willingness to accept the sinking of the *Lusitania* and Germany's violation of Belgium's neutrality illustrated its lack of resolve. She noted that one problem was to energize the native-born youth into doing their duty in industry and the military. She thought this could be done if people rediscovered the stern discipline that she believed was found in the American tradition. The other question was how to construct among immigrants feelings of national loyalty so that they would aid the country. The answers that Kellor gave for Americanization were to end dual citizenships, make every immigrant apply for citizenship or leave, and require everyone to speak English (Kellor 3–5, 182–187).

Despite the popularity that the NAC enjoyed among prominent citizens, it garnered criticism from organized labor. For example, Samuel Grompers, head of the American Federation of Labor, complained in 1916 that the Americanization movement was biased and one-sided. He argued that any effort to Americanize immigrants should be accompanied by equally strong efforts to Americanize factory owners. He explained that corporations, such as United States Steel, obstructed the American spirit because their agents lured immigrants from foreign lands to come to factories where they earned inadequate salaries and worked in unsafe conditions (Hartmann 140–141).

While unionists complained about the management-oriented NAC, business leaders complained about socialistic teaching materials. In 1917, President Wilson called on school officials to increase the training in community and national life for native-born high school and elementary school children. The task fell to Charles Judd and Leon Marshall of the University of Chicago. They produced three series of lessons about such topics as the effects of war, business organization, and workers and wage systems. Educators praised these materials as advances in the field of social studies, but the director of the National Industrial Conference Board complained that the lessons were propaganda favoring industrial insurance, supporting labor unions, and calling for governmental control of business (Krug, Vol. I 410–411, 420).

Although an enormous number of organizations took part in the Americanization movement, four agencies within the federal government played prominent roles: the U.S. Bureau of Education, housed in the U.S. Department of the Interior; the U.S. Bureau of Naturalization, housed in the U.S. Department of Labor; the Committee on Public Information; and the Council of National Defense. According to John F. McClymer, the development of the Americanization movement is the story of the conflict between two of these departments, the Bureau of Education and the Bureau of Naturalization. During this interdepartmental friction, the Bureau of Education had a decided advantage because the U.S. Congress did not allocate funds to support the Americanization movement, but the NAC donated almost $90,000 to the Bureau of Education over a period from 1914 to 1919. Although McClymer acknowledged that there is conflicting evidence as to how much Kellor and the NAC influenced federal policy, he claimed that Kellor and her colleagues enjoyed considerable power. Evidence that he is correct comes from the fact that in 1919, the U.S. Congress adopted legislation that prohibited the federal government or any of its agencies from receiving such contributions (McClymer 26–32; Hartmann 195).

The various parties that advanced Americanization as educational policy held a wide range of views. The differences among these perspectives appeared almost immediately in April 1918 when the U.S. Secretary of the Interior, Franklin K. Lane, called a conference of state governors, national officials, industrialists, and educators to discuss Americanization as a war measure. To set the stage for his remarks, Lane recalled the recent Bolshevik revolution and claimed that Russia abandoned its allies in the war effort because its people lacked the education to continue the fight for political freedom. Calling such a rebellion "Russianization," he urged his audience members to become missionaries to prevent it from happening in America (Conference on Americanization 14–15).

For Lane, Americanization went beyond historical studies. It was the development of a patriotic spirit, and, to his eyes, it was the most advanced spirit to come to humankind. He argued that it depended on the ability of the nation to gather together the immigrants from many different lands and forge among them a shared sense of meaning and purpose. To accomplish this goal, he foresaw four problems. First, many people did not speak English, the language of the majority. Second, many draftees into the Army could not read. Third, the schools had not been able to correct these problems. Fourth, people failed to recognize what the immigrants wanted from the United States (Conference on Americanization 16–17).

Each state had created a council of defense to work with a national council of defense. Elliott D. Smith, of the national council, reported the establishment of an information service that would spread an understanding of the aims and ideals at issue in the war. Smith believed this service was needed to prevent enemy agents from misleading foreign-born immigrants about the nature of their adopted land. He expected the recently created series of agencies coordinated under the U.S. Council of National Defense to transmit this information throughout the United States (Conference on Americanization 22–23).

Although officials from different states and cities concerned themselves with local initiatives to encourage Americanization, these ranged in their severity. For example, the governor of Virginia described a recent but mild campaign among public schools to have children urge their parents to buy liberty bonds. Taking a more militant position, an official from Chicago recommended that immigrants be denied the right to work unless they applied for naturalization and that state legislatures require foreign language newspapers to carry articles written in both English and the foreign language. These articles were to be written by the U.S. Bureau of Education and to extol the blessings of the United States. In general, educators claimed regular public schools could not Americanize the immigrants. Thus, the chairperson of the New York City board of education described efforts to reach beyond the elementary and secondary schools through evening classes for adults to teach them to speak and read English, continuation classes for children of immigrants who left before finishing grade school, and extension classes in English in factories where immigrants worked throughout the city (Conference on Americanization 23–29).

George Creel, chairperson of the U.S. Committee on Public Information (CPI), called on the supporters of Americanization to use what might be called public relations techniques to persuade immigrants to support their new country. Creel had been a newspaper editor, and in April 1917, when President Wilson created the CPI, Creel organized an effective campaign to confirm domestic support for the war. He described that effort in his book, *How We Advertised America*. At the conference, Creel suggested that schools could make people feel more patriotic by trying to help them. For example, he noted that schools tended to separate the children from their families. To rectify this problem, he suggested that educators open the school buildings at night so that parents in immigrant families could use them as community centers to meet their neighbors, to consult with experts about a range of common problems, and to learn about their new country (Mock and Larson 48–64, Conference on Americanization 32–33).

Other conference participants urged that public schools fight against all ethnic loyalties. For example, one participant—identified as Mr. Young of Iowa—complained that in the northwest region of the United States many schools allowed the German people to use their language and practice some of their customs in the schools. He claimed this practice began in a misguided effort to help the immigrants adjust to school. Mr. Young quoted from a grade-school textbook published in the United States that favorably compared democracy in the United States with the political system in Germany. Finally, he asserted that 90 percent of the German language teachers in the United States sympathized with Germany and were traitors to the United States. He concluded that state legislatures should forbid the teaching of any foreign language before high school (Conference on Americanization 33–35).

At the close of the conference, the Committee on Resolutions recommended that the federal government begin a program of Americanization to be carried out in cooperation with the states, that industries assist in programs to teach English to adults, and that all elementary schools teach only English. In a fairly short period of time, thirty states enacted laws establishing Americanization programs. As the conference had recommended, these measures required factories to offer classes in English and in civics to immigrant workers. Schools had to offer adult evening classes, and labor unions, such as the United Mine Workers, encourage immigrant workers to apply for citizenship (Conference on Americanization 36; McClymer 23).

According to John Higham, the most severe measure aimed directly at forcing immigrants to become citizens was the Revenue Act of 1918. This imposed almost double the taxes on nonresident aliens as it required of citizens or resident aliens. As a result of these economic sanctions, many immigrants applied to become citizens. Higham added that private zealots urged more extreme measures such as placing time limits on naturalization, suppressing the foreign language press, and interning aliens in isolated camps. He believed, however, that need for national unity in the face of the mobilization effort prevented the federal government from proposing measures that would alienate the ethnic members of many communities (Higham 248–249).

A handbook distributed by the U.S. Department of the Interior in 1919 to facilitate Americanization of adults illustrates the department's efforts to avoid antagonizing ethnic groups. It described the process as the opportunity to inspire people who were foreign born with the ideals of democracy and to give them the resolve to work for the common good. In this way, the handbook presented Americanization as a process of education that had to depend on the attractive power of the ideals. If Americanization were forced on people, the handbook warned, it would no longer be American (Butler, *Community* 5–6, 9).

The 1919 handbook urged teachers to respect the adults in their classes. To do this, teachers had to overcome prejudices against ethnic groups, to judge individuals on their own merits, and to learn about the history and literature of the countries of the immigrants. As a result, Americanization was a mutual process wherein foreign-born people learned English and American values and teachers learned to appreciate the contributions of foreign cultures (Butler, *Community* 9–14).

Since there was no compulsion for foreign-born adults to attend these Americanization classes, the 1919 handbook recommended that teachers should demonstrate the advantages of learning English and civics. Also, since there was no federal money to support these programs, the 1919 handbook urged teachers to convince community members to support the Americanization classes. The handbook suggested that communities could sponsor campaign drives similar to those for liberty bonds to recruit adults to attend the classes. The handbook strongly recommended that employers permit adult workers to attend Americanization classes on company time and in the factory. The handbook added that the Americanization classes should provide information that enabled the families to adjust to their new homes, such as lessons in home economics that taught ways to cook available foods or discussions about proper habits in purchasing goods and services. The handbook listed various types of people who could provide important information to the students. These included public officials, lawyers, and doctors (Butler, *Community* 30–61).

Another bulletin from the U.S. Department of the Interior discussed the role of state governments in offering Americanization programs. Although the bulletin repeated that adults should not be forced to attend Americanization classes, the bulletin recommended that states should not grant citizenship easily. It held that immigrants should have to read and speak English before being allowed to file for citizenship. Further, the bulletin recommended that each state adopt laws similar to those already in force in New York. These laws required children between the ages of 16 and 20 who had left school to work but had not acquired the skills of reading, writing, and speaking to attend some day or evening school (Butler, *State* 7–13).

Other supporters of educative forms of Americanization argued that milder methods were more effective than harsher ones. Writing in 1919 in support of Americanization, Emory S. Bogardus warned against efforts to outlaw the use of foreign languages in the United States. Recounting that other countries tried to outlaw minority languages, he argued that the process caused rebellion. Bogardus cited the example of Prussia's effort to suppress the Polish language, which he claimed created four million belligerent Polish subjects. Bogardus suggested that supporters of Americanization show the immigrants how they would profit from learning English rather than outlaw the use of foreign languages. On another point, Bogardus did not approve of night schools because he believed that people were too tired to learn after a day's work. Instead, he thought that classes offered in the factories during the day would be helpful, and by offering training in industrial techniques, they could improve production as well as teach English and civics. Finally, Bogardus considered the idea of suppressing foreign language newspapers as some supporters of Americanization suggested. Bogardus believed that these papers did no harm and that they could serve as a means to reach specific immigrant groups. Thus, Bogardus concluded that Americanism could win more converts among the immigrants by cooperating in their efforts to satisfy their own needs than it could by forcing the immigrant families to give up things they loved (Bogardus 342–365).

The effort to Americanize the immigrants grew out of a fear that these groups of foreign-born adults might not help the country during war. Yet, the debates among supporters of Americanization seemed similar to the debates among school people about how to meet the needs of the students and of the society. That is, although advocates of this process agreed that the society needed loyal citizens, the different members of the movement had different ways to identify when immigrants supported their adopted country. As a result, these advocates took different positions on the best ways to encourage the immigrants to express patriotism to the United States.

How did German-American newspapers try to preserve the German-American heritage?

In his account of the German-American newspapers during World War I, Carl Wittke presented a story of the editors' efforts to preserve the language, to challenge what the editors considered to be the misperceptions of English language reporters, and to turn the Americanization movement into directions that allowed German-Americans to preserve their heritage. In this way, the papers tried to serve the needs of the wider society by retaining loyalty to the United States while maintaining what they considered to be the best of their foreign heritage.

Characterized as thrifty, industrious, and law-abiding, many German settlers retained pride in their cultural heritage. When the fighting began in 1914, German-Americans found English language newspapers condemning everything German even though the United States was not involved in the fighting. Consequently, German language newspapers in the United States printed stories and editorials to counter the prevailing views that the Allies defended democracy and Germany was an autocratic, imperialistic country. Unfortunately, the German language papers could not obtain stories directly from Germany. As a result, the German language papers in the United States argued that the English language papers offered biased reporting. In addition, they repeatedly called for the U.S. president and the newspapers to live up to the neutrality they professed (Wittke 3–9).

German-Americans tried to make clear that they supported the United States through their labor and their loyalty, but their hearts remained in what they called the fatherland. With this deep-seated affection as a motive, many citizens formed a German-American National Alliance whose members undertook writing letters to English language newspapers criticizing biased reporting, circulating pamphlets explaining their views, and raising money for relief of the relatives of German soldiers. Above all, they strove to preserve American neutrality (Wittke 22–35, 45).

In 1915, when President Wilson drew attention to hyphenated Americans and called for legislation against conspirators, German language newspaper editors claimed he was attacking German-Americans. This feeling of having been insulted was an important aspect in later efforts by German-Americans to defeat Wilson when he ran for reelection (Wittke 42–43).

Once war was declared, the German-American National Alliance, the group that had raised money for the relief of relatives of German soldiers, stopped their fund-raising activities and discussed the possibility of forming German-American regiments to fight for the Allies. Before the Alliance could take any action, the U.S. Congress threatened to investigate, and the group disbanded (Wittke 166, 171).

In October 1917, the U.S. Congress passed the Trading-with-the-Enemy Act that contained two sections that affected German newspapers. The act allowed Wilson to create a censorship board, which required that every foreign language paper submit to the postmaster an English translation of any article referring to the war. The foreign language newspaper division of the Committee on Public Information (CPI) followed these periodicals closely and offered news stories written by selected authors and containing information the division leaders thought would enhance the war effort (Mock and Larson 44–45, 68).

When George Creel wrote his account of his work as director of the CPI, he praised the editors of the foreign language press for their dedication to the war effort. Creel described the aim of his committee as seeking to carry to everyone the full message of America's idealism. Calling his campaign the greatest adventure in advertising, Creel said he did not depend on the authority of the war laws to limit the freedom of the press. He claimed that throughout the war, the German bureau offered a weekly bulletin written in German to about two hundred German language newspapers that had combined readerships of about two million people. The German bureau sent English translations to English language papers published in areas with many German-speaking residents. In stressing the unwillingness of the CPI to force editors to obey his will, Creel contended that his committee members separated themselves from the Americanizers who turned patriotism into excuses to express prejudice and violent antagonism (Creel 4, 189, 190).

The freedom that Creel claimed the foreign language press enjoyed may not have been as real as he hoped. For example, although the foreign language press could obtain permits to use mail service, several states prevented mail carriers from delivering the German language papers, and private citizens in many communities organized boycotts of the papers. In addition, citizen leagues circulated petitions to remove the study of the German language from schools and universities. Ohio and Nebraska passed laws prohibiting the instruction of the German language in public or private schools, but, in 1923, the U.S. Supreme Court declared these laws to be unconstitutional (Wittke 173–182).

In 1918, after the armistice, the German language papers reminded their readers of the high ideals the Americans professed when they entered the war. Editorials called for the creation of a new world order, and they warned against taking revenge on the defeated countries.

The newspapers condemned the continuing blockade of Germany and reminded Americans that Wilson had pledged not to wage war against the German people. By 1919, stories appeared in German language papers claiming that the German soldiers had not committed the atrocities attributed to them (Wittke 200, 208–209).

Wittke claimed the German language newspapers tried to return to cultural concerns after the war. They published stories about singing fests and related cultural events, but they took a political stand on the presidential election, urging their readers to vote for Warren G. Harding. This was an expression of hatred for the Democratic Party and for Wilson whom they saw as the causes of their misfortunes.

In all of these activities, the German-American press sought to preserve the value of their readers' heritage and to blend their traditional values with the ideals of American democracy. Many native-born conservatives disapproved and sought to censure the papers, but the disagreement represented a conflict over the best ways to make a stronger society.

How did supporters of the Americanization movement, liberal progressives, and Pope Pius XI view the social role of Catholic schools?

Writing in the 1920s, Horace M. Kallen claimed there were two parts to the Americanization movement. For example, Kallen praised Franklin K. Lane, the U.S. Secretary of the Interior quoted earlier in this chapter, for presenting an intelligent and careful description of a process for protection of the immigrants and their education. Kallen added, however, that fear gripped Americans, blocking their intelligence, and the anti-Bolshevist mania fostered by the U.S. Department of Justice overpowered Lane's voice. As a result, Americanization became an effort to force immigrants to acknowledge the superiority of Anglo-Saxonism (Kallen 144–145).

In 1919, as Kallen noted, one form of Americanism had become part of the effort to weaken labor unions. When the war was over, industrial workers sought to maintain their wages relative to rising costs of living. As unions grew and strikes occurred, industrialists claimed that immigrant radicals had caused the conflicts. Although the strikes involved native-born workers, the press blamed the intervention of foreign agitators. In response, the U.S. Attorney General, A. Mitchell Palmer, began a series of raids, arrested hundreds of immigrants, accused them of Bolshevik leanings, held summary hearings, and decided to deport them. To order the deportations, though, the Department of Justice needed the cooperation of the Department of Labor. In 1920, Assistant Secretary of Labor Louis F. Post released more than 2,000 of the prospective deportees. Standing before a congressional committee, Post made an impassioned defense and newspapers praised his action (Higham 222–232).

Although the public hysteria over communists subsided by 1920, the nativism inherent in parts of the Americanism movement turned to efforts to have all children attend public schools. Focused on Oregon, the outcome of this controversy strengthened Catholic schools in two ways. The U.S. Supreme Court limited the extent to which a state government could control the education of children. And, in reaction to the decision, Pope Pius XI delivered the first papal encyclical to speak to all Catholics about the education of children. These events confirmed the value of Catholic schools, and research later demonstrated that the ethnic parishes eased the transition of immigrants into the mainstream of American society. They were not the obstacles nativists thought them to be.

In 1922, Oregon voters approved a law that required all students to attend public schools. Although the Republican Party had sponsored the Bennett and the Edwards Laws, the Democratic candidate for governor, Walter M. Pierce, endorsed the Oregon statute. The Ku Klux Klan campaigned strongly for the measure, arguing that compulsory public schools were the foundation for the preservation of free institutions and the means to avoid racial, religious, and social antagonisms. But, this was not simply a Klan decision. Two Masonic organizations, the Odd Fellows, the Knights of Pythias, and an organization called the Federated Patriotic Society supported the measure for the same reasons that the Klan gave (Jorgenson 27–29).

A wide-ranging coalition opposed the Oregon law. Catholic organizations, such as the National Catholic Welfare Conference, took the lead, arguing that Catholic schools provided a sound education and shaped moral people and upright citizens. Some newspapers, such as the *New York Times* and the *Chicago Tribune,* argued that Oregon law went too far. While states have a right to regulate religious schools, the newspapers did not think the state governments could eliminate them. Several Protestant groups, such as the Lutheran Schools Committee of Portland, Oregon, a group of Episcopalian leaders, and several Seventh Day Adventists, complained the law infringed on religious liberty. John Dewey wrote that the Oregon law destroyed the elements of trust and faith that built good relations among the different elements in American society (Jorgenson 30–32).

The Sisters of the Holy Names of Jesus and Mary and the Hill Military Academy filed suit in U.S. District Court, listing several reasons why the law should be invalid. For example, it would deprive them of the right to use their property without due process of law. It deprived parents of the right to control the education of their children. It also abridged the free exercise of religion (Jorgenson 32).

The state's attorney countered these complaints. For example, he noted that it was an established principle not to hold state governments liable for losses resulting from changes in legislation. He added that the right of parents to control their children had to balance against the right of the state to protect the safety of its citizens. In this case, the attorney added, the voters of the state had decided that public school enrollments were the best protection against juvenile crime and the proper way to Americanize immigrants. Finally, he noted that the Oregon law did not prohibit any parents from teaching their children any religion they wanted. It guaranteed that the children received a portion of their education in an environment free of any religious bias (*Oregon School Cases* 90, 96–97, 102, 122).

In 1925, the U.S. Supreme Court delivered its decision. The justices concluded that the Oregon law would prevent Catholic schools from conducting business and using their property. The justices noted that states had a right to supervise the education of the children, to examine the teachers, and to ensure that the students learned good citizenship, but the justices claimed that the state should not force parents to accept only public school teachers. In this regard, the court's decision added that the parents had the right and a high duty to prepare the children for obligations beyond those imposed by the state government (*Oregon School Cases* 940–943).

According to Lloyd P. Jorgenson, most newspapers and periodicals in the United States congratulated the court on its decision. For example, the *New Republic,* a journal that had argued against sectarian influences, denounced the Oregon law as an effort to regiment the mental life of Americans through coerced public school instruction. Jorgenson cited one journal, the *New Age,* sponsored by the Masons that supported the Oregon law after the court published its decision. Although the Masons acknowledged the finality of the court's decision and the obligation of Americans to obey it, they promised to continue their battle against Catholic schools by urging increased financial support of public schools and by seeking to convince parents that their patriotic duty was to send their children to public schools (Jorgenson 36–37).

In addition to making the U.S. Supreme Court state the right of Catholics to support their own schools, the Oregon case prompted Pope Pius XI in 1929 to synthesize previous statements about Catholic education. For many years, this encyclical, *Christian Education of Youth,* provided direction to Catholic educators in the development of their schools.

The pope divided the responsibilities for education among three agencies. The first was the family created by God to generate and form children. The second was the state because it was obliged to advance the well-being of the community. And the third was the Catholic Church for it had the means to point humankind to eternal salvation. The pope quoted the U.S. Supreme Court in the Oregon case to show that people at each level had to respect the authority of the other agencies. For example, while the state should ensure that children receive adequate civil instruction, its agents could not prevent the parents from exercising their right and their duty to prepare the children to fulfill their obligations that may exceed citizenship (Pius XI 6, 14–15).

At the same time, the pope added, the church had to remind parents of their duties to baptize the children and raise them as Christians. To aid the family, the church offered to educate the children in ways that shape them as Christians. While such education had to prepare children for life in society, as productive workers and as religious beings, these aspects had to be united so that growth in one area encouraged development in the other aspects of life. To the pope, in countries such as the United States where there were many religious groups, this meant Catholic education in Catholic schools for Catholic youth (Pius XI 15–16, 29–32).

Thus, in the Oregon case, civil authorities, U.S. Supreme Court justices, progressive citizens, and Pius XI took different views about the ways parents and schools should cooperate to meet the needs of children and society. The civil authorities demanded state-sponsored education. The justices wanted the parents to be able to exceed the training offered by public schools. Progressive citizens, like Dewey, thought that civil authorities had to maintain good relations with the leaders of ethnic and religious groups. Pius XI argued that Catholic schools strengthened the various governments by meeting the spiritual needs of the Catholic youth. As a result, the conflict turned on the different ideas that people had about students' and society's needs.

Why did concern for Americanization and for ethnic Catholic schools decline before the Great Depression?

During the decade between World War I and the Great Depression, Americanization loomed as a major concern for native-born citizens and for Catholic leaders. Three things happened, however, to reduce the need for Americanization: The U.S. Congress decided to restrict immigration, the immigrant families who lived in the United States became more prosperous, and the Catholic Church made it more difficult for any group to open an ethnic parish.

The first change came about because the Congress decided it was easier to restrict immigration than to offer Americanization through education. In 1911, William P. Dillingham chaired the U.S. Committee on Immigration and conducted an extensive study of the conditions under which immigrants lived and worked. The report on education included results on more than two million children in more than thirty-seven cities. In 1921, Dillingham served as a U.S. senator from Vermont, and he had the opportunity to offer compromise legislation that would reduce the flow of immigration. His plan was to limit immigration to 5 percent of the number of nationalities coming into the United States in 1910. The aim of such legislation was to preserve the racial balance of the nation and prevent any major shifts. But, in 1923, some senators complained that the 1921 restrictions did not retain what they considered the racial balance in the country because the limits came from the 1910 census when most immigrants came from southeastern Europe. Contending that at earlier periods, the immigrants came from Nordic countries, the U.S. Senate approved legislation in 1924 that based the quotas for immigrants on the 1890 census. They hoped that this practice would contain immigration in ways that reflected the ethnic patterns then present in the country. These quotas remained in place until 1968 (Higham 310, 320–321).

The decision to reduce immigration rather than to encourage education fit the pattern of wavering support that the U.S. Congress gave to the Americanization movement. For example, in 1922, the Department of the Interior published a record of programs for immigrant education. In writing the report, the author, John J. Mahoney, narrowed the definition of Americanization to classes in English and civics given to adult immigrants at any hour and in any place by public education officials. Mahoney called this a new approach that meant classes were offered in factories during the day. For women, classes were offered from 8 AM to 5 PM five days each week all year long. Although the Department of the Interior recommended that such classes be established, the federal government did not offer financial support to the states to conduct the programs. Some state governments, such as Massachusetts and California, shared expenses with local governments. Mahoney claimed that these states provided extensive programs and worked out agreements with industries employing immigrants to offer incentives to those adults who attended the classes. But, Mahoney noted that other states, such as Ohio, offered no contributions to local governments. In these situations, the local schools charged the immigrants a tuition fee to cover expenses, but fewer programs resulted (Mahoney 2–18, 39).

Immigration had been low during the war, and the quotas retained a tight hold on applications. As a result, the rate with which newcomers entered the cities declined rapidly. Instead of facing foreign-born children, teachers met native-born children in their classrooms. Within the ethnic parish schools, more children spoke English. Further, as the families of immigrants remained in the United States, they became more prosperous and began to move into outlying suburban areas. This was the second change that made Americanization less of a concern.

Changes in the lifestyles of immigrant families had two effects among the formerly ethnic Catholic parishes. One was that as the members of one ethnic group moved out of an urban area, another group of Catholics moved in. Thus, the formerly ethnic parishes in the cities became English-speaking territorial ones, and the schools enrolled children from several different nationalities. The other effect was that English-speaking territorial parishes and schools opened in the more outlaying areas where the former urban dwellers moved. Although certain groups, such as the Polish immigrants, tried to resist the trends, the direction of the change was clear. There were always some Polish people who did not wish to speak Polish in church or in school. With each new generation, the number of English-speaking Poles grew, and the immigration restrictions prevented people who spoke only Polish from coming to the United States (Sanders 110–120).

The third thing that happened to ethnic Catholic parishes is that ethnic groups could not easily open parishes dedicated to their nationality. Until 1918, ethnic groups could petition the bishop of a diocese to allow them to form an ethnic parish. In 1918, a new Code of Canon Law changed the process. Although the Code required children to attend Catholic schools and allowed immigrants to attend a national parish wherein the priest was a member of the same ethnic group as the parishioners, the Code took the authority to form these ethnic parishes from the bishops and gave it to the Vatican. This made it extremely difficult to obtain permission to form a new ethnic parish (Vinyard 184).

In all, the three alternatives for Americanization described in this chapter claimed to meet the individual needs of individual immigrants and of society, but they differed on which aspect they placed the most emphasis. For example, liberal, progressive educators sought to show members of foreign-born families how to adjust to the demands of the New World. As a result, Jewish Zionists and Catholic educators complained that the settlement house moved their children away from the ideals of Judaism and Catholicism. They could have argued that the Hull House offered an education that made the children more individualistic. The liberal, progressives, such as Addams and Dewey, thought they were meeting social and individual needs. As Dewey pointed out many times, individual needs could not be contrasted to social needs because the one was best satisfied in the context of the other. That is, a progressive society required individual uniqueness because this was the source of social creativity, and an individual required the benefits offered by an advanced society to develop his or her abilities fully.

The ethnic Catholic schools offered an interesting example of the way religion could aid in assimilation. In the last years of the nineteenth and early years of the twentieth century, parishioners, priests, and bishops disagreed about the wisdom of foreign language schools. On the one side, adherents thought language brought faith, but this view seemed to insulate people from the external culture. From a practical standpoint, ethnic parishes caused the inefficient allocation of resources and the duplication of efforts. Yet, when historians look back on the effects of these schools, they find that the gradualism the schools offered served the communities and the individuals.

Finally, although the Americanization movement appeared overwhelmingly concerned with social needs and willing to trespass on the needs of different groups to retain aspects of the their heritages, the movement did prepare the way for programs through which many individuals could improve their own lives. For example, writing in 1948, Edward George Hartmann found that the movement brought about increased concern for adult education and that it paved the way for legislation in favor of educating other types of adults. In addition, Hartmann claimed that in reaction to excessive actions of the Ku Klux Klan, many native-born Americans felt responsible for their foreign-born neighbors. Thus, he claimed that brotherhood drives and national efforts to abolish bigotry came from popular revulsion to the actions of the superpatriots during World War I (Hartmann 271–273).

Thus, the three different efforts to Americanize the immigrants described in this chapter could be placed on a continuum. The mildest model was that of liberal progressive reformers, such as Addams and Dewey. Although ethnic religious groups saw this movement as a threat to their values, the overwhelming tendency of the period was in favor of helping to free ethnic groups from their tendencies to retain practices just because they were traditional. The most extreme supporters of the Americanization movement complained that when ethnic groups held on to their traditional practices, they reflected alien loyalties. The problem was that such a view led to bigotry, enforced enculturation, and deportation. Perhaps the problems were irresolvable because they did not decline until the U.S. Congress restricted immigration severely. If this was the case, it may indicate that educators could not easily find the point at which the need for social harmony began to harm the interests of individuals.

Summary

During and after World War I, three separate educational efforts sought to help immigrants adjust to their new homes and to strengthen the country as it tried to withstand external threats. One of these efforts came from liberal, progressive educators, such as Jane Addams and John Dewey, who tried to help the immigrant families adjust to their new homes. Another effort derived from the work of ethnic educators, such as Jewish Zionists and ethnic Catholics, who believed that settlement houses, such as Addams's Hull House, frustrated their cultural and religious ideals. Although ethnic Catholic schools provided a means to Americanize the children of the immigrants, the schools caused problems for progressive educators and for Catholic bishops. German language newspapers belonged to this second effort because they sought to preserve what German-Americans considered to be the best of their heritage and to demonstrate loyalty to the United States. The third effort came from politicians and business leaders who wanted the process to create loyal Americans and to unify public support for the war effort. Sometimes advocates of one direction complained that advocates of another direction were hindering the process or leading it astray. In 1922, however, when a coalition of Masons and members of the Ku Klux Klan convinced voters in Oregon to prohibit Catholics from maintaining their own schools on the grounds that every child should attend public school, the effort strengthened the Catholic schools. The U.S. Supreme Court rejected the Oregon law and sought to establish a balance between the state's need to produce good citizens and the parents' obligation to prepare children for duties that surpassed citizenship. Furthermore, the Oregon controversy prompted Pope Pius XI to publish an encyclical explaining what Catholic schools should offer. In 1921 and 1924, the U.S. Congress chose to restrict immigration, and the drive for Americanization diminished. Since the problems continued until immigration declined, it may be that educators could not easily locate the point beyond which efforts to build one country out of many people became hurtful.

CHAPTER FOUR

BALANCING INDIVIDUAL AND SOCIAL NEEDS, 1918–1929

In 1918, the National Education Association's Commission on the Reorganization of Secondary Education (CRSE) recommended that secondary institutions adopt a model of curriculum, known as the comprehensive high school, to provide a variety of vocational courses for different types of students and a set of common experiences that would teach the students to work together in the wider society. Thus, the CRSE called for a change from the ideas of the Committee of Ten that wanted all students to study similar academic subjects. As a result, historians who favor more general or more academic programs look upon this report as a problem. Other historians disagree and believe that the comprehensive high school offered a type of education that served the democracy.

Joel Spring is among those historians who believe that the CRSE reduced the opportunities for schools to liberate students. He contends that the comprehensive high school offered a mixture of social activities and a variety of curriculums to develop individual students' capacities to work productively in large corporations (Spring, *American School* 265).

In a similar manner, Herbert Kliebard contends that educators who belonged to what he calls the "social efficiency group" wanted the model of the comprehensive high school to prepare students for the different roles they might play in society. The priority of these educators was to create a smoothly running society and the ideal they held was one of efficiency patterned after the standardized techniques of industry (Kliebard 24, 99).

Diane Ravitch is more critical. She contends that the CRSE used inflated language to offer the following simple message: Many dumb students are entering the high schools, and they should be trained to be efficient workers in factories or good clerks in business or capable housewives. Although she acknowledges that the report allowed children to prepare for college, she does not think the authors of the report took this concern seriously. She asserts that the driving purpose of the report was to fit children into society (Ravitch, *Left Back* 124–125).

David Angus and Jeffrey Mirel claim that the CRSE report offered muted support for every possible educational alternative and thereby avoided any educational controversies. They contend that it favored offering different courses for different students but that it did not want the students set into their tracks when they were too young. Angus and Mirel argue that the report favored vocational education, but not overly specialized vocational training. It favored many different courses, but not all of them had to serve practical aims. According to Angus and Mirel, the important thing about the CRSE report was that it was written by educators and not by academics. As a result, they contend that the CRSE report was the first nationally recognized call for professional curriculum planning instead of allowing university academics or lay people to provide the direction for school reform (Angus and Mirel 16).

On the opposite side, historians such as Daniel and Laurel Tanner argue that the CRSE report offered a radically democratic vision that coincided with the best progressive thought of the time. It tried to teach children to live and work together in a democratic setting. In this regard, the Tanners claim that the CRSE report obeyed Dewey's desire to combine vocational and general education (Tanner and Tanner, *Curriculum* 97–98).

Joining the Tanners in claiming that the CRSE endorsed a democratic vision of education, William Wraga complains that the scholars who argue the CRSE document contained a social efficiency perspective were excessively influenced by an earlier work written by Edward A. Krug. More important, Wraga argues that Krug quoted the original documents inaccurately and thereby distorted the aims of the CRSE committee. Wraga agrees with the Tanners that the comprehensive high school represents Dewey's vision of a good education (Wraga, "Progressive" 511–513).

Unfortunately, checking the accuracy of the references will not settle the debate. Although Wraga accuses historians such as Krug, Spring, and Ravitch of drawing incorrect conclusions, both he and the historians he favors appear to do the same thing. For example, in his book, *Democracy's High School,* Wraga tries to show that Dewey influenced the writing of the report, but he does not cite an essay wherein Dewey expressed approval of a school offering separate courses for special training and general courses for citizenship training. Nor does he quote any member of the CRSE acknowledging Dewey's influence. At best, he claims that the language of the report is similar to the language found in Dewey's essays. The Tanners make a similar claim about Dewey's influence on the idea of the comprehensive high school, but they do not offer substantial evidence to show that it existed (Wraga, *Democracy's* 26–28; Tanner and Tanner, *Curriculum* 97–98).

The problem is that the disagreements among historians represent interpretations that reasonable people can hold because the CRSE tried to accomplish something that should be logically impossible. The committee members wanted to build an institution that could liberate individuals yet provide for social harmony. They wanted to offer liberal education and to provide opportunities for children to pursue special training. Any plan to resolve these contradictory impulses should be flawed, and the different historical interpretations illustrate the ways different people can look at those difficulties.

Although Angus and Mirel's concern about the domination of professional educators appears distinct, it is part of the question of whether the CRSE favored social efficiency or democracy. They fear that since the members of the CRSE were educators, they did not appreciate the ways that traditional academic studies served individuals and society. The educators' domination of the CRSE is not as clear or as unique as Angus and Mirel want it to be. While most of the members of the CRSE were principals and high school supervisors, the membership list included college presidents, and academic scholars participated on the various committees that were part of the CRSE. More important, while most of the members of earlier groups, such as the Committee of Ten that met in 1893, were academic scholars, they took pride in having experience as practical educators. Finally, as will be discussed later, the CRSE report did not cause nationally recognized professional educators to direct educational reform. Instead, school districts began processes to determine and to initiate local reforms.

More relevant to this discussion, since the CRSE met about twenty-five years after the Committee of Ten's meeting, its report illustrates how quickly Harris's opponents came to dominate educational reform. That is, the members of the CRSE did not seek to retain the distinct nature of the academic disciplines or to design them in ways acquainting the student with the historic development of society. Instead, the members sought to integrate the disciplines and to develop the curriculum around the interests and daily activities of the students.

In what ways did the model of the comprehensive high school express other ideas of curriculum reform?

In 1905, William Chandler Bagley offered what he considered a comprehensive aim of education. He noted that parents wanted schools to teach children how to make money. Academicians wanted students to acquire knowledge or to learn about the best forms of culture. Psychologists sought the harmonious development of students' powers and faculties, and educators, following Herbart, wanted to develop students' moral characters. Claiming that each of these aims overlooked the social requirements of education, Bagley argued that the best aim was to seek the development of socially efficient individuals because such people would contribute to the advancement of society, would not interfere with other people's efforts to improve society, and would sacrifice their own pleasure for the social good (Bagley, *Educative Process* 44–65).

In a review of Bagley's *The Educative Process,* Guy Montrose Whipple claimed that the most interesting part was the section in which Bagley demonstrated how different types of experiences promoted the development of socially efficient individuals. In this section of his book, Bagley sought to accommodate a number of competing ideals. For example, Bagley approved of the rise of vocational programs in high schools because these changes implied that utilitarian values were as important as intellectual or aesthetic values. At the same time, in the elementary schools, he called for more attention to sentimental values. This did not require new subjects in elementary schools. Rather, it meant that elementary schoolteachers should recognize that students could pursue grammar, mathematics, and literature for the pleasure they afforded (Whipple 419–420; Bagley, *Educative Process* 218–238).

If the schools were to ensure this more comprehensive goal, teachers had to offer more than academic subjects. To accomplish this practical aim, educators began efforts to establish social efficiency by changing college entrance requirements on the belief that these requirements dominated the formation of the high school curriculum. In 1911, the National Education Association's Committee on the Articulation of High School and College (CAHSC) issued a report that noted in its concluding statement that high schools in a democracy had the duty to return to the society that supported them citizens who were intelligent, able-bodied, and progressive. This meant that high schools had to contribute to what the report called efficiency along several broad lines. These included vocational training, citizenship training, and home management. The report called for a blending of these vocational pursuits with liberal arts training in the high school. In that way, students would see the relation of their work to the welfare of the entire society. Since these were opportunities that all students needed, the committee members criticized most high schools for requiring students to take courses in mathematics and foreign languages to prepare them to enter college. Although the chairperson of the committee, Clarence D. Kingsley, had been a teacher of mathematics, his committee's report complained that many boys and girls could perform well in other subjects but not in mathematics and foreign languages. Since the society would benefit if students of different abilities could attend, the committee requested that high schools offer and colleges accept social science and natural science courses in place of both a foreign language, such as Latin, and mathematics (NEA, *College Entrance* 97–98, 103).

The members of the CAHSC realized that liberalizing college entrance requirements placed greater responsibility on high schools to develop appropriate programs. To them, this meant that the reform of the high schools had to be more drastic. As a result, the CAHSC recommended that the NEA establish fourteen committees to draft reports about the content of various high school studies. While these included the traditional academic subjects, they added several subjects, such as social studies, household arts, and business. In addition to forming the committees, in 1913, the NEA formed the Commission on the Reorganization of Secondary Education (CRSE), to oversee the committees' work (NEA, *Preliminary Statements* 7–8; NEA, *Cardinal Principles* 5).

In 1913, with the cooperation of the U.S. Bureau of Education, the CRSE released preliminary reports of the various committees. The Commissioner of Education, P. P. Claxton, applauded the CRSE, hoping its work would be a first step in satisfying what he called "the insistent public demands for the readjustment of the work of the high school." Similarly, the committee chairpersons noted in their preliminary reports the need to change the direction of their courses. For example, the chairperson of the Committee on English asserted that the course that prepared students for life at home, in society, and in industry would best prepare them for college as well. The chairperson of the Committee on Social Studies claimed that in modern high schools, recent history was more important than stories of ancient times and the history of the United States was more important than the history of foreign lands. Even the chairperson of Committee on Ancient Languages, while asserting that Latin was an effective instrument of general culture, acknowledged that the time was ripe for a reformation (NEA, *Preliminary Statements* 5, 10, 17–18, 33–34, 40).

The CRSE did not publish final reports from the Committee on Ancient Languages nor the Committee on Modern Languages. Although the Committee on Ancient Languages submitted a final report, the reviewing committee did not accept it. The final report of the CRSE did not mention any possible value for foreign language instruction. Instead, the report asserted the need for students to master English to work and live in their communities. Thus, the report ignored the long-standing claim that foreign languages taught culture or improved logical thinking (Krug, Vol. I 341–342; NEA, *Cardinal Principles* 11, 22–23.)

To support its recommendations, the CRSE's *Cardinal Principles* report listed three changes that justified a reorganization of high schools. First, changes in the society created a more complex and urban economic order, and citizens were not prepared to participate in this complex society because their lives had been simpler a few decades earlier. Second, the *Cardinal Principles* report noted changes in the school population as more and different types of students entered high schools. Unfortunately, the report noted that less than one-third of the students who entered the high school graduated. Third, the report claimed that changes in the science of psychology recognized the importance of individual differences, called into question the idea that traditional studies could enhance general intelligence, expressed the value of applying knowledge, and recognized the changes children underwent as they grew into adults (NEA, *Cardinal Principles* 7–8).

Although the social changes noted by the CRSE appear dramatic, they did not happen overnight. For example, the U.S. Census Bureau observed in 1920 that for the first time the majority of the nation lived in urban centers, but the growth of industrial centers had been evident since the U.S. Civil War. Further, although by 1918, every state in the union had adopted compulsory education laws, the campaigns for such legislation took place much earlier as Chapter Two describes. Yet, some historians point out that when school attendance laws existed, school superintendents refused to enforce these laws because teachers did not want their classes disturbed by children uninterested in academics. After WWI, however, local districts complied with those laws because they were interrelated with newly adopted child labor regulations. As a result, by 1920, more than 85 percent of the children required to go to school were enrolled (Ensign 234–235, Katz 18, 21).

Although the Committee of Ten that met in 1893 might have used arguments of social change to justify a more varied approach to curriculum, it did not. On the other hand, in keeping with the desire of Harris's critics to build academic courses in ways that related to practical circumstances, the *Cardinal Principles* report asserted that the goal of education had to be guided by the meaning of democracy. And, the committee defined democracy in ways similar to those that Bagley had used when he spoke about social efficiency as the educational aim. The authors of the *Cardinal Principles* report contended that democracy meant each person should develop his or her personality through activities designed for the well-being of the fellow members of the society. From this definition, the *Cardinal Principles* report claimed that the goal of education should be to develop within each student the knowledge, interests, ideals, habits, and powers to enable those students to find their places in society and use those places to shape themselves and their society to ever more noble ends (NEA, *Cardinal Principles* 9).

The *Cardinal Principles* report made the connection among school subjects and social life clear by claiming that the educational objectives appropriate for a democracy could be found by analyzing the activities of adults in the community. Since people were members of families, of vocational groups, and of civic groups, it appeared reasonable to the committee members that schools should train the students in health, command of fundamental processes, worthy home membership, vocation, citizenship, worthy use of leisure, and ethical character. The CRSE members claimed these seven objectives represented statements of the students' needs and, consequently, could become the objectives for many different courses (NEA, *Cardinal Principles* 9–11).

In several other sections, the *Cardinal Principles* report indicated the direction that changes in high schools should take to meet the important student needs. For example, the report urged that districts divide the last eight years of secondary education into junior and senior periods that were usually three years long apiece. According to the *Cardinal Principles* report, the junior high schools could give students opportunities to explore different vocations, thereby catering to the needs of different individual students, and the junior high schools offered a social organization that called forth a sense of responsibility for the welfare of the group, thereby satisfying society's needs. In a similar manner, the report claimed that the ideal of democracy required secondary education to admit all the pupils who could benefit. This meant educators had to think of secondary schools as places where liberal, academic training and vocational training took place. As a result, the *Cardinal Principles* report claimed that the standard high school should be a comprehensive model that offered some different courses for different types of students. According to the report, this model allowed for students to pursue courses suited to their unique needs. If students had to change courses during their studies, they could do so without sacrificing school loyalties or relationships with other students or faculty, which would happen if the courses were located in separate campuses. Within comprehensive high schools, students could pursue such options as business, industrial, house arts, and academic curriculums. Yet, the school could offer common or unifying studies, such as social studies and English, which taught students the ideals and skills they needed as citizens in a democracy, and common activities, such as athletic contests, social events, and school government, which taught them to work together. In short, the report concluded, the comprehensive high school represented the prototype of democracy wherein small groups pursued their own interests but recognized the common ideals of the school. As a result, students prepared for life in a democratic society (NEA, *Cardinal Principles* 18–23).

Although the *Cardinal Principles* report enjoyed the largest sale up to that time of any work published by the U.S. Bureau of Education, it did not convince high school principals to change the curriculums nor did it lead to changes in the courses that students took. By 1929, the bureau sold 110,000 copies of the report, yet supporters of the CRSE were disheartened to find that of a sample of 1,200 high school principals, 255 had never heard of the report. More disheartening to the CRSE supporters, by 1930, high school course-taking patterns had not changed from the academic ideals they disliked even though secondary school enrollments grew. The CRSE members had argued that expanded enrollments brought new types of students into the school and these new, different students would not succeed in academic courses. This turned out to be incorrect. According to David Angus and Jeffrey Mirel, many high schools offered a variety of vocational courses, but most students enrolled in the traditional academic fields of English, mathematics, science, and the social studies (Krug, Vol. II 24–27; Angus and Mirel 53–54).

Surveys conducted by the U.S. Office of Education at the time reinforce Angus and Mirel's point that traditional classes retained their popularity and relatively few students enrolled in the newer, more practical courses. The Office of Education noted that high school attendance rose. In 1915, before the CRSE published its report, there were about 1,700,000 students enrolled in high schools. By 1928, this figure nearly doubled, growing to almost 3,000,000. Yet, the most popular courses remained English literature and rhetoric, enrolling over 90 percent of the students. Although the percentage of students taking algebra and geometry dropped somewhat during those thirteen years, more than 30 percent of the students took algebra and nearly 20 percent took geometry. Foreign language enrollments declined, although more students took French and Spanish classes. French enrollments increased from under 10 percent in 1910 to over 14 percent in 1928, and Spanish enrollments grew from under 1 percent to nearly 10 percent in the same period. Unfortunately, formerly popular languages suffered severe declines in enrollments. In 1915, almost 40 percent of the students enrolled in Latin, but by 1928, the enrollment dropped to a little more than 20 percent. As critics complained that studying German caused Americans to be disloyal, enrollments in German language classes fell from about 25 percent of the students in 1915 to barely 1.5 percent of the students in 1928. Most surprising to the reformers, the most popular vocational courses had modest enrollments. In 1915, some high schools offered shorthand. By 1928, enrollment in shorthand rose to about 10 percent of the students. In 1928, over 15 percent of the students enrolled in commercial arithmetic, but other business courses, such as bookkeeping, typing, and commercial law, attracted fewer than 2 percent of the students. Finally, home economics attracted few women students. According to the Bureau of Education, in 1910, when home economics was introduced, enrollment rose quickly from less than 4 percent of the students the first year to almost 13 percent in 1915. Its popularity remained near this level through 1928 (Office of Education 1057–1058).

Students may not have enrolled in the new subject matter because the new courses seemed to exclude the less academically talented students. This was the surprising result of a study conducted in 1914 by Ernest Horn of classroom recitations in twenty schools around the country. Horn defined recitation as any response on the part of the pupil, and he sought to determine whether all students had equal opportunities to make such responses. He concluded that the students did not have equal opportunities. Instead, the students that the teachers thought had the most abilities had the most opportunities to participate in the classrooms. While this finding was not surprising, Horn noticed a change in the patterns. The most equitable patterns of recitation appeared in those subjects that had been in the curriculum the longest time. In these subjects, the students had to memorize, and the teachers had developed mechanical procedures, such as calling on the students by rows or alphabetically, to increase student responses. In the newer classes, Horn found that teachers could not use these methods because they asked the students to sense problems, solve them, or to make comparisons to events in their everyday lives (Horn 1, 8, 36–37).

Horn ended his study with the plea that researchers had to find ways teachers could involve more different types of children in the newer courses. While such a hope was reasonable, Horn may have discovered why students enrolled in traditional classes more than the newer ones. Although reformers thought the newer classes were suited to the needs of the less academically inclined students, those same students had higher rates of success in the older courses than in the other newer classes.

Another reason students did not take vocational courses in the comprehensive high school may have been that the vocational programs were poorly constructed. In 1920, David Snedden complained that high schools could not afford to provide a range of vocational programs and general education classes for students pursuing college entrance. The best the school could offer would be to allow students to play at the jobs using some equipment and referring to some books in a library. Further, Snedden claimed the fear that students could not learn civics in a trade school was false. The best professionals graduated from schools dedicated to special training, such as military academies and engineering schools. In those schools, the students learned about the social order in which they lived and worked (Snedden, *Vocational Education* 92–104).

Despite the problems, most historians agree with Edward Krug that the *Cardinal Principles* report became the ideological force behind the movement for the comprehensive high school. Called a uniquely American institution, more and more school districts adopted the model of the comprehensive high school. Although some large cities retained the separate and special schools for boys or for girls or for trades that they had built before 1920, educators claimed these schools fostered distinctions between the genders or among social classes and therefore were European rather American in nature (Krug, Vol. II 53).

The most important success of the CRSE was the creation of a new course of study, the social studies. As noted earlier in this chapter, Kingsley's Committee on the Articulation of High School and College (CAHSC) recommended that high schools accept the social studies as a substitute for mathematics and foreign language. In line with this recommendation, one of the committees serving the CRSE was the Committee on the Social Studies. This cycle of courses was designed to help students develop common understandings about the development of their society no matter what other type of courses they pursued.

When the Committee on the Social Studies released its report in 1916, the members defined the social studies as those areas composed of subject matter relating directly to the organization and development of human society. These included geography, history, government, economics, and sociology. According to the report, the social studies afforded particular opportunities for students to learn what it meant to be efficient members of the society and thereby cultivate ideals of good citizenship. Although the report acknowledged that a sense of citizenship depended on loyalty to national ideals, the authors sought to inculcate in students feelings of membership in the world community (NEA, Committee on the Social Studies 9).

In many respects, the authors of the social studies report imitated the work of historians who were becoming popular. One of these historians, James Harvey Robinson, introduced what he called the "new history," and he served on the Madison Conference that described how history should be presented for the Committee of Ten.

In 1916, when the CRSE set out to reorganize secondary education, Robinson was a member of the Committee on the Social Studies, and he took an important role by defining the purpose of historical instruction. He claimed the aim of history in the schools should be to present past conditions and to compare them with those found in the present day. In line with his recommendations to the Committee of Ten, Robinson urged teachers to go beyond textbooks, to approach the study of history topically, and to describe with care the institutions found in contemporary society (NEA, Committee on the Social Studies 42–43).

Taking Robinson's pragmatic spirit as an example, the authors of the report of the Committee on the Social Studies extended Robinson's credo. For example, the report quoted Robinson as saying that it was an unsolved problem as to what conditions and institutions the teachers should select for the students to study. The report answered Robinson's problem quickly. The authors of the report adopted the principle that topics should be selected on the basis of how they could be related to the present life of the students (NEA, Committee on the Social Studies 43–44).

To illustrate how the principle of selection might be applied, the report of the Committee on the Social Studies praised a teacher in a high school of practical arts who taught young women whose parents worked in various trades. To begin a lesson about medieval craft guilds, the teacher asked each father to take his daughter to his work and show her what he did during the week. Returning to school, each girl found out something about the history of her father's craft, its problems, and the techniques the workers used. This research took six weeks because the students tried to find out how such trades as shoemaking had changed over the previous ten centuries. At the end of the six weeks, the girls reported their findings to the entire class. Since these oral presentations covered a range of industries, such as printing, construction, and weaving, the students learned the history of many occupations, and they saw several connections from past ages and from distant continents to their present lives (NEA, Committee on the Social Studies 46–47).

In another example, the report of the Committee on the Social Studies complimented a teacher in a rural area who taught students in a class called "community civics" to understand the value of roads. This lesson began with a survey of local roads that led to an evaluation of farmers' costs to haul produce to market and to a comparison of similar costs in areas where roads were superior. The lesson concluded with a study of the historical development of other methods of transportation, such as canals and railways, and their relation to the economic development of the countries where they were used. Such lessons built on the present-day interests of the children, applied to their life situations, and led to the development of feelings of membership in an international community (NEA, Committee on the Social Studies 29–30).

Although the members of the Committee on the Social Studies proposed an aim that was wide, educators construed the ideal of citizenship in practical terms and thereby narrowed it. For example, in 1917, David Snedden complained that history courses served no realistic purpose. To prove his point, Snedden sampled ten questions from the College Entrance Examination Board. The questions asked specific narrow questions such as the following: Who were the leaders of the first and third crusades? What was the result of the first crusade? Was Athens right in opposing Phillip of Macedon? Give reasons for your answer. The point Snedden made with these examples was that the answers depended on memorization of concentrated statements of historical facts. There was no connection of this knowledge to what a person needed to live in a twentieth-century democracy. As a result, Snedden called on educators to determine what social information different types of students needed, decide how much time should be allotted to the studies, and remove those objectives best obtained by other organizations such as the Boy Scouts (Snedden, "History" 272, 275–280).

In the hands of other theorists, the aim of citizenship became what they called the "sociological principle" in determining the elementary school curriculum. For example, Ross L. Finney argued that the role of the elementary school was to impart a common culture so that everybody could work together. To Finney, this meant that students had to master the principles of hygiene in elementary schools in order for the advances of science to reduce the threat of epidemics. For instance, if mothers were ignorant of germs, they would not clean the infant's nursing bottle adequately to prevent illness. Although Finney avoided making suggestions as to what should appear in the elementary school curriculum, he noted that as the culture became more complex, more information had to be included and students had to spend more time in schools (Finney, "The Sociological Principle" 338–344).

As a representative of the American Sociological Society, Finney approved of the addition of sociology and other the social sciences to prepare students to adjust to the complex society. Reporting in 1920, he noted approvingly a long list of committees and organizations that sought to spread social sciences in the schools. These included the NEA's Committee on the Social Studies, the American Historical Association, and the National Board of Historic Service. A self-constituted National Committee for the Teaching of Citizenship that included Charles Beard among its members enjoyed the support of the U.S. Bureau of Education. Finally, the National Association of Secondary School Principals sponsored a Committee on Social Sciences chaired by Charles Judd. To determine what effect this attention had in schools, Finney's committee sent out questionnaires to all the state superintendents asking about the extent to which such classes as civics were being taught. They found that elementary schools adopted civics more than high schools did. To change the high schools, Finney concluded, questions relating to civics would have to appear on the college entrance boards (Finney, "Tentative Report" 257–259).

Unfortunately, many schoolteachers did not seem concerned with students mastering information about their society. They sought the narrower and less intellectual aim of helping the students develop emotional bonds to their country. For example, in 1920, C. O. Davis reported that since the end of WWI, the public had demanded an increase in what he called full-blooded Americanism. He added that the nation had sought to eliminate any anti-

American doctrines, such as anarchism, and any divided national allegiances, such as using a hyphen to express a person's origin from another country and present residence in America. Davis praised various governmental agencies that sought to Americanize adult residents of foreign birth and indoctrinate them with the principles of the Declaration of Independence and the U.S. Constitution. But, he claimed that many native-born Americans lacked a full appreciation of the benefits they enjoyed as citizens. To find out what practices schools followed in teaching citizenship to these students, Davis's committee sent questionnaires to 1,180 schools from 18 states enrolled in the North Central Association (C. O. Davis 45–47).

In accord with public feelings of isolationism, Davis found that his respondents discarded the idea that citizenship was an expression of the fraternity of human beings. They saw patriotism as a form of public spiritedness that might be created by ministers or successful businessmen addressing the students in large assemblies. Davis found that many schools inculcated nationalism through stirring patriotic music. Other schools held public oral readings of selections chosen to fire emotional zeal. Most schools taught information about citizenship through a half-year course in civics. Contrary to the wishes of the members of the Committee on the Social Studies, the teachers used textbooks or official leaflets provided by the states rather than designing materials specifically for the community. While many schools offered discussions of current events, few schools presented considerations of the conflicts between labor organizations and industrial establishments. Davis thought developing proper psychological attitudes among the students was more important than helping them acquire information. As a result, he was pleased to find some efforts to stir students' patriotic emotions (C. O. Davis 45–59).

Although Davis approved of the direction in which schools were moving, his study showed that authorities in local school districts directed the suggestions of national committees into narrow, anti-intellectual channels. Despite this problem, national associations played less of a role in educational reform after WWI than they had earlier. Local districts became more important.

How could curriculum theory encourage educators in local districts to decide what was best to teach?

In 1925, the chairperson for the Commission on Curriculum for the National Education Association announced that the members of the commission had decided that the superintendents of local school districts should reconstruct the curriculum in line with their local needs. As a result, when the commission published a yearbook in 1928, it refused to take advantage of its position to set the example of the proper direction for curriculum improvement. The yearbook avoided specific recommendations that could be widely applied (Krug, Vol. II 27).

To aid local school districts design their curriculums, educators offered to describe the steps they should take in such a process. In 1918, Franklin Bobbitt claimed that his book, *The Curriculum,* was the first book on curriculum formation. Predicting a rapid end to the war, Bobbitt noted that the social reconstructions of the postwar years would place new demands on education, and he asserted that his book offered an introduction to the theory of the curriculum. Although Bobbitt acknowledged that the curriculum could include any experience to help people develop their abilities, he warned schools not to repeat lessons the students could learn in other places. He thought curriculum planners should find out what it is that children do not learn outside of school and try to teach those skills or abilities (Bobbitt, *The Curriculum* iv–v, 43–45).

To explain how curriculum planners could work, he described the work of W. W. Charters who asked teachers to listen carefully to their students' speech and to watch their written work for a few weeks. Charters asked the teachers to record those errors in notebooks, categorize them, and list them in order of their frequency. The teachers found that the most common error involved confusing the past tense of a verb with its past participle. The least common error was confusing superlatives and comparatives. These errors were calls for direct instruction because it appeared that the students did not learn the topics elsewhere (Bobbitt, *The Curriculum* 45–47).

Although Bobbitt's principles of curriculum planning could most easily apply to vocational or agricultural areas, he argued they could also be applied to complex studies, such as history. In this case, the curriculum maker had to determine the social deficiencies that result from a lack of historical, literary, and geographical experiences. For example, he suggested that studies in history might demonstrate the need for social cooperation in maintaining physical health by illustrating such things as the nature and seriousness of diseases, the ways that famous people had recognized the problems associated with urban sanitation, and the means by which people in the past reduced health dangers. As a result of such studies, Bobbitt argued, the students could see the need for improved social conditions (Bobbitt, *The Curriculum* 47–52, 189–196).

Bobbitt claimed that he discovered these principles shortly after the Spanish American war when he and six other individuals tried to create an elementary school curriculum for the Philippine Islands during the U.S. occupation. He claimed the director of education forced them to include only those subjects and lessons that met the social needs of the people. Bobbitt recommended that superintendents of schools should do the same. This meant the superintendent had to accept the situation found in the city at that time. Although a superintendent should strive to improve conditions, these changes had to come slowly, Bobbitt cautioned. The superintendent should gather teachers, principals, and community members together, he recommended, and ask them to review the subjects and determine what changes were demanded by community needs. He warned this process would be slow because they had to look at each subject individually, but the incremental changes should be beneficial. Above all, Bobbitt cautioned, the superintendent should avoid rushing the schoolteachers or the citizens toward distant goals because teachers and parents need time to adjust their expectations, their thoughts, and their practices (Bobbitt, *The Curriculum* 281–289).

Soon after Bobbitt published his book on curriculum, he went to Los Angeles, California, to help the superintendent construct a curriculum for high schools and junior high schools that met the needs of the community. To work on this task, the superintendent formed a series of committees composed of principals, heads of subject area departments, and teachers. Total membership on these committees came to over 300 people. Bobbitt's first step was to give the committees a list of 300 objectives that he had drawn up with the help of his graduate students at the University of Chicago. Although Bobbitt noted his students had carefully prepared the list of objectives, he meant it to serve as an illustration of the types of objectives they needed to construct. Bobbitt's second step was to ask the 1,200 teachers in the city to construct a list of abilities and characteristics that men and women in the city needed (Bobbitt, *Curriculum-Making* 1–6).

While explaining the steps he used in Los Angeles, Bobbitt admitted that he did not follow his earlier recommendations. Instead of sending out scientific researchers to determine what behaviors the people in Los Angeles needed, Bobbitt asked teachers and principals what they thought people needed. Thus, Bobbitt built his curriculum on the opinions of the teachers, not the findings of researchers. Nonetheless, he argued this was not a problem because the teachers agreed on the objectives. To him, this agreement made the objectives appear reasonable. Further, Bobbitt complained that he lacked the time for careful study because the schools had to teach the children immediately (Bobbitt, *Curriculum-Making* 6–7).

Although Bobbitt believed the teachers in Los Angeles had created important lists of objectives, Boyd Bode complained in 1927 that Bobbitt's questionnaires did not uncover useful information. The fact that the teachers agreed on the objectives did not impress Bode. He noted that the objectives were either specific, such as the ability to renew washers in faucets, or vague, such as the ability to protect themselves from fallacies. The most serious problem that Bode found with the list was that it did not offer direction for the reform of society. The list seemed to take the present adult activities as the pattern for the students' growth, and it could not offer suggestions as to whether those activities should take place. As a result, Bode condemned Bobbitt's effort because it omitted the need of what Bode called the "progressive transformation" of the students' experiences in the direction of wider social insight (Bode, *Modern* 80–88).

Although Bode did not approve of Bobbitt's method of curriculum making, he argued the problem was that the model did not do what it promised to do. It did not enable citizens to function competently in a democracy. Instead, Bobbitt's model seemed to prepare people to adapt to the society as it was organized.

How could a curriculum be designed that encouraged students to follow their own interests in ways that enabled them to become cooperative democratic citizens?

Bobbitt claimed that, with his model of curriculum reform, researchers could determine what people needed to know to improve their lives and teachers could make their classes relevant to the world outside the classroom when they conveyed those needed skills to the students. This idea of making school lessons directly applicable to life outside was one that vocational educators pursued. For example, vocational agriculture teachers found they could use home projects to turn school lessons into demonstrations of how to improve life on the farm.

In 1908, Rufus W. Stimson was the director of Smith's Agricultural School in Northampton, Massachusetts. He hired a man through the summer to assist the boys in applying the teachings of the school in their home farm work. Stimson found that, although his employee supervised the children, the fathers watched the projects and often applied the same principles on the larger efforts on the farm. By 1911, the Massachusetts Board of Education adopted Stimson's home project as a method to allow students to work in productive farming while they took classes in vocational agriculture. Stimson developed a wide range of farming projects. These included something to improve the farm, such as building a concrete walkway. Such a project involved studying the nature of cement, measuring the cost of cement relative to other building materials, and evaluating the cement's relative resistance to deterioration. In other projects, the boys would decide to plant a type of fruit tree new to the area. In this case, the student studied the soil, determined the likelihood of the tree flourishing, and surveyed the possibilities of marketing the fruit. According to Stimson, with the projects, the students avoided excessive theoretical speculation and combined their daily responsibilities with schoolwork. For example, a boy whose chores included milking the cows could take as a project a plan to feed clover to some cows, to determine the price of the different feed, to compare the production of milk between cows that ate clover and those that did not, and to decide if having the cows eat clover caused them to produce enough milk to surpass the extra cost of the clover. At all times, Stimson noted, the cost of any innovation was a primary consideration. The aim of these projects was to teach the students that profits came from receipts that surpassed expenses (Stimson 10–16).

Although Stimson described these home projects as if they were experiments, he pointed out that the teacher who supervised the project always knew what the result would be. As a result, while the students and their parents approached the projects as tests, the teacher used the projects to demonstrate innovative agricultural techniques to the families in the area (Stimson 13).

A surprising twist came in 1918, when William Heard Kilpatrick changed this narrow utilitarian model into a way for children to pursue their own interests. In an eighteen-page article entitled "The Project Method: The Use of the Purposeful Act in the Educative Process," Kilpatrick asserted that there could be an infinite number of different types of projects. A girl might make a dress or a boy might publish a school newspaper. The important point for Kilpatrick was that these projects could unify three conflicting aspects of educational theory: the need for wholehearted vigorous activity, the opportunity to utilize the laws of learning, and the development of ethical conduct. Defining the project as wholehearted, purposeful activity proceeding in a social setting, Kilpatrick argued that projects brought together the three conflicting aspects of educational theory in the following ways: First, the projects inspired the students' participation because they chose to engage in the activities. Second, Kilpatrick claimed doing these projects followed the laws of learning because the children received a stimulus, made a response, and thereby formed bonds of association in their minds. Since the students worked on projects that interested them, they thought about their actions and developed a range of responses while reinforcing the connections among the stimuli and the responses. Kilpatrick claimed that children who studied things teachers assigned did not make the same beneficial connections and made little effort to create responses. Third, these projects enhanced ethical conduct, Kilpatrick added, because the children came to view life as a series of purposeful acts rather than a sequence of events to which they must submit. Most important, they carried out these acts in a social setting and sought to blend their own desires with the welfare of the group (Kilpatrick 4–12).

A student of Kilpatrick's, Samuel Tenenbaum, writing an authorized biography, claimed that Kilpatrick was the first educator to conceive of the project method as a philosophical approach to education rather than a series of activities that could enrich school lessons. Tenenbaum thought this was a significant difference from the many references that educators had made to the project method before Kilpatrick used the term (Tenenbaum 140–141).

Although the idea of the project method was not new to Kilpatrick, his short article catapulted him to international fame. In the next twenty-five years, Teachers College at Columbia University circulated over 60,000 reprints of "The Project Method." The success of his article offered Kilpatrick the chance to occupy the senior chair in the philosophy of education.

During his career, he taught over 35,000 students from all over the United States, and a substantial percentage of those students became leaders in educational circles. As a result, most people in the United States associated the project method with Kilpatrick and the progressive reform of elementary schools (Cremin 216–220; Kliebard 139–142).

An effective method of spreading the idea came from a student of Kilpatrick, Ellsworth Collings, who reported on an experiment to provide evidence of the superiority of the project method over traditional methods of teaching. From 1917 to 1921, as part of his doctoral dissertation at Columbia University, Collings compared the work of students who attended three different eight-year elementary schools in McDonald County, Missouri. In the experimental school, forty-one students followed a curriculum built around the project method wherein the students pursued activities they found interesting. In two other schools, a total of fifty-nine students followed a more traditional curriculum. At the end of the experiment, Collings found the students in the experimental school outperformed the students in the control schools on standardized tests in such areas as reading, writing, and arithmetic. Furthermore, the students in the experimental school and their parents displayed more affection for school than did the students in the control schools and their parents (Collings 4–10, 339–341).

According to Samuel Tenenbaum, several professors who served on Collings's doctorate committee did not approve of his experiment. They accepted his dissertation after making some complaints and requesting several changes. But, Tenenbaum added, when Macmillan Company published Collings's dissertation as *An Experiment with the Project Method,* the book became popular and reformers in Switzerland and the Soviet Union used Collings's ideas as the basis for their own innovations (Tenenbaum 224–225).

Another student, James Fleming Hosic, worked with Sara E. Chase to publish in 1924 a handbook for teachers to use the project method. They claimed that people engaged in a series of projects throughout their lives and the method brought this way of learning into the classroom. Thus, Hosic and Chase refused to establish a set of procedures for curriculum planning and cautioned teachers not to confuse the exhibits of student accomplishments with the method. The problem might be that the students may not have felt responsible for their work; they may not have cooperated with others; or they may not have felt a desire to engage in the activities as they made the artifacts that were on display. Hosic and Chase claimed the success of the projects could be determined by considering whether the experience was valuable to the students, whether they participated in the activities on the basis of their individual abilities, and whether the lessons served the students' lives outside school. Although Hosic and Chase warned teachers against directing the projects too closely, they thought teachers should not allow the students absolute freedom in selecting projects. Instead, they urged teachers to use sympathetic guidance that led the pupils to plan to do things they ought to do (Hosic and Chase iii, 3, 7, 65–70, 86–88).

Other supporters of Kilpatrick, such as E. A. Hotchkiss who published *The Project Method in Classroom Work* in 1924, closely followed Kilpatrick's reasoning to explain the benefits of the project method. Hotchkiss offered several examples of projects teachers could use, such as a sand map of Africa, a department store, and building a community. In each of these descriptions, Hotchkiss listed procedures teachers could follow to initiate the projects, problems the students might encounter, and solutions that teachers might use to help the students. For example, Hotchkiss noted that projects should grow out of some social situation or individual experience. After discussing different ways teachers might entice students to attend symphony concerts or learn about France, Hotchkiss claimed skillful teachers could manipulate situations in ways to stimulate the children's native tendencies and to ensure that the reaction is pleasant for the students. He added that teachers should be ever alert to take advantage of opportunities to begin projects. Thus, Hotchkiss noted that a project of making a map of Africa grew out of an effort to find pictures of animals with which the students could decorate the classroom. A pupil asked why Africa was called the Dark Continent. The students and teacher came to the conclusion that the name came from the barriers such as dense forests and large deserts that prevented explorers from entering. As a result of this conversation, the pupils decided to make a large relief map of Africa so that everyone in the school could know more about the continent (Hotchkiss 12–16, 43, 56–58).

In 1925, Kilpatrick published *The Foundations of Method* to explain more fully how teachers could build all the classroom lessons on his model. Kilpatrick divided projects into four types. These included the producer's project wherein students made something; the consumer's project wherein students enjoyed something, such as a concert; the problem project wherein students sought to clear up some difficulties; and the specific learning project. With the specific learning project, Kilpatrick acknowledged the need for students to learn certain materials through some form of drill or exercises. These could include such things as mastering the fundamentals of arithmetic or learning to read. Although Kilpatrick acknowledged that these skills were so important to the life of the child that teachers could force the students to acquire them, he disapproved of the Winnetka Plan wherein students mastered such skills in morning classes and participated in projects in the afternoons. Kilpatrick asserted the problem with this arrangement was that the teachers planned in advance what the students had to master. For him, the requisite skills should be related to other projects the students wanted to accomplish. Thus, the skills might not appear in a logical pattern, but they would appear in a way related to the developing interests of the children (Kilpatrick, *Foundations* 347–366).

In the same way that Kilpatrick adapted the vocational model of the home project to his uses, educators who had popularized the Herbartian scheme described in Chapter One found the project method to be the way to continue to spread their ideas. For example, in 1920, Charles A. McMurry urged teachers to construct large units of study that would bring together considerable amounts of material. McMurry contended that if teachers constructed these units around generative ideas that pulled the information together into an interesting story, such as Washington's campaign against Yorktown or the building of the Panama Canal, they could pull in ample scholarship, use the project to illustrate a real-life setting, and develop ideas that applied in other areas. In this regard, McMurry claimed that when students understood steel mills in Pittsburgh, they could relate the problems of industrialism they encountered in that study to other parts of the world. As a result of these units, students should acquire patterns of thought they could use to understand the world (McMurry, *Teaching* v, 44–59).

When McMurry advocated the project method, he followed the style many Herbartians had used twenty years earlier when they disagreed with Harris. That is, he recommended that experts prepare the units of study for the teachers to use. Thus, the students could not choose to follow their interests. The teachers determined what the children's interests were. Further, using the language of Herbart, McMurry claimed teachers should follow separate steps to encourage the apperceptive use of knowledge. In his 1920 text, he defined apperceptive knowledge as the ability to apply old ideas to new situations. Teachers could encourage this quality by starting the lesson with questions that encouraged the students to recall information related to the materials they were about to study. Second, the teacher should present some material the students would need in the project. Then, the teacher should allow the students to apply the materials to some problem they had to solve. The teachers could test the effectiveness of the lesson by asking the students to apply the insights gained in one activity to another related situation. The important principle for McMurry was that the students assimilate material in ways that they could bring it to new situations (McMurry, *Teaching* 237–254).

McMurry's suggestions illustrate the similarity between the ideas of educational reformers in the 1890s and in the 1920s. Although Kilpatrick sought to design his projects around student choice more than did McMurry, they agreed that students needed to pursue their interests and that such lessons enabled them to become contributing, moral citizens.

When Kilpatrick applied the term *project method* to any whole-hearted purposeful activity proceeding in a social setting, other educators complained that his definition was overly broad. For example, in 1923, W. W. Charters argued that Kilpatrick's definition lacked direction because, following it, any activity could be a project or not depending on how the children went about it. Further, a project might fit the definition one day and not fit it the next. Charters pointed out that a student might begin making a dress as a purposeful activity but the next day the child's interest could wane. Following Kilpatrick's definition, the activity would cease to be so classified. For these reasons, Charters preferred a definition that he attributed to John Alford Stevenson: The project is a problematic act carried to completion in its natural setting. Charters claimed this was what the agricultural educators tried to do by having students grow corn at home and apply the lessons from school to their farms. Although Charters acknowledged this brought life to the curriculum, he warned that trying to teach all lessons through projects would change the curriculum. Instead of teaching arithmetic, geography, and spelling, for example, the school might turn into a place where students learned to play house and to play city (Charters 137–146).

In 1927, Boyd Bode appraised the movement toward projects. Noting that there were many definitions of the project method, Bode acknowledged that they all represented attempts to bring to the schoolroom activities found in everyday life. The efforts in agricultural education represented ways of teaching the students to solve problems, to acquire knowledge, and to apply it to things they understood. It was no surprise to Bode that this method would become popular among teachers of many subjects who wanted students to take an interest in their work. Bode warned that the projects could be overly simple or they could be overly complicated. In both cases, the students would learn nothing. When correctly applied, though, the projects helped students acquire what Bode called instrumental knowledge. To Bode, this was an advantage to the method, but it was also a limitation because the information learned was practical rather than theoretical (Bode, *Modern* 141–151).

Bode added that McMurry's idea of preparing central teaching units included theoretical knowledge, but his idea was vague. McMurry never told teachers what should be the aim of the material included in the units. The units could advance culture. They could train research specialists, or they could serve any other purpose (Bode *Modern* 151–157).

Bode complained that although Kilpatrick claimed students must undertake projects in whole-hearted purposeful ways, he included activities that people did not associate with such expressions of interest. For example, in the consumer's project, a student might attend a concert. Since listening to music appeared passive, Bode wondered if it enlisted the purposeful behavior that Kilpatrick had found when the student tried to solve a problem or build something. Worse, Bode accused Kilpatrick of confusing things by claiming there were certain essential skills the students had to master. These were so important, Kilpatrick had asserted, that the teacher could force the children to learn them. For Bode, the problem was that while

Kilpatrick made the project method appear to be a revolutionary method of enlisting students' interest in school lessons, he resorted to the traditional approach when he came to the matter of essential skills (Bode, *Modern* 157–163).

In all, Bode claimed that the various approaches of the project method came from efforts to make school more meaningful and less mechanical, but he did not think that it had accomplished this aim. Instead, he worried that teachers were more confused as a result of the innovation. As a result, he thought that educators might be better served by thinking about the proper aim of education; they could derive ideas of the best methods of teaching from the goals that they should pursue (Bode, *Modern* 165).

Bode's criticisms illustrate that even models such as the project method that was built on students' interests did not seem to encourage liberation. Instead, the teachers used the students' interests to help them adjust to the society.

How could educators construct a curriculum that encouraged students to think critically?

In making many of the curriculum innovations in the 1920s, educators sought to teach children to adapt to the society that existed at that time. This was true of Thomas Jesse Jones and Arthur Dunn's view of the social studies. But, in 1923, another social studies educator, Harold Rugg, tried to design the curriculum to encourage the students to learn about social problems. His idea was if the students learned to think independently, they would be able to participate in social improvement when they became adult voters in the community.

In 1923, the National Society for the Study of Education dedicated its yearbook to what the editors called an example of a scientific method of curriculum reform with regard to the social studies. The editors offered what they considered a systematic inventory of then current practices, a critical construction of hypotheses, and an analysis of the available experiments (Rugg, "Foreword" vii).

Rugg argued that social studies classes represented opportunities for teachers to encourage students to reflect on social problems. He complained that most adults did not exercise care when voting. Instead of thinking about what course of action would enhance the common good, they voted for or against a measure on impulse. In social studies classes, the students could learn to think more objectively about society, and they spent considerable time on the social studies subjects. For example, most school districts offered history from the fourth grade to the last year of high school and exposed students to this material four or five times per week for about thirty minutes a day. Unfortunately, when Rugg explored whether most schools taught the social studies in ways that prepared children to think about social responsibilities, he found that they did not. Rugg complained that the students learned about the rise and fall of kings, the details of military battles, and the provisions for peace treaties in history classes. Similarly, in geography classes, he found that the students learned lists of facts unrelated to social developments in the countries. Although courses in civics promised to open the curriculum to investigations of social problems, Rugg determined that these classes presented the details of the U.S. Constitution and the composition of federal, state, and local government. Thus, Rugg contended that while social problems could appear in civics courses, they rarely did (Rugg, "Do the Social Studies" 2–14).

The hypothesis that Rugg derived from this catalog of contemporary practices was that the selection of material had to change if schools were going to prepare pupils to work for social harmony as adults. He argued that texts should pay more attention to topics that are important to all people. Further, he argued that the texts the students read should be so rich in detail that the students' school experiences reproduced life experiences. Above all, Rugg argued, the students had to learn to approach social problems in ways that enhanced finding objective solutions (Rugg, "Do the Social Studies" 17–19).

From these hypotheses, Rugg suggested a different course of action. Instead of dividing the social sciences into separate subjects such as history, geography, and civics, he suggested that schools offer a unified, continuous social studies curriculum organized around social problems. He thought that textbooks should be organized the same way. That is, the authors should organize information around problems and issues rather than around divisions of subject matter such as sociology, political science, or economics. Such a plan would allow teachers to discuss immigration to the United States between 1820 and 1920 by discussing the economies of England and Ireland, the political history of Germany, living conditions in various countries, and the status of farming in northern and southeastern Europe (Rugg, "Do the Social Studies" 19–23).

While Rugg's call for a unified social studies appeared radical to many educators, it did not differ widely from the proposals that the Madison Conference made in 1894 and the Committee on the Social Studies made in 1916. Although these groups recommended that distinct subject matter courses remain, they had suggested that teachers organize the studies around topics the students could investigate. Rugg's innovation was to take the idea of topics, turn them into social problems, and make the problems the center of the curriculum.

To encourage school districts to adopt his notion of organizing texts around what he felt were pressing social problems, Rugg wrote a textbook series that provided the materials for such courses. But he did not set out with this idea in mind. His project unfolded awkwardly. In 1920, Rugg joined the experimental Lincoln School at Teachers College in Columbia University. The aim of this laboratory school was to try something as an experiment and to extend the new practice to the public schools. He persuaded a historian from the high school, a geography teacher, a history teacher in the elementary school, and a room teacher to assemble new reading materials for the elementary school children. Lacking a central focus, the participants frequently disagreed as to what they should try to accomplish. After a year, they mimeographed over a thousand pages of materials dealing with such issues as immigration, industrial development, and business for the Lincoln School children to use. From 1922 to 1927, he persuaded several school superintendents to underwrite the publication of twelve 300-page books. Rugg claimed that he and his assistants built the texts on objective studies. These included studies of existing curriculums, research to document pupils' abilities, determination of the problems and central trends of contemporary life that students needed to know, and discovery of the central concepts that educated minds used to think about the problems and the trends. For example, in the description of modern society, Rugg used the ideas of the new historians because he believed they offered attempts to see life as a whole, they traced the causes and relationships of factors, and they sought deep-founded traits and causes. In this effort, Rugg hired sixteen research assistants to help him. When he finished the first series of three trial texts, each about 300 pages in length, he sent them to teachers in 375 school districts. After using the books, the teachers suggested several revisions. With the $90,000 he had earned from the trial texts, Rugg began in 1927 writing and publishing textbooks, workbooks, and teachers' guides for wider distribution. By 1940, he had completed eight volumes in the elementary school course and six in the secondary along with workbooks and teachers' guides (Rugg, *That Men* 40–47, 214–220).

In his textbooks, Rugg blended such subjects as history, geography, and civics because his aim was to show how modern life came to be. Whenever history was needed, it was presented. Whenever geographic conditions could illuminate contemporary problems, they appeared. Rugg did the same thing with economic facts and sociological findings (Rugg, *Changing Governments* vii).

Although Rugg's books sold widely, they generated considerable controversy, which came in two forms. The first was from colleagues who noted reasonable problems with Rugg's methods. For example, in 1921, a dispute arose when Joseph Schafer, chairperson of the American Historical Association's Committee on History and Education for Citizenship, released its report. Rugg complained that, in deciding what the content should be in school texts, this committee relied on the judgment of a few specialists. In Rugg's view, this meant the Committee on History and Education formed its curriculum suggestions on the opinions of a few people. Schafer retorted that Rugg had done the same thing. He contended that Rugg had selected the crucial issues and the generalizations for his texts from a list of experts whom he called new historians or outstanding thinkers. Schafer argued that these thinkers shared particular biases and that Rugg had built his series around their prejudices. According to one commentator, Peter Carbone, Rugg would not admit that all social science research was infected by bias, and he persisted in presenting his procedures as objective. Since Rugg could not step back from his own perspective in this debate, Carbone thought that Rugg contradicted his stated aim of teaching children to accept dissenting views (Carbone 144–146).

The second form of criticism that Rugg received was from right wing patriots. Rugg claimed that, from 1939 to 1940, he collected a four-foot long shelf of these overstated criticisms. In general, they were a direct result of his organizing themes. Rugg had organized his texts around pressing problems in contemporary life. This allowed critics to complain that his books convinced students that life in America had failed. In fact, these censors made so much of this complaint that they called Rugg an un-American traitor. Rugg was deeply offended by these attacks, and he wrote his book, *That Men May Understand,* to counter them. Despite Rugg's insistence that his work was correct, the critics appeared to win. Rugg did not revise his textbook series in subsequent years (Rugg, *That Men* 71–73; Kliebard 178).

What rationale guided the efforts to reform elementary and high schools after World War I?

The educators who worked after World War I sought to balance two opposing needs. One need was the drive for individual development and the other need was the desire for social harmony. In the main, the educators' suggestions represented uneasy compromises with these contradictory points. For example, at the high school level, the CRSE's compromise muted vocational efforts. But, if the students' preferences caused them to pursue specific interests, the CRSE created the social studies in which the students pursued topics that reinforced their understandings of social harmony.

Some educators, such as Franklin Bobbitt, suggested that children needed to prepare to do the things that adults did. Other educators, such as William Heard Kilpatrick, suggested that children needed to be children and pursue their own desires through projects. These proposals represented efforts to balance the needs of the individuals and the social needs. Philosophers found that they did not succeed in making education democratic.

Educators tried to forge a course of social studies that enabled individuals to criticize their society. They believed that such independent thinking would enable students to find the balance between their needs and social obligations, but citizens complained that these lessons were excessively negative because they focused on the problems of society.

It may be that there is no way to resolve the contradiction between individual needs and social needs. Nonetheless, the CRSE, Bobbitt, Kilpatrick, and Rugg expressed approaches that were based on the Herbartian ideal described in Chapter One. This was that schools should serve the individual student's and the society's needs. The problem was that educators seemed to lean in the direction of helping students adapt to society more than they helped the children pursue their own interests.

Summary

After World War I, educational reformers advanced four innovations that educators hoped would make schools more democratic. The first is the model of the comprehensive high school that educators adopted to provide a differentiated curriculum with courses designed for many different types of students. Since the new vocational programs tended to separate students, the reformers recommended that students take courses in social studies and civics to prepare for life in a democratic society. The second innovation was an effort by local school districts to undertake the task of curriculum revision instead of relying on the pronouncements of national organizations as they had earlier. Theorists recommended principles of curriculum planning to aid the superintendents. In this model, curriculum specialists analyzed the activities of the adults in the community, determined what the students needed to learn to perform those roles, and found ways to teach those skills. The third innovation was from elementary educators who designed programs such as the project method to meet the needs that children had as children. The fourth reform was to use the social studies to teach children to criticize society in hopes that, as adults, they would find ways to solve pressing social problems. These models differed in the importance the supporters attached to academic studies, vocational preparation, and student choice. Yet, the models were similar because in each case, the supporters argued that concern for the concept *democracy* could reconcile potential conflicts that existed between individuals' desires and social needs. Unfortunately, critics complained that these models failed to fulfill this aim.

PART III

FROM RECONSTRUCTING SOCIETY TO MEETING STUDENTS' NEEDS DURING THE GREAT DEPRESSION, 1930–1940

The two chapters in this section focus on two different reforms that educators pursued during this period of economic and social problems. In one case, the educators sought to meet the society's needs. In the other case, the educators sought to meet the students' needs. Although these appear to represent different views of the relationship between schools and society, the chapters will argue that the advocates of each perspective shared the view that when traditional academic studies were tied to daily activities of the students, the students would be able to contribute to the formation of a good society.

Chapter Five covers four proposals to use education to change the social environment. The first proposal is the American Historical Association's (AHA's) efforts to consolidate the teaching of the social studies. The second is the federally created Civilian Conservation Corps, which offered unemployed young people the chance to earn money and obtain an education. The third and fourth are efforts by the federal government to revitalize the arts and crafts of Native Americans and of Hispanic Americans in New Mexico. While these efforts took different directions, they shared the common aim of trying to teach children about their societies. As a result, they tended to encourage the children to adapt to some externally imposed vision of what the society should be.

Chapter Six considers the Progressive Education Association's (PEA's) Eight-Year Study. Although many commentators think the Eight-Year Study was built on different assumptions than was the AHA's Commission on the Social Studies, this chapter will argue that this was not the case. That is, the PEA educators felt they had found ways to meet the needs of elementary students, and they believed that if they could change high school programs in similar ways, the programs would produce adults who could think independently and participate in social reform. Ironically, critics complained that since the progressive schools had children work together, the effect was to produce adults who tried to fit into the associations in which they lived.

CHAPTER FIVE

RECONSTRUCTING SOCIETY, 1930–1940

Although the economic problems that caused the depression developed over a long period, the disaster happened quickly and spread widely. In early September 1929, the stock market broke, rallied, and broke again. By November, the value of industrial stocks was half what it had been before the slide began, and, in 1932, industrial stocks held about one-eighth of the value they had before the crash began. As banks closed and factories shut their doors, more than six million men walked the streets looking for work. The crash devastated farmers. In 1929, before the crash, gross farm income reached nearly $12 billion. In 1932, the figure fell to $5 billion (Leuchtenburg 244–248).

Some writers argue that, during the depression, people's attitudes differed dramatically from the attitudes they had held during the preceding era of prosperity. Writing about the advent of the depression, Malcolm Cowley called the 1920s an "easy, quick, adventurous age." He added that, when the 1930s began, he experienced a sense of relief similar to the feeling he had when he left a room crowded with people and entered an empty but sunlit winter street. Building on Cowley's comparison of the 1920s and the 1930s, William E. Leuchtenburg claimed that the depression forced people to take on a new seriousness and a less optimistic outlook. Leuchtenburg demonstrated this transformation by noting that the 1930s brought the fall of formerly famous people, such as New York's flashy mayor, Jimmy Walker, and the silent film star, Clara Bow. Leuchtenburg added that the new attitudes caused citizens to lampoon Henry Ford as a tyrannical employer and to repeal prohibition. According to Leuchtenburg, there were two important signs that people no longer considered the United States to be the land of opportunity. In 1932, there were 250,000 fewer marriages as young people without hope of employment postponed marriage, and, although 36,000 immigrants entered the United States that year, 103,000 former immigrants returned to their homelands (Leuchtenburg 267–270).

Despite these arguments, the tendencies with which authors identify the 1930s had been present in the 1920s. For example, historians contend that labor unions became popular in the 1930s, but those unions had developed much earlier. In 1916, teacher associations around Chicago joined together to form the American Federation of Teachers (AFT) and received a charter from the American Federation of Labor. The AFT added groups in other large cities such as New York so that, by 1920, the union had approximately 100 local chapters. During the 1920s, anti-union movements spread through the country and membership in the AFT dropped. In the 1930s, school boards cut teachers' salaries, removed positions, and increased class size in efforts to cope with declining revenues. Consequently, like workers in many other industries, most teachers lost their anti-union sentiments. Many teachers turned to the AFT in hopes of protecting their jobs and their salaries (Urban and Wagoner 241–242, 264–265).

Increases in school enrollments contradict the view that people took on new and pessimistic outlooks. In 1929–30, about 4,800,000 students enrolled in secondary schools. By 1939–40, this number almost doubled, reaching about 7,100,000 students. Such enrollments suggest that people felt they could prepare for the return of opportunities. In addition, educators continued to advocate the same reforms they had advanced during the 1920s. For example, educators consolidated smaller districts causing the number of districts to decline in patterns similar to what they had done before the crash. This allowed districts to construct bigger schools with more diversified programs. Many reformers retained the view that these bigger schools and widely diversified programs meant increased opportunities for the students. At the same time, state departments of education increased in size and distributed publications about ways to improve curriculums, lesson plans, and instructional materials. The federal government augmented these efforts by publishing materials on topics, such as new methods of teaching, ideas about testing, and architectural plans for improved buildings (Cremin 274–275).

The tendency of educators to join national organizations in hopes of improving all schools continued through the depression. Membership in the National Education Association (NEA) rose from about 10,000 members in 1918 to over 210,000 by 1941. It is important to note that the NEA differed significantly from the AFT. Founded in 1857 by school leaders, the NEA leadership maintained the view through the depression that supervisors could best protect teachers' interests. Thus, the NEA did not align itself with organized labor. Instead, the organization published reports that told of the spreading economic problems, described their effects on schools, and suggested ways administrators could avoid the most damaging consequences. The NEA encouraged state governments to counterbalance the inequities that existed among various school districts, and the organization lobbied for federal support of local schools (Cremin 275; Urban and Wagoner 177, 265–266).

Despite the consistency in these efforts, C. A. Bowers contended that the depression made teachers think differently. He argued that, during these difficult days, the members of the PEA heard a set of ideas that they had ignored during more prosperous times. Bowers asserted that Stanwood Cobb, president of the PEA in 1931, expressed the popular view within the organization when he claimed that the child was the starting point, the middle, and the end of education. Cobb and his supporters sought to release children from adult domination in the hopes that the children would use their creative powers to reform society when they became adults. Bowers noted that, as the depression deepened, other educators in the PEA argued more strongly that the social environment had to change before schools could improve. Bowers wrote that George Counts expressed this view when he urged teachers to seek political power and to lead the nation to socialism (Bowers, *Progressive* 3–5).

Although Bowers acknowledged that various people in the PEA held these two views during the 1920s, he stated that the division deepened as the nation's economic problems spread. Despite Bowers's desire to separate the educators into two distinct groups, the American Historical Association's effort to unify the social studies suggests this distinction was not clear. The AHA brought together scholars and educators who designed a plan for social reconstruction that blended concerns for the children's needs with efforts to meet what they thought were the social needs of the day. Furthermore, three other projects illustrate that the ideas of social reconstruction and child-centered training were not far apart. These projects are the Civilian Conservation Corps, efforts to improve the education of the Mexican Americans in New Mexico, and changes in education for the Navajo.

How did the work of the AHA Commission on the Social Studies represent a blending of child-centered education and social reconstruction?

In 1926, the Council of the American Historical Association approved the plans of a committee made up of prominent historians and educators to conduct a study of how teachers should present the social sciences. To explain the need for such a study, the committee members claimed that teachers and administrators faced constantly increasing numbers of students, rapidly changing social conditions, and recommendations about social studies offered by several other committees that did not seem adequate. In 1928, the Carnegie Corporation offered to finance the study, and, in 1929, the Commission on the Social Studies began its work. By 1936, the commission had published fourteen of the proposed sixteen volumes including its overall conclusions and recommendations (Beard vii–ix).

Historians disagree about the nature of the committee and its accomplishments. For example, according to Edward Krug, this project involved some of the most dynamic personalities of the time among educationists and academicians. Led by August C. Krey, and known as the Krey Commission, the effort was more electrifying than soothing. But, added Krug, it demonstrates that, at least in this case, there was not a struggle for the curriculum. Krey was a historian, a pure academician, yet he was determined to help the public schools. Krey urged the formation of this committee because he felt that the traditional course work did not help students in public schools (Krug, *Shaping* Vol. II 242, 248).

On the other hand, Peter Novick portrayed historians as aligned against educators over control of the instruction of the social studies. He claimed that the American Historical Association never officially accepted or endorsed the commission's report. He added that most historians ignored the reports because the commission endorsed the idea that society was moving toward an age of collectivism and the historians wished to avoid taking stands or promoting such conclusions (Novick 190–191).

Other historians quote Novick and restate his view. For example, Gary Nash and his coauthors claimed that although the commission wrote seventeen volumes, these books held no interest for historians. According to Nash, historians did not want to teach students to take active roles in social reform (Nash et al. 38–39).

On the other hand, some historians contradict Novick and Nash. For example, Bowers noted that there was no evidence that the American Historical Society tried to disassociate itself from the commission's report. In fact, according to Bowers, numerous references in the association's proceedings praised the commission's work as the most important project undertaken by the association (Bowers, *Progressive* 34).

One indication that historians continued to approve of the work of the AHA Commission on the Social Studies and of social studies as a school subject is a resolution passed unanimously at the 1933 annual meeting of the AHA. The commission had finished its work, but several volumes awaited publication. A considerable amount of money was left from the Carnegie Fund's contribution to support the commission. In addition, Beard donated to the commission the royalties he received from writing *A Charter for the Social Sciences in the*

Schools. The AHA decided to send these monies to the accounts of the journal, *The Historical Outlook,* to publish articles on the teaching of social studies in schools. In recognition of the work of the commission, this journal changed its name to *The Social Studies* (AHA, *Annual Proceedings* 1935, 19, 25).

Nonetheless, Novick was correct when he wrote that some historians expressed disappointment with the commission's final report. For example, two social scientists and two educators refused to sign the conclusion because they found it to be overly radical. In addition, a geographer on the commission, Isaiah Bowman, hesitated to affirm the conclusions citing minor disagreements (Commission on the Social Studies 164–168).

A modern historian, Diane Ravitch, claims that Beard's introductory volume for the Commission on the Social Studies, *A Charter for the Social Sciences,* offered no guidance in how school studies should be conducted. According to Ravitch, the problem was that this commission accepted as the aim of the social studies the creation of rich, many-sided personalities among the students. She adds that she cannot imagine anyone making such a claim (Ravitch, "From History" 92–93).

In fairness, this definition reflected the multi-disciplinary perspective of the commission. Charles Beard wrote the first report, entitled *A Charter for the Social Sciences,* defining the objectives of the social studies. He composed it from the ideas of the other members of his subcommittee. These people came from a wide variety of disciplines and held wide-ranging interests. Four were educators. Among these was George Counts whom Bowers labeled as a radical social reconstructionist. Another was Franklin Bobbitt. As Chapter Two indicates, historians frequently labeled Bobbitt as a conservative social efficiency expert. Six of the members were historians, and the remaining six came from other social sciences. This disparate composition implied that the members of the subcommittee would not approve any statement that was overly radical or conservative nor would they emphasize history or political science at the expense of the other social sciences (Beard i–xii).

The commission members accepted the aim of creating rich, many-sided personalities to avoid simplistic formulas about the ways that the social sciences could improve the world. The difficulties inherent in scholarship confused any appraisal of the worth of history or political science. For example, Beard began *A Charter for the Social Sciences* by pointing out that social scientists, such as historians, used some form of the scientific method to offer objectivity within their studies. Although their findings often contradicted the ideas most people in their societies accepted as true, the scholars could not create truths to replace the ones they broke because they could not trust their objectivity to extend beyond the small areas they studied. Further, Beard and his subcommittee members noted that although the disciplines appeared related, they broke apart according to the things the scholars studied. Thus, they could find no easy way to organize the social sciences into a coherent pattern for school studies. At best, the social sciences could join into a mosaic with each concentration maintaining its own center (Beard 8–12, 17–21).

When Beard and his subcommittee members considered what social realities students should recognize, they encountered similar difficulties. They acknowledged that the important facts were that the United States was a society undergoing change, that the United States was an industrial rather than agricultural society, and that all citizens should participate in the government, but recognizing these realities did not solve the problems of instruction. They caused them. Since societies constantly changed, no one could predict what information or skills people would need in the new social order. Although the United States was an industrial nation, people expressed dissatisfaction with the industrial order. In the past, when schools sought to prepare young people to participate in government, the direction was to indoctrinate the children to accept the established order. These practices violated the principles of democracy teachers set out to protect (Beard 21–48).

When Beard described the climate of American ideas, he found three common but contradictory perspectives. The first was the ideological view that the then present social order was best. The second was a utopian hope in the perfection of humankind. And the third was the progressive belief that citizens could turn the present into a better future. There was no simple way to avoid the controversies these views represented. For example, if teachers sought to introduce only established facts, any organization of facts implied one of these perspectives. Nonetheless, it appeared to the commission members that American society had chosen ten goals that could shape social studies instruction. These included national planning in industry, business, and agriculture; expansion of insurance systems; universal education; perfection of transportation systems; coordination of local and national planning; development of recreational parks; provision of universal health care; enhancement of the arts and sciences; expansion of equality of opportunity for all men and women; and cooperation among all nations (Beard 52–80).

Surveying the framework of then current social studies programs, Beard noted that many states required teachers to cover the following topics: nationalism, health, safety, humane habits, and religion and ethics. While many state laws demanded conservative interpretations of these topics, Beard argued that many points, such as aspects of the U.S. Constitution, were too complex to explain simply and directly to young people. Further, Beard noted that his commission was restrained by the realizations that teachers were ill prepared to comprehend complex social issues and the students were too immature to grasp the ideas themselves (Beard 81–90).

Facing this complex situation, Beard and his subcommittee members concluded that the aim of the social sciences should be the development of rich, many-sided personalities among the students. This meant that the students should possess information. They needed skills to obtain that information and the ability to analyze it. They had to possess such habits as cleanliness, industry, courtesy, promptness, accuracy, and the willingness to cooperate with other people. While Beard asserted that students should develop patriotic attitudes, he quoted President Wilson to define these attitudes as allegiance to the idea of democracy and to the hope of humanity. In addition, Beard noted that the students needed willpower, courage, and imagination because these enabled them to persist through difficulties and to retain alternative ideas. At the same time, aesthetic appreciation could make social endeavors more widely satisfactory. Above all, Beard concluded, students had to retain affection for liberty. This meant that they must learn to tolerate different views and recognize the biases in their own (Beard 93–117).

As noted, a modern historian, Novick argued that the members of the AHA ignored the reports because they slanted toward social reconstructionism. Another historian, Bowers, complained that the AHA accepted the reports readily and thereby supported what he thought of as one of the most bizarre social reform proposals to come out of the depression. This was the notion that teachers should indoctrinate students into believing that particular governmental forms were superior to other forms (Novick 190; Bowers, *Progressive* 34).

When read today, the conclusions and the recommendations of the commission do not appear to be radical. The commission asserted that teachers of any social science had to be committed to scholarly, scientific ideals including the disinterested pursuit of truth. The commission urged teachers to develop in their students a critical spirit and to encourage them to seek and weigh evidence with an informed rather than a prejudicial mind. At the same time, the commission emphasized conditioning factors that influenced social studies teachers. Among these factors were the growing interrelationships among countries and among such aspects of social life as intellectual development and ethical sensibilities. The commission argued that empirical studies established the fact all branches of the economy were becoming integrated and that this made people dependent on larger corporations. Thus, the commission argued that objective social science had established that the age of individualism in government and the economy was closing and a new collectivism was emerging (Commission on the Social Studies 8, 11, 13–14).

According to the conclusions and recommendations of the commission, these conditioning factors did not imply a need for indoctrination. They required that teachers recognize completely and frankly that they and their students lived in an age of transition when the growth of cities and large industries implied that individuals needed the capacity to cooperate more than they needed the desire for self-reliance. Further, people needed the cultural equipment to enjoy the leisure that had not been available in frontier life. The commission warned that, if teachers emphasized the traditional values of individualism and acquisitiveness, they would intensify the conflicts inherent in the transition. At the same time, though, the commission urged teachers to affirm such traditional values as liberty for every person, equality of opportunity for all people, and tolerance for the differences among groups (Commission on the Social Studies 34–38).

When the statement of conclusions appeared, a review in *School and Society* described the document as portraying two social philosophies struggling for ascendancy. One philosophy was capitalism, which caused the division of social classes. The other philosophy was the collectivism of a planned economy with mass rights. The reviewer added that the commission members believed that collectivism was going to triumph, and the reviewer noted that the commission offered plans to prepare teachers and students for the change (Reports 682).

Other reviews were more critical. In June 1934, Frank Ballou, superintendent of schools in Washington, DC, and a member of the commission, published a statement explaining that he refused to sign the final report of the commission because it did not offer significant aid to teachers. Among the conclusions were several recommendations about teaching. These conclusions cautioned against relying on intelligence testing to sort students on the basis of abilities, warned against measures of character or culture, and pointed out that what were called objective achievement tests could not replace older methods of evaluation. Ballou argued that these criticisms of scientific methods of testing would cause dissension among teachers. Ballou added that the chapter on selection and organization of the subject matter was inadequate because it failed to offer concrete ways teachers could better present subject matter (Ballou 701–702).

In August 1934, Franklin Bobbitt censured the conclusions and recommendations. Bobbitt had served on the subcommittee to draft *A Charter for the Social Sciences* and appeared to approve of that document. In his criticism of the conclusions, Bobbitt complained that the commission used phrases such as "a new age of collectivism," "integration and interdependence," and "the masses" to disguise communistic intentions. At the same time, he noted the report urged the extension of democracy. Bobbitt complained that communism and democracy could not work together. Further, he noted that education had always served individuals and the commission wanted students to learn to function within a paternalistic state (Bobbitt, "Questionable" 202–207).

Other readers of *School and Society* found Bobbitt's complaints puzzling. For example, in September 1934, Percival Hutson of the University of Pennsylvania could not understand how Bobbitt found a threat to democracy in the report. Hutson wrote that he had read the report and found that the commission recommended collectivism to preserve democracy. According to Hutson, Bobbitt wanted the democracy of Thomas Paine where government was limited and small. In the days of the frontier, this was a good model. But in the modern world, Hutson continued, people depended on an intricately interdependent economy and someone had to control this economy if individuals were to flourish (Hutson 355).

Another reader, Philip Cox, claimed that Bobbitt's comments were hypocritical. Cox quoted Bobbitt's description of curriculum making and noted how he approved of conscious planning of the course of study. Although Bobbitt advocated a paternalistic approach to educational reform, Cox added, he rejected the experimentation and control the commission thought essential. In addition, Cox found nothing controversial in the statement that the world was drifting toward collectivism. This did not imply a communist government because conservative leaders, such as Charles W. Eliot, recognized that collectivism was inevitable in a complex impersonal world. Cox added that collectivism had been present for years in the development of parks, highways, hospitals, and social welfare (Cox 556–557).

Bode Boyd offered a limited defense of Bobbitt's views. In November 1934, Bode wrote that the commission offered two contradictory parts of the conclusions. One part was called the frame of reference from which all educational outcomes would be judged. This frame included the view that there would be economic planning, redistribution of wealth, and a possible modification of private property. The other part was the notion that the individual had to be free from excessive social pressures on such areas as his or her religious, economic, or social beliefs. Bode asked how the inevitability of social planning could fit with the freedom to hold any economic belief. For Bode, the frame of reference should not have been in the conclusions if the commission trusted people's intelligence to solve social problems. That is, if people were intelligent and there was a need for social planning, they should be allowed to recognize that need on their own (Bode, "Editorial" 1, 7).

High school and elementary teachers complained that the commission asked them to expose themselves to community pressure but offered no protection. In 1935, Julian Aronson complained that teachers would lose their jobs if they took the commission seriously and tried to engage in modest criticism of capitalism. Aronson predicted that corporate leaders, such as Andrew Mellon or William Randolph Hearst, would make sure they never taught again in any school (Aronson 96–97).

The members of the Commission on the Social Studies recognized the teachers had a legitimate complaint, and they sought to determine whether or how teachers could resist community or business pressures. In 1931, the commission asked Howard K. Beale to try to determine the answers to questions about the external control of teachers. In his effort to determine current conditions, Beale constructed an extensive questionnaire that he distributed to teachers through several channels. He found that the problems of freedom differed by level but were widely spread. Among elementary and high school teachers, Beale found that the controversies went beyond subject matter and included disputes over teachers' personal ideas about such subjects as international relations, patriotism, and politics. For example, during World War I, teachers lost their jobs if they opposed the war effort. After the war, superintendents wrote contracts in ways that required teachers to avoid conduct unbecoming a teacher. They decided that inappropriate behavior included any criticism of capitalism (Beale 5–11, 22, 55-56, 100–101, 277–280).

Although Beale listed seven things that could increase and protect the freedom of teachers, many of his recommendations were not things that teachers could do. For example, Beale's recommendations included reorganizing schools to allow such bodies as teachers' councils to share authority over teachers with administrators, funding schools sufficiently to allow teachers to purchase and use appropriate equipment, and increasing legal protection in the form of tenure laws and contracts. On the other hand, there were a few items that teachers could pursue. These included forming professional groups that had the cohesiveness of labor unions, pursuing better training, and demanding that only competent individuals be hired as teachers (Beale 684–739).

In 1935, M. E. Haggerty of the University of Minnesota wrote an extensive criticism of the conclusions and recommendations of the Commission on the Social Studies. He felt that the language of the report illustrated that, instead of conclusions based on solid research, the commission offered the prejudices of the members. He claimed that the commission placed unrealistic demands on teachers. He argued that, when the commission placed the observation about the emergence of an age of collectivism as a frame of reference, it was imposing a belief as if it were a fact. Worse, he added, the conclusions presented this observation as something all teachers had to accept. According to Haggerty, if teachers had to accept this frame of reference, they could be made to accept any other set of beliefs (Haggerty 275–278).

In general, the Commission on the Social Studies engendered considerable criticism because it elevated teachers to positions where they could direct social change. The commission members believed that students should learn about the nature of social life and about social change in order for them to participate in what the commission report called "social engineering." In this way, the commission believed that the development of individual intelligence would lead to social change. But this meant that students had to understand the changes underway, and they had to learn to act in the common interest. To accomplish these ends, the commission recommended that students use the information from several social sciences, such as geography, economics, sociology, and history, to learn about the ways people coped with different environments, the ways groups of people came into conflict with other groups, and the ways people could solve the tensions of industrial society (Commission on the Social Studies 44–54).

Other volumes produced by the commission offered three methods to teach the students about the nature of society. First, George Counts recommended that teachers infuse school subjects with a social perspective. Second, Harold Rugg recommended organizing texts around problems of contemporary society. The method that the members found most acceptable was the third: Leon Marshall and Rachel Marshall Goetz's process of living approach.

In *The Social Foundations of Education,* Counts criticized what he called a new group of educators who sought to free students from biases inherited from previous generations. Such a value-free orientation was impossible and undesirable, Counts claimed. Instead, he urged teachers to deliberately choose an orientation that would offer the most satisfying solution to social problems. This represented the first method to teach the students about the nature of society. Although Counts believed teachers had to develop among the students the habits, attitudes, and dispositions suited to the present living conditions, he did not claim the teacher was to impose a body of doctrine as fixed and final beliefs. Instead, he described the imposition essential to education as a type that encouraged the students to question all things while keeping in mind certain great ideals (Counts, *Social Foundations* 532–537).

Since Counts argued that his study of the social foundations showed that, in the economy, interdependence replaced individualism, he urged that the curriculum be organized so that children learned to work together instead of being rewarded for surpassing each other. Further, he thought the various school subjects should be taught from their social perspectives. This meant that art would seek to enrich the common life, and science would explore the ways that people sought to control nature. In order for the social sciences to illustrate the transition of society from individualism to some form of collectivism, Counts urged the social science teachers to illuminate the lives of most of the people in society, to demonstrate the development of the peaceful arts and culture, and to show the expansion of democracy and industrial civilization. In line with his desire for students to learn to think critically, Counts wanted social studies teachers to show students such contradictions as the simultaneous expansion of wealth and of poverty, to offer the basis for critical appraisals of society, and to introduce for consideration a wide range of proposals that might cure the difficulties (Counts, *Social Foundations* 538–553).

In his text, Counts urged that the curriculum in the social studies be organized in ways that led children from studies of their families, to considerations of their neighborhoods, of their states, of the nation, and of the world. Counts wanted students to learn about the customs, institutions, and conflicts in these widening spheres. He thought that if children moved from things near to them to things far away from them, they would come to appreciate the relationships in social life (Counts, *Social Foundations* 554).

Thus, although critics complained that Counts discouraged intellectual freedom in the classroom, this was not true. At best, he was guilty of poor word choice. Since he defined education as the process of inducting children into a social group because all education indoctrinated children into holding one set of beliefs or another, he asked for teachers to indoctrinate the children into beliefs that they should use the findings of science to recognize how society was changing and how they could advance the ideals of society. Ironically, Counts used the idea of indoctrination to encourage teachers to avoid being instruments of propaganda for vested interests.

Another member of the subcommittee that drafted *A Charter for the Social Sciences,* Harold Rugg, had written a textbook series that unified the different social sciences around presentations of urgent social problems. As described in Chapter Two, during the 1920s, Rugg advocated this orientation as the best means to prepare children to be contributing adults in society. This represented the second approach that the members of the commission considered. Rugg's texts were interesting to the students. They fit most classroom models because Rugg developed the texts in cooperation with teachers who tried them and reported how they succeeded and how they failed. The members of the commission, however, did not approve of depending on this approach.

The organizing document for the commission, *A Charter for the Social Sciences,* pointed out many problems with efforts to organize the social studies around presentations of current issues. For example, Beard claimed that there was no evidence that present-day problems would be important in the future. As a result, any list of possible problems could easily omit issues that would be most pressing. In addition, since many scholars found the social problems too complex to solve, school children could not reasonably master them. Further, when teachers considered controversial issues, citizens raised protests urging the boards of education to fire the teachers. Despite these difficulties, Beard acknowledged that the social studies had to introduce the students to the democratic process of government. This meant that the teachers had to make realistic studies of the ways that different institutions confronted problems in society (Beard 43–48).

The most acceptable way to teach the unified social studies came in one of the last volumes issued by the commission. Leon Marshall and his daughter, Rachael Marshall Goetz, offered a method of using realistic studies of the ways that different institutions confronted social problems. Since Marshall and Goetz waited until most of the critics had made their objections to the commission's conclusions and recommendations, they could shape a statement of curriculum principles that avoided most of the dangers educators saw in teaching children to participate in social engineering.

Entitling their book *Curriculum-Making in the Social Studies,* Marshall and Goetz argued that the social studies should follow what they called the "social processes approach." This method built on the view that all societies shared certain recognizable processes of living. Although each society manifested these processes in somewhat different ways, Marshall and Goetz asserted that certain constants appeared in every culture. Seeking a manageable number of processes that would fit most textbooks then available, Marshall and Goetz drew up a list of six fundamental processes. These processes included adjusting to the external world, continuing biologically, guiding human motivation, developing social organization, directing cultural change, and molding personality. Marshall and Goetz believed that when teachers organized their instruction around these processes of living, they could encourage students to consider ways to improve society without resorting to indoctrination or propaganda. They claimed that teachers could discuss controversial issues of the day in objective, scholarly ways because the questions appeared in comparisons of different groups. In this way, the schools enhanced social engineering while using a method that encouraged free thought and open discussion (Marshall and Goetz 12–21).

For example, Marshall and Goetz dealt with the question of economic planning while considering the process of adjustment with the external world. They avoided imposing any view on the students by noting that every society developed ways to determine what commodities the citizens would produce. The Incas relied on the rulers to determine how much grain or festival equipment people needed. In Soviet Russia, experts make estimates through statistical calculations. Americans make similar decisions in what is called a private economy when they rely on consumer spending to encourage manufacturers to produce certain goods. In evaluating the different methods, Marshall and Goetz observed that the Soviet system improved the conditions of many people at the cost of extreme suffering for some people. On the other hand, they continued, America's private economy produced a high living standard for an increasing number of people at the cost of great waste and inequitable distribution (Marshall and Goetz 69–71).

There is some disagreement as to how popular Marshall and Goetz's approach became. According to the contemporary historian, Novick, the College Entrance Examination Board (CEEB) overlooked the social studies and endorsed historical studies that included social, political, and economic studies (Novick 190–192).

Novick may have misread the report of the CEEB's Commission on History. In 1936, the CEEB made its report on how the history curriculum should be constructed. Rather than overlook the social studies, the CEEB report recommended Marshall and Goetz's book,

Curriculum-Making in the Social Studies, as the plan that history teachers should follow (Commission on History 554).

When the CEEB published its report, the journals of the National Council for the Social Studies carried comments for and against the report. Among the criticisms were the complaints of one member of the CEEB commission, Tyler Kepner, who argued that the commission should not have endorsed a method until there was proof that it would lead to better instruction in history. In addition, the teachers of history at Phillips Exeter Academy submitted a three-page mimeographed memorandum endorsing Kepner's dissent. The teachers complained that following the social studies approach of Marshall and Goetz would cause them to skim the surface of many subjects. Worse, it would turn the instruction of history into courses in sociology. Instead of trying to demonstrate process of social life, the teachers thought the students had to master facts of historical change. They asserted that, in this way, knowledge would precede wisdom (Editor 567; Commission on History 565–566; Teachers 258).

Thus, although Marshall and Goetz offered a method that avoided the controversies over indoctrination, their method was open to criticisms that it was ineffective, encouraged superficial instruction, and violated the methods of scholarship. In this way, the AHA Commission on the Social Studies may have turned into programs that helped the students adapt to their society. If this was the case, it was an ironic twist.

How was the work of the Civilian Conservation Corps different from or similar to the efforts of social studies educators?

In March 1933, Franklin D. Roosevelt took office as president of the United States. Issuing the warning that the American people had nothing to fear except fear itself, he declared confidence that the nation would endure. Almost immediately, he sent to the U.S. Congress a proposal to create a civilian conservation corps to employ thousands of young men in a range of projects such as forestry, flood control, and soil protection. He added that the work the corps accomplished would prevent immediate financial loss and it would provide the means of creating future national wealth. The program was enormously popular. By July 1933, there were 1,300 camps across the United States with over 274,000 enlistees. When it ended in 1941, more than 3 million young men had joined the corps. Among these were over 225,000 African Americans and thousands of Native Americans, Puerto Ricans, Hawaiians, and Alaskans (Hill xiv–xvii).

The men who enrolled were between the ages of seventeen and twenty-three, unmarried, and in good physical condition. They were unemployed and U.S. citizens. In the camps, the average age of the men was twenty years old, but few had stayed in school beyond the eighth grade. Most of the enrollees stated that school was difficult for them, and many of the younger enrollees added that they joined the Civilian Conservation Corps (CCC) to get away from school. Few of the enrollees had received any vocational training or vocational guidance. In general, the enrollees had never held substantial jobs, and the CCC offered an opportunity for vocational rehabilitation (Cruey 46; Oxley 4–6)

Since the U.S. War Department was responsible for the CCC, educational opportunities differed widely among the camps. As a result, after the first year, the director of the CCC asked the U.S. Office of Education to prepare an outline of a system of educational policy and administration for the camps. Approved by the secretary of war, these policies established a director of education for the CCC, mandated educational advisors for each geographic area to coordinate the educational programs in the camps, and recommended hiring 1,000 local edu-cational advisors each of whom worked with three or four camps. Although each camp offered educational opportunities, the enrollees did not have to take part in them. Attendance at any class was voluntary, but company commanders pointed out the advantages of these opportuni-ties and encouraged the men to use them (Harby 15–16).

At first, the camp supervisors did not welcome the educational advisors. The advisors did not have plans of what they should do to initiate educational programs. Since summer recreation had begun, the educational advisors began conducting sports activities, such as soft-ball and volleyball, and board games, such as chess and checkers. In this way, the advisors worked their ways into the camps. When the advisors began recruiting students to take classes, they tried to find out what the enrollees wanted to study. In addition, they made the work easy and attractive. As a result of these efforts, by 1934, an educational program had been estab-lished throughout the CCC camps that strove to encourage the following capacities: enjoy constructive entertainment, work cooperatively, understand economic and social conditions, possess good health, demonstrate vocational abilities, and appreciate nature (Harby 16–22).

Samuel F. Harby served as an educational advisor to the second corps area of the CCC for three years. Acting in this capacity, he conducted a survey of the educational programs in his area and found the situation to be uneven. The most important aspect should have been training for the job. Yet, Harby noted that, until 1937, no one was assigned to teach the men the skills they would need to do their different jobs. As a result, job training was haphazard and spontaneous. After technical services took over the task of job training, Harby claimed such training occurred more regularly. Harby found that the educational advisors offered several courses for the enrollees to take during their leisure time. Of these, the most popular were classes that offered some form of vocational training or entertainment, such as forestry and dramatics. The least popular were those that provided educational value, such as Latin and general science (Harby 143–154).

Part of the problem was that the purpose of the camps was unclear. While some directors saw their camps as labor camps, the educational advisors saw them as training schools. Unfor-tunately, the central administration of the CCC did not settle this question by making the pur-poses clear. At the same time, the educational advisors sometimes overlooked opportunities to introduce instruction to train the men in the skills they needed for their jobs. The biggest prob-lem may have been that the educational opportunities came after the enrollees completed ex-tensive work duties. The official workday was eight hours long. Since this included lunch and travel time, the regulations required that enrollees spend thirty hours per week on the actual project. In addition, after the men returned from the field or the woods, they had to spend considerable time doing chores around the camps, leaving them with little time or energy for study (Harby 184–194).

When Marjorie A. O'Brien surveyed the educational opportunities in the CCC camps, she found that the teachers and the facilities represented problems as well. Technical advisors were supposed to offer job skill training classes after they supervised the work in field. Al-though this teaching came in addition to their eight-hour day, the advisors received no extra compensation for the extra effort teaching required. O'Brien claimed that the other teachers employed by the CCC came from traditional high school settings and did not adjust to the lack of compulsion in the camps by organizing their classes in ways that attracted young people who had rejected high school training. Furthermore, although by 1939 every CCC camp had a library of at least 1,000 volumes, the books had not been selected to suit the ages and abilities of the men. A central office for all the camps purchased some books and magazines, but many were simply part of an odd assortment of donated volumes from citizens or books the Army had rejected. Although the camps provided texts for the classes, these were often outdated (O'Brien 69–73).

Despite the problems confronting the educational advisors, they had the opportunity to encourage the students to think about the ways they would participate in social engineering. The handbook for the educational advisors listed the third aim of education in the CCC in the following ways: "To develop as far as practicable an understanding of the prevailing social and economic conditions, to the end that each man may cooperate intelligently in improving these conditions." Unfortunately, few education advisors pursued this objective. From October 1934 to March 1935, Harby surveyed the subjects studied in 95 camps located in New York, New Jersey, and Delaware. From 570 lists with widely different course names, Harby found 97 subjects that appeared most frequently. Among those courses, the most popular of the voluntary courses were forestry and dramatics with each subject drawing about 23,000 student-hours of involvement. The only course that might meet the objective of encouraging social or economic awareness was a course in economics, but it was among the least popular courses because it drew only 1,200 student hours (Harby 131–143, 202).

From his study of course offerings, Harby concluded that the CCC had not done much in advancing the enrollees' understanding of economic and social conditions. He attributed part of the problem to disagreements among administrative departments and camp officers regarding the causes of economic and social problems, which made discussions about these topics extremely controversial. For example, the Army officers who supervised the camps often held different ideas from those of the teachers. Since the Army recognized the differences of opinions and ideals that existed between military men and civilians, it turned over the administration of the camps to reserve officers rather than regular officers. Further, it gave the teaching assignments to civilians. Unfortunately, this did not solve the problems because, frequently, the corps administration did everything it could to prevent teaching that might criticize the economic or political conditions. In addition, two other factors served to reduce the chances of intelligent discussion of economic and social problems in the camps. The wording of the aim in the handbook cautioned that these topics should be approached "as far as practicable," and the enrollees demonstrated little interest in political topics (Harby 205–206, 216).

In an effort to overcome the economic devastation of the depression, the CCC tried to teach the enrollees the skills and attitudes they needed to become productive workers. The CCC did not teach the enrollees to be critical thinkers as Beard and Counts wanted. For example, under the category of understand economic and social problems, the objectives of camp instruction included the ability to bear responsibility as members of the camps, the power to work in the fields and the woods, and the capacity to recognize the employment opportunities in local industries. If the CCC camps encouraged critical thinking and civic awareness, it took place through such activities as camp newspapers, debating societies, and daily papers (Harby 206; Oxley 4).

In conclusion, the CCC camps sought to teach young men to meet the social needs of the nation. The CCC camps taught the young men to dress neatly, to work steadily, and to take satisfaction in their labors. The administrators thought people with these qualities would increase the productivity of the nation's industries. At the same time, the young men faced the chances of having happier, more comfortable futures. As essential as these abilities may be, they represent the more superficial of the abilities that people need to participate in a democracy.

How was the education of Native Americans different from or similar to other educational reforms that took place during the Great Depression?

The educational reforms for Native Americans began during the prosperous 1920s. In 1926, then U.S. Secretary of the Interior, Hubert Work, commissioned the Brookings Institution to conduct a comprehensive study of the conditions among Native Americans and to make recommendations for the improvement of federal administration. Directed by Lewis Meriam and released in 1928, the Brookings study became known as the Meriam Report. It described the conditions of grinding poverty in which most Native Americans lived. While some groups had government-sponsored small homes, most of these buildings lacked adequate ventilation and had no sanitary facilities. In addition to being uncomfortable, the homes were conducive to the spread of disease. Food was scarce. Milk was unavailable for infants, and as a result, infant mortality was high (Brookings Institution 3–4).

According to the Meriam Report, the problem was that the government failed to help Native Americans adjust to new economic conditions. From 1887 to 1934, the basis of governmental policy toward Native Americans was the General Allotment Act. On the view that ownership of land would encourage Native Americans to develop middle-class values, the U.S. Congress allowed each Native American person to hold title to a piece of the tribe's reservation. Unfortunately, as the Native Americans acquired the patents to the lands, they sold the properties to white men for insignificant remuneration or used the money they did receive to spend time in idleness. These injustices occurred, the report concluded, because the Native Americans lacked an understanding of money and the economic system and because the U.S. government failed to allocate enough money to allow the Indian Service to employ personnel to help the Native Americans adjust to the social and economic life they entered (Brookings Institution 6–9).

Since the authors of the Meriam report concluded that the cause of the poverty among Native Americans was the absence of adequate educational resources, the first recommendation of the report was for people to recognize the primary task of the Indian Service as one of education. In general, the authors of the Meriam report considered the aim of such education to be to encourage the majority of Indians to merge into the general population. Their report urged discarding the former, prescribed curriculum that followed an established course of study and required the children to pass academic tests sent from Washington. In the place of such a rigid method of teaching, the Meriam report recommended that teachers be freed from textbooks. The teachers were to gather the material from the life of the children and to fit the lessons to the needs and interests of the children (Brookings Institution 2, 32–33).

The Meriam report criticized boarding schools for being overcrowded, for providing inadequate food to Native American students, and for enlisting the students in industrial labors that exposed young people to excessive dangers. The report noted, however, that in many places such boarding schools were the only way that promising Native Americans could prepare for schools outside reservations were they could learn professional, scientific, or technical skills. For example, the report urged closing all normal schools on reservations because they

offered poor educations and sending promising young Native Americans who wanted to become teachers from boarding schools to recognized teacher training institutions such as might
be found in state universities (Brookings Institution 33–36).

The Meriam report praised programs that sent Native American youths to public schools
near their homes on the grounds that many Native Americans liked this form of racial integration and that it offered the best chances for children to make the transition to life in the wider
society. But, the report recommended that the Indian Service provide special assistance to the
families and to the children so that they could succeed in those public schools (Brookings
Institution 36–37).

The Meriam report caused widespread and immediate changes. For example, the U.S.
Congress began to slow down parceling land to individual Native Americans and simulta-
neously raised the allotment for education, which went from $3 million in 1929 to more than
$12 million in 1932. Most important, the report prepared the way for the 1934 U.S. Indian
Reorganization Act that reduced the drive for assimilation and provided Native Americans on
reservations the ability to reject many federal decisions they disliked (Miller xii–xiv).

One question in allowing Native Americans self-government was in deciding who Native Americans were. When the U.S. Bureau of Indian Affairs accepted the view that a Native
American was anyone with some Indian ancestry who was a member of a tribe, officials found
that Native Americans lived in most states and assimilated in varying degrees into the surrounding society. Of the many tribes, though, the Navajo were the largest, homogeneous group
of Native Americans in the United States. According to the 1930 census, over 45,000 Navajo
people lived on a reservation of almost 24,000 square miles in Arizona, New Mexico, and
Utah. As a result of the size of the group and their relative isolation, the U.S. President's Advisory Committee on Education claimed in 1939 that the Navajo had the strongest chance for
survival apart from white Americans (Blauch 2–7, 10).

Despite the size of the Navajo nation, they did not constitute a unified group in the 1930s
and they had no tradition of an organization of the tribe as a tribe. Navajo people gave primary
allegiance to hundreds of extended families and neighborhoods scattered over the reservation.
In 1923, though, they formed a tribal council whose functions seemed to increase after 1933
when the U.S. Indian Service encouraged more local control among Native American groups
(Collier 164–165).

According to Kenneth R. Philp, John Collier, who was the U.S. Commissioner of Indian
Affairs from 1933 to 1945, sought to change the direction of the U.S. Bureau of Indian Affairs
from one that encouraged assimilation to one that supported cultural pluralism. In part, Collier
did this for personal reasons. In 1920, as a young man, he lived in the artists' colony in Taos,
New Mexico, with such luminaries as Mabel Dodge and D. H. Lawrence. Like the other members of the colony, Collier spent a great deal of time learning about and discussing the culture
of the Pueblo Indians. Philp contended that Collier came to the conclusion that the Native
American cultures offered important examples of communities of people who lived for shared
purposes. As a result, Collier decided that he should work to save those cultures because they
offered an antidote to the intense individualism he feared in the industrial society (Philp
xiv, 24).

Although Collier held romantic notions of the Native American cultures, he did not trust
their ability to preserve themselves. For example, Philp argued that Collier sought to impose
on the different tribes his own ideas of Native American heritage and how it should be served.
As a result, he alienated many Native Americans who did not want to be members of a separate

class of people with their own institutions. Philp pointed out that, in the early twentieth century, many middle-class settlement workers expressed similar contradictions as they endeavored to help European immigrants in cities, and Collier had spent his formative years in such projects where he came to believe that experts could engineer the society in the direction of greater spiritual benefits for all (Philp 10, 20, 24–25, 211–213).

In 1933, there were about 13,000 Navajo children of school age, but only about 5,000 went to any type of school. Collier proposed enhancing the education of the Navajo by constructing eighty buildings to serve as day schools and community centers throughout the reservation. In addition, he wanted to limit instruction of academic subjects to no more than one and a half hours each day and to open the schools to young children, adolescents, and adults. Instead of the traditional curriculum, the schools offered a series of educational efforts coordinated with other government programs designed to combat soil erosion, prevent disease, and improve homes (Parman 193–195).

As the department built a few of the school house–community centers, called "hogan schools," controversies developed among the directors of the U.S. Bureau of Indian Affairs. One group of directors advocated keeping the schools as places for the education of the young. An opposing group of officials urged that the schools be under Navajo direction and that the schools should not advance conventional subject matter such as the learning of English and academics. In an effort to end the controversy in 1934, the Indian Service hired fifty young Navajos as community workers. The service trained them in such things as land use, health, and community relations, and sent them out to head the hogan schools (Parman 195–197).

Few of the Navajo trainees became teachers in hogan schools. Almost immediately, critics complained that semieducated adolescents could not teach schools. As a result, in 1935, the Indian Service relented and hired only qualified teachers. These teachers were white and had little desire to use the schools to provide sewing machines, showers, laundry services, or mechanics' tools to local Navajo community members. Nonetheless, the teachers maintained the drive for progressive education implicit in the hogan school concept by tying lessons for the children to daily life in the reservation (Parman 195–197).

By 1935, on the Navajo reservation, forty-seven day schools offered four grades of instruction, but enrollment was low. This happened for two reasons: One was that when Navajo parents disliked any governmental action, they withheld their children from the school as a form of protest. The second reason was that transportation posed serious problems. For example, the unpaved roads on the Navajo reservation became impassable during bad weather. Another difficulty was that the children had to walk several miles to a place where a bus could stop and pick up several of them at one time because the Navajo families lived far apart in scattered small groups. At the least, in favorable conditions, travel to and from schools consumed most of the students' day (Parman 201–203).

Since the schools were isolated and conditions were primitive, few teachers persevered for longer than one year. Most of the teachers were women who had recently graduated from teacher training programs but who could not find jobs near their homes. They moved on to other teaching posts or married as soon as they could. The few teachers who stayed for longer periods felt affection for the Navajo and wanted to help them. Some of these women teachers gained fame for delivering babies, treating illnesses, and helping to settle personal disputes among the Navajo (Parman 203–204).

In 1936, Willard Beatty became the chief of the Branch of Education in the U.S. Bureau of Indian Affairs. According to Donald L. Parman, since Beatty was president of the Progressive Education Association, he encouraged teachers to use Dewey's approaches to education. For Parman, this approach included employing games in which Navajo children identified objects in Navajo and English; using lessons in cooking to teach health, language, and geography; and constructing various audiovisual materials, such as charts, pictures, and dioramas, to convey ideas of how to solve common problems, such as sanitation, on the reservation. In some schools, such as the Fort Wingate School, instruction aimed at teaching the Navajo children to improve their traditional arts and crafts of jewelry and rug making. Most important, in 1940, Oliver La Farge and John P. Harrington developed a simplified system of written Navajo to teach children to read their own language. The hope was that this would shorten the time the students needed to learn English (Parman 204, 208–211).

To some extent, these so-called progressive practices went too far because they tended to prepare the Navajo children for life on the reservation in conditions of poverty and did not allow them to develop the skills they could use to move into the outside society. At least, this was the verdict of an inquiry sponsored in 1939 by the Phelps-Stokes Fund.

Thomas Jesse Jones headed the committee sponsored by the Phelps-Stokes Fund that investigated what the members called *The Navajo Indian Problem.* According to their report, the problem was that the Navajo had too many sheep. The land on the reservation would support about 550,000 sheep. But, in 1938, the Navajo, who saw sheep as symbols of wealth and prestige, had more than double that number. The result was overgrazing and soil erosion that threatened the livelihood of everyone on the reservation. The committee asserted that the cause of the difficulty was a conflict between traditional Navajo customs and modern scientific methods of soil conservation (Phelps-Stokes Fund 1–3).

The Phelps-Stokes report claimed success for the federally sponsored program to reduce the number of sheep and horses that the Navajo held. Officials in Washington, DC, had required that the Navajo be paid for such reductions and that local administrators solicit Navajo participation rather than require it. But the report noted that, sometimes, local agents forced the Navajo to remove stock. The result was that by 1938, the Navajo resisted the program and refused to participate. Although the number of sheep had been drastically reduced, the Navajo maintained about 350,000 more sheep than the land could support (Phelps-Stokes Fund 8–9).

As in the problems in stock reduction, the Phelps-Stokes report noted that there were discrepancies between the excellent plans for education on the reservation and the resulting and flawed practices carried out in specific areas. The authors praised the development of vocational programs of home economics and agricultural instruction that were related to improving conditions on the reservation (Phelps-Stokes Fund 21–24).

The authors of the Phelps-Stokes report agreed with the spread of day schools around the reservation. The report claimed that such schools staffed by one teacher allowed parents to care for their children, encouraged children to pass on to parents lessons from school about such things as sanitation, and prevented the development of an educated class of Native American youth separated from their parents (Phelps-Stokes Fund 41–42).

Despite this praise, the Phelps-Stokes report noted three serious problems. The first was the lack of adequate teachers. The report suggested that teachers should be trained in pedagogy, genuinely like the Navajo, speak the language, and be able to endure the loneliness of the reservation. These conditions implied hiring Navajos as teachers. As a result, the report urged authorities not to be dissuaded by the critics who prevented the earlier attempts to hire Native Americans to teach in the hogan schools (Phelps-Stokes Fund 45–46).

The second criticism was that there had been wide swings of policy that left the day schools without any courses of study. In 1915, the Indian Service had introduced the *Uniform Course of Study.* Revised in 1922, this curriculum offered the same academic course work for all Native Americans in all parts of the country regardless of their backgrounds or rate of progress. Further, the lessons appeared to be irrelevant to their home lives. In 1930, the Indian Service discarded this curriculum and urged teachers to discontinue drill and repetition as a method of instruction. Unfortunately, the reservation teachers seemed unable or unwilling to create syllabi or organize studies for their students or their parents. As a result, the Phelps-Stokes report noted that no one could determine if the children were progressing or achieving at reasonable rates (Phelps-Stokes Fund 42–43, 52–53).

Finally, the Phelps-Stokes report complained that the education in the reservation schools was oriented exclusively to everyday life on the reservation. Although most Navajo children stayed on the reservation as adults, this form of training was unfair, the report argued, because it denied those Navajos who wished to leave the reservation the opportunity to prepare for such a life. To bring about a compromise, the report recommended that teachers infuse lessons in the academic subjects with what it called the social essentials. For example, the report suggested that teachers use such subjects as arithmetic to teach about health, agriculture, and the home. In this way, the report added, schools could combine the traditional Navajo sense of community with the technical advances found in the wider society. In another place, the report recommended that teachers give elementary science a more central place in the curriculum. The authors claimed that this subject could dispel some of the Navajo people's dependence on superstition to bring about prosperity, and lessons in general science could serve as the basis for more extensive technical instruction in agriculture or home economics (Phelps-Stokes Fund 48–49, 70–71).

When the Phelps-Stokes report recommended teaching Native Americans about modern science, the authors had in mind a notion of education that would eventually weaken the Navajo culture though it may have increased the alternatives available to individual Navajo children. This was contrary to Collier's original aim as U.S. Commissioner of Indian Affairs. He wanted to preserve Native American culture, and the programs he sponsored concentrated on information and skills needed by the children to become Navajos.

Thus, at different times, officials offered different types of education to Native Americans. To some extent, these types derived from models applied in the mainstream society, but at each point, the reforms of Native American education sought to enable the children to adapt to society. At one time, they sought to help the children enter mainstream society. At another time, the teachers were to help the children adapt to their native culture. Personal liberation seemed to be less important than some form of social adjustment.

How was education for Hispanic Americans in New Mexico during the New Deal different from or similar to other educational reforms?

According Suzanne Forrest, when John Collier tried to enhance the social and educational conditions of Native Americans, he shared his interests with other members of Roosevelt's administration. These individuals turned the New Deal toward problems in rural Hispanic villages in New Mexico (Forrest 76–78). Whether Collier deserves such praise or not, the federal government took an approach to helping the people in rural New Mexico that was similar to the ways the U.S. Bureau of Indian Affairs helped the Navajo. In both cases, education in traditional cultural vocations played important roles.

Many people in New Mexico thought that the Great Depression would have little effect on the Hispanic villages. For example, in 1929, the governor of New Mexico, Richard C. Dillon, claimed that his state had no unemployment problem because the people lived in rural, self-sufficient villages, but this apparent independence was deceiving. For years, Latino and Latina residents of the villages had traveled outside New Mexico to work as migrants and had sent the money they earned back to the villages. When the depression struck, such opportunities disappeared, and, by 1932, the villagers faced possible starvation (Forrest 79, 80–81).

From 1933 to 1935, a variety of federal projects subsidized by the Federal Emergency Relief Administration, the Civil Works Administration, and the Works Progress Administrations began in New Mexico's villages. Since these programs required decentralized projects that were local in character, officials used the money to preserve village life and agriculture. Thus, every agency, from those concerned with public health to those dedicated to road construction, had educational goals and used former or unemployed teachers to achieve these goals. Most important, the projects sought to reinforce the traditional Hispanic culture of the village (Forrest 90–91, 103–104).

An example of the aim to use federal funds to reinforce Hispanic culture is the work of Brice Sewell. After studying sculpture at Washington University in St. Louis, Sewell moved to New Mexico in 1930. In 1932, the New Mexico State Department of Education hired Sewell as state supervisor of trade and industrial education. Believing that young people in New Mexico disliked academics and that they discounted its value in preparing them for any future livelihood, Sewell urged local educators to determine what work was available in the communities and to design vocational courses that prepared youth for those opportunities. Several elementary and high school teachers took Sewell's suggestions to heart and introduced native handicrafts into their vocational programs. These schools offered instruction in weaving spinning, canning, and various types of wool work (Getz 109–110).

In November 1933, using federal funds, Sewell established what he called "community vocational schools" in each county. These paid young people between the ages of sixteen and twenty-four to take classes in spinning, weaving, iron working, and leather tooling. In writing an account of the effort, Lynne Marie Getz contended that Sewell's reasoning was as follows: There was small chance that villages would industrialize. Therefore, the best chance for the Latino and Latina residents to learn and practice a trade existed in areas of traditional village crafts (Forrest 107–108; Getz 109).

Some of Sewell's endeavors enjoyed limited success. For example, in Chupadero, in Santa Fe County, after the Hispanic residents learned tanning, woodworking, and saddle making, they sold $28,000 worth of goods in the Santa Fe market in 1935. Unfortunately, since such success depended on the tourist trade, it was seasonal and unreliable (Getz 109, 111).

In 1940, the New Deal moved away from encouraging local cultural heritages and began incorporating patriotism in its programs. When the war began, the New Deal ended, but new industries related to the war effort opened in New Mexico. Although the influx of high-paying professional and industrial jobs should have been an opportunity for Hispanics, they were ill prepared to take advantage of the newly created jobs. Their schools had trained them for village crafts and for work in construction or service-level positions (Getz 116–117).

Ironically, as the community vocational schools enjoyed popularity, local Hispanic newspapers warned against the narrowness of the training. For example, Lynne Marie Getz found that newspapers such as *La Bandera* and *La Revista Popular* urged rural schoolteachers to adopt classes that would prepare children to go on to college because the villages needed such professionals as doctors, dentists, and pharmacists. Despite these pleas, the village school movement did not include efforts to create an intellectual elite among the rural Hispanic people (Getz 117).

How did contradictory efforts to meet social needs share philosophical assumptions?

As the Great Depression revealed serious social problems, educators tried to reinforce students' faith in democracy and to help them meet the pressing social needs of the time. The three types reforms described in this chapter seemed to fall prey to the tendency to help children adjust to society. Although the Commission on the Social Studies encouraged the intellectual development of the students, critics accused the commission members of substituting indoctrination for education. The other two types of education discussed in this chapter may be more appropriately called life adjustment training. The content of the programs differed because each program represented an effort to train people to adjust to a particular style of life. For example, the Civilian Conservation Corps taught young men who left school early to work hard, dress appropriately, and keep clean. The men had to learn these attitudes or skills to succeed in a modern industrial society and to improve their society. On the other hand, the Navajo education and the vocational schools in rural New Mexico taught children to live within the traditional cultures from which they came.

Despite these differences, each of the four reform programs shared the view that students should learn things that related to their lives. The problem was that, in each case, the teachers were to do so by encouraging the students to accept a particular version of the culture.

Summary

During the Great Depression, most educators argued that schools had to reinforce people's faith in democracy and teach them how to meet society's needs. This chapter describes four different reforms to meet the social needs. Although these methods contradicted each other, they shared the view that students could cope with the distressing social conditions if school studies were tailored to the experiences of the students. One plan was proposed by the American Historical Association to unify the social studies and teach children to change the society. Critics complained that this commission's report directed teachers to impart one acceptable view of society to the students. The second approach was proposed by the federal government to remedy the effects of the depression. This was the Civilian Conservation Corps (CCC), which gave unemployed young people the opportunity to earn money and to obtain an education that would help them when the economic conditions improved and jobs became more plentiful. The third and fourth efforts came from federal agencies that encouraged teachers to revitalize the arts and crafts unique to Native Americans and Hispanic Americans. Since the CCC and the cultural reinforcement for minorities were vocational in nature, they sought to meet social needs by helping students advance their social group. While the federal programs encouraged a sort of multiculturalism that contemporary readers may recognize as liberating, these vocational programs contradicted wider democratic aims.

CHAPTER SIX

COOPERATIVE ACTIVITIES VERSUS ACADEMIC STUDIES TO MEET STUDENTS' NEEDS, 1930–1940

From 1930 to 1940, two groups of educational leaders argued about the appropriate way to design the curriculum. Although the groups were not equal in size, they took opposite positions on questions about the content of the curriculum. The larger group of educators, the progressives, claimed that schools should be tailored to the interests of students. The membership in this group was disparate because various progressive educators took different positions on the extent to which students should be allowed to select the lessons and the attention teachers should give to traditional subject matters. The smaller of the two groups, the essentialists, formed in reaction to the successes of the progressives. Since relatively few educators joined the essentialists, the members seemed to agree about the appropriate nature of the curriculum. They took a more traditional position arguing that schools should promote understanding of the liberal arts.

Although the progressives and the essentialists disagreed about the appropriate content of the curriculum, two groups of educators shared the belief that schools should enable students to advance the society. The progressives did not think that any particular subject matter was better than any other for students to learn. To the progressives, it was more important that the students engage in activities that they found interesting and that the school curriculum should be fashioned in ways that enabled the students to understand the meaning of democracy. On the other hand, the essentialists argued that the students had to acquire the discipline and the values that were engendered in the academic studies if they were to contribute to social improvement. The essentialists complained that the progressives held an excessive faith in the benefits of student choice. As a result, they created programs that lacked the essential studies.

The debate between these groups began with the creation of the Eight-Year Study in which the progressive educators sought to prove the worth of their principles. According to Lawrence Cremin, the Eight-Year Study brought success to the Progressive Education Association (PEA) while it hastened the end of the organization. The PEA had begun in 1919 as an association of parents and teachers. Through the 1920s, the PEA remained a small organization devoted to elementary education. In the 1930s, the PEA sought to diffuse the ideas of progressive education by forming commissions, conducting studies, and publishing reports. When the PEA initiated its Eight-Year Study, philanthropic organizations contributed such enormous amounts of money for the study that the association became dependent on such funding. Attracted by the money and the prestige of this organization, membership grew. In 1932, the association had 5,400 members. But by 1938, the membership reached a peak of 10,440. Unfortunately, these new members were the type of educators who initially attacked the association. They broadened the positions of the PEA and changed the association to a more conventional group. Further, when the foundations stopped donating money, the PEA had no financial program of its own (Cremin 258–259).

Other historians complain that the Eight-Year Study caused many problems that continue to beset high schools. For example, C. A. Bowers argued that the directing committee of the Eight-Year Study wanted the participating schools to plan curriculums that grew out of the students' needs and interests. He adds that these progressive educators felt contempt for any systematic acquisition of knowledge. Instead of having students learn mathematics, for example, Bowers claimed that the directing committee wanted the students to learn from life situations that involved mathematics (Bowers, *Depression* 217–219).

Bowers may have overstated the case, though. For example, the directing committee claimed that the members did not want to undervalue traditional subject matters. They did feel, however, that, in most high schools, teachers presented the traditional curriculum in predictable, formal ways and that students could not see the value in the materials. As a result, they wanted the curriculum to begin with the problems the students faced and to use those to enable the students to see the relationships among the subject matters. In this way, they thought they could break down the artificial barriers that had grown up among teachers and among subject areas (Aiken 20–21).

In a manner similar to that of Bowers, Diane Ravitch contends that the Eight-Year Study exacerbated the differences among students. She claims that colleges held to their academic requirements and would not admit high school students who lacked traditional college preparatory courses. Battered by criticisms to include programs of general education to meet the needs of youth, high school teachers offered them to non-college-bound students. As a result, only college-bound youth received academic preparation (Ravitch, *Left Back* 281–283).

Unfortunately, Ravitch does not offer evidence that colleges held to their academic requirements. Furthermore, during the Eight-Year Study, the progressives did not notice resistance from colleges over entrance requirements. They claimed to have succeeded in changing college requirements because some colleges had modified their entrance requirements and many colleges allowed for the flexible interpretation of their traditional rubrics for admission. Thus, the progressives argued that all colleges were moving toward policies of accepting students from any coherent program of four years in a school with good repute provided the students had satisfactory ratings on a scholastic aptitude test and a recommendation from the principal (Chamberlin xxii).

The story of the Eight-Year Study is important for this chapter because it demonstrates that the division among different groups of educators was not as great as some historians suggest. One such difference was among the members of the PEA itself. According to Henry Perkinson, the progressive educators followed John Dewey's ideas selectively throughout the 1920s. To make this point, Perkinson quotes Harold Rugg who complained that, in the 1920s, the progressives tried the radical methods of instruction that Dewey seemed to prefer, but they did not seek to engender the political or social changes he had described. Perkinson adds that in the 1930s, the progressives changed. An example of the change is the challenge that George Counts made to the members of the 1932 convention of the Progressive Education Association to be progressive. In his speech, Counts urged the teachers to ignore their fears of indoctrinating the students and impose those values that would lead to human progress. Perkinson points out that most educators and members of the PEA did not want to engage in what he called "social reconstruction." They preferred to remain child-centered and try to meet students' needs (Perkinson 200–201, 205–207).

Contrary to Perkinson's claims, though, the Eight-Year Study shows that the child-centered educators sought social reform although they differed in their choice of methods from that of such social reconstructionists as Counts. That is, the child-centered educators thought they could improve the society by determining and satisfying the students' needs so they became healthy adults. On the other hand, the social studies educators described in Chapter Five, of whom Counts was an active member, believed it was more important to help students analyze social problems or recognize the ways different societies fulfilled various social processes.

During the depression, how did child-centered educators seek social change?

In 1930, impressed with the changes they had encouraged in elementary education, two hundred members of the PEA met in Washington, DC, to consider ways to improve secondary education. Although elementary schools had come to allow for more student freedom and activity, secondary schools remained more traditional and subject matter oriented. The PEA members thought this happened because high schools had to prepare students for college entrance. As result, they complained that high schools lacked a clear and specific purpose. Although the students learned skills necessary for college, such as the ability to complete assignments, they failed to gain an insight into the political, social, and intellectual problems of the time. They did not learn to work in groups on something that interested them, and they failed to appreciate the importance of art or to develop a taste for good literature (Aiken 1–12).

In 1932, the directing committee of the commission secured the cooperation of over 200 colleges to modify their entrance requirements. Few colleges required students to take the College Entrance Examination Board tests. Every college that did, except Harvard, Haverford, Princeton, and Yale, agreed to waive those tests. The only requirements that the other colleges maintained were that the principal of the high school recommend the students and that the students show some measure of the quality of their work, such as adequate scores on scholastic achievement or aptitude tests (Aiken 12–13).

The directing committee chose thirty high schools to participate in the plan. In fact, there were more than thirty schools because among specific public and private junior and senior high schools were entire school districts, such as Denver, Colorado; Des Moines, Iowa; and Tulsa, Oklahoma. Other schools extended from the radically organized University School of Ohio State University to the more conservative Milton Academy in Massachusetts (Aiken 14–15).

The participating high schools were to be free to arrange the curriculums as the faculty thought best because the study sought to determine the effect of freedom on the students rather than the benefits of any particular curriculum plan. Instead of dictating a course of study, the directing committee held annual meetings in which representatives of the experimental schools discussed the progress the faculty members had in reshaping the curriculums. During these meetings, the schools agreed to follow two principles of curriculum reconstruction. The first was that life and studies in the schools should conform to what was known about the way students learn and grow. The second was that the schools would reinforce the importance of high schools by demonstrating the meaning of democracy to the students (Aiken 15–19).

The social characteristics and environment of the participating schools fell along a wide continuum. At one extreme was a private academy of about 300 students. This school was located in the country with a well-stocked library. Thirty highly trained faculty members enjoyed adequate salaries, and they met five classes per day, each containing about 25 students. On the other extreme was a high school in a city with about 2,500 students and 80 faculty members. The building was old, and the surroundings were dingy. The library was unattractive and the classrooms, forbidding. Although teachers' salaries were better than average, they met six classes per day, each containing about 40 students (Aiken 28–29).

In the fall of 1933, the schools began their work, constructing and teaching a new curriculum. In some schools, the changes were modest. In the more conservative schools, separate classes continued to teach traditional subject matters, such as science, foreign languages, mathematics, and English. The difference was that these lessons followed what the members of the directing committee believed were the concerns of youth. Thus, a mathematics course might apply the principles of logic to the analysis of local housing problems or a Spanish class might consider the effect of geography on the life of South American peoples. In other, more radical schools, the traditional subjects disappeared altogether. Instead of studying biology or chemistry, the students investigated questions such as the effect of vitamins on growth. Thus, rather than learn information, the students developed habits of critical thinking and the ability to understand cause-and-effect relationships (Aiken 46–50).

At first, the directing committee expected the participating schools to report the characteristics of the students applying to the colleges and to amass information appraising the effectiveness of their programs. Since the schools were creating new curriculums, they could not use available achievement tests or traditional measures. Thus, the directing committee organized technical staffs to assist in constructing evaluation devices. They worked to ensure that the measures related to the particular school's purpose, that the evaluation included all the school's objectives, and that the teachers helped construct the measurement devices (Smith and Tyler xviii, 4).

The procedures that the evaluation staff followed with each school were based on the view that education represented a change in the students' behavior and that the changes the school wanted were its objectives. The steps began with school faculty members formulating the objectives for the curriculum. The faculty had to draw these objectives from evidence gathered about the demands of society, the characteristics of the students, and the contributions from the subject matter. From these potential objectives, the faculty retained those that matched the philosophy of the school and that students could accomplish according to information from the psychology of learning (Smith and Tyler 9–10, 15–16).

Second, the evaluation staff helped the faculty classify the different objectives according to whether they accomplished such things as enhanced methods of thinking, aided the cultivation of appreciation, or led to better personal social adjustment. The evaluation staff assumed that teachers could achieve specific objectives within each type with similar models of instruction and use-related forms of assessment. Different types of objectives required distinct methods of instruction and evaluation. For example, under the effective thinking classification, the evaluation staff listed the objective, "to interpret data." This objective required the abilities to perceive relationships among data and to recognize the limits of certain information. These abilities varied with different types of data, such as information expressed in prose, on maps, or on graphs. While essay answers offered a means of measuring these abilities, measurements of appreciation of literature differed. These measures might include records of the extent to which students read without interruption or a list of books students read during their free time (Smith and Tyler 15–18, 39–45, 250–251).

Since the ways of measuring the objectives varied, the evaluation staff asked the school faculty to decide on the situations in which the measurements should be done and what method of sampling students' behavior they would use. From these plans, the evaluation staff and the faculty members tried to refine the measures and interpret the results. In some cases, the last step led to changes in the instruction. For example, in one school, students showed that they had considerable information about social problems, but they retained the social attitudes they had held earlier. The teachers decided this showed that the lessons covered too much material for the students to absorb and apply. Consequently, the teachers reduced the scope of the lessons, concentrated the material more tightly, and found the students' social attitudes changed (Smith and Tyler 20–27).

The ideas of the evaluation staff of the Eight-Year Study provided a common basis for developing the wide range of curriculums found in the different schools. Although some of the participating schools followed more traditional, teacher-dominated lessons and other schools depended on more student involvement, the evaluation staff tied all of the schools to objective measurements. In each school, the faculty defined the educational objectives as changes in behavior. From this common assumption, the evaluation staff contended that such things as students' interests could be determined through pencil-and-paper tests and that tests, such as measures of the students' ability to interpret data, reflected their thinking skills. According to Edward Krug, these ideas became part of the Tyler rationale, and they remained major preoccupations in curriculum thinking throughout the twentieth century. Tyler published his formula describing how evaluation could direct the development of the curriculum as a syllabus for a class he taught at the University of Chicago. In 1949, the University of Chicago Press published his syllabus as a book entitled *Basic Principles of Curriculum and Instruction*. Throughout the twentieth century, this book maintained sales of several thousand copies per year and was translated into more than a dozen languages (Krug, Vol. II 264; Willis et al. 393–394).

In 1936, the first class of students left the participating schools and entered the selected colleges. To determine the effect of the high school experience on the students, the college study staff matched each graduate of a participating school with another student in the same college who graduated from a school that had not participated in the study. These students, who served as controls, had met the college entrance requirements and they resembled the graduates of the participating schools with whom they were matched in age, gender, race, scholastic aptitude, home and community background, interests, and probable future (Aiken 108–109).

In 1942, the college follow-up staff published the results of the comparisons of the students' success in college. Contrary to the predictions of skeptics, the graduates from the participating schools earned grades that were slightly but consistently higher than did their matches from traditional high school programs. It appeared that the graduates from the progressive schools adapted themselves quickly to college work regardless of the type of preparation they had in high school. The students from each group had enrolled in roughly similar areas of specialization, but the experimental group earned higher grades in all subject fields. Thus, the experimental students did not succeed because they took easier courses than the graduates of the traditional schools. Furthermore, the students from the participating schools received more honors, such as appearing on the dean's list or honor roll more often than did the control students (Chamberlin et al. 24–32, 40).

Despite the fact that the students from the participating schools had different high school training, the college follow-up staff found that these experimental students took on the bad habits of their peers. They spent less time on some courses, concentrated on other courses, and in these ways, found time to enjoy the many social activities that college offered. Nonetheless, when the college follow-up staff surveyed the intellectual habits of the students, the staff found that the students from the participating schools had somewhat better work habits. In addition, at least in their first years of college, the students from the participating schools showed more intellectual curiosity and a sounder sense of the meaning of education (Chamberlin et al. 43, 63).

The overall conclusion was that the study had proved its point, but the college follow-up staff found a sharp distinction when they compared the graduates of the most experimental and of the least experimental of the participating schools. The graduates of the most experimental schools had the highest academic achievements, enjoyed the most honors, and exhibited the best intellectual attitudes. These graduates were more likely to think logically, to be aware of the world around themselves, and to be more aware of democratic values. These students were healthy, well-oriented individuals whose outlook was broadened by their high school experiences. Thus, the college follow-up staff concluded that the colleges should seek students from these most experimental schools because these students were superior to all other students (Chamberlin et al. 173–174).

How did educators use their freedom to shape the curriculum during the Eight-Year Study?

Although historians focus most of their attention on the evaluation of the Eight-Year Study, the curriculum proposals had the greatest effect. These came from a commission that included some of the leading intellectuals of the day. Among its members, the commission included Margaret Mead, the anthropologist; Helen Lynd, the sociologist; and Willard W. Beatty, from the Bureau of Indian Affairs.

Since the concept of democracy permeated the Eight-Year Study, the Commission on the Relation of School and College hesitated to impose any curriculum pattern on the participating schools. Instead, the directors did two things. First, they asked teachers and administrators of the participating schools to agree on two important principles. One of these principles was that teachers should change the way they presented the subject matter found in the conventional curriculums of high schools. The directors wanted subjects such as English and art to illuminate the problems common to young people growing up in the United States. Claiming they valued the cultural heritage schools usually transmitted, participating educators wanted to shape the humanities in ways that met the vital needs of youth. They did not want the studies to focus on the memorization of grammatical rules or acquiring specific artistic techniques. The other principle was that the teachers agreed to improve the unity and continuity in their curriculums. This meant that they would try to break down divisions that separated different subjects and teachers. In doing this, they hoped that students would see how different subjects related to each other, and teachers could glimpse the unity of knowledge (Aiken 20–21).

The second thing the directing committee did to shape the curriculums was that they formed in 1932, two years after the initial planning for the Eight-Year Study began, the Commission on Secondary School Curriculum to offer information to the participating schools. The PEA hoped that educators in the participating schools could use the findings in their efforts to change their curriculums. As a result, the directors charged the curriculum commission to accomplish three goals: to determine the educational needs of adolescents, to suggest ways to study curriculums, and to experiment in curriculum revision. Since the commission considered the period of adolescence as beginning with those ages appropriate for junior high schools and extending to those ages appropriate for junior college, its members hoped to assist schools and colleges develop closer relations (Thayer, Zachry, and Kotinsky v–vi).

Headed by V. T. Thayer, the Commission on Secondary School Curriculum created two types of investigations that the commission hoped would reinforce each other. One of these was the Study of Adolescents. The other type of investigation involved the work of a series of committees in the various subject areas, such as science, art, English, and the social studies. These committees described ways to select and order appropriate educational experiences for young students (Thayer, Zachry, and Kotinsky vi–viii).

As the teachers and administrators in the participating schools tried to reconstruct their curriculums, they sought assistance from the Commission on Secondary School Curriculum. To help the school people, members of the Study of Adolescents disseminated their research findings to the school people through conferences and summer workshops held by the PEA. Based on the collection of more than 600 case studies of young people, the Study of Adolescents tried to discern the interests and character traits in the different students. By working with the staff in the participating schools, members of the study could offer suggestions as to the ways reforms could meet the developing needs of youth (Thayer, Zachry, and Kotinsky vi–vii).

In a similar fashion, the committees working on the various subject areas cooperated with faculty and administrators in the participating schools. The members of these committees received preliminary findings from the Study on Adolescents, and they based their suggestions on these psychological discoveries. At the same time, the committees shared their curriculum ideas with teachers in the participating schools to see if they succeeded in practical situations. Consequently, when the committees released their reports in 1940 at the end of the Eight-Year Study, their ideas fit what scientists had found to be the needs of adolescents and they satisfied the practical and social demands of schools (Thayer, Zachry, and Kotinsky vii–ix).

The Commission on Secondary School Curriculum justified its work by contending that new social and economic conditions prepared the way for new conceptions of childhood. As a result of the depression, young adults could not participate in the world of work but had to remain dependent on their families when they wished to have the independence that jobs and salaries once offered. Although adolescents had to postpone accepting responsibilities and developing independent judgment, the commission report argued that this problem offered opportunities as well as problems. The schools could help adolescents to develop deeper awareness of their places in their personal, social, and economic relationships (Thayer, Zachry, and Kotinsky 4–6).

The report added that the economic problems of the depression forced more adolescents to stay in schools and the schools to reconsider their aims. Before the depression, high schools could offer vocational training to the students who lacked academic interests. But, as a result of the depression, there were no jobs for which students could prepare. Nonetheless, the report noted that schools could use this problem as an opportunity to help adolescents become aware of their unique status and its distinctive qualities and problems (Thayer, Zachry, and Kotinsky 7–9).

Finally, the report noted that the decreasing economic opportunity the depression caused made people more aware of the need to preserve the democratic faith. In other parts of the world, people reacted to their unstable conditions by turning to fascism. These totalitarian regimes extended the undemocratic aspects of the capitalistic society and offered people the illusion of security. People may not have been aware of the social problems during the prosperous times because there were reasonable opportunities for them to succeed in economic competition and prove themselves. The report urged educators to find ways for young adults to accept new roles, to form new relationships, and to take on new missions. If educators refused this opportunity, the report noted, adolescents would remain pressed in a culture that, on the one hand, forced them to find their statuses and identities in the economic sphere but, on the other hand, denied them opportunities to work (Thayer, Zachry, and Kotinsky 9–11).

For the members of the Commission on the Secondary School Curriculum, the way to improve education was to create educational experiences that were relevant to the needs of young people growing up in the society. The problem the commission faced in doing this was that schools followed one or another of two different notions of needs. One view of needs was popular among elementary schools. It derived from the project method and from William Heard Kilpatrick who held that children's needs were their interests, desires, or wishes. The other view derived from the work of Franklin Bobbitt whose definition of scientific curriculum making was the view that schools should teach students to learn the skills they lack for their vocations, their citizenship duties, and their responsibilities of family life (Thayer, Zachry, and Kotinsky 25–26).

The commission's report argued that each of these views lacked important aspects. For example, the report contended that needs could not reside within young people because children developed their desires and wishes from interactions they had with their environments. To support this claim, the report noted that people thought children were naturally curious, but anthropologists demonstrated that in some cultures, children learned to be inquisitive and, in other cultures, they learned not to inquire about things. On the other hand, the report claimed that adolescents would not learn the skills they needed to survive in society. Instead, the report cited evidence showing that young people reformed their inner desires to fit social requirements rather than simply adopting socially acceptable behaviors (Thayer, Zachry, and Kotinsky 26–29).

Recognizing that each conception of needs became fuller when integrated with aspects of the other, the commission's members agreed that the word *need* had to include both the students' internal desires and the skills they lacked for adult successes. This was possible if educators considered students' wishes and their lacks on a continuum. The wishes came from their previous experiences. Each experience changed those wishes. Thus, the things students lacked could be thought of as those experiences that would change their desires in ways that enabled them to control the environment. To provide students with experiences that included their present wishes and created the conditions for new ones to emerge, teachers had to know the adolescents fully and to recognize the environment in which they lived. But, it required continual study because a continually repeating pattern would emerge. The environment would change the students who would reform the surroundings and that would reshape the students (Thayer, Zachry, and Kotinsky 37–38).

Relying on its Study of Adolescents, the commission claimed that case studies of young adults from widely varying backgrounds suggested that students' needs grouped themselves into four areas: immediate social relationships, wider social relationships, economic relations, and personal living. The needs appeared in the form of relationships because the students formed their personalities in relationships with other people. Most important, due to the depression, problems in economic relationships reduced the possibilities of success in other sets of relationships. The commission hoped that schools could enable the students to understand and reconstruct the various relationships in line with improved human values (Thayer, Zachry, and Kotinsky 42–46).

In arguing that school could do for adolescents what the world of work had done in the past, the commission avoided appeals to restructure the economic system. When they explained the preferred direction for student growth, they called on educators to shape schools and students in the direction of society's traditional allegiances. This meant that the schools should seek to affirm democratic views whose popularity stemmed from promises to enhance individuals by protecting their rights and extending their opportunities (Thayer, Zachry, and Kotinsky 63–64).

The commission had trouble defining democracy or determining how to achieve it because the concept changed as the people changed their desires. Nonetheless, the report listed the important democratic values with regard for the worth of the person, reciprocal individual and group responsibility for promoting common concerns, and the free play of intelligence in solving problems. Contending that these values should direct the social arrangement, the report noted that, as social conditions changed, the arrangement of institutions should change to preserve democratic values. Most important, people had to overcome primitive aspects of their personalities and assume a high degree of socialization, taking on qualities of tolerance, cooperativeness, and skill in reflective thinking (Thayer, Zachry, and Kotinsky 66–80).

According to Edward Krug, innovations such as the core curriculum were the most important curriculum development that emerged from the work of the Eight-Year Study and its Commission on the Secondary School Curriculum. The directors of the study suggested this was the case, as well. For example, in describing the ways that teachers shaped the curriculums to meet the needs of youth, they claimed that many schools sought to integrate traditional subjects into broad fields. Thus, students would seek to investigate problems of artificial lighting or water purification, and their research crossed the subjects of physics, chemistry, and biology. Other schools sought to arrange the studies around the four common needs of youth. To meet the need called "personal living," the Denver schools offered lessons, such as "analyzing our use of time." These were organized into units related to a central idea, such as "understanding ourselves." Other lessons formed units to satisfy the needs in areas such as immediate social relationships and social–civic relationships. In these ways, they shaped a core curriculum (Krug, Vol. II 261–263; Aiken 46–59).

Although commentators claimed that ideas of a core curriculum permeated the Eight-Year Study, the reports of the various committees on the subject areas did not represent such a common focus. Most of those reports appeared in 1940, after the Eight-Year Study concluded. Written for educators who did not participate in the project, these descriptions of curriculum offered suggestions teachers could apply in a wide range of circumstances. Instead of advancing any particular curriculum model, the reports encouraged teachers to think about how they might meet the needs of the individual students in ways that promoted the realization of the student's personal potential and encouraged his or her effective participation in a democratic society. Two examples illustrate this approach. They come from the fields of English and art.

How could the subjects of English and art be restructured to meet students' needs?

The Committee on the Function of English in General Education argued that students related themselves to the world through the skillful use of language, and this ability was tied to their interests and concerns. Through language, students expressed themselves, communicated with others, and gained control over experiences. According to this report, teachers could trust facility in language to advance democratic values in three ways. First, students depended on communication for optimum development of their personalities. Second, through language, they could maintain and define their relationships with other people. Further, the free play of intelligence demanded the effective use of words. The report noted that motion pictures and radios overwhelmed people with information they could not confirm. But, people might grasp a sense of what was right by analyzing language. Thus, the committee contended, the future of democracy depended on this skill (Committee on the Function of English vi–vii).

The members of the Committee on the Function of English claimed that correct language use was important to every subject, and this made it basic to general education. The report did not advocate, however, any particular administrative or curricular procedure, such as a core curriculum, that might correlate the subjects to language as a center. Instead, the members wanted teachers to realize that good education was inductive. Teaching began with children's experiences and moved into academics to clarify, order, and amplify the experiences (Committee on the Function of English 51).

To illustrate the members' approach to language study, the committee report considered the teaching of grammar. Although grammatical instruction taught the students to clarify and order experiences, the report claimed that it had been crowded out of the curriculum by instruction in such activities as telephoning, table conversation, and appreciation of movie pictures. According to the report, grammar was unpopular because it followed a deductive technique. Typically, teachers began with rules and went to specific applications. According to the committee, the process should be reversed. Students should begin with the language they used and develop understandings of correct language from it. For example, a teacher might say, "We will give simple rules to you now." From this sentence, students might determine the elements of a sentence, and they might experiment to find the ways they can change the meaning of a sentence by altering the order of the elements. The committee members gave the name "functional grammar" to this inductive approach (Committee on the Function of English 52, 65, 69, 82, 84).

The Committee on the Function of English expressed views that other important organizations had expressed. For example, in 1935, the National Council of Teachers of English (NCTE) published a report of the principles and examples of a curriculum that would extend from kindergarten to graduate school. The NCTE committee recommended that the curriculum be formed into experience strands. A course would contain six or eight strands. For example, the seven experience strands for oral communication were as follows: conversing, telephoning, discussing and planning, telling stories, dramatizing, reporting, and speaking to large groups. Each strand presented opportunities to practice similar types of skills relating to language use and they ran from the elementary school level to the secondary school. Each strand was divided into units that centered on specific types of experiences. These units took from five to fifteen days and were so organized that the students succeeded at increasingly difficult tasks (Hatfield vi–vii).

While the example of the oral communication strand makes the NCTE curriculum appear anti-intellectual, it may illustrate a desire to accommodate to existing conditions. As noted, the report of the Committee on the Function of English acknowledged that, years earlier, activities such as using the telephone had replaced traditional literature studies in English classes throughout the United States.

Most important, the NCTE committee claimed that by building the curriculum on experience it was encouraging the self-direction essential for a democracy. Unlike authoritarian systems that followed fixed rules of conduct, the NCTE report claimed its system enabled students to learn to confront a multitude of situations, to modify the conditions, to adapt to the unchangeable and thereby to learn to live in an evolving world (Hatfield 3–4).

Although the PEA's Committee on the Function of English built on many of the ideas of the NCTE report, it was far less popular. By 1940, the NCTE report sold over 25,000 copies. This far exceeded the sales for the report of the PEA's Committee on the Function of English. Since the two reports shared similar rationales, the popularity of the NCTE report must have rested on the wealth of illustrative material it offered. Of the over 300 pages the NCTE's report, fewer than 25 described the NCTE's theoretical orientation. The rest of the pages were lists of strands, the different objectives within the strands, the enabling objectives to reach the primary objectives, and the materials needed to reach the objectives. Examples of literature, reading, creative expression, communication, corrective teaching, and electives in the NCTE report extended in an increasingly complex fashion from kindergarten to grade twelve. On the other hand, the report of the Committee on the Function of English devoted almost every one of its 224 pages to a description of its theoretical orientation. It did not offer patterns that teachers or textbook authors could follow (Krug, Vol. II 267–271).

The report of the PEA's Committee on the Function of Art in General Education claimed that, in the nineteenth century, art education took place in two forms. One form took place in academies of art where gifted students imitated authoritarian masters to learn valuable techniques. The other form took place in girls' finishing schools and some secondary schools where students learned to embroider, to paint on velvet, and to use watercolors. In the late nineteenth century, impressionistic art focused artists' attention on light and color. Similarly, art teachers simplified design principles and taught the students to use such tools as value scales and color charts. In the twentieth century, expressionism changed art into an individual form. At the same time, progressive art teachers left the children unhampered by rules or doctrines. While the members of the Committee on the Function of Art appreciated the freedom the expressionist view offered, they claimed that art education should enable children to develop their abilities and to apply them to improve life for everyone. Further, the report claimed that all students should have the opportunity to enrich their lives through art. Finally, the report added that art should enter into every aspect of human life (Committee on the Function of Art 1–18).

Claiming that people's emotional lives were related to their experiences in art, the report of the Committee on the Function of Art examined aspects of adolescent growth the teacher could take into account to help students develop fruitfully. For example, to the young person yearning for independence and adult status, planning and executing arrangements for festivals or exhibitions may offer opportunities to grow in responsibility (Committee on the Function of Art 19, 43).

When the committee came to describe teaching methods, the members took care to note that everything had to be related to the needs and interests of the students. For example, the committee noted that among adolescents murals sparked some interest because the students could work together. Without exception, drawings of the human figure were the most popular exercise. Although the committee noted that few schools allowed students to draw from living models because of the association with sex, the members thought drawing from live nudes could help students develop a wholesome interest in the human form by treating it as an aesthetic form. One way the practice could begin was for students to pose for each other in bathing suits. The report added that if parents and administrators would agree to allow students to draw from human nudes, the practice could help the adolescents understand sex differences and their meanings (Committee on the Function of Art 61–64).

The report offered many less controversial applications of the principle of relating instruction to the needs of the students while fostering skill and ability. For example, in painting, a teacher could approach a student struggling with a drawing and say, "Let me show you how to handle the brush." But the report warned that any such demonstration of technique had to be done in an effort to further the student's expression. In this way, the artist's technique transmitted his or her emotion to the work without overemphasizing either skill or feeling (Committee on the Function of Art 68–70).

The Committee on the Function of Art called for a conception of evaluation that included the teacher's approach to the class, the value of the experience the teacher sought to promote, and the effects of the experience on the life of the student. The report offered several questions in each category such as the following: "Do I recognize and respect creativity in other people?" "Does the experience arouse the student's interest?" "Is there evidence in the student's personal appearance of sensitivity to art values?" Warning that letter grades fostered false standards, the report urged teachers to send home written descriptions of progress. Should the teacher not have time to write individual notes, a secretary could type and mimeograph the comments covering common situations as a substitute (Committee on the Function of Art 96–120).

How could public schools apply the ideas of the Eight-Year Study?

The PEA's committees on the function of English and art recommended principles that could be adopted in almost any school setting. In each case, the committees decided that teachers should use a sort of inductive method that allowed the students to begin with activities that captured the students' interests and served their needs. The committees recommended that the teachers work with guidance counselors to determine what activities would fit the students' interests and needs. The committee reports noted that these principles could apply to schools that constructed a core curriculum where all activities related to a set of central concepts, such as cultural epochs, or they could apply to more traditional settings where subject matters followed more traditional disciplinary lines.

Although schoolteachers could follow the recommendations of the PEA's committees on the subject matters without reconsidering classroom arrangements, the results of the Eight-

Year Study argued for extensive restructuring of the curriculum. According to the evaluation report, the students who enjoyed the most success in college came from the participating schools that followed the most experimental programs. Further, the evaluation committee noted that the more radical the high school program, the more success the graduates enjoyed in college (Chamberlin et al. 208–209).

As the Eight-Year Study gathered momentum, state governmental agencies sought ways to encourage local schools to reduce concern for college preparation, blend subject areas, and offer the students opportunities to practice democratic ways of life. In this way, state departments of education encouraged the more radical reform recommended by the evaluation committee of the Eight-Year Study. For example, in 1935, the Regents of the University of the State of New York organized an inquiry into the character and cost of education in the state. At that time, under the constitution the Regents of the University held responsibility for leadership but not management of the state's entire system of education. As part of their report, the members of the Special Committee on the Inquiry outlined recommendations for a new educational program. Included among the suggestions was the recommendation that a greater part of the secondary program should be taken up by general education. Complaining that college preparatory classes took up an excessive amount of the high school programs, the special committee preferred students to take such courses as general science, human relations, and community life whose broad fields covered many academic topics. At the same time, the special committee recommended that the schools establish opportunities for students to develop an understanding of the democratic system and that the schools offer guidance services (Regents' Inquiry ix, 46–47).

Other states imitated the Eight-Year Study more closely. For example, in 1937, the Michigan Department of Public Instruction initiated a study that imitated the Eight-Year Study. After applying for and receiving grants from the General Education Board, the McGregor Fund, and the Children's Fund of Michigan, the directing committee of the Michigan study set out to reorganize the instructional program in fifty-four secondary schools over a twelve-year period. As in the case of the Eight-Year Study, the cooperating high schools came from a range of school districts. Some schools were located in rural areas. Other schools were in urban areas. Some schools were large while others were small. The state department considered some of the cooperating schools to be good and others to be bad. But the teachers and the administrators in all the schools volunteered to be in the study. To allow the teachers the freedom to experiment, the directing committee secured agreements from thirty colleges in the state to accept graduates of the cooperating schools without reference to the pattern of courses the students pursued provided the principals recommend them (Parker, Menge, and Rice 3–4, 16, 30–31).

The purpose of the Michigan study was to help schools develop democratic ways of improving the schools. The study asked the teachers and administrators to attend summer workshops to enhance their understanding of democratic methods of curriculum reform. Teachers and administrators in the schools determined the previous experiences of the pupils, they sampled the needs of the community, and they created appropriate methods of evaluation. During these activities, most of the schools found ways to adapt the subject matter to fit the experiences of the students. Teachers gave students opportunities to do things rather than asking them to learn about processes. In chemistry classes, girls removed stains. Students learned to drive automobiles safely, and teachers asked students to solve problems involving space and number in the classrooms. To show the relationships among the subjects, teachers in about half of the schools formed some sort of core course often called a unified studies course or an arts of living course (Parker, Menge, and Rice 15, 34–36, 49–50, 95–97).

Although the Michigan study ran through the war, the participants thought that the national crisis lent more significance to their effort to adapt traditional courses to fit the needs of youth and society. The directing committee contended that the study had helped schools prepare students for a democratic society by having them work cooperatively with other students and teachers. It offered increased opportunities to improve the health and fitness of the youth. Cooperative problem solving prepared everyone for new ways of thinking about global politics. Furthermore, the practical thrust of the courses encouraged school people to contribute to the material needs of the war (Parker, Menge, and Rice 105–107).

In 1945, after the war ended, evaluators assessed the success of the Michigan study. They noted that the impact of the war resulted in students organizing, administering, and conducting student councils, war councils, and youth centers. Despite the student participation in extracurricular affairs, the evaluators found that many classrooms had not changed. Some schools had developed unified studies, core courses, and offered increased opportunities for student and teacher planning. Usually, these schools combined the required social studies and English classes and assigned the same teacher to conduct both of them with the same students for two consecutive periods. Such arrangements did not disrupt other, more traditional arrangements, yet many schools did not go this far. They retained the idea that the classrooms were places where students followed previously arranged materials to acquire skills the teachers selected. The evaluators blamed the problems on the unwillingness of teachers to attend summer conferences in which staff from the Department of Instruction helped teachers to see the school program as a whole, to form school philosophies, and to eliminate inconsistencies in practices. Nonetheless, according to the evaluators, members of the Department of Instruction had shown remarkable willingness to participate in school planning rather than restrict their duties to those of inspection and enforcement (Rice and Faunce 27–31).

What problems did critics find in the work of the Eight-Year Study?

While the Eight-Year Study was proceeding, some supporters of progressive education raised concerns. For example, in 1938, Boyd Bode published his book, *Progressive Education at the Crossroads*. Noting that progressive education was the strongest and most evangelistic movement in American education, he warned progressives that they could become dogmatic by relying on concern for the needs, interests, and freedom of the child. While Bode praised progressive educators for their concern with the individual and their faith in intelligence to solve social problems, he disliked the hope that teachers could find the purposes of education in studies of children's development. In what could have been a criticism of the Eight-Year Study, Bode noted that an understanding of the needs of youth could not emerge from studies of young people any more than the proper design of a building could emerge from a study of the materials that would go into its construction. To Bode, the concept of needs was so fluid that authoritarian educators could use it to serve their own ends. Instead of starting with ideas of what students need, Bode thought that teachers should think about educating the students so the children could find out for themselves what were their own needs. Otherwise, teachers might flit from satisfying one presumed need to satisfying another while forgetting their obligation to enhance the understanding of intellectual affairs and ignoring the need for continuity in the classroom (Bode, *Progressive Education* 9, 40–41, 67–70).

Bode disagreed with the desire to teach essential subjects in any strict, demanding form. For example, the traditional approach to science was for teachers to transmit the organized results of science as something to be learned. This approach did not allow the students to use the concepts in science in ways that organized their own experiences. Worse, science teachers mistook the ability of students to remember facts as the cultivation of methods of thinking (Bode, *Progressive Education* 95–96).

The answer for Bode was for teachers to recognize how subjects in the natural sciences could illustrate the patterns of free intelligence. For example, students could learn how a new fact is considered true when it fits into a body of previous knowledge. In turn, the students would revise and use this knowledge to control their own experiences. Bode approved of progressive teachers allowing students to investigate things that interested them. He asked that the teachers make sure the students had some ways to measure their success (Bode, *Progressive Education* 96–97).

When the Eight-Year Study ended in the 1940–1941 school year, other critics began to debate the benefits and difficulties of the study. Writing in *Harpers* in 1941, Dorothy Dunbar Bromley expressed envy at the fine education offered to the students in the participating schools, whom she called the guinea pigs. She claimed the reports of the participating schools curriculums made her feel that they learned much more than she had when she attended school. When Bromley looked at the students' performance in college, she was not as impressed that they had done well academically as she was appreciative that several of the students had organized lecture series or dramatic presentations in their colleges. Finally, she noted that the guinea pigs were surer of their direction in life. Although Bromley noted that the results were not explosive, she predicted that they would work extensive changes over time. She found that admission requirements had already become more flexible at such colleges as New York University, Cornell, Dartmouth, Sarah Lawrence, Bard, and Bennington. While some colleges, such as Harvard, Princeton, and Smith, retained particular requirements for certain subjects or specific exams, she noted that more and more colleges looked toward simply a scholastic aptitude test offered by the College Board. Most important, she found some schools, such as in Denver, Colorado, to be so pleased with the study that they maintained their revised curriculum regardless of college entrance requirements (Bromley 409, 411, 413–414, and 416).

Bromley's article inspired critic G. Wakeham to point out that conservative educators expected students from the participating schools to equal the academic performance of the students from traditional schools. He noted that in the past several years, as the number of applicants to colleges increased, colleges had lowered their academic expectations. As a result, many colleges used ninth grade texts for their classes. More important, he wondered if students from the participating schools had been better prepared for life (Wakeham 12).

To some extent at least, the debate over the validity of the experiment continued. In 1950, on reading a comment that then contemporary practices in secondary education derived from the Eight-Year Study, Helmer G. Johnson complained the study was a hoax and a fraud. Johnson argued that the study was biased because the students from the participating schools had more ability than the students from the traditional schools. According to Johnson, this happened because the students from the participating schools shared many characteristics, but the evaluation staff chose students from traditional schools on the basis of their scores on aptitude tests. Thus, a student from Lincoln School, where most students had high IQs, was matched with a student from an average high school because the two students had the same aptitude test score (Johnson, "Some Comments" 337–338).

In reaction, Paul E. Diederich, who had been member of the evaluation staff, pointed out that Johnson ignored the fact that the evaluation staff did not match by aptitude test scores alone. They matched students on the basis of aptitude scores and, among other factors, the type of school from which they came. As result, he considered Johnson's criticisms to be based on misinformation and misreading (Diederich 41–42).

Johnson replied that his complaints were reasonable because matching schools by size and type did not match the schools by composition of the student body. The students in the matched schools would have to have similar academic abilities for the comparison to be reasonable. He added that the irrelevance of the Eight-Year Study was illustrated by the fact that, in the 1950s, most of the participating schools were undoing their experimental programs (Johnson, "Here" 41–42).

While Johnson's criticisms of the statistical controls of the Eight-Year Study were controversial, he may have been correct in asserting that most of the experimental schools returned to conservative practices within eight years after the Eight-Year Study. In 1950, the former director of the Progressive Education Association called a meeting of the heads of the schools that had participated in the study. Two of the participating schools had closed. Many of the schools had new headmasters or principals. A few school leaders reported that the faculty members in their schools retained liberal educational viewpoints and sought to overcome subject matter distinctions. Yet, no school engaged in developing programs of general education as the Eight-Year Study emphasized. Only one school continued work on the core curriculum that had been popular among the participating schools. Most important, no school reported that the needs of the adolescents dominated curriculum planning as they had during the study. Most of the officials admitted that their schools had retreated to traditional college preparatory programs (Redefer 33–34).

Redefer found that the principals believed that the advent of the war diverted attention away from the important findings of the study. This seemed true as Redefer recounted poor sales of books about the study. The basic volume sold about 6,400 copies. The others sold about 1,000 copies. Since there were over 325,000 secondary teachers in the United States and more than 500 institutions of teacher training, Redefer worried that the Eight-Year Study did not command sufficient attention in the profession (Redefer 35).

Other studies found that the Eight-Year Study had an extensive impact. For example, in 1950, William Brinkman published a review of the educational literature then available. He concluded his examination by noting that most of the descriptions of principles and practices for secondary schools derived from the Eight-Year Study. The authors accepted the conclusions of the study as if they were some set of gospel truths instead of subjecting the ideas of core courses, student planning, and curriculum revision to critical examination. Although Brinkman appeared to approve of the direction the Eight-Year study had taken, he did not think educators should apply the findings in a mechanical fashion. Echoing the intent of the study, Brinkman declared that educators should adopt the stance of experimentalism that characterized the study rather than try to apply strictly any of the findings (Brinkman 90–91).

If the Eight-Year Study continued to influence educators after World War II, part of the reason must have been that people who had participated in the study became college professors who encouraged teachers and school administrators to think in ways similar to those reform efforts. For example, in 1947, Harold Alberty, professor of education at the Ohio State University, published his book, *Reorganizing the High School Curriculum,* to demonstrate to teachers and administrators how they could clarify the purposes of the high school in American society. Although Alberty included a list implying that high schools followed traditional subject matter divisions and teachers heard endless series of student recitations, he noted a promising trend in each case. According to Alberty, high schools had been selective institutions, but he believed many schools tailored the curriculum to meet the needs of all normal youth. Instead of depending on tests of facts and information, schools offered evaluation procedures that measured thinking, cooperativeness, and creativity (Alberty v–vii, 21–23).

When Alberty considered different curriculum patterns, he noted that the subject-centered approach remained popular. Although Alberty warned that the subject-matter approach could not teach students to be democratic citizens, he thought that this difficulty might be reduced when it was combined with other methods, such as the experience-centered curriculum or the core curriculum models. For example, within the experience-centered curriculum, Alberty noted that teachers could plan such things as field trips, work experience, or projects to supplement the subject-centered organization. Since teachers had to organize knowledge around these experiences, Alberty claimed the core curriculum offered the most guidance. This would consist of a program designed to meet the needs of students, and every student had to take part in this integrated course. In his example, Alberty borrowed the four categories of needs as relationships the Eight-Year Study had defined, and he turned them into problems. Thus, instead of listing the relationships as "immediate social relationships" or "personal living," Alberty recommended that the core curriculum be designed around such categories as "immediate personal-social problems." Within that category, Alberty thought students in grades seven, eight, and nine could participate in activities labeled "orientation to school" or "living in the home." Within a core period of two hours, students would develop the skills they needed to cope with problems in those areas. During such a core period, teachers could meet the students' needs, Alberty added, and this period would replace homeroom and its guidance and counseling activities (Alberty 117–118, 147, 173–178).

During the 1950s, popular writers, such as William Whyte, complained that progressive education encouraged a sort of tyranny of the majority because the teachers sought to teach the children to cooperate and always to work in peer-led groups. When Whyte interviewed administrators and teachers in a new suburban development, he found that teachers conceived of the peer group as the vehicle of discipline. According to Whyte, the teacher strove to influence all the children's attitudes so that they learned correct behavior without being punished individually. Whyte found that the teachers did not select the lessons but asked the students what they would like to know about particular subjects. After recounting the results of his interviews, Whyte made a criticism commonly aimed at progressive education. The problem was that educators and parents agreed that the job of the schools was to help the children learn how to get along with people. It was not to teach subject matter (Whyte 424, 425, 434; Cremin 126).

In fairness, conformity among adolescents is always a problem. Although the reports of the PEA's Commission on Secondary Education School Curriculum sought to emphasize the teaching of minority rights and tolerance, the teachers in the participating schools may have been unable to protect teenage diversity.

As the Eight-Year Study gathered prominence, a group of traditionalists gathered to complain about the direction in which the study was taking American educators. A spokesperson for the traditionalists was William C. Bagley. In 1934, Bagley warned Americans that experiences in the Soviet Union demonstrated the dangers of tailoring instruction to the interests of the students. He wrote that, shortly after the revolution, the Soviet Union replaced teacher-dominated schools with institutions where students pursued projects or activities that captured their interest. The Commissary for Public Instruction reversed this order less than fifteen years later, however, asking teachers to reestablish discipline. Bagley claimed that the reason for this change was that the teacher was the trustee of the spiritual heritage that every generation must receive in order for the society to progress. While Bagley acknowledged that students should pursue their interests to some extent, he thought the teacher had to direct the class, offering direct oral instruction that made the lessons vibrate with life and meaning. As a result, Bagley urged researchers to seek the best way for teachers to impart instruction, but he feared progressive educators would resist these efforts because they refused to value the achievement tests that demonstrated the relative worth of different methods (Bagley, *Emergent Man* 179–181, 186–189).

In making these statements, Bagley appeared to change the recommendations he had made in 1905 when he wrote *The Educative Process*. As Chapter Four describes, Bagley called for a curriculum that would teach the children to become what he called socially efficient adults. At that time, he claimed that schools had to offer more than academic subjects. For example, in 1905, he approved of the introduction of vocational courses because this showed that intellectual or aesthetic values did not dominate over other considerations.

In 1938, Bagley wrote the platform of the Essentialist Committee for the Advancement of American Education. This committee consisted of seven educators who opposed what they called soft pedagogy. Bagley asserted that American high school students lagged so far behind their counterparts in other English-speaking countries on scores of achievement tests as to warrant calling them illiterate. He blamed this poor academic standing on the rapidly expanding high school enrollments and the acceptance of educational theories that encouraged teachers to relax academic standards to allow the ever-increasing numbers of students to pass their courses. According to Bagley, when teachers tried to organize the curriculum around the students' interests and needs, they discredited discipline and the need to acquire what he called the "race-experience" (Bagley, "Essentialist's" 241–245).

According to Bagley, students in the upper grades lacked academic abilities because teachers in the lower levels promoted them on the fear that they would suffer psychological damage if they did not progress with their peers. At the same time, teachers did not think it was important to teach the fundamental academic skills to the students on the grounds that the students would acquire these skills as they engaged in interesting activities. Bagley objected to teachers thinking students could acquire skills in an incidental manner because psychologists showed this belief to be a false hope (Bagley, "Essentialist's" 246–247).

Not only did Bagley accuse teachers of accepting theories that promoted slack standards, but also he thought that they discredited those subjects that required effort and exactness, such as Latin, algebra, and geometry. Although Bagley acknowledged that psychological experiments showed these subjects did not produce what was called mental discipline, he accused educators of overgeneralizing these studies and removing the courses so that not even intelligent students could profit from them. At the same time teachers discredited the exacting sciences, they substituted less demanding courses in the social studies. Although these courses promised to teach citizenship, Bagley argued that they did not encourage students to understand or to apply the principles of history, sociology, or economics (Bagley, "Essentialist's" 247–248).

Since Bagley believed that a democratic state needed citizens who were informed and intelligent, he urged teachers to train their students in the skills needed for literacy in such ways as to form what he called a "community of culture." To Bagley, this meant that the citizens of a civilized society had to share a common core of ideas, meanings, and ideas. Finding this common core in traditional studies, Bagley wanted educators to determine the order and placement of studies so that schools across the country could follow the same curriculum (Bagley, "Essentialist's" 252–253).

Bagley and other members of the essentialist committee served as officers in the National Society for the Study of Education (NSSE) so the society devoted its 1939 yearbook to ways to construct such a sequence of courses. Entitled *Child Development and the Curriculum,* the yearbook was divided into three parts. It presented articles on child development, on materials and activities essential to the curriculum, and on those aspects of child development that would guide curriculum organization. The articles provided significant information indicating when certain subject matters should be presented to children. For example, in an overview of research on the children's development of oral and written language, Leo J. Brueckner showed what might be appropriate to teach children in different grades. He claimed that he had found dependable data to support such lessons as teaching students in third grade to use a capital letter at the beginning of a sentence. He asserted that other studies showed that fourth-grade students could master the use of capital letters for land and water forms and that fifth-grade students could understand how to use question marks at the end of questions (Brueckner 231–235).

One critic, Ernest Melby, found the essays in the NSSE yearbook to be of little use to teachers because they were written in a scholarly fashion, but Melby acknowledged that he disagreed with the fundamental assumption of the yearbook. Unlike the essentialists, he did not think there were bodies of subject matter independent of the students. As a result, he did not think teachers could profit from studies of what age to introduce which topics or skills. Instead, he believed that students should pursue activities that they wanted to pursue, learning from the teacher whatever academic skills they needed (Melby 439–440).

Writing in 1974, G. Max Wingo claimed that most Americans held the essentialist perspective about education. Crediting Michael Demiashkevich with coining the term *essentialist* in 1935, Wingo noted that the idea became popular because various conservative educators, politicians, and journalists adopted the view. At the same time, Wingo explained how Bagley may have maintained a consistent perspective though he appeared to shift from a position favoring vocational education in 1905 to a view supporting liberal arts subjects in 1938. In these apparently distinct propositions, Bagley argued that school subjects should help the students learn things they could use to improve the society. Thus, in 1905, Bagley found vocational courses useful, while in 1938, he claimed that academic courses produced socially useful abilities (Wingo 28, 61).

It should be clear that Bagley did not imitate W. T. Harris who wanted the schools to teach only academic subjects. As Chapter One describes, Harris's view was that the academic subjects were correct at all times because they correlated the students with the society in which they lived. Harris might have agreed with Bagley that such ways of thinking as found in the various subject matters helped to advance society, but he thought students had to master those ways of thinking in order to advance their spiritual development. Such considerations went far beyond Bagley's claims because he shared the progressive notion that curriculum should help students gain the skills and abilities that the society needed.

The essentialists shared the progressive bias in favor of a strong role for research. For example, Brueckner's reports about the best time to introduce certain skills to children illustrate a bias similar to that found in the Tyler rationale. That is, Brueckner defined learning as a change in behavior, and he saw objective tests as the means to determine the effectiveness of various teaching strategies.

In what ways did cooperative activities and academic studies meet the needs of students?

The progressive educators wanted the students to develop a sense of social responsibility and a concern for the common welfare. They thought the schools and the colleges could work together to help the students understand the democratic way of life instead of teaching them to succeed at lessons and gain diplomas. Thus, they sought to encourage the students to regard education as an enduring quest for meaning rather than to view school as a place to accumulate credits. Their hope was to help students in high schools to find meanings in their life experiences, and they expected the students to continue to find meanings in their college work (Aiken 4–5, 22–24).

In these ways, the progressives who worked in the Eight-Year Study imitated the ideas of the Herbartians discussed in Chapter One. They thought the lessons should relate to the students' lives. They tried to set up ways the teachers could determine what the children needed to learn. From those studies of adolescent needs, they thought they could construct a curriculum. Finally, they believed that objective measures of the effectiveness of those lessons would improve the curriculum. In this way, the Study of Adolescents and the Tyler rationale provided a common underpinning to a wide variety of curriculums among the participating schools.

During the depression, other educators took this progressive mind-set and applied it in ways that opposed the direction of the Eight-Year Study. For example, conservative educators, such as Bagley, thought that scholars could determine the intellectual qualities that all students should have if the society was to advance. They added that studies of youth could indicate when teachers should introduce particular lessons and in what ways the teachers should construct those lessons. Thus, while Bagley's call for academic studies sounds similar to the appeal that W. T. Harris made in 1895, the two educators differed considerably. Harris held the idealistic view that academic courses enhanced students' spiritual dimensions. Bagley took the more pragmatic view common to the progressives. He argued that academic courses provided practical benefits because they imparted the information and qualities that all people in a democracy should share.

Ironically, critics in the 1950s complained that progressive education caused excessive peer pressure and led to conformity. Critics could easily complain that the conservatives led to conformity because they wanted all students to pursue academic subjects regardless of the students' interests. Thus, although the progressives and their critics, including the essentialists, disagreed about the content of the curriculum, they agreed the curriculum should be aimed at benefiting the society.

Summary

According to some historians, progressive educators split into two groups during the 1930s: the social reconstructionists and the child-centered theorists. The important point in this chapter is that the story of the Progressive Education Association's (PEA) Eight-Year Study indicates that, if the two groups differed, it was in the methods they preferred not in the aims they pursued. Chapter Five described the social reconstructionists' efforts to meet the students' needs to think critically in hopes that, when the children became adults, they would recognize the need for social change. This chapter shows that the other group, the child-centered educators, did not ignore the question of social change. They believed that when students followed their own interests, the students would not develop prejudices and they would become independent adults capable of participating in social reform. During the 1930s, the Eight-Year Study gave the PEA prestige out of proportion to the size of the organization. Participants in the study developed systems of evaluation and of curriculum planning that enabled educators to design effective programs no matter what content the curriculum contained. A surprising number of educators adopted this model although they supported different types of curriculums. For example, a group of conservative educators, the essentialists, felt that the best way to teach children to be democratic citizens was to have them study the traditional academic courses. Although they disagreed with the progressive practice of tailoring the humanities to fit the individual student, they shared the progressives' assumptions that curriculums should benefit society. As a result, critics could complain that the PEA and the essentialists led to some form of social conformity.

PART IV

CONTRADICTORY REFORMS TO SERVE THE NEEDS OF THE DEMOCRACY, 1940–1964

The two chapters in this section describe the ways that the schools responded to the military threats in the 1940s and 1950s. Chapter Seven, "Balancing Individual and Social Needs after World War II," describes the ways that educators tried to aid the war effort. At first, the educators called for students to train for military service, to prepare for a war-related industry, and to develop patriotic feelings so they would sacrifice their individual interests to help the society in this time of need. During the uneasy peace that followed, educators tried to balance the social needs, individual student needs, and requirements that everyone understand democratic ideals. Although some educators urged separate vocational schools and other educators recommended liberal arts training for everyone, educators such as James Conant claimed the comprehensive high school could blend the contradictory impulses of providing for gifted elite students who could become scientists who could devise technological advances and ordinary citizens who understood the democratic values that had prevailed during the Eight-Year Study. Unfortunately, the model of the comprehensive high school seemed to exacerbate the distinctions among social classes because it sought to prepare children for the work they would do as adults.

Chapter Eight, "Academic Excellence to Meet Society's Needs," explains how scientists tried to create curriculums that would teach the students to think in the manner of scientists. Sharing Conant's fear of an overly independent and technologically competent elite, these scientists sought to help every student understand science. To justify their efforts, they claimed that subject matters could be interesting in themselves. This view of student interest differed from the view held by progressive educators during the Eight-Year Study that students were interested in subject matters that helped them in activities outside school. Nonetheless, the scientists thought they could use it to construct ways to reach students of all ability levels and all ages. Critics complained that the projects threatened to impose social orientations that contradicted traditional values.

CHAPTER SEVEN

BALANCING INDIVIDUAL AND SOCIAL NEEDS AFTER WORLD WAR II, 1940–1964

A contemporary author, Joel Spring, contended that the fears caused by the cold war with the Soviet Union led the federal government to influence public secondary schools to serve national interests. According to Spring, the public school educators acceded to these requests and increased vocational guidance, grouped the students according to ability, and separated students into different programs according to their probable occupational destinies (Spring, *Sorting* 1–2).

Spring correctly pointed to the changes in vocational guidance and ability grouping that took place in secondary schools during World War II and the subsequent cold war. To Spring, these accommodations served the national interest. While there can be no doubt that Spring is at least partially correct, this was an unintended consequence of the best efforts of intelligent people.

After the emergency of the war passed, the educators sought to strike a balance between the needs of society and the needs of the individual. Some public figures called for separate trade schools and high-quality scientific institutions to improve the international standing of the country. Other educators thought that all students should study the academic subjects because this prepared them to participate in a democratic society. The educators who supported the comprehensive high schools complete with vocational guidance and ability grouping tried to balance these forces that would separate students by offering such courses as social studies and by providing opportunities for students to learn to live and work together in a democratic fashion.

How did educators think schools should meet the country's needs during the war?

As noted in Chapter Six, progressive educators sought to meet society's needs by serving the students' needs. They held this view through the trying times of the Great Depression. Immediately after the bombing of Pearl Harbor, however, influential progressive educators joined with more than fifty other educators on a Wartime Commission formed by the U.S. Office of Education to determine how schools could help defeat the enemy. They agreed that until the national emergency passed, schools would have to serve national interests at the expense of the students' individual needs.

Among the educational leaders who served on this commission were representatives from the American Federation of Teachers, the National Educational Association, the American Library Association, the National Catholic Welfare Conference, the Progressive Education Association, various state departments of education, and several colleges and universities. In August 1942, the commission called a conference—the National Institute of Education and the War—attended by 700 educators to determine what schools could do to preserve the nation (National Institute of Education and the War ix–xii).

President Franklin D. Roosevelt sent a letter to the conference in which he asked for three things. First, he wanted teachers to mold men and women who would fight through to victory. Second, he asked that every schoolhouse become a service center for the home front. And finally, he hoped that young people would acquire the wisdom and the patience to bring about a lasting peace (National Institute of Education and the War iii).

Following the requests in Roosevelt's letter, the conference participants suggested ways that the schools could perform the three functions. The National Institute of Education and the War printed these recommendations in the form of a handbook for teachers. First, military leaders presented statements asserting that the schools had to offer more technical training if they were to mold men and women who would fight through to victory. For example, the chairperson of the War Manpower Commission, Paul V. McNutt, noted that soldiers in World War I did not need mathematics to fire a rifle, but that, in the twenty-five years between the wars, technology had advanced to the point that soldiers were trained for specific jobs. The Army and the Navy needed skilled mechanics, engineers, and radio technicians. To meet these requirements, McNutt made some specific suggestions. He thought that high school teachers should direct their students into courses that would prepare them for service as pilots, mechanics, or nurses. He asked that young men in college join the Reserve Officer Training Corps and enroll in courses directly useful to the war effort (National Institute of Education and the War 1–3).

Second, in order to make schools into service centers on the home front, participants at the conference recommended simple things that elementary school children could do to advance the war effort. One example was for the students to engage in a campaign to buy War Stamps. Although the amount of money the students could raise was small, it aided the war effort and the drives taught the children how they could participate in national movements. Another example was to have the children collect scrap metal that could be turned into steel for armaments. A third example was to grow vegetables in victory gardens to produce food needed by the country (National Institute of Education and the War 239–243).

Third, to help the students acquire the wisdom and the patience to bring about a lasting peace, participants at the conference recommended that schools offer students opportunities to determine the causes of the war and to realize that the United States has to play a part in world organizations to prevent future wars. Another suggestion was that children could begin by studying the ways the war affected people in the children's neighborhoods. From this point, the children could realize the interconnections among nations. Above all, the participants recommended that, for the children to learn the meanings of democracy, the teachers should foster attitudes of community service among the students (National Institute of Education and the War 305–312).

Educational organizations offered their own suggestions of ways the schools could aid the war effort. In a manner similar to the National Institute of Education and the War, the recommendations focused on offerings that advanced the war effort rather than serving individual desires. For example, in a statement on teacher education, the American Council on Education (ACE) suggested that school authorities expand the educational programs to meet new demands. In this regard, the ACE recommended that schools add nurseries and kindergartens to care for children of parents working in war industries. For teachers to deepen their loyalty to democratic principles and to strengthen their capacities for democratic behavior, the report urged that teachers make suggestions on how the school could save resources. At the same time, the report warned against false economies, such as hiring unprepared teachers and increasing class size in unreasonable manners. To help the students appreciate the war effort, the report advised that teachers introduce curriculum materials to explain the necessity of such measures as rationing, compulsory savings, and wage controls (Evenden 104–107).

In 1943, the National Education Association published a handbook of practical procedures the schools should follow. As in the cases cited above, this handbook gave suggestions for enlisting the children's aid in the war effort. For elementary schools, the handbook recommended that the children learn to obey expert authority, learn to read, and acquire accuracy in arithmetic because these qualities and skills were essential in emergencies. For the high schools, the NEA noted that the U.S. Office of Education offered $94 million for programs specifically aimed to train workers for war-plant production. This was the third year such federal funds were available to schools. To aid school people participating in these programs, the NEA handbook described the types of training the students could pursue. In describing how general education courses could serve war aims, the handbook noted that choirs and school bands could play for ceremonies when men departed for military training camps. Science classes could provide opportunities to learn things that would aid the military, such as using air currents for gliding, food preservation, and simple mechanics. Geography teachers should show students the locations of those places where the war was being waged (NEA, *Wartime* 4–7, 11–12, 25, 29, 33).

At about the same time, the Educational Policies Commission (EPC) of the National Education Association issued a more theoretical statement, *What the Schools Should Teach in Wartime*. In this case, the recommendations varied by the age of the students. According to the EPC, the younger students should be taught basic instruction in academic skills. They should learn to avoid hatred of the enemy, to maintain good health, and to express the democratic spirit through service work. On the other hand, the schools should prepare the older students according to their abilities to serve the war effort. A few of the students should prepare for the professions, but most of the students should develop their fitness for war-related industries or for fighting in battle (EPC, *What* 3–5).

The EPC recommended that teachers consider every high school student to be a reservist in the armed forces. Thus, when offering occupational guidance, teachers should consult lists that the War Manpower Commission was producing of needed workers to direct the students. The students' vocational choices should serve the national interests, not their personal preferences. The EPC thought courses in general education, such as mathematics and science, had to serve practical ends. A few students who would go to college required theoretical mathematics, but the majority of the students needed only basic arithmetic. As far as foreign languages were concerned, the EPC stated that it was more important for a few people to learn a modern foreign language thoroughly than for thousands of students to be exposed to the rudiments of French, German, or Spanish (EPC, *What* 6–19).

Thus, during World War II, educators and public officials of all types made repeated statements calling for schools to offer more practical courses directly relevant to the war effort. They urged that students be assigned to vocational training in line with national needs, and they called for changes in formerly general education courses to prepare students to face the challenges of war. But, at the same time, these educators and officials wanted teachers to explain to their students the reasons why the country was at war, the necessity for the many personal privations the war caused, and the need to support international organizations to keep the peace when the fighting stopped. In this national emergency, educators seemed to agree that students had to learn to place the needs of the country before their own desires.

When the war ended, how did educators change their ideas about serving the needs of the children?

In 1944, confident of the United States triumph in the war, the EPC issued the document, *Education for All American Youth,* warning that unless the high schools stopped catering to an intellectual minority of students, the federal government would take over the schools. This meant that high schools had to cater to the needs of a wide variety of young people. While such a task might seem daunting, the EPC suggested it was not as complicated as it appeared. All children had what the report called individual or divergent needs that came from differences in occupational desires, intellectual pursuits, and recreational desires. At the same time, the EPC added that students in all communities shared several common or unifying needs. These included education in the responsibilities of citizenship, in family living, in health, and in appreciating the cultural heritage (EPC, *All* 35–37).

In another section of the report, the EPC expanded its definition of the common needs of youths. Calling them the ten imperative needs of youths, the authors of the report listed them as developing salable skills; maintaining good health; understanding the rights and duties of citizenship; recognizing the significance of family life; knowing how to purchase goods intelligently; understanding the methods of science and their influence on human life; developing capacities to appreciate art, music, and literature; using leisure time effectively; respecting other persons; and thinking rationally (EPC, *All* 225–226).

According to the EPC, teachers had to present subject matters in ways appropriate to students' capacities and interests. By taking the view that all teachers had to meet students' imperative needs, the EPC continued the tendency to call for applied versions of traditional subject matters. For example, in subjects such as mathematics, every student acquired a basic mastery. Some students went ahead and studied applied mathematics that would aid in their occupational pursuits. Gifted students had opportunities to study individually with teachers. The same pattern took place in English. The faculty tried to ensure that students had a reasonable mastery of reading and listening by the end of the ninth grade. After that point, the students applied those skills in making reports on various subjects of interest or in dramatics. The EPC claimed that, under such a system, teachers could begin with the students' interests and lead them to learn more about the world (EPC, *All* 140–141).

The EPC offered at least two different ways to reorganize the curriculum to meet the individual and the common or imperative needs of youths. Small or rural schools could retain the classes in certain subjects as the chief unit for organizing instruction, but classes could not be conducted solely to provide abstract information the students had to master. The teacher tried to shape the material to meet students' needs, such as personal and health matters, or to understand far-reaching changes in society (EPC, *All* 52–53).

Larger urban schools could use another method of organizing the curriculum. In this case, the EPC recommended dividing the curriculum into four areas: vocational preparation, individual interests, common learnings, and health and physical education. The first two areas catered to individual interests or needs, and the second two areas referred to the common studies. The traditional subjects fell into a broad continuous course called common learnings. It was in this area that the students learned about their responsibilities as citizens, their roles as producers and consumers in the economy, and the skills for cooperative living. Guidance of individual students was an important part of this broad course or area. Furthermore, science was such an important area in the modern world—and knowledge about science was an imperative need by itself—that urban schools should devote an entire course or area to developing an understanding of the methods, principles, and facts of science (EPC, *All* 232–244).

Under both systems of curriculum organization, the EPC noted that learning about citizenship took place when students engaged in such activities as investigating issues relevant to their community and when the teachers tied the issues to questions of politics and to democratic ideals. While the EPC recommended that rural school students could work directly in external service projects, such as agricultural extension, urban schools were too large to permit sending the pupils to work in different agencies. Thus, urban teachers depended on field trips and reports from experts (EPC, *All* 78–100, 258–259).

In the EPC report, guidance was the keystone of the school plan in rural and urban communities. As a result, it took place in elementary schools and in high schools. The EPC recommended that both rural and urban schools employ specially trained counselors who had been teachers. These specialists assisted regular teachers in providing direction for the students. Together, the specialists and the teachers helped the students to select appropriate courses and to work through many of life's problems (EPC, *All* 40–43, 309–310).

Finally, the EPC recommended that procedures of curriculum planning include community members. In smaller rural areas, community members attended meetings and voiced their opinions about plans drawn up by the board of education, the principal, and the teachers. In urban schools, planning took place through a series of committees headed by experts but including citizens (EPC, *All* 34, 184–188).

In its report, *Education for All American Youth,* the EPC warned against the influence of university faculty members who believed that specialized training in subject matter was adequate to prepare teachers for public schools. While the EPC recommended that teachers have a liberal education and specific preparation in a field of study, the commission members did not think that such training was adequate. In addition to knowing subject matter, teachers had to recognize the purposes of education in a democratic society, to possess an understanding of how schools could impart a sense of civic responsibility to students, and to recognize the importance of offering guidance to students (EPC, *All* 368–370).

Shortly after *Education for All American Youth* appeared, Isaac Leon Kandel claimed the report suggested that teachers should have a liberal education but that it did not expect the students to have one. The EPC had complained that traditional high school programs ignored the nonacademic students and concentrated on providing courses to meet college entrance requirements. Yet, Kandel pointed out that the EPC went too far in the opposite direction. He wrote that the report ignored the needs of the youth who could profit from a liberal arts education (Kandel 117–118).

According to Kandel, when the National Association of Secondary School Principals published a short summary of *Education for All American Youth,* the pamphlet suggested that superintendents appoint commissions on postwar education to determine what changes should happen in the schools. But, Kandel added, the pamphlet did not recommend that superintendents appoint any representatives from colleges to serve on these commissions (Kandel 117).

While Kandel's criticisms were accurate, he neglected to point out that, when the EPC wrote *Education for All American Youth,* two college presidents were members of the commission. One of them, James Bryant Conant, president of Harvard University, went back to his university in 1945 and received the report of a faculty committee to determine the objectives of general education in a free society. In his memoirs, Conant did not connect the act of appointing the committee to his participation on the EPC. Instead, he contended that the idea came up in conversations with deans on the college campus in 1942. At that time, Harvard had become a war college. Scientists had dropped their other research interests and directed their attention to work related to the war effort. Special schools for the Army, Navy, and Air Force took over parts of the university. According to Conant, he and his colleagues thought that if the faculty members could take time off from their regular duties to help the country in wartime, the faculty might be willing to take time to consider how to plan an education that would preserve civilization (Conant, *Lives* 363–364).

Despite Conant's disavowal of calling the committee to aid the EPC in its work, the two documents complement each other. In making his charge to the committee on general education, Conant rejected the name, "liberal education," because he wanted the committee to consider what students in high schools and colleges should learn to continue the liberal and humane tradition. The term *liberal education* implied that traditional courses in the classics, available at the university level, would suffice. Conant was concerned that general education should provide not only the knowledge and skills found in the arts and the sciences but also contact with human beings' emotional experiences as individuals and their practical experiences as social animals. To achieve this end, he believed that general education had to take place at each level of the educational process. As result, he urged the committee to determine what would be appropriate for the general public, not for the select group of students who came to Harvard (Harvard University viii–ix).

In defining general education, the committee members divided the curriculum into three areas that everyone should study. The first was mathematics and the natural sciences because these subjects enabled people to understand the physical world. The second was the social sciences because these subjects enabled people to understand human institutions. And the third was the humanities because they helped human beings understand their humanness. The methods used by scholars in each area differed from each other, the committee noted, but common mental traits should come from the study of each of the areas. These qualities included the abilities to think effectively, to communicate accurately, to make relevant judgments, and to discriminate among values (Harvard University 58–59, 64–71).

The problem the committee faced was how to adapt general education so that it could appeal to students of radically different abilities and interests and yet preserve its essential qualities. In an effort to solve this problem, the committee urged that teachers recognize the different ways and distinct rates that students learn. Further, the committee added that teachers should adopt the principles that provoked the rise of vocational education. This was the realization that students could take an interest in some abstract study, such as literature or history, if they could see how a particular book or historical study related to occupations they planned to pursue. At the same time, though, the report warned against allowing students to choose the subject matter. For example, in literature, teachers should try to select books that students would enjoy and in which they could discover meaning. But the books should be the type that the students could not or would not read without the help of the teacher (Harvard University 93–95, 115–116).

The basic plan that the committee constructed was for instruction in the four areas to form a core for all students and take up about half of the students' time at each level. At the levels of the public high school, there would be different courses of each subject. For example, general mathematics would be offered and so would algebra. These would vary in difficulty so that students with differing abilities could master the material. Some students, such as those preparing for industrial work, might avoid some subjects, such as foreign languages, and take something more useful to them instead, such as music (Harvard University 98–102).

The Harvard committee offered an idea of general education based on the belief that there were things that all people should know. Since the committee claimed that students should pursue such subjects for about half their time in schools, this meant that the students could pursue their own special interests for the other half. Such a compromise resembled the structure of the EPC report, but the Harvard report offered a substantially different content from that of the EPC.

According to Kandel, the EPC report and the Harvard report emphasized the importance of common understandings, but the authors of the EPC report wanted to prepare children for life, not college. As a result, they thought the subject matter and the activities the students in the comprehensive high school had in common differed from what went on in college. On the other hand, Kandel continued, the Harvard report claimed that the instruction the students had in common in high schools should be consistent with the instruction available in colleges. This consistency was essential because the academic courses that formed general education developed skills and knowledge that fulfilled the students' human need for freedom (Kandel 120–121).

Interestingly, vocational educators followed similar directions when they sought to reshape education after the war. In 1947, several educational leaders participated in a conference about the effectiveness of vocational education. At the close of the meeting, Charles Prosser, director of the Federal Board for Vocational Education, summarized the participants' remarks in the form of a resolution. According to Prosser, the high schools failed to serve the needs of the 60 percent of students who did not plan to enter college or to enter a profession directly after graduation. He noted that vocational education served 20 percent of the students and academic studies served another 20 percent. As a result, he proposed that the U.S. Office of Education create the Commission on Life Adjustment Education to determine what steps should be taken to help the majority of high school students (U.S. Office of Education 16).

Once established, the commission claimed that its work was to encourage educators to accept the work of such committees as the EPC. It defined life adjustment education as programs to enable all youth to live democratically as family members, workers, and citizens. The commission claimed it faced two problems: First, most people thought of the high school as a place to study academic subjects instead of a place to solve personal problems. Second, teachers did not know how to present traditional subject matter in ways that served the needs of youth. Nonetheless, the commission wanted to encourage schools to meet the students' needs (U.S. Office of Education 8–11).

Contemporary historians disagree as to the influence of life adjustment education. On the one hand, Diane Ravitch claimed that all the progressive efforts joined together in this movement and that it exerted significant influence. Worse, she claimed that the effect of the movement was unabashedly anti-intellectual. On the other hand, Daniel and Laurel Tanner claimed the greatest influence of the life adjustment movement was that it gave critics a label they could ridicule. According to the Tanners, there were two commissions of life adjustment education, and by 1954, the commissions disappeared. The Tanners claimed the problem was that the term *adjustment* implied the children learned to surrender to the social settings. Despite the fact that many progressives wanted to help students achieve some mastery over their environment, critics derisively labeled every progressive effort to serve the needs of youth as life adjustment education (Ravitch, *Left Back* 327–335; Tanner and Tanner, *History* 246–249).

If the life adjustment movement influenced educational reform in the 1950s, it was to continue reform in the direction in which it had been moving. For example, when the EPC offered a revision of its report in 1952 entitled *Education for All American Youth: A Further Look,* the only mention this revised volume made of the life adjustment movement was to note that a school employed some materials produced under that name in a course on family relationships. In general, the volume continued to stress the need for schools to meet the needs of youths. But the revised version of the EPC report added a chapter in which it claimed the peace that people expected had not followed the war. As a result, society had many needs and most of the students would serve in the military. Consequently, the report listed the ways in which the schools could help youths adjust in ways that would serve the needs of society. These included making the students aware of the need to enter the service and the value that sacrifice offers to the country, home, and school. In addition, the school should train students in subjects such as mathematics, mechanics, and electronics that would enable them to fill national needs. Finally, students had to appreciate the need to defend the freedom and liberty found in a democracy (EPC, *Further* 21–22, 360–361).

Thus, in the revised version of the EPC report, academic subject matters not only served individual intellectual needs but also social or common needs because the skills in science, mathematics, and engineering could help in the military defense of the country. Academic subjects also remained to satisfy individual intellectual needs and to prepare for college entrance. As in the case of the earlier report, the EPC assumed most students did not have intellectual interests and that few students went on to college (EPC, *Further* 216).

What faults did critics find in educators' attempts to balance students' needs with social needs?

At the end of World War II, a red scare swept the United States similar to the one that passed over the country after World War I. As a result, conservative politicians became more popular, and in various cities, citizens' groups complained about the progressive influences in schools and the high taxes needed to support the comprehensive school programs. At the same time, popular authors complained that progressive practices replaced traditional subject matters with efforts to teach the children to get along with each other. In response, the progressive educators claimed that conservatives were plotting against them. While the progressives' fear of a conservative rebellion may have been realistic, some of the critics wanted to reappraise the educational reforms. According to Lawrence Cremin, the American historian Arthur Bestor worked from such higher motives (Cremin 338–343).

In his main text, *Educational Wastelands*, Bestor criticized the EPC's belief that schools should serve the ten imperative needs of youths. He complained that the authors failed to explain how the traditional functions of the school served the students. That is, Bestor argued that the EPC had tried to define education by listing what children need instead of considering what schools should provide. As a result, he found no mention in the report of how academic disciplines could improve life. For example, the ten imperative needs did not contain a statement about understanding the past to grasp the difficulties of the present. Furthermore, statements of needs about such things as recognizing the importance of family living implied that the school should perform functions that belonged to other social institutions (Bestor 61–80).

Bestor criticized the life adjustment movement because it illuminated the tendencies of educators to confuse incidental activities with essential ones. For example, he quoted an Illinois Curriculum Program that offered as its goal to organize what it called common learnings into large units on the basis of youth and social needs. This was the pattern that the EPC had recommended as well. To determine what those needs were, the project leaders conducted several surveys asking parents, citizens, teachers, and students what were problems of the youths. After compiling that information, the program developers sought to organize materials to teach students to confront the difficulties. Although Bestor found a great deal to complain about in the organization of these materials, the primary failing was that the curriculum leaders felt that the required courses for all students were discussions of personal problems, such as improving one's appearance or selecting a dentist, while academic subjects, such as history, economics, and sociology, appeared as electives (Bestor 81–89).

According to Bestor, the denigration of academic disciplines was misguided because he believed that human beings had accumulated the academic disciplines as methods to overcome the various problems that confronted them. Since he was convinced that academic disciplines liberated the mind and organized its powers, he argued that a concentrated study of the liberal arts was the best road to human freedom. As a result, he complained that when the life adjustment educators had made academic studies optional while placing at the center of the curriculum the students' personal troubles, they had confused the essential with the incidental (Bestor 18–23).

In addition, Bestor argued that educators should not serve social needs. For example, he complained that when educators accused academic subject matters of serving elitist values, they undermined democratic education. Bestor believed that a liberal education did not preserve an aristocracy. According to Bestor, academic subjects disciplined a student's mental abilities. For him, the schools served democracy when they enabled every citizen to study literature, art, and philosophy and thereby develop his or her intellectual powers to the fullest (Bestor 25–35).

According to Bestor, the problem was that specialists in pedagogy had determined the content of public school instruction. These so-called professors of education sought to improve the methods of instruction, Bestor added, but they undermined the content as well by continually applying it to practical situations. For example, he noted that these educators recommended that children develop their knowledge of arithmetic by adding three apples to four apples to arrive at seven apples. Although he acknowledged that such lessons were reasonable, the problems arose when the professors of education wanted the children to play store, plant gardens, and lay carpet to continually practice these concrete operations in increasingly com-plicated settings. The result was that the children never saw that mathematics was a theoretical, abstract subject divorced from concrete objects (Bestor 40–51).

The anti-intellectual evils found in public schools were the result of historical forces, Bestor argued. In the 1890s, scholars from important universities sat on national committees to determine what public schools should teach, and they sought to combine the best of academics with the particular needs of the students. In the twentieth century, the normal schools moved into the universities to improve the training of teachers by making such training part of a broad liberal education. Separate education departments undertook the practical training component for the prospective teachers. Instead of aligning themselves with academic subjects, the profes-sors of education tied themselves to practical school affairs and lost interest in traditional sub-ject matter. When these professors of education occupied the positions on the national commissions, such as the EPC or the Commission on Life Adjustment Education, they made anti-intellectual proposals for schools to follow. As a result, these professors formed what Bestor complained was an interlocking directorate of professional educationists who focused on practical affairs and lacked concern for scholarly standards (Bestor 101–121).

In order to break the effects of this interlocking directorate, Bestor circulated a petition to members of the American Historical Association and other learned societies. Gathering almost 700 signatures, Bestor's resolutions asserted that education required concentrated study at every level in traditional subjects such as history, science, mathematics, and art because these disciplines represented the best ways of thinking. The resolutions claimed that vocational education could not substitute for intellectual preparation and that committees to determine educational policy could not be dominated by educational administrators but that scholars and scientists had to participate. To effectuate changes in public schools, Bestor's resolutions rec-ommended that colleges and universities strengthen their admission policies (Bestor 197–205).

While Bestor disapproved of the curriculum the EPC recommended, Bestor justified an intensive study of academic studies on a rationale similar to the one the EPC used to describe the curriculum. In arguing that the academic studies grew out of people's efforts to solve prob-lems, he expressed a view to which most progressive educators had agreed. As Chapter One explains, John Dewey made a similar point in his essay, *Child and the Curriculum.* In making this point, Dewey reinforced the view of the Herbartians against the ideas of Harris. Dewey went on that children should not learn the academic studies on their own. Instead, as Chapter One describes, Dewey wanted the children to learn to use the subject matters to achieve the ends that interested them while Harris wanted children to learn subject matters so they could identify with the progress of society.

In this argument, Bestor took a position roughly similar to that of Dewey. That is, Bestor's view that the liberal arts protected democracy because they encouraged the skills of independent thought was far more individualistic than Harris believed. As Chapter One de-scribes, Harris wanted children to develop thinking skills but he saw these skills as necessary for the children to form worldviews that enabled them to recognize the progress of society and the spiritual development of human beings. Although Dewey may have wished for the children to develop worldviews wherein they could recognize when and if society progressed, he would measure progress in more concrete terms than those Harris sought. As Dewey noted in *Democracy and Education,* he measured a good society by looking to see how numerous and varied

are the interests that people consciously share and how full and free is the interplay or cooperation among the different groups that make up the society (Dewey, *Democracy* 83).

Bestor's view did not differ greatly from the perspective found in the report of the Commission on the Reorganization of Secondary Education. As Chapter Four points out, this report
called for people to see education as a process of growth in which students would begin working on problems that interested them and move outward applying the command of fundamental processes such as mathematics and the insights of subjects such as history in ways that
enabled them to understand the world in which they lived. As noted, the EPC called for teachers to enable the students to master some basic academic skills and apply them to problems or
issues of interest to them.

Bestor's complaint was that educators had taken the progressive principle to extremes.
Thus, he preferred the model illustrated in the Harvard report on general education in which
teachers took students' interest into consideration when they planned the curriculum. But the
teachers' aim was to introduce the students to the classic subject matters rather than to satisfy
their immediate needs. Nonetheless, it is important to realize, as noted, that the Harvard report
asserted that these subject matters met deeper needs, such as the development of critical thinking skills.

While the EPC favored the comprehensive high school and Bestor argued that teachers
had to emphasize the academic studies, vocational educators sought to advance vocational
education as the integrating principle for high school curriculums. Franklin J. Keller, principal
of the New York City Metropolitan Vocational High School, published in 1953 the results of a
study sponsored by the Edgar Starr Barney Project. He claimed that vocational and academic
studies could best be integrated without harming either in what he called double-purpose high
schools.

Keller claimed that comprehensive high schools failed to offer a reasonable combination
of vocational and academic preparation even in the best circumstances. Small towns lacked
adequate resources to provide reasonable vocational and academic training together. In larger
cities, academic preparation overshadowed vocational programs and made the practical
courses appear inferior. Keller visited twelve double-purpose schools that overcame the difficulties by offering extensive vocational programs. These included Keller's Metropolitan Vocational High School in New York City. Founded as a continuation school in 1920 for students
who dropped out of regular school, the Metropolitan grew into a full four-year vocational high
school program offering courses in such areas as auto mechanics, dress making, and the performing arts with an enrollment of 2,000 full-time students and 1,000 part-time students. The
Metropolitan was not a comprehensive high school because it did not offer a straight academic
program, and the students were admitted on the basis of interest in a vocation or, in the case of
the performing arts, the evidence of talent. Although students could take courses in mathematics and foreign languages to prepare for college, every student had to prepare for one of the
vocations covered by the school program. Keller described other similar examples in other
parts of the country, such as the San Antonio, Texas, Vocational and Technical High School,
and the Paul Hayne Vocational High School in Birmingham, Alabama. Although these schools
prepared students for specific jobs, the students had sufficient academic credits upon graduation to enter college (Keller, *Double* 11–12, 87–126).

To explain how students in these vocational or double-purpose schools could prepare for
a vocation and for college, Keller noted that they went to school longer and used the time more

efficiently than did students in other high schools. Students in the dual-purpose schools attended six hours per day while students in most comprehensive schools went for five hours. In addition, in academic or comprehensive high schools, the students had a number of free or study periods. The double-purpose high school did not offer such free time. In the morning, the double-purpose students went to academic classes for three hours. In the afternoon, they went to shop classes for another three hours (Keller, *Double* 95, 164–165).

According to Keller, the University of Illinois, the University of Georgia, and Virginia Polytechnical Institute accepted courses in vocational agriculture, industrial arts, and commerce to replace one year of such academic courses as foreign languages, history, or mathematics. In taking advantage of this option, students did not have to pursue any specific field. They could use the vocational courses to enter any college course. Quoting one study, Keller claimed that the students with vocational preparation did as well in college as the students with only academic training. Thus, he urged other colleges to accept vocational courses toward admission (Keller, *Double* 174–176).

When he looked at other plans, Keller approved of the EPC model and considered it an ideal plan, but he found the life adjustment education to be unnecessary. He described the dual-purpose or vocational schools as doing what life adjustment sought. Those schools helped students who wanted to go to college, students who wanted to enter the work force, and students who had no plans. Keller claimed that vocational preparation created free human beings because the students arrived at a concern for culture by developing their occupational skills. Consequently, he believed that vocational training could be the integrating principle in education (Keller, *Double* 178–180).

In 1955, Keller released the second study supported by the Edgar Starr Barney Project, *The Comprehensive High School.* Keller began this second study because most educators claimed that the comprehensive high school was the best plan for secondary education. As in the first study, Keller surveyed available literature and visited high schools held to be exemplars of the model. When he finished his visits, Keller was disappointed. He noticed that school people applied the word *comprehensive* to anything they wished. Usually, it was an academic high school with a course in homemaking, another in typing, and a third in woodshop. Keller found the best models of blending academics and vocational preparation were found among double-purpose schools that began as strictly vocational institutions. Although the advocates of the comprehensive high school claimed their model served society's needs by reinforcing democracy, he could find no evidence to prove the democratic nature of the model. To Keller, it appeared that the democratic atmosphere of the school depended on such factors as the personality of the principal, the morale of the teachers, and the standards for graduation. He added that placing different children in the same building did not teach them to live and work together (Keller, *Comprehensive* xiii–xv, 254–256).

Keller ended his book with a plea for more research. If most Americans preferred the comprehensive high school, educators should be able to demonstrate its effectiveness. If the model was a poor one, the people should know it. Unfortunately, he concluded, there was little data to prove either side of the argument (Keller, *Comprehensive* 267).

According to Richard Wraga, the principal contribution that Keller made was to widen the analysis of specialized versus comprehensive high schools (Wraga, *Democracy's* 74). If Keller's book, *The Comprehensive High School,* widened the analysis of comprehensive high schools, one reason was that it encouraged James Bryant Conant to begin his own study.

In 1957, after resigning his post as ambassador to Germany, Conant met with officials from the Carnegie Corporation, the Educational Testing Service, the dean of the Harvard School of Education, and a school superintendent. According to Conant, he had been much impressed by Keller's book *The Comprehensive High School* and decided to use the schools that Keller thought were truly comprehensive as the starting point of a study of the education of talented youth in comprehensive high schools. When he presented this proposal to the group, they received it enthusiastically and granted him financial support to proceed (Conant, *Lives* 618–619).

How did James Conant recommend that schools balance attention to students' and society's needs?

Conant's study turned out to be one of two forces that combined to increase the popularity of the comprehensive high school model. The other was the National Defense Education Act of 1958. The relation among these forces might be illustrated by the following story. In 1957, the Soviet Union launched a space satellite. During the resulting Sputnik crisis, many people in the United States urged that public schools could contribute to military defense if they concentrated on producing gifted scientists. As President Dwight D. Eisenhower prepared his plans for a possible education program, he received a lengthy telegram from James Conant describing the condition of education in the United States. According to Barbara Barkdale Clowse, the message that Conant sent appealed to the president because it urged Eisenhower to avoid any drastic reforms or crash programs. The schools were in good shape, Conant asserted. Although he believed that foreign language instruction should be reinforced, he had found many students with fine backgrounds in math and science. As a result, Eisenhower used Conant's telegram as the basis of his speech to the nation (Clowse 56–57).

Conant's standing among leaders such as Eisenhower contradicted Bestor's accusation that an interlocking directorate of professional educationists who lacked concern for academic standards controlled schools. Trained as a research chemist, Conant joined the EPC in 1940 when he was the president of Harvard University. At that time, the committee consisted of the president of Cornell University, four professors of education, five public school administrators, and a classroom teacher. In 1944, Conant had helped in the preparation of the EPC's *Education for All American Youth*. He was chairperson of the EPC in 1951 when the organization published *Education for All American Youth: A Further Look* (Conant, *Lives* 395, 614).

During World War II, Conant served as deputy to Vannevar Bush in the U.S. Office of Scientific Research and Development. In this position, he was one of the leaders of the Manhattan Project, which developed the atomic bomb. Although the project created the bomb, Conant was not sure the project was a success. In his autobiography, Conant wrote that he feared the enormous potential for destruction from the bomb outweighed the possible peacetime benefits of atomic power. James G. Hershberg contended that Conant was deeply shaken when he witnessed the first test of an atomic bomb. On 16 July 1945, Conant lay on his stomach on the desert sands looking at the horizon away from the center of an explosion that took place about ten miles away. A burst of light filled the sky and lasted for enough time to convince Conant that the bomb had started a chain reaction that would engulf the entire atmosphere. Forty seconds later, an enormous growl reverberated off the surrounding mountains that grew into an awesome roar as a ball of flame billowed into a giant reddish purple mushroom cloud. Hershberg quoted notes that Conant made indicating Conant thought, for a moment, he was one of the last people to live on earth, and he believed he had helped to create the apocalypse (Conant, *Lives* 272–273, 304; Hershberg 233–234).

Apparently, the experience in Alamogordo, New Mexico, never left Conant. When the Sputnik crisis grew, Conant urged restraint. He claimed that the country did not need more and better scientists. It needed more political leaders with wisdom, courage, and devotion who could solve intricate human problems. Conant's distaste for weapons development had grown to such an extent that when government advisors asked him if he would serve on the President's Science Advisory Committee, he replied that he would not take part because it would do harmful things to the country by pushing technology (Hershberg 710–711).

Conant believed that his study of high schools would improve democratic traditions and provide an alternative to the drive to enhance military defense. Writing in a letter in 1957 to a prospective member of his staff about his study of high schools, Conant asserted that he was committed to the idea of one high school that enrolled all the youths of a given area. He added that such institutions could break down barriers among groups of children, engender a spirit of democracy, and enhance respect for all forms of labor. At the same time, he realized this type of schooling raised problems of how to encourage talented children to prepare for academic careers. His hope was to identify schools in which academic students did not exceed fifty percent of the enrollment in communities that were not suburban or primarily white collar but that were successful in preparing youth whose IQ scores exceeded 115 (Hershberg 707).

Conant told his colleagues that he designed his study to give him the practical experience to fortify his prejudices. Although this statement may appear as self-deprecating humor, the statement was accurate. Conant did not set out to determine the effectiveness of the comprehensive high school model by comparing that form against other forms of schooling on a variety of measures. Instead, Conant and his staff made a list of criteria to evaluate a comprehensive high school. These criteria might be said to represent Conant's prejudices. They included adequacy of general education, adequacy of vocational programs, effective arrangements for academically talented students, adequacy of guidance services, and success in promoting understanding among students with different academic abilities. Armed with the list of criteria, he and his staff compiled a list of 103 high schools in twenty-six states that they thought would fit the criteria, sent detailed questionnaires to the schools, and visited 59 of them. They then tried to determine which schools fulfilled the criteria. In these ways, Conant sought to determine if the idea of a comprehensive high school was reasonable and how a school could accomplish the goal of becoming one (Conant, *American High School* 18–22, 97–101).

Conant found eight schools that fulfilled the objectives he and his staff defined as essential for a comprehensive high school. Although these schools offered reasonable programs in general education, vocational training, and special opportunities in math and science for the gifted students, he noted two general faults. None of the schools provided adequate instruction in foreign languages, and, in most of the schools, the gifted students did not work hard enough. The problem of gifted female students was especially severe, he added, because bright girls avoided the sciences and math. Despite these reservations, Conant proclaimed that most schools could be improved by relatively minor changes (Conant, *American High School* 22–23, 40).

For Conant, the key to balancing individual needs with social requirements was school size. On the one hand, he noted that small schools could not meet students' needs for specialized courses. Many small schools could not offer courses in advanced mathematics, physics, and chemistry because there were few teachers. And when small schools tried to offer these courses, the teachers lacked training in the subject matter. The situation was reversed if well-qualified physics or chemistry teachers accepted jobs in small schools. Their abilities were often ill used because they had to teach introductory biology or general science. On the other hand, Conant argued that large specialized city schools did not provide for social needs. Cities had enough students that they could set up specialized schools for students with high academic talent or vocational abilities. While these students received fine academic or vocational training, they did not have the opportunity to work with students of remarkably different abilities (Conant, *American High School* 77–89).

In 1959, Conant published his report, *The American High School Today*. In his memoirs, Conant bragged that the timing of its appearance was perfect. The public criticism of high schools over Sputnik was at its height. School board members in all parts of the country wanted to know what they should do. Conant added that he boldly provided the answers in twenty-one specific recommendations (Conant, *Lives* 621).

A prominent critic of the comprehensive high school was John Francis Latimer, a professor of classics at Georgetown University. In 1958, he took advantage of the Sputnik crisis to urge educators to return to what he thought was the wisdom of the report of the Committee of Ten. The report was written in 1893 and is discussed in Chapter One. According to Latimer, this report urged all students to take some form of broad, general education in the liberal arts and sciences. These were the subjects that provided the foundation for civic and cultural development as well as mental and moral growth. Latimer claimed that high schools worked together for almost thirty years following this plan to train and discipline students' minds. But by 1922, he complained, educators began to see education as a process of developing social and civic awareness. The result was the expansion of nonacademic subjects to make education more practical (Latimer 114–120).

According to Latimer, students in the Soviet Union followed a curriculum roughly similar to the one the Committee of Ten had prescribed. But during the same period, fewer students in the United States enrolled in courses of mathematics, science, or foreign languages. When the Soviet Union succeeded in launching a satellite, he claimed this showed the wisdom of the Committee of Ten. The academic courses were the most practical (Latimer 121–132).

To Latimer, the main core of education was the same for every country: mathematics, science, foreign languages, history, and one's own native language. He recommended that every student have the opportunity to learn these subjects. To account for differences in students' abilities, teachers might offer different amounts of material to different groups. But Latimer urged teachers to ask all students to learn the same kind of material. Slower students should be given the basic principles of the subjects that to Latimer made modern life possible (Latimer 135).

Another more polemical critic of the comprehensive high school was a vice admiral of the U.S. Navy, Hyman G. Rickover. In 1959, Rickover used the Sputnik crisis as reason to demand the radical reorganization of the schools. Repeatedly comparing U.S. schools to European or Soviet institutions, Rickover noted that Soviet students, who were able to pursue professional study in those systems, moved ahead two or three years faster than their U.S.

counterparts because the teachers placed them at an early age in upper-track sections. Attending these sections or special schools for six or nine years, the Soviet students pursued required courses with each subject arranged to follow the others in logical sequence. Rickover added that the instruction was effective in these special schools because the students' abilities were uniform and the students were motivated. When criticized for offering an undemocratic vision of schools, Rickover replied that a democratic government should throw open the schools to all students who made the effort to succeed. He added that the U.S. tendency to try to bring all children together hurt the schools and the country. Furthermore, Rickover claimed that by tailoring the education to fit the aptitudes of the children, the European and Soviet countries spent less on education but enjoyed the benefits of more and better scientists than did the United States (Rickover 150–151).

In writing *The American High School Today,* Conant did not mention any public school critics by name. Yet, many of the comments appeared to be directed at Latimer and Rickover, who believed that European or Soviet systems were more efficient than the U.S. schools. Conant noted that those systems ruthlessly selected a few children to move ahead in a narrow track system. The result was a waste of talent because the system gave no chance to students who might be called "late bloomers" because they developed their talents later than other children. Further, while a European visitor would find the American educational patterns to be chaotic, Conant believed that they fit the American economic history and public devotion to the ideals of equality of opportunity and status. Thus, he concluded the only acceptable model for a high school in the United States was a comprehensive high school that educated all youths from the community (Conant, *American High School* 8–9).

In his specific recommendations, Conant met the objections of academics such as Latimer who complained that high schools allowed some students to avoid traditional subject matters. In this regard, Conant applied the suggestions of the Harvard Committee on General Education, which he had organized in 1945. He demanded that in order for students to graduate from high school, they had to complete four years of English, two years of history, one year of social studies, one year of mathematics, and one year of science. These academic courses with homework were to occupy about one-half of the students' time no matter what elective program they selected (Conant, *American High School* 47–48).

To meet the objections of people like Rickover who wanted more special attention given to students who were gifted and talented, Conant recommended grouping the students by abilities and offering advanced placement courses for which students could receive college credit. At the same time, though, he argued against tracks labeled "college preparatory" or "vocational." Instead, he suggested that students should take most subjects on the basis of their aptitudes for those disciplines. Thus, a student might pursue advanced English but middle-level algebra. In addition, Conant urged improving the counseling system so that students could take advantage of individualized programs. To encourage students to pursue appropriate classes, he recommended that students receive small, durable cards they could carry in their wallets instead of diplomas. On such a card, there would be a record of the classes the student took and the grades he or she received (Conant, *American High School,* 44–47, 62–63).

To meet the objections of vocational educators, Conant recommended that schools offer vocational programs, such as typing, stenography, vocational agriculture, or industrial programs. In this regard, Conant noted that school administrators had to monitor the local employment situation so that the schools could provide appropriate training for the opportunities for employment. He argued that some academic courses, such as English and social studies, could offer training in marketable skills (Conant, *American High School* 52–55).

Finally, to retain the idea of the common learnings found in the EPC reports, Conant recommended that students attend the same homeroom throughout their high school years with students of different abilities and interests. He added that all students of varying abilities be required to attend together a twelfth-grade social studies course about the problems of American government. Such a course, focused on discussion of controversial issues, would teach the different types of students to work and to think together about topics important to them (Conant, *American High School* 74–76).

Although Conant's book remained a best-seller for several weeks, he was disappointed in the limited influence it had. In 1967, Conant sent questionnaires to about 18,500 schools asking for information about their organization, size, and offerings. On the basis of enrollment, about one-half of the schools fell into the range Conant considered reasonable for a comprehensive high school. This was a student population that ranged from 750 to about 2,000. Noting that the advantage of a comprehensive school was the opportunity it provided for students with different backgrounds to meet one another, he claimed that there would be no problem with racial segregation if every city had adopted the model (Conant, *Comprehensive* 7–8).

When Conant looked at the schools that fell into the acceptable range of enrollments, he found several problems. Few of the schools had an adequate number of counselors for their students. The educators appeared to group students in tracks by ability rather than follow Conant's suggestions of grouping students class by class. Although 71 percent of the schools had a course in the problems of democracy, most schools placed too many students in the English classes for the teachers to assign and grade many compositions. Only about 40 percent of the schools offered advanced placement courses for their students, but these were not evenly distributed around the country. In some states, such as New York, almost 50 percent of the schools offered advanced placement courses, but in other states, such as Alabama, about 8 percent of the schools had them. Further, few schools reported that they used such technology as television, and most schools lacked adequate library facilities (Conant, *Comprehensive* 26, 30, 36, 42, 70–73).

Despite the problems that he found, Conant believed the situation was better than it had been. The situation regarding the academic studies depended on the ambition of the community and the money available. Therefore, unless the methods of funding schools changed, he predicted that many students attending small, disadvantaged schools would not have the opportunities open to students attending genuinely comprehensive schools. And he believed the communities would suffer because students would not develop the democratic sensibilities that they could in comprehensive schools (Conant, *Comprehensive* 2, 80).

Although Conant was disappointed with the influence of his report, Daniel and Laurel Tanner credited him with rescuing the model of the comprehensive high school from the critics who called for a system of separate academic and vocational high schools. They asserted that Conant's suggestions were widely adopted (Tanner and Tanner, *Curriculum* 424–425, 493).

Other historians agreed with Conant's gloomy observations. For example, James G. Hershberg asserted that *The American High School Today* had little long-term impact on schools. He believed that some schools organized programs for the gifted students, yet most school boards ignored most of the suggestions (Hershberg 713–714).

Although the U.S. National Defense Education Act should have combined with Conant's recommendations to encourage more school boards to strengthen offerings in science and math, this seems not to have happened. For example, David Angus and Jeffrey Mirel contended that mathematics enrollments rose in high schools from about 55 percent of the students in grades nine to twelve in 1948 to about 66 percent in 1963. They contended this is a modest increase and that overall patterns of course taking in the sciences and mathematics remained unchanged from 1948 to 1960. More disturbing to Angus and Mirel, the enrollment increases that took place were in such courses as consumer mathematics or mathematics for modern living. They added that special science projects, such as those described in Chapter Eight, had little impact on enrollment patterns. Instead, graduation requirements remained relaxed, and the type of courses that dominated were life adjustment classes aimed at helping students solve personal problems (Angus and Mirel 117–120).

The U.S. Office of Education came to conclusions that reinforced those of Angus and Mirel and of Conant when it conducted a national survey of the scholastic performance of pupils of various abilities. The study included almost 6,000 students who graduated in June 1958 from three different sized public high schools. When the researchers classified the students into four levels of ability, they found that the students from each ability level worked below their ability and took fewer courses then they could have, as Angus and Mirel would suggest. But the survey noted some important differences. As Conant might have predicted, the size of the school seemed to determine the equality of educational opportunity. That is, pupils in large schools were more likely to have programs compatible to their abilities than did students in smaller schools. Also, in large schools, able girls were more likely to pursue academic courses than were girls with similar abilities in smaller schools. Yet, low-ability boys in small schools earned more credits in business but fewer in industrial arts than similarly ranked boys in large schools. Low-ability girls in small schools earned more credits in college preparatory classes than did similarly ranked girls in large schools (Greer and Harbeck 7–10, 119–123).

In what ways did educators' ideas of serving national needs and individual needs change as a result of World War II and the subsequent cold war?

Educators wanted to balance the desire to meet the needs of students and of society. Yet, during wartime, even formerly child-centered pedagogues worked together with more traditional educators to find ways to meet the national emergencies. In peacetime, the educators tended to return to their previous alignments. The situation seemed to determine how the educators reacted.

During peacetime, many educators believed the comprehensive high school with its range of options for different types of students would allow some students to excel in academics and other students to pursue vocational courses. Many educators argued, however, that the comprehensive high school aggravated the problems it was supposed to solve. Educators who favored academic training for everyone complained that traditional subject matter was optional in the comprehensive high school. Vocational educators complained that vocational subjects received little attention in comprehensive high schools.

After working in colleges and on educational councils for many years, James Conant thought he had found a way to meet most of the objections. He recommended that high schools offer a blend of required courses in traditional subject matter, elective classes in advanced academic or vocational classes, and common learnings in social studies. Most important, he found eight schools that operated in this manner successfully. Thus, he contended that other school districts could adapt the programs to their situations.

Unfortunately, Conant's major contribution may be that he prevented radical revision of school programs. Politicians and educators seemed to find solace in his suggestion that they could avoid extensive changes. As a result, students continued to enroll in practical or life adjustment courses, to the dismay of people who favored academic studies. Furthermore, traditional subject matter and grouping students by ability into separate programs remained important parts of secondary education, to the dismay of the progressive educators.

While the schools tended to sacrifice the needs of the students to the needs of society when something threatened national security, this does not mean that the federal government was the force behind the change. In fact, when Conant expected the NDEA to help schools adopt his reforms, he found that communities and school people were unwilling to invest the time and the money to make the changes.

Educators may have tried to accomplish the impossible. They wanted to form a balance between social obligations and individual needs, but social needs often contradict individual ones. As a result, the comprehensive high school remained a model that tended to send children from lower social classes toward vocational training that prepared them for work similar to that of their parents. And the high schools tended to prepare wealthier children for college and more professional work. This seemed to happen because the different educators shared the view that schools should enable children to satisfy their needs in ways that met social requirements.

Summary

During World War II, educators joined together and urged that all schools reorganize the curriculum to meet the needs of the country. They agreed that the individual needs of the students had to wait until the national emergency passed. After the war, educational organizations such as the National Education Association issued statements seeking to realign the curriculum in ways that balanced individual needs with social obligations. In doing this, they returned to the progressive notion that schools served the country when they met the needs of individual students. Thus, the educators called on high schools to become comprehensive and allow individual students to pursue their interests while teaching them how to live and work together. Conservative critics, such as Arthur Bestor, complained that educators supporting the comprehensive high school made traditional subject matters optional but required all students to take courses aimed at helping them adjust to society. At the same time, vocational educators complained that vocational courses suffered from low status in the comprehensive high school. In 1957, critics used the Sputnik crisis to call for radical reforms of the comprehensive high school. These calls took two important directions. One reformer, John Latimer, wanted schools to offer a liberal arts curriculum for all students. Another critic, Hyman Rickover, believed the United States should set up separate types of schools to allow the gifted students to develop into productive scientists. A chemist and former president of Harvard University, James Conant, sought to form a compromise among these options, and he championed the model of the comprehensive high school as an institution that could balance the needs of the students and of the country. As a result, Conant adapted the image provided in 1918 by the Commission on the Reorganization of Secondary Education to provide for schools to build on the interests of the students, to prepare them for the professions they would pursue as adults, and to advance democratic values. Conant could provide such a compromise because the supporters of liberal arts training and the advocates of separate trade schools sought to meet student needs in ways that produced a better society. Unfortunately, since Conant accepted this assumption as well, his efforts appeared to reinforce the distinctions among the social classes.

CHAPTER EIGHT

ACADEMIC EXCELLENCE TO MEET SOCIETY'S NEEDS, 1940–1964

An uneasy peace followed World War II, and scientists warned that technical and scientific superiority was important to national security. As Chapter Seven demonstrates, many educators, such as James Conant, considered the comprehensive high school as a means to produce an elite corps of scientists while at the same time inculcating in all students the democratic values that would prevent the outbreak of military violence. At the same time that the federal government supported Conant's efforts, federal agencies supported scientists who took a different view. These scholars considered it essential that all people come to understand science and mathematics. They argued that if only an elite group learned to control technology, these technicians could use their abilities to serve their own interests at the expense of the common good. Further, the scientists feared that if small groups of researchers controlled technical developments, they would resist new ideas to such an extent that they would retard scientific progress. Thus, these scholars created programs to spread an understanding of science among students of every ability level.

Before the end of World War II, Vannevar Bush, director of the U.S. Office of Scientific Research and Development, urged President Franklin Roosevelt to create a federal agency to advance scientific research in the United States. Despite such requests, it was not until 1950 that the U.S. Congress created the National Science Foundation (NSF). In signing the legislation, President Harry S Truman noted that the end of World War II had not brought peace. He added that the United States had to retain leadership in scientific progress in order to deter threats from the Soviet Union. He expressed the hope that the NSF would stimulate basic research and improve instruction in science to provide the knowledge needed for the growth, prosperity, and defense of the nation (Schaffter 11).

At first, the NSF concentrated on work at the university level. But as some educators sought to change the training of elementary and high school students, their successes encouraged the NSF to change its focus. In 1951, the University of Illinois Committee on School Mathematics (UICSM) published a list of mathematical competencies that they thought students would need before they entered an engineering program. The hope was that this list would aid high school students prepare for university studies. The next year, teachers in the university laboratory school and in two nearby public schools used this list to help the children develop understandings of basic concepts in mathematics. The program was unique in that the teachers sought to have children discover and use concepts such as numbers, functions, and equations without receiving direct instruction about the terms. In this process, called "guided discovery," the teacher helped the children work through a series of problems, but the teacher did not offer nor did the students express the definitions of the concepts they learned to use. The rationale was that children should not verbalize their discoveries. Instead, they should apply their insights in a variety of settings in order to assimilate the ways that the concepts worked (Hayden 100–107).

In 1956, the annual report of the NSF noted that the foundation had to extend support beyond university instruction to include high-quality elementary and secondary school programs. Otherwise, the report warned, the country would face a shortage of qualified scientists in the coming decade. As a result, the NSF offered to support Jerrold R. Zacharias of the Massachusetts Institute of Technology who wanted to convene a group of eminent scientists to find ways to improve the instruction of physics. Calling themselves the Physical Science Study Committee (PSSC), Zacharias's group began evaluating textbooks in physics. They found the books offered too much material, paid excessive attention to practical applications, and often misrepresented theoretical concepts. The solution they offered was to produce a set of ninety films. Each of the films offered a complete lesson, had a teacher's guide, and contained supplementary questions for further research and classroom discussion. The films were organized so that the students began with a study of particles, considered laws of force and motion, and were introduced to some of the mathematics necessary to test theory with experiments (Marsh and Gortner 16–23).

It is important to note that academicians, like Zacharias, did not want to train a select group of students to become productive scientists. They wanted to spread an understanding of science throughout the population, and they believed this was how better science teaching would improve society. In March 1958, Bentley Glass, president of the American Institute of Biological Sciences, expressed such a view by recommending that science become the core of the curriculum in order to preserve the democratic nature of our society.

When Glass urged elementary and secondary school educators to make science the core of the curriculum, he did not want science classes to displace other courses. Instead, he thought teachers should present science as an integral part of modern life. Texts should demonstrate the uniqueness and the limits of scientific methods. In all, Glass wanted teachers to explain how science and mathematics offered imaginative ways to explore nature, to integrate experience, and to develop a philosophy of life (Glass, *Science* 66).

According to Glass, the problem was that schoolteachers had not taught science as a way of learning. They presented scientific concepts and facts as bodies of information separate from other studies. Glass acknowledged that the problem was not exclusively the fault of science teachers. He complained that teachers of the humanities and the social studies had ignored the ways that science and mathematics shaped their own subjects. The result was that students tended to think of science as a modern sort of magic, and they viewed scientists as people who had authoritative answers to modern problems (Glass, *Science* viii–ix, 68).

Glass warned against the tendency of people to idolize scientists and to think that science was incomprehensible. Glass noted that the society would be oligarchic if a few scientists controlled people's lives and the rest of the population could not understand what happened. As a result, he claimed the only way to protect democracy was for everyone to become what he called truly scientific (Glass, *Science* 68–69).

Other scientists adopted Glass's viewpoint. For example, in 1959, the leaders of various academic programs met at Woods Hole, Massachusetts. One of the points they made in the final report was that they wanted to spread the pursuit of excellence beyond those students recognized as gifted. In fact, they warned that the desire to improve the science and technological training in schools could cause schools to reward students who mastered the material easily. The result would be that students who acquired academic interests later in their lives would fall behind and be unable to make up the difference. Further, they complained that schools could become dependent on some sort of standard examinations. In this regard, they quoted C. P. Snow who claimed an examination in English universities, the Cambridge University Tripos, separated graduates considered most promising from those who appeared less deserving. But the scholars warned that the effect of the Tripos was to force students to learn the information for the test to the point where they gave up creative thinking about the material (Bruner 70–80).

How did the federal government want schools to meet national needs?

On 4 October 1957, the Soviet Union launched a space satellite, and newspaper reports claimed that the United States had lost the race to control space because elementary and high schools did not teach the students enough math or science. In reaction to the Sputnik crisis, the federal government allocated funds to do two different things. On the one hand, it sought to select and train the best scientists to work to improve the nation's defenses. On the other hand, it offered money to spread an understanding of science to all children.

In an effort to calm the controversy, on 9 October 1957, President Dwight D. Eisenhower issued a statement claiming that the United States could have sent a satellite into orbit earlier if it had merged military and scientific programs. He added that the federal government decided not to do this because the missile program was designed to provide maximum research benefits. On 7 November 1957, in an address on radio and television, Eisenhower announced that he would recommend programs to improve science education in schools, and he would rearrange the federal agencies to facilitate the production of military technology (Eisenhower, "Statement" 733–734; Eisenhower, "Radio" 789–799).

Eisenhower assured the public that the Soviet Sputnik did not pose an immediate threat to national security. He noted that the United States had enough military power to annihilate the war-making capabilities of any other country. Further, he claimed that the federal government spent over $5 billion per year on research and development for defense, and he listed several accomplishments such as missiles that carried nuclear warheads, atomic submarines, and many new warplanes. To preserve this technological lead, he made two important recommendations. The first was to make science education an important part of school life. The second was to increase scientific research by removing legal barriers to the communication of scientific advances among scientists from different but friendly nations and to facilitate the funding and manufacture of armaments by rearranging the relevant governmental offices (Eisenhower, "Radio" 789–799).

On 27 January 1958, Eisenhower sent a special message to the U.S. Congress asking for additional support to improve the training in science and engineering in elementary and secondary schools. In his message, Eisenhower asserted his belief that local residents should control the schools that serve their areas, but he claimed that the emergency in national security meant the federal government had to offer additional help. Thus, he requested that the U.S. Congress allocate funds to allow the NSF and the U.S. Department of Health, Education, and

Welfare (HEW) to improve science instruction. He requested that the role of the NSF be to improve the subject matter knowledge of science and mathematics teachers and to support the revision of course materials. The role he wanted the HEW to play was to provide funds for the construction of facilities to aid in science, math, and foreign language study and to support the improvement of counseling and guidance procedures to encourage able students to pursue these rigorous fields (Eisenhower, "Special" 127–131).

Scientific leaders serving the military wanted the government to create special educational opportunities for gifted students to become scientists and to improve the nation's defense. For example, when the U.S. Congress began hearings to determine what action the federal government should take to change the training in schools, the committee called Werner von Braun, director of the U.S. Army Ballistic Missile Agency, to testify. Comparing the education that he had received in Germany to the education he saw in the United States, von Braun claimed that U.S. schools offered lessons on family relations and human relations, the teachers tried to make learning fun for the students, and prospective teachers concentrated on courses about methods of instruction. In Europe, he believed the students took required academic courses, they had to pass stringent examinations, and the prospective teachers learned the subject matter they were to communicate. In conclusion, he recommended that the federal government create an inspection agency that established national standards for promotion and graduation at all levels, that U.S. educators imitate the Soviet Union in offering the best opportunities to the gifted students, and that all Americans eschew anti-intellectualism (U.S. Committee on Labor and Public Welfare 63–69).

Thus, von Braun represented a point of view distinct from that of scientists such as Glass. While von Braun wanted the high schools to encourage gifted students to pursue scientific studies, Glass wanted to spread an understanding of science throughout the population. Most important, they thought about protecting the society in different ways. On the one hand, von Braun wanted science training to produce increased military strength that would protect against foreign invaders. On the other hand, Glass thought of the information and knowledge that science produced as the sources of power in a technological society; he wanted to spread scientific understandings throughout the social classes so that everyone could share in the control of social change.

Despite the desire of scientists like von Braun to have schools adopt procedures that would develop an intellectual elite, Eisenhower requested that the federal agencies not impose a program on state and local education agencies. To some extent at least, the agencies refrained from imposing any programs. For example, Title III of the NDEA was written in such a way that the HEW could not control what the states or the local school people did with the funds. The state agencies reported to the HEW the sum of money the agency spent and the name of the project on which they spent it. Since the agencies offered no other information, federal supervisors could not determine how or if the projects improved science teaching. Further, the NDEA made no provision for any agency to judge what effect a project had (Marsh and Gortner 87–88).

The NSF made similar efforts to avoid influencing educators. In 1966, an evaluator of the NSF stated that the NSF had a significant influence on the nation's educational system by supporting the introduction of new textbooks and the training of teachers. The evaluator added that the NSF did not control what went on in the classrooms nor did it initiate any programs. The role of the NSF was to react to suggestions from outsiders by providing money or not providing money for their proposals (Schaffter 115).

While the HEW and the NSF may not have sought to control schools, they did influence different orientations. By encouraging the testing and counseling of gifted students, the HEW supported school systems that treated the students differently in hopes it could produce an elite group of scientists who would improve national defense. On the other hand, by supporting academics similar to Glass, the NSF encouraged the development of curriculums that tried to spread the central ideas of science and math throughout the population and thereby reduce the chances of society becoming oligarchic.

Although the federal government supported different directions for reform, it devoted considerably more money to support school districts that treated students differently than it devoted to efforts to spread an understanding of science throughout the public. For example, the HEW claimed that, during the first complete year of funding, fiscal year 1960, the department sent about $50 million of NDEA Title III funds to school districts to acquire equipment and to remodel classrooms for better science, mathematics, and foreign language instruction. During the same period, the HEW sent about $15 million of NDEA Title V funds for states to provide such measures as testing services to identify gifted students and about $6 million to train guidance counselors. On the other hand, the NSF claimed that it spent about $13.5 million on what it called course content improvement from 1952 to 1960. This category included the work of scientists, such as Zacharias. In another category, special projects in science education, the NSF spent about $10 million on projects directed to secondary school students, college programs, teacher improvement programs, and programs to aid the public understanding of science (U.S. Science Policy Research Division 133–134; U.S. Department of Health, Education and Welfare 7, 17–20).

As the controversy about the teaching of math and science grew, academics from almost every scientific discipline organized groups to improve the curriculum. For example, the American Institute of Biological Sciences (AIBS) appointed Glass to chair a committee that would consider ways to reform the biology curriculum in elementary and secondary schools. The committee organized a team of sixty-nine authors who met in Boulder, Colorado, for seven weeks during the summer of 1960. They prepared three different versions of a course for high school biology students. The Blue Version presented fundamental concepts of biology through experimental methods of physiology and biochemistry. The Green Version was built around natural history and ecology. The Yellow Version presented the topics usually covered in a high school biology course but concentrated on the important concepts involved (Grobman 9–18; Glass, "Report" 100).

Mathematicians began a similar process. In February 1958, a group of research mathematicians and the presidents of the American Mathematical Society, an association of theorists, and of the Mathematical Association of America, a society of college math teachers, held a conference in Cambridge, Massachusetts. They began a series of activities that led to the creation of the School Mathematics Study Group (SMSG), headed by Edward G. Begle (Wooten 10–14).

The SMSG formed teams of mathematicians to write the texts during relatively short periods of time, usually over the summer. These texts covered material for most grades and mathematical subjects, such as geometry and algebra. For example, during the summer of 1958, a team met for four weeks to write texts for grades seven and eight. The members decided to remove references to what they called "social mathematics," not to include drill and repetition, and to concentrate on what the authors called "mathematical structure." This meant the texts would seek to expand the students' appreciation of abstract concepts, to help them understand the role of definition, and to encourage them to develop precise vocabularies (*Philosophies* 2).

Similarly, the Chemical Education Material Study group produced a high school course in chemistry. This included a text, a teachers' guide, a set of motion pictures, wall charts, and other supplementary materials. The chemists who wrote the materials sought to create a course that was based on laboratory work, that emphasized the importance of concepts in correlating chemical facts, and that showed the wide scope of the field of chemistry (Campbell 82–83).

In addition to preparing the programs, these various study groups arranged for experimental centers to try out the materials in classes with students. From the reactions of the teachers and the students, the writing teams revised the materials before they produced them in large numbers. Although the groups wanted to reach children of different abilities, they did not always use the same materials. For example, the SMSG prepared sets of mathematics texts for college-bound high school students and another set for non-college-bound students. In addition, SMSG set about constructing a set of texts for children who lived in large cities and whose parents earned between $2,000 and $4,000 per year. As Chapter Nine shows, these children were considered culturally deprived and were said to pose unique educational problems. At the same time, the SMSG translated their texts into Spanish for students in Puerto Rico (Leiderman, Chinn, and Dunkley 1–3, 89; Wooten 130–131).

What was the theoretical basis of the new math and science programs?

In September 1959, the NSF sponsored a conference of thirty-five educators, scientists, and scholars in Woods Hole, Massachusetts. Among the people attending this conference were four members of the UICSM; Zacharias who had founded the PSSC; two film makers; Begle who led the SMSG; the biologist, Glass, and his colleague from the Biological Sciences Curriculum Study (BSCS), Arnold B. Grobman. The psychologist, Jerome S. Bruner, wrote *The Process of Education* to express the general themes that circulated throughout the conference. As a result, this document expressed the aims and the working principles of the different programs (Bruner vii–xiii).

Looking at various projects organized by the participants, Bruner argued that an understanding of the importance of the structure of academic studies should guide the reform of curriculum. Bruner believed that each discipline, such as mathematics, history, or literature, had a structure. This structure was the way that scholars in the field thought when they were at work. Another way to think about the structure was to imagine it as the fundamental ideas or the general principles that enabled a scholar to proceed. Bruner thought these fundamental ideas or structures were the things the curriculum should seek to convey to students. He wanted the curriculum to form a spiral so that the material learned by elementary school students was related to the material covered in a university course in the same subject (Bruner 27–30).

Bruner claimed that, if the material or the lessons were organized around the structure or the fundamental ideas in a discipline, the students could learn, recall, and use a great deal of information because the structure provided a pattern of organization. Over time, students would forget the details of many of their studies. Bruner believed that, if they recalled the structure of the discipline, they could reconstruct the missing details. When he considered how this structure could be taught, Bruner believed they had to discover it. This presented some problems because the students worked slowly when they discovered everything on their own. It was quicker for teachers to tell them some things. Thus, Bruner felt that teachers had to find some balance that preserved the excitement implicit in discovery but allowed for the efficiency found in teacher presentations (Bruner 20–26).

For Bruner, the importance of structure and discovery was related to the best ways that teachers could balance what he called intrinsic and extrinsic rewards for learning. He noted that typically teachers kept students by rewarding them, but that good teachers used more effective measures. They recognized that leading students to make discoveries on their own enabled them to feel the pleasure of their minds functioning fully. In this way, the students became absorbed in the activities, and they spent longer hours at the activities than teachers imagined possible (Bruner 49–51).

The question was who should identify the fundamental structure of any discipline. To Bruner, it was clear that the scholars in the fields were the people who should make such determinations. He pointed out that this was the rationale of programs the NSF sponsored. For example, the members of the Woods Hole conference came from projects, such as UICSM, PSSC, SMSG, and BSCS, that sought grants from the NSF to hire eminent scholars for a summer or a year to devise ways to select and organize these concepts (Bruner 18–20).

Although Bruner was convinced that any subject could be presented in an intellectually honest way to any child at any stage of development, he acknowledged that this did not mean a young child could learn complex mathematics. The concepts had to be presented to the students in ways consistent with the children's own patterns of thinking. Bruner quoted Swiss psychologist Jean Piaget to explain how children below the age of six years are in the first stage of mental development, the *preoperational* stage. They cannot learn many ideas in mathematics because they do not recognize that a sum of objects remains the same when divided into groups. At the age of six until about ten children enter the second stage of mental development, the *concrete operational* stage. Children at this age can gather information by moving objects in ways that would solve problems. With these abilities, children can use logic to understand changes among objects that are immediately present. Somewhere between ten to fourteen years of age, children enter the third stage of mental development, the *formal operations* stage. These children can use theoretical ideas to understand the relationships that exist among objects treated in particular ways (Bruner 31–38).

Bruner used this discussion of Piaget and the stages of mental development to explain why the teachers in the UICSM did not ask the children to explain what they discovered. He described how a teacher from that project demonstrated to the conference members at Woods Hole how children in the fifth grade grasped the central ideas of the theory of functions but they could not explain the theory nor could they understand a teacher's explanation of it (Bruner 38).

While Bruner asserted that the structure of the discipline had to be organized in ways that conformed to the stages of the children's mental development, he did not think the instruction should be tightly controlled. He added that children did not follow the patterns of mental development in any mechanical sense. Some children moved faster than other children. Another group of children moved more slowly. According to Bruner, sometimes, children benefited from attempting lessons that belonged more appropriately to a stage beyond the one they occupied. In this regard, Bruner quoted a teacher from the UICSM who noted that no subject is difficult for any student if the teacher asks the questions that can lead to an understanding of the topic (Bruner 39–40).

Although Bruner placed considerable importance on the structure of a discipline, he could not easily define the structure of any discipline. Nor could he describe the ways in which the scholars in different fields thought. At first, he called for more research on the ways that scholars did their work in hopes that such studies would explain more fully how the subjects should be taught. When he began to organize a curriculum for social studies, however, he abandoned the idea of constructing the instruction around a single discipline. Instead, he tried to draft broad questions that focused the students' thinking in important directions.

As he wrote the *Process of Education,* Bruner did not describe the central concepts or the structure of any discipline. He offered examples of students working with materials in ways that illustrated how the children had acquired some idea. For example, he described a group of sixth graders undertaking a lesson on economic geography trying to decide why cities grew in certain places. They located the cities on a map that contained the physical features of the land but lacked all place names. In another example, he described students who learned about the triangle of trade in colonial America as an example of the fundamental idea that nations must trade to exist. In a third instance, Bruner noted that students reading *Moby Dick* should recognize that Melville offered a study of evil in society. He noted that students could understand literature better when they realized that novels dealt with a limited number of themes. For biology, Bruner claimed the organizing questions focused on discovering the function that something served (Bruner 21–24, 28).

Bruner thought structure was important because he believed that scientists made discoveries through the use of deductive logic. That is, they began thinking about general theories and applied those ideas to particular instances. The physicist who began the PSSC and attended the Woods Hole conference, Jerrold Zacharias, disagreed with Bruner on this point. According to Zacharias, it was a misconception of laypeople that science was a collection of principles. As a result, he thought that laypeople wanted to tie these principles together into some sort of structure. But, added Zacharias, scientists did not start with these principles and apply them to concrete problems. Instead, Zacharias believed that when scientists faced a problem, they made guesses in rather disorganized fashions. Further, Zacharias claimed that such intuitive thinkers could not explain how they achieved an answer. At best, they might employ concrete illustrations or examples to point out some relationships that might exist. Thus, Zacharias recommended that students be encouraged to think inductively by moving from particular examples to general principles (Dow 35).

Bruner acknowledged Zacharias's objections in a chapter devoted to the relation of intuition and analytic thinking. Bruner agreed that intuition was an essential part of any act of analysis. He felt that it was wrong for teachers to discourage students from guessing, but that it was not correct to encourage wild guessing either. Bruner noted that a student could learn methods of guessing such as use of analogy, appeal to symmetry, or visualization of the solution though these limited the role of intuition. He found it ironic that people in fields of mathematics and physics, such as Zacharias, relied on the word *intuition* to explain their methods of work because these fields held solid conceptions of fundamental principles. Nonetheless, he acknowledged that specialists in other fields, such as history, did not have such clear statements of principles, yet scholars in those areas made rough or intuitive judgments. In the end, Bruner called for more research on the subject (Bruner 63–68).

In the early 1960s, several organizations—for instance, the Association for Supervision and Curriculum and Development and the National Educational Association—convened seminars of scholars and educators seeking to determine the structures of the different academic disciplines. In 1963, San Jose State College hosted such a seminar. During the conference, Joseph J. Schwab argued that the different disciplines had distinct structures and that the structure of each discipline varied as a result of scholars' work in accumulating knowledge. Schwab quoted Aristotle to claim that there were different types of academic disciplines. He argued that the physical and biological sciences were theoretical, political science and ethics were practical, and the fine arts and engineering were productive. The result was that the different disciplines organized the subject matters in distinct patterns. Second, among the different disciplines, specialists worked differently. Schwab claimed that biologists assembled small fragments of knowledge while physicists worked to develop comprehensive theories that encompassed vast ranges of material. Third, Schwab added that scholars combined the information they pursued in different ways as they accumulated data. He noted that a biologist might seek the explanation of animal behavior by considering what stimulus provoked it. But Schwab noted that as scientists amassed information, they changed their conceptions, and he argued that, often, the scientists held distinct images of their subject matter at the same time. For example, psychologists who studied human personality portrayed it to be a complex structure made of parts that were similar to the physical organs in a body. At the same time, these psychologists would explain that personalities were the products of the various relationships people formed with other people. Thus, for Schwab, the structure of a discipline was not a simple, fixed way of thinking. He did not think that students should learn one body or structure of any type of knowledge. He wanted the students to see how structures of knowledge change and mature (Schwab 14–30).

Bruner realized the many problems in locating or using the structure of knowledge. Therefore, when he had the chance to construct a program around the structure of a discipline, he looked for the most general propositions he could find. He did not tie his studies to the basic pattern of any specific discipline. In September 1964, Bruner became director of the program to create a social studies curriculum. Entitled "Man: A Course of Study" (MACOS), the curriculum offered a cross-cultural, cross-disciplinary perspective by covering various topics in a comparative manner. The structure that the lessons spiraled around was the following simple but profound question: What makes human beings human? For example, an anthropologist working in Bruner's project sought to devise ways to teach about social organization by asking the students to compare the behavior of individuals who lived in different groups. To make the comparisons as broad as possible, the different groups included Eskimos, urban Americans, and free-ranging baboons. The lessons offered opportunities for students to discover how the groups provided protection and how cooperation among group members helped each of the members overcome problems of scarcity. At the same time, they noted the place of the individual within the group and predicted how the behavior might change in new settings. Thus, the children had the opportunity to recognize the central aspects of any social organization, such as reciprocity and exchange (Dow 72, 83).

According to one of Bruner's assistants, Peter Dow, the fundamental concepts or the structures that Bruner sought to convey were not the structures peculiar to anthropology or to sociology or to history. Dow argued that Bruner wanted MACOS to help the students to draw information from many different fields and to develop deeper understandings of what it meant to be human. In line with Glass's democratic urgings, Bruner wanted the students to learn a vocabulary that explained the quality of humanness and that they could share with people who lacked academic interests (Dow 138).

In searching for more general ways of thinking about society than the practitioner of any discipline would use, Bruner appeared to abandon the search for the structure of a discipline. In response, though, Bruner might reply that he sought the structure of knowledge by searching for fundamental ideas that could organize information from many disciplines and direct it toward matters of serious import to every person. Instead of pointing to the structure of a discipline, Bruner might argue that he wanted the MACOS curriculum to point to the structure of knowledge in general.

How did Bruner and his colleagues use the idea of student interest when they constructed their curriculums?

In his report of the 1959 Woods Hole conference, Bruner noted that the effort to teach children who did not have a natural affection for academic study raised the problem of appealing to their interests. He believed that there were many different ways to attract students' attention. While many teachers used films or games as enrichment, Bruner thought they could play central roles in the instruction. In this regard, he considered all devices such as books, films, and programmed teaching machines as ways to extend students' experiences. They were best used when the entire course was designed in the way that the UICSM, SMSG, and PSSC had designed materials for math and physics. In these cases, films enabled the students to recognize some central idea. The problem was to integrate these experiences (Bruner 84).

Bruner described the experiences of Zacharias's group, PSSC, in which the group tried to produce a set of films that furthered the presentation of the physics course. Thus, the films presented experiments that the students could conduct in their own classroom laboratories. In the films, the researchers used more sophisticated laboratory equipment than the students might have, but the films introduced new topics to the students and directed the students' attention to the central ideas of the course. For example, Bruner noted that a film on work and mechanical energy described the rise in temperature of a nail as a carpenter hammered it. This led to a discussion of thermal energy that was the subject of the next class, and it showed real scientists in action dealing with real problems and deriving excitement and pleasure from their work (Bruner 86–87).

The fact that two cinematographers attended the Woods Hole conference indicates the interest that different groups of academics had in making films. As Bruner noted, Zacharias's group had constructed an entire course of physics around the films. Biologists tried to imitate the physicists. In 1958, the AIBS began to construct a series consisting of 120 films, each thirty minutes in length, to augment high school biology courses in a manner similar to the films made by Zacharias and the PSSC (Grobman 9–11).

The people in Bruner's social studies project, MACOS, shared his interest in films as teaching aids. One example is particularly clear. In 1963, the project commissioned an ethnographer, Asen Balikci, to film the Netsilik Eskimo in a remote village above the Arctic Circle. In making this film, Balikci sought to recreate the ways of life the group followed when the members subsisted as hunter-gathers using stone and bone tools. He found willing actors and began filming scenes in what would have been a summer fishing camp. The result was a series of thirty-minute silent film selections such as *Fishing at Stone Weir* (Dow 60–63).

When Bruner became director of MACOS, he praised Balikci's films, and he liked the fact that the films lacked dialogue, sound effects, and narration. Without the explanations a narrator might give, the children could come up with multiple explanations for the behaviors they observed. This meant that, in class discussions, after seeing some of the films, the children became detectives searching for clues to describe the culture that they had witnessed on the screen. As the students saw more films, they accumulated evidence to test their theories and to work through to their conclusions. Bruner hoped that, with the help of the teacher, the children would come to understand the internal order of the culture, realizing that it was equivalent to yet different from their own (Dow 82).

A weakness in this effort was the inability of teachers to lead the discussions. Bruner noted in 1959 that the teacher was the principal teaching aid in the classroom. Yet, he complained that several surveys had shown that primary and secondary school teachers could not communicate the knowledge of the subject matter and the joy that comes from its mastery. The teachers were not even sufficiently well trained to introduce children to the subjects (Bruner 88).

An obvious answer was that the various projects had to train the teachers. In 1964, when Bruner became director of the MACOS project, he decided that the project should create one course that could work as a model or prototype for other social studies courses. He reduced the emphasis on depending on scholars that he described in *The Process of Education* and invited teachers, writers, and media specialists to work together to create a course that drew on the latest findings of behavioral sciences but presented the material in a variety of ways. During the period of development, the project staff tried their lessons with children and employed evaluators to determine how the materials fared. But by 1966, as the staff completed the materials, they realized that teachers felt uncomfortable when using the course. As a result, MACOS staff constructed a parallel course of over twenty seminars designed to show teachers how they could use the wealth of materials the staff had prepared (Dow 72–73, 101–104, 154–155).

Other groups had found the same problem with teacher preparation. In 1958, after completing work on a text in physics to accompany its films, the PSSC offered summer seminars to help teachers use the new materials. Similarly, when the SMSG tried to write textbooks to introduce new math, they found that teachers knew little mathematics themselves. According to one study more than 25 percent of the mathematics teachers had never studied calculus. As a result, the SMSG wrote a series of study guides for teachers in such areas as set theory, geometry, and algebra (Marsh and Gortner 47–50; Wooten 48–53).

The teachers were important to these projects because the rationale of these curriculum reform efforts was that it was the teachers' task to infect the children with the idea that the structure of a discipline was interesting. For example, the teacher of mathematics had to ignite in the students a feeling of the beauty and the power of the subject. According to Bruner, the teacher inspired interest in the subject in two ways. First, the teacher showed students that they could succeed in doing something that was worthwhile for any person to do. Thus, there was a sort of external reward that came when the students imitated the actions and feelings of the teacher. The second way the teacher inspired interest was that by helping the students understand the structure of the discipline, the students came to feel pleasure as they felt their intellectual abilities grow. This second point held that intellectual mastery was self-rewarding. That is, the students rewarded themselves by experiencing the cumulative power of their learning as one skill led to another. Since Bruner and the other scholars believed that no external praise could match the students' recognition of their own achievements, they hoped that the students would become independent lifelong learners (Bruner 50, 90; Dow 76).

In 1967, Robert B. Davis, professor of mathematics and education at Syracuse University, asserted that the new mathematics was a direct extension of the progressive movement as described by Lawrence Cremin in *The Transformation of the Schools.* In making this assessment, Davis looked at several types of innovations. The SMSG and the UICSM were among these innovations. The reason that he thought the innovations continued the progressive legacy was that they did not depend on textbooks and they encouraged the students to discover important ideas (Davis 4, 51–57).

Davis's judgment is only half correct. While there are several similarities among the innovations made by such groups as UICSM and SMSG, the important difference is the emphasis the scientists placed on the structure of the discipline. These groups had joined with Bruner at Woods Hole to create a movement in curriculum innovation based on the belief that intellectual, theoretical disciplines could be organized and presented in ways that captured students' interest. For the scientists, the subject matter did not have to appear relevant to social problems or life situations to be interesting to the students. In this way, Bruner and his colleagues at Woods Hole challenged part of the basis of progressive educational reform.

As Chapter One shows, the Herbartians challenged Harris on the ground that teachers had to construct lessons in ways that built on the students' interests. From the Herbartians, the progressive educators took two ideas. One idea was that the children came to school with interests. The second idea was that the teacher should present the material in such a way that the children saw the connection between the new lessons and something they found appealing. For this reason, the Herbartians claimed that children naturally found some things pleasurable, such as the act of cooperating with other people. They thought teachers could use the children's interest in people working together to introduce a series of lessons about planting, reaping, threshing, and grinding wheat and to connect the lessons to a larger point about bread.

As other progressive educators followed the Herbartians' pattern, they provided more sophisticated explanations of the relation between children's interests and the curriculum. For example, in 1896, John Dewey built the curriculum of his laboratory school around what he called "occupations." He claimed that he chose occupations that involved the relationship of human beings to their environment, such as working with wood, cooking, or sewing. Since these activities were essential to human life, he believed that they were part of the children's inherited instincts and interested them. By 1915, when he wrote *Democracy and Education,* Dewey pointed out that the word *interest* meant what lies between or connects two distant things. Thus, Dewey concluded that something is of interest to children because it lies between their present powers and their desires or purposes. When Dewey discussed the source of a person's desires, he noted that these could derive from needs such as original instincts. By 1936, when he wrote *Experience and Education,* Dewey noted that what he called the "students' natural impulses" were the starting point of any effective education, but he warned that education could not end with these desires. That is, Dewey thought an education should be something that teaches children to transform their impulses into purposes. For Dewey, having a purpose was the same as forming a plan and it meant that the children changed their impulses or desires as they considered the range of possibilities ahead of them (Dewey, *School* 132–137; Dewey, *Democracy* 107–108, 127; Dewey, *Experience* 65–68).

By the time of the Great Depression, progressive educators dropped the view that children's impulses derived from their inherited characteristics, but the progressives continued to think that teachers should begin curriculum planning by determining children's interests. For example, as described in Chapter Six, in 1938, the Progressive Education Association established the Commission on the Secondary School Curriculum as part of the Eight-Year Study. The commission report claimed that children developed their interests from their interactions with their environments. As a result, the commission urged teachers to learn about the past experiences of children and to adapt the lessons in ways leading the children to form new desires.

When Ralph Tyler served as director of evaluation for the Eight-Year Study, he developed his ideas of how to form curriculum. As pointed out in Chapter Six, Tyler's book, *Basic Principles of Curriculum and Instruction,* published in 1949, became an important guide for teachers. According to Tyler, no single source of information provided the basis for decisions about educational objectives. Tyler defined education as changing the students' behavior. Consequently, he began with studies of students to determine what they needed to change. He noted that the studies could reveal the children's interests, and they could reveal what the community needed them to do. Tyler thought it was important for the teacher to build lessons on the students' interests because the students would want to participate actively in them (Tyler, *Basic* 5–10).

Although Tyler recommended consulting subject matter specialists, he warned that these should not dominate the curriculum. In fact, Tyler feared that subject matter specialists wanted to shape the curriculum for students who would pursue advanced studies in college. But Tyler approved of some reports that came from groups such as the National Council of English Teachers in the 1940s. He noted that their recommendations aimed at helping students who would not take any advanced studies, and he was gratified to find these reports offered suggestions regarding the functions the subject served and the contributions the subject could make to life in general (Tyler, *Basic* 25–28).

By 1959, none of the groups of scholars that revised the science and math curriculums worked in the fashion recommended by Tyler. They sent a group of academics to a central location for a few weeks during the summer. These scholars reviewed existing texts in their areas, and they made suggestions to revise them. They tested the materials with teachers in various centers and revised the texts and the films according to the reports they received.

While the Tyler rationale would have required the scholars who wrote the new curriculums to determine how their plans would serve the specific needs of the students or the particular social needs of the community, the scholars did not follow this model in their team meetings. In short period of time and under considerable pressure, they tried to make materials that presented the central ideas of the subject areas in ways that challenged the superior students and remained accessible to less able students. They believed that if they succeeded in doing this, they would satisfy the children's intellectual needs. Further, they thought the materials would fulfill the social need to affirm democracy because the materials aimed to spread the basic understandings of science throughout the citizenry. Not surprisingly, when the new curriculums appeared, Tyler complained that the subject matter specialists had selected the objectives without thinking about the needs or the interests of the children and they sought to deliver the learning rather than to involve the learner in an active process (Tyler, "Rationale Reconsidered" 395–396).

While Tyler's complaint is incorrect, the basis of his accusation arises from his unwill-ingness to believe that the structure of any subject matter could be presented in interesting ways to students. On the other hand, Bruner made theoretical subject matter more important than an inventory of students' interests or of community needs. Following Bruner's rationale, subject area specialists could construct curriculums without considering the ways that the les-sons helped children do other things.

Thus, the Herbartians, Dewey and Tyler conceived of interests as things the children brought to school while Bruner and his colleagues thought of interests as things that could be placed into a lesson. Despite this difference, the progressives and the scientists shared the view that lessons should capture the interests of the students and that they should provide some external reward by developing a set of skills that would be socially useful.

What happened to the effort to design new curriculums?

Three forces combined to end the academicians' efforts to revise the curriculums. First, they encountered serious criticisms from members of their own disciplines. Second, public atten-tion turned away from the need to engage in such programs to defend national security. Third, the programs suffered from extensive political controversies.

First, as the various writing groups worked on the innovations, some academicians criti-cized the projects. For example, in 1961, as the SMSG released their texts for elementary and secondary schools, a well-publicized dispute began what Benjamin Demott called the "math wars." Demott claimed that Morris Kline made four major complaints against the SMSG. First, Kline rejected the idea that a new orientation had to replace the old mathematics. Second, Kline complained that the new topics, such as symbolic logic, Boolean algebra, and set theory, had few scientific or practical applications. Third, Kline argued that the new topics did not teach the central ideas of the field because the students could master them without learning to add or subtract numbers. Fourth, Kline claimed the new math ignored students' interests be-cause it offered few social or practical applications and the texts' concentration on abstract reasoning made them appealing only to an esoteric group (Demott 58–59).

In 1962, Kline and a group of seventy-four university mathematicians signed a petition protesting the movement toward a new mathematics. Written as a set of principles to be fol-lowed in any revision, the document was actually a list of seven criticisms of the work of the SMSG in drafting and publishing new texts. First, the petition claimed that mathematics could not be taught as a discipline without reference to the particular needs of different students. The signers of the petition disliked the fact that the SMSG texts tried to present mathematics as an abstract method of thinking. Second, the petition claimed that students required the practice that applied or social mathematics offered, and the SMSG texts sought to reduce the use of practical applications. Third, the petition asserted that mathematics could not be presented without reference to other sciences. Fourth, the petition criticized the deductive approach found in the texts by claiming that most mathematicians actually used inductive reasoning in which they worked from particular concrete examples to general rules. Fifth, the protesting mathematicians wanted more historical coverage of the development of mathematics. Sixth, while the protestors agreed that mathematics teaching lagged behind modern needs, they be-lieved that traditional areas, such as algebra, trigonometry, and calculus, remained essential and all had to be taught. Seventh, the protestors complained that the texts could not depend on repeating abstract concepts. They had to apply these concepts to concrete situations for the students to grasp them (Kline 112–118).

In 1973, Kline extended his criticisms when he published his book, *Why Johnny Can't Add: The Failure of New Math.* Robert W. Hayden cast doubt on the reasonableness of Kline's complaints. He claimed that many of Kline's complaints were vague, based on distorted facts, and resulted from overgeneralizations. Hayden accused Kline of bias by calling Kline an applied mathematician who had never been involved in elementary or secondary education (Hayden 165, 214).

Ironically, though, when Hayden quoted a critic whom he believed to be most competent—Howard F. Fehr, a professor of mathematics education at Columbia University—the criticisms were similar. That is, Fehr complained that the new math put too much emphasis on verbal formulations and that the texts lacked opportunities to practice with concrete objects. Fehr added that several elements of the new mathematics had no place in the elementary school. These elements included using set theory, teaching arithmetic in bases other than ten, and making distinctions between numbers and numerals. Kline had made these same comments (Hayden 213–214; Kline 60–61, 80–83).

The second force that conspired to end the academicians' efforts to create new curriculums was that the concern for military dominance subsided. By 1 February 1958, the United States successfully launched a satellite into space, and Eisenhower announced that he had formed a group of scientists to begin planning travel to the moon. Instead, as Chapter Nine explains, people became concerned for children living in poverty. By 1965, the programs offered under the NDEA were absorbed into the Elementary and Secondary Education Act (Michael 249–250).

These changes in public opinion caused mathematics teachers to jump from rags to riches, according to Eugene Smith, president of the National Council of Teachers of Mathematics. Speaking to his association in 1973, Smith recalled that, in 1958, mathematics teachers had more federal money available to them than they knew how to use. In 1973, the U.S. Congress reduced the NSF budget. This forced NSF to end its support of in-service programs, academic year programs, and summer institutes that provided many of the new curriculums. As a result, Smith complained that the money disappeared by the time the mathematics teachers knew how to use it (Smith 568).

The third force that hurt the NSF programs was that they suffered from public distrust. Although there were several reasons why the U.S. Congress began to cut funds for education, one of them was that critics complained that the federal subsidies were upsetting the traditional organization of American education. These complaints came out most clearly in the debates about the social studies programs, MACOS.

By 1970, conservative critics complained that MACOS threatened traditional values. In this case, the conservatives attacked what Bruner and his colleagues believed to be the strength of the program. Although many complaints were exaggerated, the conservatives disliked the fact that Bruner tried to have the students compare cultures, find similarities among social practices, and avoid making judgments about the cultures. While Bruner thought the students had to remain tolerant of particular cultural characteristics if they were to locate the common humanity that people shared, conservative critics argued that Bruner was showing children that primitive cultures were as good as civilized cultures. Thus, while Bruner and his critics wanted the schools to produce children who upheld what was best about society, they wanted to do this in different ways. Bruner wanted the students to learn to suspend judgments, to hold relativistic stances, and to think deeply about issues. The conservative critics thought the schools should reinforce the beliefs of the parents (Dow 178–187).

The controversy reached the U.S. Congress in 1975 when Congressman John B. Conlan of Arizona attacked the proposed NSF budget on the grounds that MACOS influenced children's attitudes away from the values of their parents. Other conservative politicians supported Conlan's attack although they did not share the antagonism toward MACOS. Senators such as Barry Goldwater, Jr. disapproved of NSF funding projects to print texts because those texts competed with books published by private companies. Thus, for Goldwater, the NSF disturbed the traditional arrangements of schoolbook publishing. After considerable controversy, the U.S. Congress approved the budget for NSF, but the bill included an amendment demanding that the NSF prove how funded proposals would foster the national interest (Dow 200–201, 214–215).

Conservative attacks against NSF continued until Ronald Reagan took office as president. His administration exerted such pressure that the U.S. Congress voted to close the educational programs offered by the NSF except the graduate university fellowship programs (Dow 240–241).

In what ways were the new curriculums similar to and different from the reforms the progressive and the traditional educators attempted?

In the aftermath of the Sputnik crisis, politicians turned to academics to refashion the curriculums and to improve instruction in science and mathematics. Not surprisingly, many politicians conceived of serving the nation's needs in different ways than did the academics. While many politicians wanted schools to select and train a few excellent scientists, the academics wanted to spread the ability to think scientifically to all students. In a short time, the federal government supported both concepts. To some extent, the scholars working on the curriculum projects reversed the traditions of school reform. That is, instead of trying to locate what interests or needs the children had, they sought to construct intellectually honest lessons in ways that would inspire the students to take an interest in the lessons and to acquire the qualities of mind that would be socially useful. Thus, an important idea of the scientists was that subject matter well constructed and well presented could fascinate children. Since this notion reversed the progressive ideal, it was revolutionary.

As groups of scientists and academics began to work on the new curriculum projects, complaints appeared from all directions. Academics complained that the materials were badly designed. Public opinion drifted away for supporting endeavors aimed at academic excellence. Progressives argued the new curriculums ignored student needs and interests. And conservatives complained that the federal support disturbed traditional educational arrangements.

In several ways, the conservative objections to programs such as MACOS resembled the complaints that Harold Rugg, Charles Beard, and George Counts suffered when they advanced social reconstructionism in the 1930s. As Chapter Five describes, Rugg, Beard, and Counts thought the Great Depression illustrated the need for social studies programs to prepare the children to participate in social engineering. Although Rugg, Beard, and Counts thought they were advancing traditional American values of independence and community control, conservatives claimed the social reconstructionists opposed free enterprise.

In a similar manner, conservatives in the 1970s objected to the comparisons of cultures that MACOS offered, on the grounds that Bruner wanted to discredit traditional American values. Although the MACOS materials avoided the suggestion that cultures evolved and they resisted any implication that civilization was preferable to savagery, this was not a value-free orientation. Instead, it holds that all cultures provide ways to maintain themselves, and it implies that the cultures and the practices of the different peoples are equally good and bad. Although Bruner believed that such an orientation would enable students to recognize what was best and what was worst about their society, the conservatives disagreed. They wanted a view closer to the notion of indoctrination that Counts had advanced in the 1930s.

The point of this discussion is not whether Bruner, the progressives, or the conservatives were right or wrong. Student interest is difficult to determine. Further, the relativism MACOS offered threatened typical understandings of traditional values. The progressive educators, such as Tyler, appeared to overlook how completely Bruner and his colleagues depended on student interests, and conservative critics seemed to overlook the way the new curriculums depended on such traditional values as independent thought, impartial evaluation, and fair representation.

While commentators such as Peter Dow complained that conservative politicians defeated MACOS supporters, the results of the controversy were not that clear. Although the new texts and the films disappeared from schools and libraries, the contributions of the writing and curriculum teams did not. For example, according to Robert Hayden, many of the changes suggested by the SMSG remained in elementary school mathematics texts through the 1980s, but the texts supplemented the theoretical developments with increased use of manipulation of concrete objects. Thus, he believed that the new math fused with the progressive tradition that had preceded it (Hayden 240–241).

In a similar manner, criticism of MACOS did not end the effort of social studies teachers to ask students to think about what makes societies different. In the spirit of Bruner, as multicultural education became popular through the 1980s, social studies teachers tried to have their students understand the functional similarities among cultures, and they remained on guard against value judgments that could lead students to develop xenophobic tendencies.

It may be that conservative critics attacked the new programs because the content of the curriculums differed considerably from what traditional schools offered. For example, Bruner wanted children to understand human society in ways that roughly conformed to the model Marshal and Goetz had urged during the Great Depression. This was an effort described in Chapter Five that sought to understand the processes that all societies share. Like Marshall and Goetz, Bruner wanted the children to learn about these processes so they could participate in social change. It should not be surprising that Bruner would meet the same criticisms as Marshall and Goetz did. Conservatives complained the reformers wanted to impose liberal values on the children.

On the other hand, the new programs had what might be called staying power because they were built on the assumptions that other groups of educational reformers shared. For example, the scholars who created the new curriculums seemed to adopt the ideas the progressive educators had about building on students' interests. The difference was the scientists constructed a different way of thinking about the ways that students developed and held those interests. Similarly, the new curriculums sought to enhance democracy by ensuring that all people could understand the way the technological society moved and changed. Since these are traditional American values, the scholars who designed such programs as new physics and new math shared this orientation with their conservative critics.

Summary

In 1950, the U.S. Congress created the National Science Foundation (NSF) to promote scientific research in universities throughout the United States. After the Soviet Union launched a satellite into space, the NSF found itself supporting programs that contradicted the aims of the National Defense Education Act (NDEA). As described in Chapter Seven, the NDEA sought to aid elementary and secondary schools to train an elite group of future scientists who could improve the military. On the other hand, the NSF promoted efforts to develop curriculums in physics, mathematics, biology, chemistry, and social studies that tried to teach students of different abilities to follow the same types of thinking used by scholars in the academic disciplines. Unfortunately, the scientists could not agree as to how scholars thought. Further, although the scholars wanted to utilize the interests of the children, they thought that academic lessons could be made to be interesting. This turned around the traditional and progressive idea of student interest. That is, progressive educators such as those who conducted the Eight-Year Study believed children brought their interests to school and teachers should show the students how academic subjects could help the students achieve their own goals. The scholars, however, thought that films and other devices could inspire the students to take an interest in academics. Thus, although all educators shared assumptions about the role of interest, the benefits of meeting student needs, and the requirement to advance democracy, progressive and traditional educators joined in opposing the advocates of the new curriculums because the new curriculums assigned a different role to subject matters. The scholars who designed the new curriculums believed that the subject matters could be designed in some way that the students became intelligent independent thinkers and thereby enabled the school to improve the democratic society. The progressive and the traditional critics thought the satisfaction of the students' needs and the reinforcement of the value of democracy should be the primary aims of the schools. They thought of the subject matters as tools to reach those goals. As a result, although the conflicts were real, the competing parties shared views that placed a primary importance on helping children become responsible citizens.

PART V

CHANGING SCHOOLS BY PROTECTING STUDENTS' RIGHTS, 1964–1981

In the 1960s, the Civil Rights movement changed the ways that educators thought about curriculums. As the previous chapters illustrate, from 1890 until 1964, different groups of educators assumed that teachers should meet students' needs. After the March on Washington and the resulting federal legislation, educators claimed that teachers should affirm students' rights. Although educators could not agree what those rights were nor how teachers should affirm them, they held the affirmation of those rights to be essential. In this way, the more contemporary educators shared an assumption in ways similar to ways the educators in the first half of the century had agreed that teachers should meet students' needs though they disagreed about the ways to accomplish this end.

In this section, Chapter Nine discusses the efforts to establish the right of African Americans to equal education and the related efforts to provide equal education to children from low-income families. To achieve these goals, the U.S. Congress passed the U.S. Civil Rights Act of 1964 and the Elementary and Secondary Education Act of 1965 (ESEA). Although different, these laws reinforced each other. On the one hand, Title VI of the Civil Rights Act gave the federal government the authority to require local school officials to desegregate the schools and ESEA offered about $1 billion to aid in the education of children from low-income families. Neither of these efforts enjoyed significant success. By the 1990s, federal courts began releasing most public school districts from desegregation plans. Furthermore, studies showed that compensatory education did not enhance the education of children from low-income families. Nonetheless, the successes that the NAACP and the SCLC enjoyed caused the advocates of other groups of children to imitate their strategies and seek to establish for their constituents the right to appropriate educations.

Chapter Ten shows how two other groups imitated the strategies of the Civil Rights movement. First, advocates for children with disabilities sought to establish that the children had the right to an equal education. As a result, they sued in federal courts and used the resulting decisions to shape legislation requiring schools to adopt a set of procedures and rewarded the schools for following those recommendations. Second, advocates for children with limited English abilities tried to do the same thing, but they were less successful. Although these advocates wanted schools to meet the children's special needs, they adopted a legalistic model that contradicted the progressive ideal of serving the democratic ethos. In the case of the special educators, the model was overly open-ended. In the case of the bilingual educators, critics complained that the ideal of pluralism threatened social harmony.

CHAPTER NINE

AFFIRMING STUDENTS' RIGHTS THROUGH RACIAL INTEGRATION AND COMPENSATORY EDUCATION, 1963–1981

On 17 May 1954, Chief Justice Warren delivered the opinion of the U.S. Supreme Court in the case of *Brown v. Board of Education of Topeka.* In a short, clear statement, Warren noted this decision involved the question of whether African American children could enter public schools designated for whites. Warren pointed out that this decision depended on an interpretation of the Fourteenth Amendment of the U.S. Constitution that forbade any state from making laws that restricted the privileges of citizens or eliminated the protection they should receive without due process of law (Kluger 47, 779–780).

Warren acknowledged that, in the 1896 decision, *Plessy v. Ferguson,* the U.S. Supreme Court had decided state governments could prohibit white and black people from sitting together in public transportation. He added, however, that the justices had never considered whether states could segregate black students in public education. In fact, in subsequent cases, such as *Sweatt v. Painter* in 1950, the justices had declared that separate facilities restricted the benefits available to black graduate students (Kluger 780–781).

In the *Brown* case, Warren quoted a lower court decision acknowledging that segregation with the sanction of law retarded the educational and mental development of African American youths. Thus, it appeared that separating black high school students from white students of their same age caused the black students to feel inferior, and he noted that "modern authorities" supported this finding. Thus, Warren concluded, "separate educational facilities are unequal" (Kluger 782).

Shortly after the decision became public, scholars warned that Justice Warren had made a mistake connecting the end of segregation to the harm that segregation caused to African Americans. The critics complained that if social psychology proved that segregation did not cause harm, the decision might be undone. If the decision had simply asserted that the U.S. Constitution demands equality before the law, the decision would have been stronger because the effects would not have been central (tenBroek 23–24).

Many African Americans greeted the *Brown* decision with caution though it represented a significant accomplishment in the NAACP's legal campaign against racial segregation. For example, in cities such as Memphis, Tennessee, editorials in African American newspapers wondered if the decision would change things. The skepticism turned out to be warranted. In 1963, Martin Luther King, Jr. complained that although the decision had been made nine years earlier, only 9 percent of the black students in the South attended racially integrated schools (Kluger 710).

To speed up the process, King called on people to participate in a public, peaceful demonstration against segregation in Birmingham, Alabama. He selected Birmingham because city officials, such as the Commissioner of Public Safety, Eugene "Bill" Connor, resisted any form of racial integration and had made the city a symbol of white supremacy. Second, King wanted the demonstration to take place in April 1963 because the Easter season was the second biggest shopping season in the city and a demonstration would hurt local business people. Unfortunately, Birmingham had a reputation of intimidating civil rights activists. From 1957 to January 1963, segregationists bombed seventeen Negro churches and homes of civil rights leaders in the city, yet police never convicted anyone for these bombings. As a result, King realized the demonstrators faced the threat of violence. It came as he had expected. On 4 May 1963, newspapers and televisions carried images of Birmingham police officers clubbing prostrate African American women. Pictures showed vicious police dogs attacking young children and police sweeping people down streets with the water from high-pressure fire hoses (King 18, 48–55, 100).

In King's eyes, when the police resorted to violence, they weakened their position. He claimed that the demonstrators defeated their opponents by remaining nonviolent and absorbing the abuse. Although many protestors suffered, King believed that the Birmingham officials lost their spirit during the contest. For example, at one point, Conner ordered his men to turn their fire hoses on a group of African American men and women who were on their knees praying, but the police refused. More important to King, a tide of moral indignation swept the nation (King 100).

On 7 May 1963, President John Kennedy used his press conference to describe the problems in Birmingham and to emphasize that the opposing sides had to come to an agreement. Three days later, the city leaders and King's group accepted a pact that promised to bring desegregation to the southern city (King 101–105).

After intervening in the Birmingham crisis, Kennedy sought a wider solution. On 12 June 1963, he addressed the nation and called for legislation to strengthen the role of the federal government in the protection of the rights of African Americans. A week later, his administration sent a version of the 1964 U.S. Civil Rights Act to Congress. It came to the floor of the House shortly before his assassination. In the tempestuous days following Kennedy's death, President Lyndon Johnson promised that he would ensure the passage of the civil rights bill (Orfield, *Reconstruction* 34–35, 39).

Although opponents tied up the U.S. Senate for more than thirteen weeks in a filibuster, the Civil Rights Act passed almost unchanged. One point, Title VI, escaped most people's notice as they considered the larger bill. Title VI held that no person could be excluded from any program receiving federal financial assistance. Although one senator, Albert Gore from Tennessee, father of a future vice president, expressed the fear that this particular title would give the administration excessive power, most senators went along with Senator Hubert Humphrey who advanced the administration's contention that the title was a moderate requirement to prevent the federal government from supporting programs that contradicted the decision of the U.S. Supreme Court (Orfield, *Reconstruction* 41, 44).

On 2 July 1964, Johnson signed the U.S. Civil Rights Act. In January 1965, the Office of Education sent out warnings that no federal funds would be available until the commissioner of education had determined that local school districts complied with Title VI. Despite the confusion in federal offices with the rush to organize information and to set guidelines, the results were dramatic. For as long as Title VI was enforced, it had a powerful effect. In 1964, when the law passed, 2 percent of the black students in the South attended majority white schools. By 1986, the high point for desegregation, about 44 percent of the black students in the South attended majority white schools. Unfortunately, after 1986, the U.S. Supreme Court justices allowed schools to end desegregation programs, and segregation rose (Orfield, "The Act" 116–118).

The 1964 U.S. Civil Rights Act became part of a complicated legislative effort. During his campaign for election in 1964, Johnson claimed that improved education was essential for the "Great Society." Winning a landslide victory, Johnson set task forces to work on programs that would fulfill his promises. On 11 April 1965, he signed the U.S. Elementary and Secondary Education Act (ESEA), which promised more than $1 billion of special aid for schools with children from low-income families. As a result of this unprecedented infusion of federal monies into local school districts, Title VI of the 1964 U.S. Civil Rights Act became more than a means of punishment; it was a condition for progress (Bailey and Mosher 39–41; Orfield, *Reconstruction* 94).

For what reasons did the federal government initiate programs to improve schools?

According to Stephen K. Bailey and Edith K. Mosher, ESEA was successful in bringing federal support to public schools because it offered to reduce the problems of poverty. These authors contend that the *Brown* decision may not have increased school integration, but it made people aware of the problems of poverty that race discrimination reinforced. Thus, the court decision offered reasons that supporters of federal aid to public education could use to nullify the long-standing opposition voiced by Southern Democrats, conservative Republicans, and Catholic educators (Bailey and Mosher 8–9, 23).

In the 1960s, most authors considered African Americans to be the group who suffered from "educational deprivation." For example, in 1961, James Conant published his book, *Slums and Suburbs,* acknowledging that many African Americans lived in difficult conditions in large cities. He claimed they accepted low-paying jobs because they could find no other openings. Worse, Conant believed that the lack of educational experiences among these families caused them to have different attitudes about schools, and these views limited the chances of educators' succeeding with their children. Thus, Conant recommended that school people in urban situations do things such as offer classes for parents of school children to try to alter the parents' attitudes about schools (Conant, *Slums* 1–3, 60–61).

At the time, Conant was an influential public figure. As noted in earlier chapters, he had been president of Harvard University. Since 1944, he had been involved in national efforts to improve elementary and secondary education. And, in 1957, President Dwight D. Eisenhower had incorporated many of Conant's ideas into his recommendations for the National Defense Education Act. Thus, educators were apt to accept Conant's thoughts about how to improve schools in the cities.

Another influential author, Frank Riessman, a psychologist, noted that most educators considered black urban youths to be culturally deprived. Although he argued that this term was misleading because he believed these children had a unique culture, he used it because it was the then current term. In describing the culturally deprived children, Riessman noted that these children felt alienated from the wider culture, they disliked the ambitions that they attributed to middle-class people, and they preferred the sense of security that they derived from their friends and family. Riessman added that culturally deprived children were anti-intellectual, preferring to think by manipulating objects rather than using language (Riessman 3–30).

Many federal officials accepted Riessman's explanation of the problems of cultural deprivation, and they spread his ideas widely. For example, in May 1962, the U.S. Office of Education held a conference about teaching children who were culturally disadvantaged. Organized in response to Conant's report about the problems facing urban youth, the conference began with a presentation by Riessman, who had become head of Mobilization for Youth. Riessman quoted extensively from his book about the cultural differences of disadvantaged youth (Conference on Teaching 1–3).

In 1962, the surprising success of Michael Harrington's book, *The Other America,* made many people aware of the possibility that low-income people shared what he called "a culture of poverty." Although Harrington based his theme on the idea that poor people held to attitudes and values different from those found among affluent people, he did not coin the phrase, *a culture of poverty.* He borrowed the term from Oscar Lewis probably because it was a catchy way to demonstrate the ways that capitalism harmed lower-class people (Rigdon 170, 244).

The term offered policy makers several advantages. It suggested the solution to poverty was some form of compensatory education that corrected the deficits from which the children were said to suffer, and thereby, it avoided the controversial issue of racial integration. In fact, neither Conant nor Riessman recommended integration as a remedy for the educational disadvantages these children suffered. For example, Conant claimed that he opposed any form of racial segregation, but he urged reformers to improve urban schools by adapting their programs to the unique family situations found in the slums. He complained that when educators sought racially mixed schools, their actions implied that black schools were inferior because of the race of the students and this undermined the efforts to improve urban schools. On the other hand, Riessman remained silent on the issue of racial integration. He noted that segregation seemed to prevent African American youths from aspiring to pursue advanced education. The solution he recommended was for teachers in urban schools to recognize and to compensate for the cultural deficits of the children (Conant 29–32; Riessman 19–21).

In addition to avoiding the question of racial integration, the idea of cultural deprivation or the related concept of a culture of poverty gave federal officials a direction in which to form several related programs. These ideas offered a rationale for these programs that appealed to people's sense of justice. For example, writing in 1964, Senator Hubert H. Humphrey explained why Americans had to join in the War on Poverty that President Johnson had recently announced. Humphrey quoted Harrington to show that poor people had attitudes such as an unwillingness to plan ahead, a lack of trust in other people, and a tendency to be depressed. Humphrey argued that these attitudes condemned poor people to remain in poverty. According to Humphrey, the answer was not to give poor people welfare or direct subsidies but to provide the children with the appropriate education to learn to hold well-paying jobs. As a result, Humphrey praised Johnson's effort to create the Jobs Corps, and he complimented such school programs as Higher Horizons, which introduced adolescents to employment opportunities. Nonetheless, Humphrey noted that the problems of poverty were too great for local school districts to solve. Although he believed that the effort required large amounts of federal funds, he claimed that the country was morally bound to expend these funds and make this effort. Paraphrasing Johnson, Humphrey wrote that since the country had the power to offer everyone full participation in society, every citizen had the duty to make sure that it happened (Humphrey 20–30, 131–141).

Not only politicians affirmed the right of low-income people to enjoy the material comforts available to other people, but also labor unions agreed that this War on Poverty was morally necessary. For example, in 1964, the United Auto Workers financed a study by the Conference on Economic Progress as an illustration of the union's commitment to end poverty. In that study, the conference's chairperson, Leon H. Keyserling, noted that the problems of poverty required federal intervention because they were too large for any local or small-scale effort to control. While Keyserling was convinced that the reduction of poverty would improve life for all people, he contended that Americans had to enlist in the war on poverty because the Golden Rule required it (Keyserling 14–15).

Some business organizations opposed the effort as costly and counterproductive. For example, in 1964, the National Association of Manufacturers urged senators not to approve the Economic Opportunity Act on the grounds that it would resurrect impractical, costly, and discredited welfare programs. In the same year, the U.S. Chamber of Commerce criticized the Jobs Corps and the Neighborhood Youth Corps for encouraging students to drop out of school so they could collect wages while pursuing vocational training (Lander 15, 32).

In general, though, most supporters of the War on Poverty argued that children from low-income families had the right to an education that changed their outlooks, enabled them to function successfully in schools, and permitted them to take their places in mainstream society. Although these supporters claimed the culturally deprived children suffered from the same set of deficits that Riessman and Humphrey had listed, the programs ESEA supported in 1965–66 did not fit any organized approach to change the personalities of children from low-income families. During that academic year, most Title I funds went to provide individual attention for what were called "deprived children." School districts hired teacher aides or formed teams of specialists to work on specific needs of each student. Many districts offered cultural enrichment activities such as visits to zoos or tours of museums. In 1966, the National Advisory Council on the Education of Disadvantaged Children made a survey of the summer programs that ESEA funded. The consultants found fragmented efforts at remediation and vaguely directed enrichment programs instead of strategically planned comprehensive efforts (Subcommittee on Education 917–920; National Advisory Council on the Education of Disadvantaged Children 3–9).

Perhaps the most well known of the federal efforts to change the personalities of children called "disadvantaged" was Project Head Start. Unlike ESEA, Project Head Start was not the result of legislation that a planning task force submitted to Congress. One person, Sargent Shriver, created and funded the program. According to Shriver, he did this because, as director of the Office of Economic Opportunity, he controlled a large budget, he was in charge of programs such as Job Corps and Neighborhood Youth Corps that catered to adolescents, and he thought he should do something for young children. While helping his wife at the Joseph P. Kennedy, Jr. Foundation, he learned about Susan Gray and her research trying to raise the IQs of young children suffering from mental retardation. Gray's idea was that appropriate interventions made when the children were very young could raise their IQ scores. Thinking that he could offer something similar for children of low-income families, Shriver began to talk with other psychologists. In December 1964, he formed a committee chaired by Dr. Robert Cooke from the Kennedy Foundation and made plans to start an experimental project in the summer of 1965 (Shriver 50–55).

Although Project Head Start included early education, it sought to improve children's health, to employ family members, and to feed children. Since it covered several aspects of child and family life, it made some sense for the Office of Economic Opportunity to sponsor Head Start rather than the U.S. Office of Education. In keeping with this so-called ecological approach to the problems of poverty, the original plan had five components. First, the children received periodic medical examinations and immunizations. Second, the children had some form of educational experience that included the use of language in ways that encouraged the enhancement of self-esteem. Third, parents were involved in the program as aides, cooks, or storytellers. Fourth, each day, the program gave the children one hot meal and one snack to improve nutrition. Finally, the program offered family counseling or other mental health assistance (Brain 74–75).

In short, the federal government sponsored a multitude of programs designed to affirm the right of children from low-income families to appropriate education. With such programs, the federal government began a tradition of supporting local school programs. Although many conservative politicians tried to end the federal involvement in education, they seemed unable to overcome the argument that children from low-income families have the right to such special attention. This assumption protected the programs because the sponsors of a wide variety of otherwise contradictory initiatives based their efforts on this desire to fulfill what Humphrey called "the Golden Rule."

What did studies reveal about the effectiveness of the compensatory programs in raising academic achievement of youths from low-income families?

In approving the 1964 Civil Rights Act, Congress requested a survey of the availability of educational opportunities for minority students in the United States, and the U.S. Office of Education commissioned James Coleman to conduct it. Although critics complained about Coleman's techniques, his was the first major attempt to use sophisticated social science to evaluate education across the country. On completion, Coleman found that most African American students attended schools with other African American students wherever high concentrations of African Americans could be found, such as in the South and in urban centers in the North, the Midwest, and the West. Further, he noted that the programs, the teachers, and the materials in these segregated, black schools were inferior to those found in the white schools (Bailey and Mosher 177–178; Coleman et al., *Equality* 3–20).

Coleman offered an innovation in his survey by seeking information about results, such as student achievement, as well as asking questions about resources, such as the programs, the teachers, and the materials. In this way, he could compare what he called the outcomes, student achievement, to what he called the inputs, the resources. Since he had not been asked to do this, he claimed that he did not spend much time on this comparison. He described the comparison in one section of one chapter in the more than 700 pages in the report. Yet, he argued that by including this section, he had changed the nature of the debate about compensatory education. Instead of simply looking at whether the educational resources were equivalent, people wanted to know if the materials were effective (Coleman, "Evaluation" 150).

Coleman found an unexpected correlation when he compared resources and student achievement. According to his analysis, the most important factors influencing student achievement were the educational backgrounds and the aspirations of the members of the students' peer groups. This meant that, if African American students from low-income families went to school with other low-aspiring students, their academic performance was poor. If they attended school with more upwardly mobile middle-class children, their performance improved (Coleman et al., *Equality* 22).

Although Coleman qualified this finding in many ways, it was as eloquent testimony for racial integration as any statistician could offer. Coleman noted that this effect was true for African American students more than for white or for Asian students. Thus, if a white student from a family that supported education attended a school with low-aspiring youngsters, his or her academic achievement would not suffer. Further, it appeared that more than any other group, African American students from low-income families profited from well-qualified teachers (Coleman et al., *Equality* 3–20).

In line with Coleman's conclusion that racial integration was the most effective way to boost the academic achievement of African American youths from low-income families, the U.S. Commission on Civil Rights endorsed this approach in 1967. Comparing the academic achievement of African American children in several Title I programs to the academic success of African American children in racially integrated schools without such programs, the commission found that, in almost every instance, the children in integrated settings outperformed the children in segregated schools (U.S. Commission on Civil Rights, *Racial Isolation* 205).

Coleman's findings did more than describe an important benefit of racial integration; they called into question the educational assumptions of the War on Poverty. The rationale of Title I of ESEA and of Project Head Start had been that better schools, improved curriculums, and well-trained teachers would break the circle of poverty, but, Coleman wrote, "it appears that differences between schools account for only a small fraction of differences in pupil achievement." Although the statement was vague and unclear, it meant that improving the condition of schools, hiring good teachers, and changing the curriculums would not improve the achievement of students from low-income families. This was so surprising that scholars pursued the possibility that academic intervention could not break the cycle of poverty (Coleman et al., *Equality* 22).

During the 1966–1967 academic year, the Carnegie Corporation sponsored a faculty seminar at Harvard University to evaluate the so-called Coleman report. They soon received other information that claimed schools could not change the academic performance of low-income children.

In 1968, the first nationwide evaluation of Head Start reported that academic enrichment had failed to improve the school performance of the young children. After comparing the performance of almost 4,000 children, the researchers found that Head Start had not improved school cognitive performance. In first grade, the children who had been in the Head Start programs scored better on the standardized tests than did their age mates who were also from low-income families but had not attended Head Start programs. Unfortunately, the Head Start children soon lost their advantage. After that first year, the Head Start children did not score higher (Cicirelli 235–243).

Critics complained that this evaluation of Head Start was unfair for a variety of reasons, and some subsequent, carefully focused studies found some compensatory education programs to be successful. To further the understanding of remedial education, several educators, economists, and statisticians reanalyzed Coleman's data and combined it with the results of several other studies. In 1972, Christopher Jencks and several coauthors released the book, *Inequality,* extending Jencks's contribution to the Harvard seminar and summarizing the research efforts of eight different scholars.

Jencks and his colleagues noted that Americans considered equality as a basic social value, and that most of the reforms of the 1960s had been predicated on the notion that children had the right to equal opportunities. The authors made three significant findings from their studies that called these efforts into question. First, they argued that reformers overstated the idea of the cycle of poverty. Not only did the authors find a surprising amount of economic mobility from one generation to the next, but also they noted that family traits did not seem to be the important influence. There was as much economic inequality among members of the same families as appeared in the society as a whole. Second, though reformers had asserted that economic success depended on academic abilities or competence on the job, the authors found this was not the case. There was as much economic inequality among people with identical academic test scores as in the general public. To the authors, economic success appeared to be related to personality traits and luck rather than to knowledge, skills, or effort. Third, Jencks and his colleagues could not find evidence that school reform would improve cognitive inequality as measured by standardized tests. According to the authors, neither school resources nor segregation influenced students' test scores or educational achievements in appreciable amounts (Jencks et al. 3–9, 110).

Believing that society should provide the greatest good for the greatest number, Jencks and his colleagues argued that the reasonable way to end poverty was to increase the taxes of wealthy families and provide income supplements to low-income families. Jencks and his coauthors argued that this was a better strategy to reduce inequality than offering educational interventions (Jencks et al. 8–9).

In general, studies of the effectiveness of programs sponsored by ESEA seemed to confirm what Coleman and Jencks suggested. That is, the compensatory education did not seem to change the academic achievement of children from low-income families. For example, in 1984, Launor F. Carter reported the results of the largest study conducted up to that time of children receiving special aid from ESEA. It covered the results of 120,000 students over three academic years from 1976–1977 to 1978–1979. The study showed that students from low-income families seemed not to profit from the instruction available to them from ESEA. While some ESEA programs did report successes, the successes were among students who were not poor or educationally disadvantaged. Such students could be enrolled in the ESEA programs, Carter explained, because some of the federal money went to school districts that contained a mix of social classes. Special efforts, such as summer school, had no beneficial effects on the academic achievement of students from low-income families. Most distressing to the author, he could not locate any instructional programs that were particularly effective in helping disadvantaged students. As a result, Carter concluded that there was no simple solution to the problem of educating children from low-income families (Carter 11–12).

In part, the reason that neither compensatory education nor racial integration improved the academic performance of children described as disadvantaged may have been that the rationale behind these efforts was misguided. In the 1970s, researchers criticized the assumption that children from low-income families shared deficits that would cause school failure. For example, in 1972, a psychologist, Herbert Ginsburg, published *The Myth of the Deprived Child* in which he criticized the notions that culturally deprived children suffered from lower intelligence, used a language that limited their abilities to think, and developed in different ways than did middle-class children. Writing from the perspective of a cognitive theorist, Ginsburg argued that there were modes of language and thought that all children shared regardless of their culture and upbringing. While Ginsburg acknowledged that children from different social classes might express themselves differently, he believed that these differences were superficial and did not represent deficits that hampered their ability to learn academics (Ginsburg x, 14).

According to Ginsburg, an important thrust in compensatory education was correcting the language of poor children. Such efforts were based on the views of sociologists such as Basil Bernstein who held that poor children learned restricted codes from their parents. Bernstein believed low-income parents used brief commands, such as "shut-up." On the other hand, Bernstein argued that middle-class parents used expanded codes to explain what they wanted and why they wanted it, such as "please be quiet because I am talking on the phone." Ginsburg wrote that Bernstein attributed poor children's inability to use abstract thinking to familiarity with restricted rather than expanded codes (Ginsburg 60–64).

Objecting to Bernstein's arguments, Ginsburg quoted several researchers, M. C. Templin, W. D. Loban, and W. Labov, who offered empirical studies of the speech of lower-class American children. These researchers found differences between the speech of African American children from low-income families and the speech of children from middle-class white families, as Bernstein would have predicted. But according to Ginsburg, the differences were not sufficiently great to affect the ways the children thought. He claimed that the researchers found African American dialects or forms of speech to be complex, and people who used such speech could understand what he called Standard English (Ginsburg 64–82).

To offer a sort of case study that illustrated his point that African American children from low-income families did not share deficits that kept them from learning, Ginsburg quoted the book *36 Children* by Herbert Kohl. Describing his year teaching sixth grade in a school in the Harlem section of New York City, Kohl offered several examples of his students' work. These samples showed to Ginsburg's satisfaction that children of poverty could be as literate as any other children when offered the opportunity to create (Ginsburg 89–92).

At the same time, sociologists attacked Oscar Lewis's idea that poor people shared a culture of poverty. For example, in 1968, Charles A. Valentine offered an extended criticism of this idea, which he contended appeared in the work of several sociologists. Valentine noted that the concept of culture had allowed anthropologists to make sense of different patterns of life and, as a result, the concept is an intellectual reaction to racism and ethnocentrism. But Valentine noted that when the War on Poverty adopted the idea that poor people share a culture of poverty, it meant that they caused their own problems (Valentine 2, 15).

Although Valentine acknowledged that poor people had somewhat different patterns of living than did more affluent families, he rejected the broad assertions that many sociologists and anthropologists made about the culture of poverty. For example, he noted that Oscar Lewis used many traditional methods of collecting information about poor people and their values.

Lewis tape recorded extensive interviews in which he had his informants describe their life stories. To these, he added a battery of psychological tests. Unlike other anthropologists who usually limited their conclusions to the sphere in which they were working, Lewis jumped from this information about individuals and families to make global statements about a way of life that all people in roughly similar circumstances were supposed to share. The expected problem occurred. Valentine noted that the facts Lewis recorded did not substantiate the conclusions that he made. In fact, Lewis's theoretical construction of the culture of poverty seemed unrelated to the enormous amount of evidence he collected (Valentine 100–104).

Like many other sociologists who had shared the idea of a culture of poverty, Lewis became aware of the problems in his research, and he backed away from his own thesis. According to his biographer, Susan M. Rigdon, Lewis was shocked to find sociologists, like Valentine, accusing him of blaming the poor for their poverty. He realized that this happened because his words made the cause and effect relationship appear to be between culture and poverty rather than between poverty and capitalism as he had intended. Consequently, Lewis began to claim that the notion of a culture of poverty was an idea to be tested. Later, he asserted that the culture was an adaptation to the conditions of lower-class life. These qualifications did not protect him from criticism, however, and by 1968, when he left to conduct a study in Cuba, he seemed to have given up on the idea. He never finished this work because he died of a heart attack at the age of fifty-six in 1970 (Rigdon 88–104).

In some ways, Oscar Lewis appeared as a tragic hero. He wanted to help children from lower-income families enjoy the education to which he believed they had a right. Yet, critics complained his studies reinforced programs that continued the inequities under which those children suffered. The proponents of programs of compensatory education, such as Conant and Riessman, had advanced their plans in efforts to affirm the students' rights to effective educations. Researchers who found those programs ineffective agreed with the assumption that the children had a right to an appropriate education. They did not approve of the various forms of compensatory education that schools employed.

What did studies reveal about the effectiveness of racial integration in increasing the academic performance of African American youths?

Soon after the Coleman report showed that racial integration of schools improved the academic achievement of African American youths, researchers began to find this effect to be more complicated than it appeared. For example, during the Harvard seminar on the Coleman findings, David K. Cohen, Thomas F. Pettigrew, and Robert T. Riley compared the Coleman findings with some later research conducted in specific schools. The authors noticed that while African American students in desegregated schools earned higher scores on standardized tests, they had lower aspirations than did African American students in segregated schools. To the authors, this suggested that, in desegregated schools, the children chose more realistic career objectives and worked harder to realize those goals (Cohen, Pettigrew, and Riley 363–366).

In 1972, David Armor published a report of his evaluations of an exchange program in the Boston area, METCO, and studies of programs in four other cities. These showed that sending black students to white schools did not close the achievement gap. Before the article appeared in print, national newspapers described its findings, and President Richard Nixon quoted the article to bolster his plans to stop busing for racial balance. As a result, questions about the effects of racial integration on black achievement became a national issue (Crain, Mahard, and Narot 69–70).

To frame his research, Armor quoted the U.S. Supreme Court's decision claiming that segregation generated feelings of inferiority that affected the minds of African American children. Although Armor acknowledged that social science research bolstered that earlier opinion, he thought that intentional desegregation might not have the beneficial effects people expected (Armor 90–91).

When Armor analyzed his data, he found that no study demonstrated conclusively that racial integration had a positive effect on academic achievement as measured by standardized tests. Although the METCO study was the only one to include high school students, it did not show any changes in the students' levels of aspiration or in the relationships the students had with members of other races. When he interviewed thirty-two of the METCO students who had graduated two years earlier, he found racial integration seemed to have encouraged them to attend college. Unfortunately, this optimistic finding was contradicted by the observation that these students dropped out of college in higher numbers than did African American students who had attended black high schools. As a result of these findings, Armor recommended that massive mandatory busing should not be pursued as public policy because it would not lead to improvements for African Americans. He thought voluntary desegregation should proceed because those parents who thought it would make a difference should be allowed to try (Armor 99, 101, 102, 105, 115–116).

A few months later, Thomas Pettigrew and his colleagues published a rejoinder to Armor's article presenting four ways in which they believed that Armor had distorted his evidence. First, they claimed that Armor used criteria to evaluate change that were the highest and the most rigid ever employed in educational research. Second, they argued that Armor selected his few studies in ways that ignored the many other studies showing black students improved as a result of racial integration. Third, they contended that most of the antibusing evidence came from Armor's small study of METCO, and this appeared to be faulty. In designing his study, Armor chose to compare a control group to METCO students. The control group should have remained in black schools if he was going to study the effects of racial integration. Pettigrew and his colleagues claimed many of the students in Armor's control group attended integrated schools. Fourth, Pettigrew and his colleagues asserted that Armor was wrong to base the continuation of busing on beneficial effects on black achievement. To them, racial integration was not for academic improvement. It was to affirm students' rights (Pettigrew et al. 89–91).

After this interchange, studies began to focus on whether racial integration influenced the achievement of black students. In 1972, Robert L. Crain and Carol Sachs Weisman released their survey of 297 randomly selected male adults living in twenty-five metropolitan areas in the North. The authors wanted to determine what effects attending integrated or segregated schools had on these men. The results were positive. Integration increased the African Americans' sense of security and inhibited aggression. While the authors thought this set the stage for higher achievement, they found success in schools and work depended on other factors, such as the consistency of the experiences. Thus, African American children who moved from segregated conditions to integrated settings did not benefit as much from the integration (Crain and Weisman 176–178).

In 1975, Nancy H. St. John published her review of over 120 studies about the effects of racial integration of schools on the achievement, attitudes, and behavior of children. She found that the results were mixed to such an extent that she could not call integrated schooling a success or a failure. To her, it did not seem to close the achievement gap. Sometimes racial integration harmed the race relations among the students, and other times it seemed to benefit them. Despite these inconclusive findings, St. John recommended that policy makers stop trying to balance the ratios of black and white students among schools. Instead, she thought educators should concentrate on helping black students succeed and on improving racial relations within a school (St. John 118–121).

In 1977, Meyer Weinberg published a review of the literature and agreed with St. John to the extent that he noted the research findings were confusing. He did not think racial integration should be suspended. Instead, he complained that few scholars had studied the effects of desegregation on student achievement because the federal government had not extended many grants to measure the successes of the policies. For example, the only national study of the effects of desegregation Weinberg could find was a study of the Emergency School Assistance Act that was made in 1973. This study found that achievement scores among black male high school students in desegregated schools were one-half grade higher than the scores of their age mates in segregated settings. Although the study found that white students achieved more in predominantly white schools than in predominantly black schools, it noted that the white students performed best in racially balanced settings (Weinberg 109–110).

The other studies that Weinberg reviewed measured the effects on small populations in specific settings. Nonetheless, of those studies, twenty-nine had shown a positive effect, and nineteen had shown no effect. According to Weinberg, the beneficial effects seemed to happen when the teachers and the students accepted and supported the minority pupils. Weinberg noted that these studies measured the effects of a few African American students attending majority white schools, and Weinberg warned that this tokenism encouraged the white administrators, teachers, and students to adopt attitudes of paternalism that poorly served everyone involved (Weinberg 122).

In 1978, Robert Crain and Rita Mahard published their study on the effects of desegregation on the college attendance rates and achievement test scores of African American students. Unlike most previous work, this was a national study. Using data from the National Longitudinal Study of the High School Graduating Class of 1972, the researchers had information from more than 1,300 high schools about almost 24,000 students that extended from their senior year to two years after graduation. The researchers found that the effects of desegregation differed by region. In the North, black students graduating from predominantly white high schools were more likely to attend college than those who attended predominantly black schools. In the South, the opposite was true. Similarly, in the North, black achievement as measured by test scores was higher among African American students in predominantly white schools. In the South, achievement was not related to the racial composition of the school. Thus, the researchers noted that desegregation had the least positive effects in the area where the most desegregation had occurred (Crain and Mahard, *The Influence* 44, 58).

When the authors conducted statistical tests to isolate what might be causing the regional differences, they attributed the variations to the race of the teachers in the schools. Although they could not prove their assumptions, they assumed that black teachers in black schools were more supportive of their black students than white teachers were. In northern and southern schools, the grades of black students were lower in white schools, yet northern schools seemed to offer more encouragement for success than did southern schools. Remaining optimistic, the authors pointed to other studies indicating that the attitudes of white teachers changed as they became accustomed to the presence of black students (Crain and Mahard, *The Influence* 74–75, 130–131).

In 1978, Crain and Mahard reviewed the studies conducted up to that time about the influence of school desegregation on black achievement. They noted that almost every researcher concluded that desegregation did not affect white students' achievement. Out of thirty-nine studies of districts with mandatory desegregation, twenty-four studies showed gains for black students and five studies showed losses. The studies made one point clearly. This was that the earlier the grade at which the desegregation began, the more likely it was to influence the achievement of African American students. On other points, the researchers found less agreement. Finally, they concluded that the studies could not show that desegregation was the only factor leading to improvements in black achievement because, when the districts desegregated, many of them improved the quality of the school settings and the curriculum materials the students used. Thus, they thought that improvements in the quality of education might have caused the improved achievement (Crain and Mahard, "Desegregation" 18, 34, 48–50).

In 1982, seeking to determine what sort of desegregation plans would increase the achievement of African American students, Crain and Mahard considered the ways that the extent of desegregation influenced black achievement. Analyzing the methods and the findings of ninety-three studies, the authors found that black achievement reached a peak when the schools were 72 to 81 percent white. This level of achievement dropped on either side of this optimum mix at a steady rate (Crain and Mahard, *Desegregation Plans* 6, 7, 32, 33).

In 1983, Mahard and Crain went back over some of their studies and asked why desegregated schools increased black achievement. Although they had little evidence for their conjectures, they believed that the reason lay in the tendency of black students in integrated schools to see reality differently than did black students in black schools. According to Mahard and Crain, African American students in integrated settings appeared to think that many opportunities were open to them, while the black students in the black schools thought those opportunities were only for white people (Mahard and Crain 121–124).

Unfortunately, some researchers noted that the racial desegregation of schools did not always lead to the racial integration of the students. For example, in 1983, Janet Eyler and her coauthors noted that the students in desegregated schools could attend segregated classes because of the way the students were divided. According to Eyler and her coauthors, ability grouping or tracking in elementary schools could lead to black students being assigned to lower groups more frequently than were white students. Other similar practices that spread from elementary schools to high schools included the practices of assigning minority children to compensatory education programs, to special education, or to bilingual education. The authors added that if disciplinary practices centered on black students, they could force black students to drop out more frequently than white students (Eyler, Cook, and Ward 126–145).

Thus, although the researchers found the effects of racial integration to be complicated, many studies found that such programs as busing for racial balance tended to be more successful than programs of compensatory education. Those researchers who disagreed wanted to replace mandatory racial desegregation with some type of program that would enable school people to affirm the rights of African American children to an equal education. Thus, everyone assumed that schools should affirm the children's rights to an equal education.

What reasons did officials give for slowing the movement for racial integration of schools?

Although the racial integration of schools appeared to be more successful than compensatory education, the movement toward desegregation slowed in the 1970s and began to recede in the 1980s. Three events explain this change. First, the U.S. Department of Health, Education, and Welfare (HEW) stopped enforcing Title VI of the Civil Rights Act. Second, after steadily extending the meaning of racial desegregation, in 1974, the U.S. Supreme Court blocked efforts to integrate white students in the suburbs of northern cities with African American students in the city schools. Third, the U.S. Supreme Court began to allow school districts to end their desegregation plans and return to segregated neighborhood schools.

After a successful period forcing desegregation in the South, officials in HEW turned their attention to northern cities. In 1965, their first objective was to change the schools in Chicago, but the resulting controversy was so intense that they withdrew their sanctions. Nonetheless, members of the U.S. Congress who had formerly supported civil rights legislation joined in the criticism of HEW to the extent that by 1967 northern senators began to call for legislation forbidding the transportation of students for racial balance (Orfield, *Reconstruction* 185–207).

In 1969, President Richard Nixon ordered HEW to stop using the threat of an end of federal funds to bring about the racial integration of school districts. As a result, HEW and the Justice Department did not enforce Title VI, and the U.S. Justice Department began entering desegregation cases arguing that remedies were not necessary. As a result, in 1972 and in 1973, civil rights groups sued in federal courts to force HEW to enforce Title VI. Although the civil rights groups won, HEW did not substantially alter its policies (Orfield, "Act" 109–114).

The second event that changed the pace of racial desegregation was that the U.S. Supreme Court ruled against the NAACP in the case *Milliken v. Bradley.* This halted the string of victories the NAACP lawyers won in the U.S. Supreme Court from 1954 until 1974 to extend the meaning of desegregation. For example, in 1968, they won *Green v. County School Board of New Kent County* that declared a school board had to do more than simply offer the freedom of choice to desegregate its schools. According to this ruling, the officials had to adopt policies that made significant differences in all sorts of factors, such as facilities, faculty, and extracurricular activities. In 1971, in *Swann v. Charlotte-Mecklenberg,* the court approved cross-district busing because the plans had to affect student attendance patterns as much as possible. In 1973, they won *Keyes v. Denver School District* by showing the school officials had intentionally segregated the schools through such things as the selection of building sites and manipulating school attendance zones (Orfield et al. xxi–xxii).

In 1974, however, the NAACP lawyers lost in their efforts to merge the students from the fifty-four surrounding predominantly white suburban schools with the predominantly African American students in Detroit. Although lower courts had ruled in favor of such a plan because it represented the only way to bring about meaningful integration, the justices on the Supreme Court rejected it, arguing that the lawyers did not show that school officials had created the suburban districts for the purpose of segregating the students (U.S. Commission on Civil Rights, *Statement* 87–89).

The decision in *Milliken v. Bradley* had a greater impact in the North and the Midwest than in the South because the schools districts were formed differently. In the South, most states formed the school districts by including the entire county. Since this would usually involve a city and its suburbs, it was easy for officials to include both in any program to alleviate racial imbalance. On the other hand, in the North and the Midwest, usually school districts followed the city limits and *Milliken v. Bradley* forbade merging them together unless lawyers could show that officials had drawn the district lines or engaged in other practices for the purpose of segregating the students. Since such evidence was difficult to obtain, city schools the North and Midwest that tended to contain the African American students remained apart from the suburban schools that tended to contain the white students living in the area (Orfield et al. 60–61).

The third event was that in 1986 the U.S. Supreme Court refused to hear the case of *Riddick v. School Board of Norfolk County.* In this case, lower courts had allowed the school district to dismantle a desegregation plan on the grounds that it caused white flight that prevented further improvement of the schools. According to Gary Orfield and his colleagues, the school district had hired David Armor to conduct a study that showed mandatory busing for racial balance caused white students to leave the system. Armor predicted that many white students would remain or return to the public schools if the practice of busing stopped. Although subsequent studies claimed Armor's figures were incorrect, the lower courts released the school officials from the desegregation plan. When the U.S. Supreme Court refused to hear the case, other lower court justices looked to information gathered by social scientists showing that an end of busing would cause there to be more white students in the system to bring about meaningful integration, and they agreed to allow schools to return to neighborhood schools (Orfield et al. 118–124).

In 1991, in *Board of Education of Oklahoma City v. Dowell,* the U.S. Supreme Court relied on the concept "unitary status" to end mandatory desegregation. According to this decision, after a school board took the steps to integrate students, faculty, and other facilities, a judge could declare that the district could return to policies such as those of neighborhood schools if these policies served an educational function. With this possibility before them, school districts filed for such decisions. For example, in 2002, the board of education in Dayton, Ohio, won such approval from the federal district judge and returned to a policy of neighborhood schools. This was important because the busing program Dayton had adopted in 1975 was hailed as one of the most successful programs for racial desegregation. Other schools districts in Ohio, such as Cleveland, had returned to neighborhood schools earlier. Thus, in 2002, when Dayton returned to neighborhood schools, no school district in the state of Ohio followed a desegregation plan (Orfield et al. 3).

Unfortunately, the end of busing that resulted from *Riddick v. School Board of Norfolk County* did not stop the decline of white residents and students in Norfolk, Virginia. Instead, more schools became almost exclusively black. Similar changes took place throughout the nation. For example, a desegregation plan began in Cleveland, Ohio, in 1976 and ended in 1996. According to an analysis by the Lewis Mumford Center for Comparative Urban and Regional Research, in 1999–2000, released from court supervision, the Cleveland elementary schools experienced the most rapid increase in racial segregation of students in the United

States. Other cities experienced rapid increases in school segregation during the 1990s. These included Columbus, Ohio; Milwaukee, Wisconsin; and Minneapolis, Minnesota (Orfield et al. 140–141; Lewis Mumford Center, "Choosing Segregation" 7).

Although some judges appeared willing to remove desegregation plans on the belief that busing caused white flight, social scientists did not agree that white people abandoned urban schools because of school desegregation plans. For example, in 1975, James Coleman claimed that his research showed that school desegregation caused white flight. The next year, Thomas Pettigrew and Robert Green argued that other researchers had used the same data as had Coleman, but they came to different conclusions because they included more years in their studies. Pettigrew and Green claimed that desegregation plans involving the city and the suburbs in a metropolitan area plan reduced the problems of white flight (Coleman et al., *Trends* 73–79; Pettigrew and Green 20–26, 40).

In 1976, Coleman replied to Pettigrew and Green. He wrote that the situation was worse than he had claimed a year earlier. After five years of school desegregation, white people continued to leave cities to avoid integration plans. More important, Coleman did not think that metropolitan desegregation would lessen white flight because the data supporting such a contention came from areas that were growing and had few black residents (Coleman, "Correspondence" 217–224).

In 1977, the U.S. Commission on Civil Rights accepted Pettigrew and Green's explanation. The commission members reported that white families had been leaving cities for many decades prior to any school desegregation because their places of employment changed or because they wanted a larger living space. Nonetheless, the commission asserted that whether racial desegregation caused white flight or not, the U.S. Supreme Court decided in 1972 not to allow school districts to use this excuse to avoid racial integration (U.S. Commission, *Fulfilling* 161–162).

At the same time, some researchers changed their minds about the effectiveness of busing for racial balance. For example, in 1978, Christine H. Rossell noted that, on average, city schools with less than 35 percent black student enrollment lost about 5 percent of their white students in the first year. Schools with more than 35 percent white students lost about 8 percent of the white students. Rossell added that as school desegregation has proceeded, racial intolerance has declined. While this may not be caused by school integration, she noted that after three years most communities that had elected antibusing politicians voted those people out of office and voted in black candidates. In all, she noted that plans where students were forced to attend certain schools appeared to be beneficial and necessary. Yet, in 1990, Rossell changed her mind about mandatory desegregation plans and decided that voluntary magnet schools were best. The hope behind magnet schools was that special schools with highly attractive curriculums in areas where concentrations of minority students lived would attract middle-class white students. In this way, racial integration would take place by the students' choices rather than by school officers assigning them to certain schools (Rossell, "School" 181–183).

Rossell came to the conclusion that plans depending on students' choices were superior after she studied twenty school districts. She compared the success of magnet programs in districts that had to follow a strict court ruling to the success of magnet programs she called voluntary because there was no court order demanding certain ratios in all schools. Rossell chose the twenty schools from information about 119 school districts that extended from the 1960s to 1984. Dayton, Ohio, was an example of a magnet program functioning under a strict court order while Buffalo, New York, was a similarly sized city with a voluntary magnet program. When Rossell compared the experiences of matched pairs such as Dayton and Buffalo schools, she found that the measures of interracial exposure in the voluntary plans, such as Buffalo implemented, surpassed the measures of interracial exposure in court-ordered compliance plans similar to Dayton's. This happened because there was less white flight associated with the voluntary plans. In Dayton, white enrollment dropped 51 percent from 1975 to 1986 while Buffalo experienced a 29 percent decline over the same period (Rossell, *Carrot* 80–90).

Rossell's conclusions were controversial. To measure racial integration, Rossell had used what she called "interracial exposure." She defined this as the percentage of white students in the average black student's school. But, in 1992, Brian Fife argued that interracial exposure indexes were inaccurate measures of integration because they offered average conditions. He preferred what he called "an index of dissimilarity" that indicated the percentage of black students that would have to be reassigned to give racial balance within the school district. Although an index of dissimilarity could be the same in a situation where most students were white and in another where most students were black, Fife contended that the index measured the integration present in the schools. On the other hand, he argued that Rossell's interracial exposure index tried to capture racial integration in the schools and the presence of white students in the district at the same time. He claimed this was impossible because the white students could congregate in separate buildings (Rossell, *Carrot* 34; Fife 16–25).

Although Rossell and Fife used the same data from the same twenty school districts for their studies, they came to different conclusions. While Rossell thought voluntary plans were best, Fife concluded that white people and African Americans had to be coerced into attending schools together (Fife 137).

Considering the question of white flight separately, Fife recommended that courts continue to coerce the different groups to attend schools together. Since Fife found that offering incentives, such as magnet schools, would not help to bring about desegregation, he concluded that court-ordered metropolitan plans of desegregation would be the most effective means of ensuring that school districts had enough white and African American students for desegregation to take place. Unfortunately, he did not believe that this was not an option the federal courts would pursue (Fife 176).

Thus, the problems that critics found in the original court decisions appeared to be real. In 1954, critics warned that future justices could reverse the *Brown* decision because Justice Warren had used social science data to argue that racial segregation denied African American students their rights to an equal education. By 1986, as the critics had warned, federal courts began a process of releasing many school districts to return to being neighborhood schools because social science data seemed to indicate that mandatory racial desegregation did not enable schools to affirm the rights of African American students. Not surprisingly, racial segregation of schools returned to the levels that existed before court-ordered busing for racial balance (Orfield et al. 54–55).

Ironically, experts on both sides of this controversy based their arguments on similar assumptions. That is, some social scientists supported racial integration because they felt that this was the best way to affirm the African American students' rights to an equal education. At the same time, other social scientists argued against mandatory plans of racial desegregation on the grounds that such court orders created situations in which it was impossible to bring about the racial integration that would affirm the African American students' rights to an equal education.

What were the effects of programs of compensatory education and of efforts to racially integrate the schools?

Neither the effort to racially integrate the schools nor the War on Poverty succeeded in alleviating the problems they confronted. In part, the problems were so large that, in the 1960s and 1970s, some federal programs contradicted each other. For example, in 1967, while HEW forced schools to desegregate, the U.S. Department of Housing and Urban Development sponsored the Model Cities Program that encouraged low-income urban residents to develop self-help programs to improve their neighborhoods. Since Congress removed requirements for the racial integration of housing or of schools from this legislation, the monies could reinforce segregated conditions and in some places, such as Dayton, Ohio, Model Cities programs encouraged segregation (Sundquist 79–82; Watras 114–128).

In a similar manner, the effort to provide compensatory education seemed to contradict HEW's interpretation of Title VI of the 1964 U.S. Civil Rights Act requiring school integration. For example, when ESEA offered funds for the education of educationally deprived children in 1965, school officials could claim that these children were best served when they were grouped together in their home schools. Further, in areas where the desegregation plans involved freedom of choice, officials could tell black parents that their children would forfeit ESEA assistance in a white school. In 1966, in the face of these problems, the director of the U.S. Office of Education decided that the ESEA funds should follow the children in desegregation programs. This seemed to alleviate the contradiction (Bailey and Mosher 149–152).

In other ways, though, programs of compensatory education seemed to replace integration. For example, after the U.S. Supreme Court prohibited merging African Americans students in Detroit with white students from suburban schools, the justices required the state to provide compensatory education to repair the damages caused by segregation. Although the state provided this aid while desegregation took place within the city, merging the students in a metropolitan plan should have reduced the number of schools that were overwhelmed by poverty and exposed children from low-income families to middle-class children with higher educational and occupational aspirations (Orfield et al. 146–148).

In the main, the War on Poverty was fueled by the idea that poor people held to a culture that prevented them from succeeding. The reasoning was that if schools could break this cycle of cultural deprivation, they would close the gap in educational achievement between affluent students and those less fortunate. The failure of compensatory education to eradicate the educational disadvantages associated with poverty led many researchers to claim that teachers had little influence on student achievement. To many researchers, this was an overstatement. They claimed the failures of compensatory education derived from teachers basing their strategies on a faulty theory of deficiency.

Although anthropologists and social scientists criticized the concept of a culture of poverty, it remained in various forms as an important part of educational research. For example, in 1966, the U.S. Department of Health, Education, and Welfare published Catherine S. Chilman's overview and analysis of studies of child-raising patterns among low-income families. Acknowledging that by the time she was writing concepts such as culturally deprived and a culture of poverty had lost favor among educators and researchers, Chilman claimed this was unfortunate because she believed these notions offered insights about family patterns that caused children problems in later life. Although she qualified her use of the term *culturally deprived,* she confined her analysis to studies about the ways interactions in low-income families contributed to high rates of mental illness, school failure, and delinquency. In this way, she retained the idea that there was something about the way low-income families raised children that caused a cycle of poverty. Chilman's study remained so popular that HEW reprinted it in 1969 (Chilman 1–3).

Other researchers retained the idea of a culture of poverty but turned it to include political or social oppression. For example, John U. Ogbu published in 1976 the results of his research in a bilingual education program in Stockton, California. Although Ogbu disliked the notion of a culture of poverty because it implied that poverty was the important factor in personality development, he preserved the idea by adding to it a view that social and economic domination was most important. According to Ogbu, groups that he referred to as "subordinate minorities," such as blacks and Mexican Americans, adopted what he called a "retreatist subculture" when they believed that they could not advance through the traditional avenues of success. Consequently, he argued that the school failure of children from subordinate minorities derived from their awareness of their limited opportunities in the wider society (Ogbu 5–13).

Whether there was a culture of poverty or not, studies continued to show that programs aimed at children from low-income families were unable to improve their academic performance in significant ways. Racial integration might have been more successful than compensatory education in raising black achievement scores. But in order for desegregation to improve the chances for success among low-income African Americans, the desegregation plans would have had to spread wider to include entire metropolitan districts and it would have had to involve more middle-class children. Unfortunately, popular opinion prevented local and national legislators from adopting such rules, and, in 1974, the U.S. Supreme Court refused to order the racial desegregation of contiguous school districts because there was no evidence the officials who created those districts did so in an effort to deny African American students their rights to equal education. Further, after 1986, the courts began to argue that mandatory desegregation could not affirm the African American students' rights to equal educations. Consequently, the courts released school districts from desegregation plans.

Despite these practical problems, the 1964 U.S. Civil Rights Act and ESEA had a profound effect on educators in the United States. Built on efforts to affirm the rights of African Americans and of deprived children, these pieces of legislation set the model for later efforts. For example, according to Gary Orfield, Title VI of the 1964 U.S. Civil Rights Act was the most important element in federal involvement in education. He claimed that the legislation for children with disabilities and changes prohibiting discrimination against girls in schools imitated the mechanics of this act (Orfield, "The Act" 99).

While Orfield noted two groups that imitated the NAACP and the Civil Rights movement, the number is far greater. From the 1960s, increasingly larger numbers of groups turned to the strategies used by civil rights advocates to advance the education of their constituents. Thus, during the 1970s and 1980s, it was common for groups to claim that public schools had discriminated against particular groups. Usually, these groups advocated some change so that the children could enjoy their rights. In some cases, such as the advocates for children with disabilities, the reforms surpassed those made for African Americans and children for low-income families. In other cases, such as bilingual education, the results were less successful. But successful or not, an important legacy of the 1964 U.S. Civil Rights Act and of ESEA was the idea that advocates of particular groups should engage in legal and political campaigns to force schools to affirm the rights of students.

Summary

In 1954, the U.S. Supreme Court decided that when public officials required African American children to attend segregated schools, those officials illegally violated the students' rights. Unfortunately, the decision had little practical effect on schools. Nine years after the *Brown* decision, most African American children remained in segregated schools. Things changed quickly following the protest in Birmingham, Alabama; the March on Washington; and U.S. President Kennedy's assassination. The U.S. Congress passed and President Lyndon Johnson signed the U.S. Civil Rights Act of 1964. A year later, they approved the Elementary and Secondary Education Act (ESEA). These laws reinforced each other. The Civil Rights Act gave the federal government the authority to forbid local boards of education to receive federal funds unless they racially desegregated the schools, and ESEA offered educators over $1 billion dollars in federal money to improve the education of children from lower-income families. As a result, racial integration increased throughout the South, and most schools developed programs of compensatory education. It was called compensatory education because an important component of the War on Poverty was that schools could repair or compensate for the personality deficits of children from low-income families that caused the children to repeat the cycle of privation inherited from their parents. Despite the intentions of the legislators, compensatory education could contradict the racial integration of schools because some educators argued that students from low-income families shared certain deficits and should receive a compensatory education distinct from the type of training appropriate for middle-class children. After a short period, some studies showed that racial integration was more effective in improving the academic performance of children labeled deprived than was compensatory education, but neither approach made much difference. Despite these apparent failures, the laws that inspired the new programs served as models for educational reform. Instead of trying to persuade schools to meet the students' needs, educational reformers saw themselves as advocates who should engage in legal and political campaigns to force schools to affirm students' rights.

CHAPTER TEN

SPECIAL EDUCATORS AND BILINGUAL EDUCATORS IMITATE THE NAACP, 1963–1986

In his book, *The Sorting Machine,* Joel Spring contended that the Civil Rights movement of the 1950s and 1960s increased federal control of American education. Spring took the ironic view that Title VI of the 1964 U.S. Civil Rights Act, which gave the power to officials to deny federal funds to racially segregated school districts, broke down people's resistance to national regulation of education. Claiming that the War on Poverty released an army of social scientists who sought to train poor people for the culture of the schools, Spring argued this reinforced the view that schools should prepare children to enter what he referred to as the opportunity structure of society. Although Spring acknowledged that the different parts of the federal government worked independently of each other, he claimed that the effect of the combined efforts of different agencies was to create a national policy that was never stated. He believed that the policy was to separate students according to abilities, to guide them into specific programs based on their abilities, and to prepare them for specific slots in the labor force. He argued that the apparently philanthropic programs, such as the racial desegregation of schools and the War on Poverty, actually represented efforts to control the conflicts that could have arisen because of discrimination and income inequalities (Spring, *Sorting* 1–2, 93, 122, 150, 173, 175).

Another author, Gerald Grant, took a different but equally caustic view of the effects of the Civil Rights movement. Grant argued that the Civil Rights movement destroyed the bases of authority that made education possible and the increased bureaucratic control of teachers removed the chances of them controlling their profession. Grant made these accusations in his account of a particular school that he called Hamilton High. Located in a northeastern industrial city, Hamilton High was an elite academic, all white high school in the 1950s. In 1966, the school district began a program of racial desegregation. Although the U.S. Civil Rights Commission praised Hamilton High for improving the academic performance of African Americans and developing classroom climates that encouraged respect and sensitivity, the school was torn by riots from 1968 to 1971 (Grant 5–6, 11, 24–29, 44).

According to Grant, the desegregation plan and resulting racial violence disrupted people's conceptions of authority in two ways. First, teachers and administrators lost control and had to rely on police to quiet the students. As a result, by 1971, about 72 percent of the teachers who had made the school an elite institution had left the school. Second, the new teachers eschewed traditional discipline and tried to allow the students to decide what they should learn. In a similar manner, administrators sought to protect the students' rights in matters of discipline and academics. Unfortunately, the students abused their new power. For example, when a teacher confronted a student for disruptive behavior, the student responded by filing a legal complaint and police arrested the teacher (Grant 45–57).

In 1980, another change came to Hamilton High when children with a wide range of disabilities enrolled. To affirm these students' rights, the school board created new programs for them. Grant claimed that, although the special teachers held master's degrees, they had few workable suggestions about techniques with which a regular teacher could help these children. Nonetheless, the special teachers were ideologically committed to placing the students with disabilities in regular classes. Since those classes were large, the regular teachers had difficulty meeting the varied needs of their students. As a result, according to Grant, the special students received less help, the other students learned little, and, because they were overwhelmed with work, the teachers lost more control of their classes (Grant 77–86).

Despite the differences in their interpretations, Spring and Grant believed the educational reforms of the 1960s and 1970s reduced the freedoms available to students and teachers. On the other side, advocates for the education of children with disabilities claimed those reforms were necessary steps to prevent school people from arbitrarily excluding children with special needs from classrooms. These advocates did not see themselves as opening the schools to federal imposition nor did they think they reduced the freedom of teachers. Calling those reforms a quiet revolution, the advocates noted that they established a right to an education for children with disabilities. From a few legal cases, the advocates recommended a process of planning the curriculum wherein teachers were to use scientific knowledge to diagnose a child's problems, and the teachers were to consult with parents about the planned instruction. According to the advocates, neither the courts nor any state or federal agency imposed a curriculum plan because the legislation described a process wherein teachers, administrators, parents, and children could use their own best judgments and thereby protect their rights.

What Spring and Grant ignored is that campaigns led by the National Association for the Advancement of Colored People (NAACP) and the Southern Christian Leadership Conference (SCLC) combined to change the ways that educators thought about school reform. As a result, the campaigns for the education of children with disabilities and for children with linguistic differences illustrate the change in the concepts that educators employed to improve schools after 1963. During the Great Depression and the postwar years, educators tried to convince other school people, public officials, and parents that they had not met the needs of the children. At the same time, the NAACP challenged local schools and appealed to the state and federal courts to force local schools to fulfill the rights of African Americans to an equal education. From 1963, Martin Luther King, Jr.'s SCLC enlisted public support to adopt laws and extend federal funds that would either force or entice local schools to design appropriate educations for the children. Looking on these successes, the advocates for children with disabilities began to take more militant, legalistic, and politically charged approaches to encourage school reform. They claimed that schools had denied the rights of children with disabilities and linguistic differences. In making these complaints, the advocates shifted the concepts that inspired school reform. Instead of simply urging teachers to meet students' needs, the advocates sought to affirm students' rights to have schools satisfy students' special needs.

In what ways did the advocates for children with disabilities change their campaigns as a result of the Civil Rights movement?

After World War II, advocates for children with disabilities sought to cooperate with educators and public officials to expand the programs to help the children. For example, in 1944, the U.S. Office of Education published Elise H. Martens's leaflet, *The Needs of Exceptional Children*. Noting that the needs of the children should determine the programs, Martens recommended that state legislatures require local schools to offer special classes and to establish state-supported residence homes for the children. She argued that these programs should serve the many different types of exceptional children, including gifted children as well as children suffering from such disabilities as orthopedic handicaps, mental retardation, or limited vision. In addition, she urged that educational, health, and welfare agencies coordinate their services for these children (Martens 4, 12–14).

When John F. Kennedy became president in 1961, the advocates of exceptional children may have felt that their strategy of seeking cooperation among different agencies was appropriate. The Kennedy family had taken on mental retardation as their important philanthropy. In 1945, Joseph P. Kennedy, President Kennedy's father, established the Joseph P. Kennedy, Jr. Foundation, named in honor of one of his sons who had died. Although at first dedicated to the general care of the sick and the poor, by 1958, the foundation devoted most of its resources to support research into the causes and cure of mental retardation. According to Edward Shorter, the foundation changed directions for two reasons. First, Joseph Kennedy, Sr. was concerned about mental retardation because his daughter Rosemary was mentally retarded. Second, another daughter, Eunice, and her husband, Sargent Shriver, became involved in the center's work (Shorter 35–36, 43, 50–51).

President John F. Kennedy followed his family's interest in mental retardation after his inauguration. In October 1961, he appointed a panel of physicians, scientists, educators, lawyers, and psychologists to consider the problems of mental retardation and to propose methods of eliminating it. The following year, the panel made its report, and among the topics covered in the report was the question of legal requirements for the education or treatment of the mentally retarded. Although the panel asserted that people suffering from mental retardation had the same legal rights as other people, the members hesitated to enact legal requirements for their education on the fear that these strictures could prevent physicians or educators from offering the widest variety of services for the children. Thus, the panel recommended avoiding mandatory legal requirements and seeking voluntary compliance of agencies and educators. If legal intervention was necessary, the panel's report continued, advocates should look to the general laws and only as a last resort should they seek legislation for a specific handicapped group. In addition, the panel called on the U.S. Department of Health, Education, and Welfare (HEW) to expand its efforts to stimulate and coordinate treatment and research of mental retardation (President's Panel on Mental Retardation 148–150, 179–183).

In response to the President's Panel on Mental Retardation, the secretary of HEW formed a committee to make recommendations. In the area of education, the secretary's committee urged three types of endeavors: development of statistical reports showing the need for specialized classroom services, advancement of recruitment and training of teachers by offering fellowships, and augmentation of vocational training for mentally retarded children and adults (Secretary's Committee on Mental Retardation 27–40).

In 1965, following this pattern of pursuing general improvements in education rather than seeking legislation specifically for mental retardation, advocacy groups, such as the Council for Exceptional Children (CEC), cooperated with the National Education Association (NEA) for the passage of ESEA. Unfortunately, when the U.S. Congress approved ESEA, the U.S. Office of Education chose not to direct funds for children with disabilities but concentrated on aid for children of low-income families (Colachio 51–52; Salomone 143–144).

When ESEA came up for renewal the following year, special educators changed their strategy and pushed for increased educational opportunities specifically aimed toward children with disabilities. The CEC joined with such groups as the American Psychological Association and the National Association of Mental Health to present information to the U.S. Congress about three needs: funds for the education of children with disabilities, a central office within the administration to advance the cause of children with handicaps, and regulations requiring states to provide free, appropriate education for all children with disabilities (Levine and Wexler 20–28).

The interest groups enjoyed remarkable success. In 1966, the U.S. Congress approved and President Lyndon B. Johnson renewed a version of ESEA that contained Title VI authorizing $50 million in 1967 and $150 million in 1968 to assist in the initiation and expansion of what the bill called programs for handicapped children in the preschool, elementary, and secondary schools. Title VI did not require states to provide such education for the handicapped. Rather, it offered the money if the states would follow the federal guidelines for such education (Levine and Wexler 31–33).

According to Erwin Levine and Elizabeth Wexler, the most important aspect of the legislation was that it established the Bureau of Education within the U.S. Office of Education. This bureau could direct congressional committees to important advocacy groups about the need for the education of exceptional children. President Johnson made the bureau even more important when he appointed a person who had encouraged adoption of the legislation to direct this bureau rather than select a longtime administrative aide who might prove disinterested (Levine and Wexler 32–33).

Most educational advocacy groups had to be careful in the 1960s and 1970s because they faced what Stephen K. Bailey described as a lobbying dilemma. These educational organizations incorporated under a provision of the tax code, 501 (c) (3), that prohibited them from devoting more than 5 percent of their activities to influencing legislation. This tax-exempt status was important to the groups because it allowed major foundations, such as the Ford Foundation or the Carnegie Corporation, to offer support without jeopardizing their own tax-exempt status. According to Bailey, what most organizations learned to do was to dodge the restrictions. For example, a group might state in its constitution that the organization was not a lobbying organization but that it offered information to congressional representatives at their request (Bailey 50–52).

The CEC was particularly effective in advocating reforms in the education of children with special needs. The CEC's aims differed from those of similar groups, such as the National Association for Retarded Citizens, because the CEC organized and served teachers who worked with children. To advance their interests, the CEC monitored proposed legislative actions, advertised these proposals to their members, and urged them to communicate their feelings to their congressional representatives. The CEC supplied information about the education of children with special needs to members of Congress, and members of the national CEC served as consultants to court cases, such as *PARC,* that established the right to education for children with disabilities (Colachio 62–67).

As a result of their actions, the members of the CEC exerted considerable influence in the U.S. Congress. In 1973, Bailey compiled a list of the fifteen most effective educational advocacy groups from a total of 300. The CEC ranked as the fifth most able to manipulate policy writing in Washington, DC. On this ranking, the CEC fell behind such groups as the AFL/CIO, but it appeared ahead of other important organizations such as the NAACP (Bailey 28).

When advocacy groups shifted from speaking about students' needs to affirming students' rights, they faced the difficulty of having courts and legislatures legally recognize the students' rights. This was not easy because the U.S. Constitution does not spell out a right to education. As a result, the advocates for children with disabilities used the same tactics the NAACP lawyers had used. First, several associations adopted declarations stating that children with disabilities had the right to an appropriate education. For example, in 1968, the International League of Societies for the Mentally Handicapped adopted the "Declaration of General and Specific Rights of the Mentally Retarded." This declared that people with mental retardation had the right to medical care and education that would enable them to develop their abilities as much as possible (Lippman and Goldberg 7).

Second, advocacy organizations sued in federal courts to establish the right of children with disabilities to an education. In 1969, the Pennsylvania Association for Retarded Children (PARC) filed suit in U.S. District Court in 1969 against the Commonwealth of Pennsylvania arguing that the children with mental retardation did not have equal access to an education. The suit was similar to the appeal made by the NAACP in *Brown v. Board* because it argued that public officials kept the children out of public schools by official exclusions, postponements, waiting lists, and excusals. In these ways, according to PARC lawyers, public officials segregated these children and denied them their right to an education. This trial was extremely brief. After four witnesses testified, officials from the Commonwealth of Pennsylvania agreed to search out children requiring special education and place them in programs as similar as possible to those available in public schools (Lippman and Goldberg 16–44).

In 1971 and in 1972, in *Mills v. Board of Education of the District of Columbia,* U.S. Justice Joseph Waddy extended the right to an equal education to groups of children other than mentally retarded children. This case began when seven children complained that they had been excluded from regular classes simply because they were labeled as suffering from behavioral problems, hyperactivity, or emotional disturbances. In these decisions, Waddy forbade the schools to exclude these children by placing them in separate classes unless the board provided alternative education, a prior hearing, and periodic review of the child's progress. Further, he would not accept the argument that the school district could not afford to pay for the special education and required that the education of these children had to be on equal terms with the education provided other children.

Other cases followed rapidly. By 1975, forty-six similar cases took place in twenty-eight different states. Together, these accumulated decisions seemed to support the right of children with disabilities to participate in publicly supported education (Zettle and Ballard 14).

In 1973, Paul R. Dimond, a lawyer who had worked with the NAACP, summed up the ways that these cases pointed out the proper type of legislation to prevent school authorities from excluding children from public education. In his article, "The Constitutional Right to an Education," Dimond argued that the cases implied the child had a right to a hearing. Through some sort of notices or advertisements, school officials had to inform people about the opportunity to receive special education. An expert had to evaluate any child who might benefit from such treatment and teachers had to use that evaluation to develop an educational plan. Finally, the officials had to share the plan with the child's parents and notify them that they could appeal the decision. According to Dimond, the advantage of such an approach was that it did not ask judges to decide if school districts offered a good education. The only question that justices needed to ask was whether or not school officials followed the proper procedures (Dimond 1111–1118, 1124–1127).

In order to encourage local schools to adopt these practices, advocates sought legislation that enabled federal officials to threaten schools that ignored the right of children with disabilities and to reward schools that affirmed them. As Chapter Nine pointed out, Title VI of the 1964 Civil Rights Act gave officials in the U.S. Department of Health, Education, and Welfare the authority to reduce federal funds to a segregated school district and the ESEA gave them the ability to offer substantial sums to schools to help with the education of disadvantaged youths. As a result of these combined powers, officials desegregated large numbers of schools. Consequently, the different interest groups such as CEC and the National Association for Retarded Citizens joined together, sent witnesses to testify in hearings, and advised congressional staff about ways they could structure legislation to prevent the problems in the education of children with disabilities that the federal courts had acknowledged (Colachio 132–135).

After extensive hearings and compromises between the House and the Senate versions, Congress approved the Education for All Handicapped Children Act, Public Law 94-142 by wide margins. In the U.S. House of Representatives, the vote was 404 in favor and 7 opposed. In the U.S. Senate, the vote was 87 to 7. On 29 November 1975, President Gerald Ford signed the bill into law.

As the advocates wanted, PL 94-142 had two parts. One part guaranteed all children with handicaps the right to a free appropriate public education and described the procedures by which school people had to deliver it. The second section offered to financially support the states for special education, and it described the formula by which the amount would be determined. When the U.S. Bureau of Education for the Handicapped began to determine how to meet the law's requirements, the officials made it clear that a state's schools would lose the opportunity to receive the federal funds provided by the law if the state did not follow the outlined process. Thus, PL 94-142 required school districts to set up programs for special education, and it offered to pay some of the expenses. The law mandated that states ignoring the processes could not receive the monies. As had been the case with Title VI of the Civil Rights Act, states began to adopt special education classes and implement them in ways suggested by the procedures. In the academic year 1976–77, the law served 3.48 million children. This number grew to 4.3 million children in the academic year 1983–84 (Salomone 146–147).

As a result of the Public Law 94-142, spending for special education grew considerably. For example, in a detailed study of nine typical U.S. school districts, researchers for the Economic Policy Institute estimated that special education consumed the biggest share of new funds coming into schools. The researchers concluded that "special education growth consumed 38 percent of net new funds in 1991" (Rothstein and Miles 49).

Advocacy groups for special education achieved many of their goals because they encountered little opposition. Three factors insulated their drive to use federal legislation to advance special education: (1) They did not pursue any particular curriculum nor did they seek to remedy any particular sort of disability. As a result, critics had difficulty criticizing the general desire to help children with disabilities. (2) Unlike other areas of federal intervention, such as racial integration or the War on Poverty, there was no way to determine if the increased expenditures for special education brought about increased student achievement. As a result, critics could not complain that the money was wasted. (3) Special education programs served every social class and ethnic group because anyone's child could have a disability. Therefore, the increased programs did not elicit opposition because of changes they might cause in the social composition of schools. The paragraphs that follow explain these points in turn.

First, advocates did not require any particular curriculum proposal. The Education for Handicapped Children Act required schools to set up procedures that were similar to those Dimond had listed in 1973. The school had to identify, locate, and evaluate children needing special attention. School officials had to notify the parents indicating they thought the child should be evaluated. Experts had to evaluate the child in a nondiscriminatory way, and a placement team that included the special teacher or the regular teacher, the parent, and perhaps the school principal or the child drew up an individualized educational plan based on that evaluation. This plan had to include long-term goals for the child, short-term objectives to reach those goals, and methods to determine if the child met these goals and objectives. If the parents did not approve of the suggestions at any point, they could object, ask for an impartial hearing, and, ultimately, pursue judicial review.

According to proponents of individual educational plans, these procedures meant courts did not have to examine whether teachers did particular things or covered particular subject matter. According to some special education advocates, the process of evaluating the children, involving the parents, and planning the children's programs were simply procedures any intelligent teacher should take in preparing classroom lessons and they represented a reasonable amount of accountability. For example, H. Rutherford Turnbull pointed out that, under the Education for Handicapped Children Act, teachers had to show the parents or guardians what they planned to do with the children, and they had to provide evidence indicating their success. Turnbull added that this was no more than any professional should be willing to do. Although Turnbull noted that there was a difficulty in the required paperwork, he thought the benefits of improving education for the children with special needs outweighed any inconvenience for the teachers (Turnbull 367).

Although some professionals feared the new legislation, they thought the problems could be corrected. For example, writing in 1977, Maynard C. Reynolds and Jack W. Birch noted that the system might encourage state bureaucracies to describe every detail of the teacher's proper actions, and they worried that the system could place parents against teachers. Reynolds and Birch argued that federal, state, and local agencies could reduce these dangers by launching extensive educational efforts to teach parents, teachers, and administrators the proper ways to approach the education of children with special needs (Reynolds and Birch 685–687).

As if acting on such prescriptions, organizations such as the CEC and public agencies sought to help everyone understand the requirements of PL 94-142 after its adoption. Some things, such as the individual educational plans and the opportunities for parents to be involved in all phases of the curriculum planning, had been parts of previous legislation. Thus, many educators were familiar with them. Nonetheless, in states such as Ohio, Regional Centers for Handicapped Children published and distributed manuals explaining how individual educational plans were opportunities for parents and teachers to cooperate. In these manuals, administrators encountered suggestions on such things as offering parents access to the children's records as part of that cooperation (Miami Valley Regional Center ii–viii).

Second, although supporters of the Education for Handicapped Children Act claimed the law asked teachers to be accountable for their actions, there was no way for critics to assess whether the increased monies spent on the education of children with disabilities led to increased student achievement. Since the category of children with disabilities was extremely broad, experts could not make such measurements. Instead, evaluations of special education tended to focus on specific techniques for children exhibiting particular syndromes. Even in these cases, though, clinical evidence about the ineffectiveness of a particular intervention did not slow its use. For example, in 1972, a U.S. Congressional hearing discovered that Ritalin seemed ineffective in controlling the impulsive behavior of children. In response to the hearings, HEW called together a blue ribbon panel to consider the issue. This report acknowledged the inconclusive nature of the research, yet the panel members were unwilling to condemn the prescription of stimulants to control what they called "hyperactivity." Thus, the conference's report concluded that physicians should make their own decisions, and sales of Ritalin for children increased (Schrag and Divoky 94–95).

Third, the Education for Handicapped Children Act did not call for dramatic changes in schools. It did not threaten to bring students from different social classes to previously homogenous schools. Nor did the law require that teachers learn difficult skills such as master a foreign language. As a result of the conservative nature of the requirements, school people could meet them without rearranging their institutions.

Since the legislation was insulated from criticism, the advocacy groups, such as the CEC, did not have to fight for their own survival, and they could maintain careful watch over legislation alerting their members to any administrative changes that might threaten their gains. For example, in 1982, following President Reagan's effort to reduce the federal regulation of schools, the U.S. Department of Education announced a proposal to change the regulations required by PL 94-142. The changes would have reduced the necessary record keeping and ended the required reevaluation of the children. In reaction, about 23,000 letters and comments flowed in to the agency from supporters of the legislation claiming the proposed changes would strip parents of their rights, release school systems from their obligations, and eliminate progress in special education. After a flurry of resistance, the administration dropped its proposal (Salomone 163–164).

On the other hand, advocacy groups, such as the NAACP, could not oppose challenges to racial desegregation in the 1990s because they struggled for survival themselves. Thus, with the largest civil rights organization weakened by internal struggles and facing bankruptcy, critics of desegregation could mount successful campaigns against busing (Orfield et al. 22).

PL 94-142 underwent some criticism as a few legal cases rose to the U.S. Supreme Court. Some of these cases limited the extent to which schools had to go to provide equal opportunity for students with disabilities. For example, in 1982, in the case *Board of Education of the Hendrik Hudson Central School District v. Rowley*, the lower courts had ruled that the schools should provide a sign-language interpreter for a child with a hearing impairment. But U.S. Supreme Court justices concluded that the school did not have to provide the student with such an interpreter even though this might have enabled her to excel in her studies. The justices noted that the student was performing adequately without such attention and the law required only that her education be substantially equal to the education other students received.

Despite the federal administration's and the U.S. Supreme Court's attempts to temper PL 94-142, during the 1980s, the U.S. Congress extended and renamed the Education for Handicapped Children Act in 1990. The new name was the Individuals with Disabilities Education Act (IDEA). In adopting IDEA, legislators changed the phrase "handicapped children" to "children with disabilities." According to some educators, this change was important because it reinforced the concept that all children share the same human rights by pointing immediately to their common humanity and then to the particular fact of their disabilities.

The change also demonstrated that advocates for children with disabilities had succeeded in changing the ways that people thought about school reform and about democracy. As the earlier chapters illustrate, in the first half of the twentieth century, educators sought reforms that enabled children to satisfy their own desires while teaching them to contribute to the common good. By adopting the legalistic and political tactics of the NAACP and the SCLC, the advocates for special education transformed the aims of education.

The Education for All Handicapped Children Act defined the appropriate education for the children as that expressed on an individually guided educational plan. This was a plan that the teachers, the specialists, and the parents would shape during a placement team conference. Thus, the competing parties attending the conference could shape a curriculum that reinforced the progressive ideals of developing creative self-expression and cooperative attitudes, but the model did not require it. On the other hand, they could create a plan that would teach the child to master academic fundamentals and to conform to social expectations. There was nothing in the model to prevent the team from developing such conservative aims.

In short, the model of curriculum planning in the Education for All Handicaped Children Act left out any effort to describe what constituted a good education. Special educators may have adopted this inadequate model because the people who proposed it, such as Paul Dimond, did not think of themselves as curriculum theorists. They served as advocates for the children. Thus, they proposed an adversarial model of curriculum planning that was similar to the forums in which legal negotiation took place. To the advocates, this model advanced democracy because it allowed everyone the opportunity to help the children to develop their abilities to the maximum extent possible. Although the advocates may have thought of this as a democratic aim, the notion turned into a more pluralistic view because they implied that the appropriate education for the children is whatever everyone accepts provided it is expressed in terms that can be measured and reevaluated.

In the case of education for children with disabilities, few critics complained about the openness of the mode. In the efforts of advocates for children with linguistic differences, however, the question of whether or how the children would learn to advance the democratic nature of the society became an important consideration. Despite this difference, the campaign for bilingual education followed patterns that were similar to those used by the special educators.

In what ways did the advocates for bilingual education change their campaigns as a result of the Civil Rights movement?

During the 1960s and 1970s, bilingual educators imitated the tactics of the NAACP and the SCLC in the same way that special educators had. Advocacy groups for children of linguistic minorities argued that these children could not avail themselves of educational opportunities and that they had a right to an education that met their special needs. As a result of these campaigns, the U.S. Congress added legislation supporting such programs to the ESEA, and the U.S. Supreme Court required that schools offer such programs. The advocates of bilingual education disagreed, however, about the way schools should affirm these students' rights. Most advocates argued that bilingual education should help children whose native language was not English become proficient in English, and this was the direction that the federal legislation took. Yet, some advocates complained that this effort to bring the children into what they saw as the mainstream culture denied the children's rights to retain the cultures of their families. At the same time, supporters of English as the language of instruction argued that the programs reinforced the language and culture of the children's families instead of creating a national identity.

In 1966, the NEA conducted a survey on the teaching of Spanish to Mexican Americans in the Southwest. The members of the NEA committee found that many Mexican Americans lived in poverty, felt alienated from the surrounding society, and developed a set of attitudes and values that prevented them from succeeding in Anglo society. The report added that the schools exacerbated the problems. The children used poor English and spoke low-level Spanish, but the lessons in school aimed at teaching them the Anglo ways. Feeling compelled to ignore their culture, the children dropped out of school at early ages. Thus, the NEA committee reported that the schools refused to recognize the culture in which these children were raised and recommended that schools adopt programs of bilingual education to enable the children to fulfill their rights to become functioning citizens. In such programs, instruction extending from preschool to the early grades would be in Spanish and English. While English would be taught as a second language in later years, instruction in Spanish would continue through high school (NEA, *Invisible* 5–12, 17–18).

Senator Ralph Yarborough of Texas approved of the NEA's position on bilingualism. In 1967, when the ESEA came up for renewal, Yarborough submitted a bill that became Title VII of ESEA. Although a number of interest groups had sought to act as advocates for linguistic minorities, these groups did not seem to take an interest in bilingual education until Yarborough introduced his legislation. More important, during the hearings, the activists disagreed over what form the legislation should take (Stein 30–32; Moran 7–8).

In an effort to encourage the schools to become more pluralistic, Monroe Sweetland, legislative consultant for the NEA, urged Congress to draft legislation that would provide programs to teach Mexican American Children about their culture and their language. He recommended that these programs extend from kindergarten through high school (Committee on Education and Labor, 90th Congress 302–307).

On the other hand, in an effort to encourage intercultural understanding, John A. Carpenter of the University of Southern California, urged Congress to design legislation that would create programs to teach students about the cultures and languages of the different peoples in the United States. Carpenter complained that there was an imbalance in the schools because the Mexican American children had to learn Anglo culture. Yet, he added, few Anglos had consistent, coherent exposure to Hispanic language or experiences (Committee on Education and Labor, 90th Congress 254–255).

Taking the view that the students should use their native language as an aid in their transition to English, school people, such as Sarah Folsom, Arizona superintendent of public instruction, recommended that the legislation support efforts to help the children acquire facility in English. She referred to her efforts to have people recognize that Spanish was her state's second most important language (Committee on Education and Labor, 90th Congress 444–445).

At the same time that the committee heard testimony about the need for bilingual education, the members heard witnesses complain about the difficulty of finding adequately trained teachers for bilingual education classes. There were some ironies in the question of qualified teachers, however. For example, Herman Badillo, president of the Borough of the Bronx in New York, noted that adults who had been trained as teachers in Puerto Rico could not obtain positions in the New York City schools because they had strong Spanish accents. As a result, the schools refused to hire the teachers who could implement or conduct bilingual programs (Committee on Education and Labor, 90th Congress 248–249).

After the hearings, the U.S. Congress passed the Bilingual Education Act, Title VII of ESEA, but the legislation did not take any side in the controversies about the direction such programs should take. The act sought to create new imaginative elementary and secondary educational programs for low-income students who had limited English-speaking abilities. The bill sought to provide appropriate training for teachers and teacher aides. It listed several approaches that would be acceptable. These included bilingual education, programs to teach children about the culture associated with their language, and efforts to bring homes and schools closer together (U.S. Commission on Civil Rights, *A Better* 180–181).

Despite the unwillingness of the federal officials to choose among the possible options, the move for distinct, separate bilingual and bicultural programs grew as Mexican Americans pushed for increased political power. For example, in 1969, a protest took place in Crystal City, Texas. Beginning with a request for a homecoming for former Mexican American students, the protest grew into demands for recognition of the rights of Mexican Americans to bilingual and bicultural education. Since the Crystal City demonstrations were part of an effort to build a third political party in Texas, protests developed in other cities. In response to these demonstrations, the director of the U.S. Office of Civil Rights, J. Stanley Pottinger, issued a memo in 1970 to school districts with more than 5 percent national origin–minority students. In his memo, Pottinger quoted Title VI of the U.S. Civil Rights Act of 1964 barring discrimination. He noted that many practices in schools with Hispanic American students denied those students their rights to equal opportunities. Thus, he recommended that the schools take steps to remedy the students' language deficiency. He warned against segregating such students in low-level classes or classifying them as mentally retarded. And, he concluded, school officials may have to communicate with the parents of these students in their native language (Garcia 37–61; U.S. Commission on Civil Rights, *A Better* 204–205).

In 1971, a similar political protest arose in San Francisco, California, as Chinese community groups protested the city's proposed racial desegregation plan. Under the proposed racial desegregation, Chinese American children would move from the downtown Chinatown schools into areas where the teachers would be less likely to speak both Chinese and English, and, according to the parents' groups, would be less concerned with the students' achievement. Their complaints made little difference. Consequently, when the desegregation began, about 1,000 Chinese American students enrolled in so-called private freedom schools to avoid being bused to outlying schools. To bring the Chinese students back to the public schools, officials exempted them from the desegregation plan. Nonetheless, the controversies over desegregation made Chinese Americans aware of concerns over equality of opportunity, and they filed suit over the need for bilingual-bicultural education (Kirp 103–104, 108, 114–115).

The case from San Francisco, *Lau v. Nichols,* was the only U.S. Supreme Court decision on bilingual education. Released in 1974, the decision affirmed that children with limited English-speaking abilities had the right to receive supplementary education. According to the U.S. Supreme Court justices, there were about 2,856 Chinese-speaking students in the school district, and the schools gave supplementary instruction in English to about 1,000 Chinese-speaking students. This left almost 1,800 Chinese-speaking students without such aid, but the U.S. District Court had contended that California law required schools to use English as the language of instruction. Consequently, bilingual instruction was not necessary. At the U.S. Supreme Court, the justices agreed with the Chinese American families that the students who lacked knowledge of English could not make sense of their education. Further, the justices quoted Pottinger's memo from 1970 to show that the schools discriminated against these students and violated Title VI of the U.S. Civil Rights Act of 1964. Although the justices ordered the schools to provide some sort of remedial attention for the students, they cautioned that they arrived at this decision because a large number of students were involved. Since they would not order such changes for one or two students with limited English-speaking abilities, the justices implied that practical circumstance would limit this right to equal opportunity (*Lau v. Nichols*).

The same year, 1974, Title VII of ESEA, the Bilingual Education Act, came up for renewal. Although the U.S. Congress claimed the act was to establish equal educational opportunity, it did not require schools to set up such programs. It suggested that the funding was to encourage schools to develop programs such as instruction given in children's native language when this was necessary to allow students to progress effectively. Furthermore, the act recommended that instruction include consideration of the child's native culture, and to avoid excessive segregation, the act allowed some children who spoke English to participate in the bilingual and bicultural education (U.S. Commission on Civil Rights, *A Better* 186–187).

According to Ursala Casanova and M. Beatriz Arias, since the 1974 act did not specify an instructional approach, many instructors assumed this allowed them to stress the development of literacy skills in the child's native language. A split developed among bilingual education teachers. Some teachers wanted to use the native language to help the children learn English and enter the mainstream of society. Other teachers wanted to maintain the children's abilities in their native languages and in English even though the law forbade using bilingual education funds to help children maintain their abilities in two languages (Casanova and Arias 10–11).

Another boast for bilingual education came from an unexpected direction. In Title II of the Educational Amendments of 1974, the U.S. Congress listed among those acts that would deny students' their rights to equal opportunity the failure of an educational agency to help children overcome language barriers that could impede equal participation. Although Congress intended these amendments to end busing for racial balance, this section reaffirmed students' right to some sort of bilingual education (U.S. Commission on Civil Rights, *A Better* 174–175).

In keeping with the federal concern for bilingual education, the U.S. Office of Civil Rights issued in 1975 the findings of a task force to help school districts comply with the *Lau v. Nichols* decision. The task force suggested that districts with more than twenty students with limited English-speaking abilities should assess their language proficiencies and provide instruction in the students' native language until they could function in English. Called the Lau remedies, these guidelines indicated that techniques known as English as a Second Language

(ESL) were inadequate because this technique made no reference to the children's native tongue and lessons took place in English alone (Hakuta 201–202).

Critics found four weaknesses, which they used to challenge the practice of bilingual education: (1) Major studies commissioned by the federal government found the programs did not raise students' achievement test scores nor did they change students' attitudes toward school. (2) Federal officials sought to enforce the Lau remedies before the officials had followed the procedures to change these recommendations into required guidelines. (3) Programs of bilingual education could cause segregation and thereby frustrate the social advancement of the students. (4) The bilingual educators could not clearly show how the methods of bilingual education could lead to the goals they proposed. The following paragraphs explain these weaknesses in more detail.

First, in 1977, the American Institutes for Research (AIR) published the results of its study of thirty-eight Spanish/English bilingual programs that enrolled students from grades two to six. The U.S. Office of Education commissioned the study. The students in the programs came from families with occupational levels equivalent to a machine operator or service worker, and about 75 percent of them were Hispanic. The programs had received Title VII of ESEA funds for four or five years (Danoff 1–5).

Despite the high hopes of the bilingual educators, the results of the study were devastating. In English or mathematics achievement, the students in the bilingual program did not surpass what they could have accomplished without the programs. In fact, in comparisons with similar students in regular programs, the students in bilingual programs performed worse in English and in mathematics. In comparison to national norms, the students in bilingual programs scored in the twentieth percentile in English and in the thirtieth percentile in mathematics. There was no relation between success in mathematics and the extent to which teachers used Spanish in mathematics lessons. The bilingual programs did not lead to improved attitudes toward school. There were gains in Spanish fluency among some students in the bilingual programs, but this was related to student grouping procedures, not to instruction (Danoff 9–14).

When researchers interviewed the project directors and the teachers, they found that the programs seemed to ignore the legislative guidelines. That is, less than a third of the students had limited English ability. About 60 percent of the students spoke only English or spoke better English than Spanish. Further, when the researchers asked the program directors what happened to children when they could function in English, the directors replied that they stayed in the program. According to the researchers, this ran against the transition approach called for in Title VII of ESEA (Danoff 5–6).

Almost immediately, supporters of bilingual education complained that the AIR researchers had ignored such important concerns as the initial language dominance of the students and the qualifications of the teachers. In reply, the researchers claimed these accusations were untrue, and they explained where the information could be found (Nickel 261; Danoff and Coles 262).

Second, despite the disappointing evaluations, the federal administration continued to enforce bilingual education, but they encountered considerable difficulty. Since 1975, the U.S. Office of Civil Rights (OCR) had urged school districts to follow the Lau remedies, but the OCR had not followed the steps outlined in the Administrative Procedure Act to change these suggestions into required guidelines. As a result, school district officials in Alaska sued in federal district court, complaining that the OCR enforced the guidelines as rules but no one had been able to comment on their applicability. As a result, officials from the OCR agreed to go through the steps needed to make the guidelines binding (Moran 23).

Instead of publishing the Lau remedies as proposed regulations, officials in the ORC issued a notice of proposed rule making. These proposed rules suggested that children should learn English immediately. In this way, the new rules ignored the emphasis on bicultural education that had been present in the earlier Lau remedies. Feeling the OCR overlooked their concerns, several Hispanic groups argued against the new rules and joined with civil rights advocates asking that OCR protect the rights of linguistic minorities. Many school officials, however, and such teacher organizations as the American Federation of Teachers asked the OCR to give local schools more flexibility in determining how to meet the needs of students with limited English abilities. In the face of the controversy, the OCR withdrew the guidelines, returned to the looser standards Pottinger had formed in 1970, and provided schools with little guidance in organizing programs of bilingual education (Moran 23–25).

The third weakness was that programs of bilingual education could cause segregation. During the U.S. Senate hearings to reauthorize the Bilingual Education Act in 1977, Gary Orfield noted that he had formerly supported bilingual education but that concern with the ways the programs were conducted had caused him to change his mind. He claimed that fewer than ten percent of the students involved were Anglos. To Orfield, this was a serious problem since Spanish-surnamed children were the most segregated group in the United States. Bilingual education seemed to aggravate their segregation (Moran 21).

The fourth weakness was a lack of clarity in the methods of bilingual education that led the educators to make inflated claims about the goals of such instruction. In 1977, Richard Pratte, a philosopher of education, complained that bilingual educators made fuzzy statements about their methods and seemed to expect the programs to accomplish more than they could possibly deliver.

According to Pratte, a common claim among advocates of bilingual education was that the children learned that no culture was supreme and they lost their prejudices when teachers used the culture of the children's families and their language. Pratt complained that these advocates mixed bilingual education with bicultural education when the connection was not always direct. For example, Pratt noted that Mexican Americans in Texas spoke Spanish and held to what might be called Tex-Mex culture, but he added that a Jew in New York could share two cultures while speaking only English. In addition, Pratte complained that bilingual educators expected children to learn tolerance when they learned about different cultures and languages, but that he did not see how such school lessons could break down intense social attitudes. Further, Pratte added that the idea of bilingual education glossed over problems in selecting the languages. In this regard, he wondered if the bilingual educator would teach a Mexican American child who spoke a version of Spanish called Tex-Mex to read that slang language though the language did not appear in literary works or in governmental documents. Finally, Pratt noted that advocates for bilingual education suggested that their practices would break the cycle of poverty. Pratt concluded that this was more than any school program could do (Pratte 178–198).

These conflicts about bilingual education came before the U.S. Congress in 1984 when the legislators reconsidered Title VII of ESEA. At the congressional hearings, Gumecindo Salas of the Michigan State Board of Education pointed out that Title VII had helped Michigan to adopt a bilingual education law and to develop programs of bilingual education for 20,800 students from 60 different language groups. At that time, the state paid about $3.8 million for a year and received an additional $2.5 million from Title VII of the ESEA. Although this was significant, Salas added that there were children from 45 more language groups that would qualify for such aid if the state had adequate teaching staff. As a result, he urged more attention to the teacher-training component of the bill (Committee on Education and Labor 51–62).

Taking the opposing viewpoint, Senator S. I. Hayakawa testified at the hearings that he feared the Bilingual Education Act was misdirected. He claimed that he did not oppose bilingual education if it was severely limited. According to Hayakawa, several supporters of bilingual education used the issue to increase the importance of Spanish and change the United States into a polyglot country. He exhibited advertisements for college scholarships that were written in Spanish, and he claimed that the ads demonstrated how institutions made Spanish into an official language (Committee on Education and Labor 63–68).

The executive director of the organization, U.S. English, Gerda Bikales, supported Hayakawa's testimony at the hearing. She urged that the bill be renamed the English Language Acquisition Opportunity Act. In addition, she recommended that the U.S. Office of Bilingual Education within the U.S. Department of Education that would administer this act should be renamed the Office of English Language Acquisition. Above all, she urged that the funding for bicultural education should be removed. Ethnic cultures could remain in homes, and she thought that families should celebrate their cultures. She argued that public schools should form a common culture by transmitting common understandings among students. Most important, she noted that studies had not demonstrated the method of bilingual education to be effective, yet studies had shown that immersion, often called "sink or swim," worked well with disadvantaged youth in Canada. Above all, she urged the committee to draft legislation that would allow schools flexibility in choosing their approach to teaching (Committee on Education and Labor 68–70, 139–140).

Contradicting Hayakawa and the organization, U.S. English, the president of the National Association for Bilingual Education, Gloria Zamora, urged the U.S. House's subcommittee to extend the bilingual education act. In her presentation she made three points. First, she noted that in 1984, there were 3.6 million children with limited English proficiency, but that this number would increase by 35 percent by the year 2000. Second, she reaffirmed that the aim of the bilingual programs was to teach the children to acquire abilities to speak, to read, and to write in English. Third, she praised an aspect of the act that allowed children to learn and develop a second language. She claimed this was essential to preserve the linguistic resources in the country (Committee on Education and Labor 70–77).

Guillermo Lopez, chief of the Office of Bilingual Education in the California State Department of Education, took exception to U.S. English's position and some of Hayakawa's statements. Lopez complained that when Hayakawa accused bilingual education of promoting a language other than English, Hayakawa was mistaken. Lopez contended that neither the *Lau* decision nor any of the statutes adopted by twenty-two state legislatures in reaction to that U.S. Supreme Court case mentioned anything about one language over another (Committee on Education and Labor 114).

The NEA's prepared statement urged the subcommittee to frame legislation that would allow school districts flexibility. The NEA statement refused to support programs that maintained the children's native languages. Instead, the statement praised bilingual education claiming that it helped some students overcome feelings of alienation and that it allowed the school to develop a rich pattern of cultures in the community. In another breath, the NEA's statement praised English as a Second Language claiming it could develop a child's proficiency through systematic instruction. These programs differed because bilingual education used the children's native language and culture as part of the instruction. On the other hand, in English as a Second Language, the teacher ignored the children's language and culture and taught English. Despite the differences, the NEA supported both approaches as methods to provide equal educational opportunity to students with limited English proficiency. The NEA statement concluded by asserting that the goal in these programs should be proficiency in English (Committee on Education and Labor 137–139).

After the hearings, the U.S. Congress approved the Bilingual Education Act in 1984, but they set aside 4 percent of the appropriations for use in programs that would not use the students' native language. Almost immediately, there were controversies about whether the U.S. Office of Education made sure that school districts provided the supplemental instruction to the children with limited English proficiency. For example, in 1986, the U.S. Secretary of Education, William Bennett, claimed that 94 percent of the eligible 1.2 million children received special language programs. On hearing Bennett's comments, bilingual educators argued that Bennett grossly understated the number of eligible children and thereby expanded the percentage served. They claimed that school districts had many more students with limited skills in English because immigration had expanded and, according to a decision of the U.S. Supreme Court decision in *Pyler v. Doe,* schools had to serve illegal immigrants who were not counted (Casanova and Arias 14–15).

In 1988, the Bilingual Education Act came up for reconsideration again, and the U.S. Congress chose to give local school officials more discretion in deciding what methods to use in offering supplemental aid to children with limited English proficiency. Further, the bill limited a child's participation in a bilingual education program to three years. While it offered 500 fellowships to increase the number of qualified teachers, the bill discontinued grants for the development of instructional materials and eliminated the National Advisory and Coordinating Council on Bilingual Education (Bangura and Muo 89–92).

While federal officials did not remove bilingual education during the 1980s, they increased the flexibility in selecting appropriate methods. According to Rachel F. Moran, such conservative politicians as Ronald Reagan celebrated the flexibility in the Bilingual Education Act claiming that it allowed local school districts to experiment with a range of new programs for children with limited English proficiency. Moran noted, however, that many bilingual educators lamented the changes, asserting that in the 1960s when there was no law and school districts had complete freedom to experiment, they ignored the children who did not speak English as a native language (Moran 29).

From Moran's perspective, federal policy toward bilingual education retained its basis in the civil rights throughout the 1980s, but the politicians she called the "new federalists" were able to reduce the role of the federal government and offer more discretion to local officials. It is also important to note that while federal spending on all forms of bilingual education increased over the years, it remained significantly less than the amount devoted to other programs, such as Title I of ESEA or Head Start. Since increasing amounts of the money for bilingual education went to proposals that did not employ the students' language or culture, educators such as Colman Brez Stein, Jr. advised bilingual educators in 1986 to move away from federal funding for compensatory education and to develop high-quality maintenance programs wherein all children learned another language and another culture. Calling this positive integration, Stein recommended that programs that mixed children of all social classes could be constructed as magnet schools. He thought that such programs could attract English-speaking majority children to schools with Hispanic or Asian children. In this way, he thought bilingual education could become part of regular education and no longer be dependent on short-term federal grants (Sevilla 52; Stein 178).

Despite Stein's proposal to separate bilingual education and compensatory education, he repeated the claim that bilingual education was essential to affirm the rights of children with limited English abilities. That is, he reminded language minority parents and advocates to bring suit in federal courts if programs became experiences where teachers immersed children completely in English. Such legal complaints depended on the right to bilingual education.

Advocates for the education of children with limited English proficiency sought to establish programs by arguing that these children had a right to some sort of bilingual education. In part, they endured more controversy than special educators suffered because their proposals illuminated the problems of pluralism. That is, the claims that children had a right to an education that met their special needs changed the pattern of education that had prevailed in the years after World War I until the 1960s. During the first half of the twentieth century, progressive educators argued that schools should meet students' needs in ways that advanced democracy. In the 1960s, bilingual educators took a more legalistic direction. They built their campaigns on the view that children had a right to an education that met their special needs. Unfortunately, critics could complain that the special programs for these children did not enhance the democratic society. The critics thought that bilingual education enabled children with limited English proficiency to withdraw into small cultural enclaves. Thus, they protested that such training placed the schools in positions that divided the society. These critics wanted schools to serve the more progressive notion of forging one society out of many cultures.

What were the effects of the campaigns by special educators and bilingual educators to establish students' rights to appropriate educations?

Special educators and bilingual educators followed similar strategies to advance the curriculums for their students. Both groups based their reforms on efforts to establish a right to education for the students in their programs. Since federal courts could establish such rights, these groups sued in federal courts in the same way that the NAACP had. This represented a unique strategy because the laws governing schools and making education compulsory appeared in state constitutions or in state legislation rather than in the U.S. Constitution. Their hope was to win some cases and use those court victories to create central offices within the federal administration from which they could influence federal legislation.

In addition to seeking federal support to change the practices of local schools, advocates for both movements worked under roughly similar conditions. They were composed of a variety of narrowly focused interest groups. For example, among advocates for children with handicaps, a multitude of organizations catered to children with specific disabilities. Among the advocates for bilingual education, a range of political and cultural groups supported each different language and ethnic group.

Despite these similarities, the advocates for special education differed from the advocates for bilingual education in the aims they pursued. Special educators did not have any specific curriculum or program in mind to satisfy the rights of children with disabilities. On the other hand, advocates for children with limited English proficiency found themselves defending specific formulas.

By adopting a model of curriculum planning that could be used in a variety of ways by different teachers, advocates for children with disabilities could form coalitions with the various groups that agreed with them. Controversies developed about what should be the level and the extent of the opportunities for children with disabilities. Nonetheless, special educators remained convinced that the model of the individual educational plan with distinct steps of appeal provided equality of opportunity for the students. No matter what techniques a group of special educators favored, they accepted the overarching procedures outlined in the public laws as a model that would encompass their various notions. To obtain such universal support, this model remained neutral. It required that such people as the parents, the teachers, and specialists form a consensus on the aid the children should receive. It did not try to define the aims or the nature of a good plan.

On the other hand, bilingual advocates and educators disagreed about the methods the programs should use and what aims they should seek. Some advocates urged that programs maintain the children's original language and culture. Other programs called for rapid transition into English. Thus, unlike special educators, bilingual educators could not construct a consensus. Worse, the internal debates among bilingual educators made them vulnerable to the arguments of conservative politicians in the 1980s. Seeking to reduce the role that the federal government played in local school affairs, these conservatives called for more flexibility and more opportunities for local school districts to make their own decisions on how to spend federal aid. While special educators could mobilize parents and teachers to protest these efforts to undercut their reforms, bilingual educators could not as easily resist. Not only were they more divided but research studies had called into question the effectiveness of their methods.

Thus, by 1986, the law supporting the education of the handicapped required certain procedures and offered funds to aid in those efforts, but the law supporting bilingual educators offered funds and required few procedures. When bilingual educators tried to salvage their programs by urging that all students should become bilingual or bicultural, they solved some of their problems and created new ones. Universal programs of bilingualism would overcome the difficulties in receiving federal and local support that derived from linking bilingual to compensatory education. Further, in such schoolwide programs, bilingual education would not segregate students, but the possibility of every student learning another language removed the rationale that had made bilingual education a force in the curriculum. There was no way to show that everyone had the right to speak another language in addition to English.

As the introduction of this chapter describes, historians such as Joel Spring and Gerald Grant noticed ironic effects of the Civil Rights movement. They contended that the effect of such campaigns was to cause schools to become less educative. These authors may have been correct but they overlooked an important effect of the the Civil Rights movement. When advocates for special education and bilingual education imitated the strategies that the NAACP and the SCLC had used to advance concern for African American students, they altered the progressive tradition of meeting the students' needs. To meet the special needs of their constituencies, these advocates sought to establish that the children they wished to serve had the right to an education that met their special needs. The problem was that by taking an approach from a legal campaign for the students' individual rights, educators seemed to reinforce the personal aspects of education at the expense of social concerns. Thus, instead of advancing a democratic society as the progressives had urged, these advocates seemed to define a good education as whatever the people receiving it considered it to be. They did this because they seemed to think of themselves as advocates for the children more than they considered themselves educators in the broader sense that the progressive educators had adopted.

In the chapters that follow, readers will find that advocates for other groups continue to imitate the NAACP and the SCLC. In order to reform elementary and secondary curriculums, conservative politicians campaign for vouchers to pay for private school education and for charter schools based on the view that parents have the right to select an effective education for their children. Not surprisingly, critics complain that conservatives make these arguments to destroy the common basis the public schools provide. Ironically, liberal educators, such as critical pedagogues and advocates for gay and lesbian students, follow the same strategies by arguing that students have the right to form supportive communities. Although these distinct groups of advocates campaign for different programs, they base their views on a similar assumption. This is that the schools should affirm the parents' or the children's rights.

Summary

Following the success of the Civil Rights movement, several groups of advocates sought to establish the right to education for their constituents. Advocates serving children with disabilities were the most successful of these groups. They claimed that public schools denied the rights of the children. They sued in federal courts for redress. They pointed to the resulting legal victories of requiring local school officials to follow a set of procedures as evidence of equal educational opportunities. Imitating the earlier civil rights groups, these advocates wanted legislation with two different tendencies. On the one hand, the legislation should reward schools that acted correctly. On the other hand, it should punish those schools that ignored the requirements. This was the way the Civil Rights Act and ESEA had functioned.

In a similar manner, advocates for children with limited English abilities sought legislation that would reward schools that offered special programs for the children and they sued in federal courts seeking redress against schools that ignored these recommendations. The supporters of bilingual education succeeded in garnering federal aid for their programs, and the U.S. Supreme Court established a right to supplemental assistance for children with limited English proficiency. But unlike special educators, bilingual educators could not extract their federal aid from compensatory education nor could bilingual educators clearly establish what would satisfy the right to equal education for these children. At the request of many school officials, legislators decided that most plans to aid in the children's acquisition of English satisfied that right. Some bilingual educators contended, however, that the children had a right to learn their own culture and native language. Thus, although educators disagreed about what methods they should employ in bilingual education, the teachers agreed that the programs should affirm the children's rights.

In making these campaigns, advocates for children with disabilities and for children with limited English proficiency broke with the earlier progressive ideal that schools should meet the needs of the students in ways that advanced the democracy. The legal, adversarial nature of the model for curriculum making implied that whatever the placement team thought was good for the child was acceptable. The advocates made no effort to describe what constituted a good education. On the other hand, bilingual education fell apart because the advocates could not agree on what schools should do for the children with linguistic differences. Some advocates wanted bilingual education to help children adjust to the wider society. Participants of the campaigns for special education and bilingual education shared difficulties in defining a good education because they did not focus on this concern. They wanted to force schools to affirm the children's rights to an appropriate education.

PART VI

AFFIRMING PARENTS' RIGHTS TO EFFECTIVE SCHOOLS AND STUDENTS' RIGHTS TO SUPPORTIVE COMMUNITIES, 1981–2000

The two chapters in this section describe what appear to be different campaigns to support contradictory ideas. Despite the differences, the advocates and educators who shaped these campaigns shared concerns that schools affirm the rights of individuals. Since these reformers saw themselves as representing the interests of particular groups, they tended to overlook the wider social aims that consumed the progressives during the first half of the century.

Chapter Eleven, From the Right to an Effective Education to Charter Schools, describes the efforts of federal officials to have parents assert their rights to effective schools and to force teachers to concentrate on teaching basic academic skills. Unwilling to offer federal funds for the purpose, the federal officials tried to persuade parents to organize and pressure school administrators and local officials to make the changes. To help parents make intelligent choices, the officials tried to adopt national standards and uniform testing. Although the federal government did not adopt such policies, these officials and the educators who supported them encouraged state governments to approve the formation of charter schools as a method of allowing parents to exercise their rights to choose their children's school. They hoped that this would cause competing schools to develop more effective educational programs.

Chapter Twelve, Affirming People's Rights to Community through Schools, describes the efforts of another group of educators who sought to affirm the students' rights to form communities. This chapter explains the efforts of three groups of educators: critical pedagogues, feminists, and gay and lesbian teachers. In varying degrees, the members of each of these groups followed the ideas of Paulo Freire who developed a philosophy while he conducted programs for adult literacy in South America. Under this model, the students formed learning communities and decided among themselves what direction their education should take. Unfortunately, critics complained that the pursuit of liberation could exacerbate the problems of oppression rather than reduce them.

CHAPTER ELEVEN

FROM THE RIGHT TO AN EFFECTIVE EDUCATION TO CHARTER SCHOOLS, 1981–2000

In 1981, Ronald W. Reagan took office as the U.S. president after conducting a campaign in which he cited high levels of unemployment and a rising international trade deficit as evidence that the Democratic incumbent, Jimmy Carter, failed in office. But, one year after Reagan's inauguration, the rate of unemployment rose even higher and the trade deficit increased.

In the face of apparently unsolvable economic problems, Reagan and his Secretary of Education, Terrell Bell, created the National Commission on Excellence in Education (NCEE) to examine the quality of education and to make recommendations for its improvement. In making its report, the NCEE claimed that the mediocre performance of public schools threatened the economic prosperity of the country because the graduates were ill prepared to become productive workers. To prove its claims, the NCEE offered some indicators. For example, U.S. students were never first or second on international comparisons of academic achievement, SAT test scores had declined steadily from 1963 to 1980, and business and military leaders complained they had to spend millions of dollars to train workers in basic academic skills (NCEE 1–9).

The NCEE recommended that schools become more subject matter oriented, that administrators require the students to perform on objective measures of achievement, and that students spend more time in school and doing homework. For example, although high schools could offer some vocational courses and fine arts opportunities, students would have to take more courses in English, mathematics, science, social studies, and computer science to graduate. Standardized tests would be administered at major transition points, such as high school graduation. Further, the NCEE recommended that schools stay in session for seven hours each day and extend the academic year to 220 days per year (NCEE 24–29).

The premise of the NCEE was that excellence had to replace mediocrity in schools. According to the committee, general track courses had replaced the traditional college preparatory and vocational classes. While general classes tied the subject matter to some topic of interest to the students, the report complained that they deterred students from studying substantial material. In this way, the report *A Nation at Risk* claimed the cause of low educational achievement was that teachers followed methods of instruction similar to those approved by the Herbartians in Chapter One and by the progressive educators in Chapter Six. To remedy the problem, the report recommended that teachers hold to high standards and require the students to work at the most difficult level possible. Defining this procedure as excellence, the NCEE asserted that this quality enabled people to respond to the challenges of a rapidly changing world (NCEE 12–13, 18).

Although the NCEE was a federal commission, its report did not describe mechanisms to reform schools. Instead, the NCEE subtitled its report as "An Open Letter to the American People." The authors stated that they were confident that the American people would do what was right for their children if they were properly informed. Thus, according to the report, the driving force behind the reform was to be the parents asserting their rights for the best education that schools could provide for their children. Once the parents made their complaints, the public officials, school administrators, and parents could work together to make the changes. Public officials would recognize and advance the national interest in effective schools, and school administrators would provide leadership in creating school and community support for the reforms (NCEE 6, 32–34).

A year after the NCEE made its report, the U.S. Secretary of Education, Terrell Bell, maintained that the public took the message to heart and had begun the work of school reform. For example, he claimed that forty-eight states were in the process of strengthening their high school graduation requirements, eight states had extended the length of the school day, and seven states had lengthened the school year. To Bell, these changes showed that the people and their public officials could work together to improve schools (U.S. Department of Education, *Nation* 7–8, 11–16).

Despite Bell's optimistic pronouncements, the reforms that appeared among the states ignored two important areas. The first area was academic standards. Although several states revised the graduation requirements, school systems responded by creating new courses that appeared to be academic but were not. For example, when Thomas Toch visited schools in Florida, Texas, and California, he found that these states had mandated more academic courses for the students, but the schools allowed students to meet this requirement with such offerings as "Science by Investigation," or "Introduction to Physical Science." According to Toch, these new courses did not cover the material usually associated with the subject area disciplines. When the schools retained the academic courses, Toch found that administrators assigned the classes to teachers who had insufficient training in the academic areas (Toch 102–111).

The second area where schools subverted the NCEE's recommendations was the use of standardized measures of academic achievement. When the NCEE recommended standardized measures of achievement, the report warned that minimum competency examinations did not encourage excellence because people tended to think that the minimum requirements were the maximum necessary. Nonetheless, according to the National Center for Fair and Open Testing, the number of states requiring students to pass a standardized test for high school graduation increased from 15 in 1985 to 24 in 1987. These tests measured minimum requirements (NCEE 20; Medina and Neill 6).

Minimum competency tests may have become popular because school administrators could create the tests or design the curriculum in ways to ensure that most students succeeded on the exams. Then, the school officials could point to increasing scores as measures of the schools' success. For example, Thomas Toch pointed out that, in some states, the people who created the exams worked in the state department of education. They designed the tests to fail only those children who knew nothing. If too many students failed, they revised the tests. Nonetheless, the fact of the test and evidence that most students could pass the test allowed many administrators to claim that they were doing a good job (Toch 211–213).

Despite the possibility of manipulating the tests, elementary and high school teachers complained that what they called "high stakes testing" reduced the level of instruction in their classes. At the school district level, superintendents could urge teachers to link the curriculum directly to specific tests. Textbook companies aided this effort by producing texts that introduced lists of basic skills the students would need to excel on certain standardized tests, and teachers admitted that they gave less attention to what they called higher-level thinking or extended projects. They concentrated on imparting basic skills throughout the year so the children would perform well on the standardized tests. As a result of these problems, organizations, such as the International Reading Association, issued statements opposing the use of standardized tests to make important decisions about the students, such as whether they would be promoted or graduate; to make decisions about the teachers, such as linking merit pay or tenure to children's scores; or to make decisions about the schools, such as threatening to remove certain administrators if students' scores fell. The organizations claimed that using the tests to judge the students, the teachers, or the schools changed the tests. Under those conditions, the tests did not serve to help the children learn. Instead, they became methods of controlling the instruction (Toch 211–227; Shepard and Dougherty 14–15; International Reading Association 1).

In what ways did government officials and parent advocates seek to establish parents' rights to an effective education for their children?

In general, government officials and advocates took three directions to enable parents to establish the right to a basic education. The first was the method employed by officials in the U.S. Department of Education. It consisted of providing information on the ways that schools should be organized and on the rates of progress of the students in acquiring academic skills. The officials hoped that the parents would use this information to engage in political action to change schools.

When Bell left the position of U.S. secretary of education, his successor, William Bennett, maintained the practice of providing information that parents and citizens could use to assert their rights to send their children to effective schools. For example, in 1986, Bennett released the report, *What Works: Research about Teaching and Learning.* In the foreword, Bennett wrote that the aim was to provide the American people with accurate and reliable information about what works in the education of children so that they could improve their schools. He added that parents had to take action because most of the then current educational theory discredited the most effective suggestions. According to Bennett, the best types of instruction followed simple principles of common sense, yet most teachers disagreed with them (U.S. Department of Education, *What* v–vi).

In the section about schools, the report, *What Works,* claimed that one of the most important achievements of educational research was accomplished when researchers studied schools that successfully taught basic skills to children from low-income families. The researchers found that these so-called effective schools shared seven characteristics. They maintained vigorous instructional leadership. The schools' principals made clear, consistent decisions. The schools' policies emphasized order and discipline, and the teachers' instruction centered on academic achievement. The teachers shared a sense of collegiality in support of student achievement, and they held high expectations for the students. Finally, the schools offered frequent reviews of student progress (U.S. Department of Education, *What* 45).

To some extent, these characteristics of effective schools matched the recommendations the NCEE had urged people to make in the high schools. According to NCEE, it was important for teachers to hold to high standards, to measure progress, and to concentrate on academic achievement. Furthermore, the NCEE report claimed that schools had to create atmospheres encouraging all faculty and staff to accomplish their jobs. The difference is that unlike the effective schools research, The NCEE listed five subjects the students should study because the students had to have such skills if they were to become valuable employees who could provide economic prosperity for themselves and the society. Unlike Bennett, the NCEE report did not tie the recommendations to any specific model of school improvement such as the effective schools plan.

By the mid-1980s, though, the effective schools research became so popular that at least one advocate made it an important part of a strategy to enable parents to force state and federal courts to establish their rights to a basic education. This was the second method that advocates recommended to parents' groups.

In 1986, Gershon M. Ratner published an article in the *Texas Law Review* arguing that groups of parents could use the due process rights of the Fourteenth Amendment of the U.S. Constitution in filing suits to establish their rights. They could force schools to adopt the effective schools model of instruction. According to Ratner, research findings agreed that, if schools accepted and implemented the characteristics of effective schools, the children from low-income families would master basic academic skills. Ratner's rationale for the legal claim was that states deprived young people of their liberty through compulsory education. In order to be legitimate, such a deprivation must serve the purpose it was designed to accomplish. In the case of compulsory education, the purpose was to adequately educate children in basic skills (Ratner 315, 325).

When Ratner republished his article in 1994, he urged the federal government, state agencies, and business leaders to try to persuade schools to adopt the characteristics of so-called effective schools. As a last resort, he noted that class action suits in state and federal courts could establish the legal right of parents to an effective education, but, he did not list successful cases that had carried out his ideas (Ratner 339–340).

In making his pleas for legal action, Ratner overlooked the tendency of courts not to become involved in matters of educational methods. For example, as described in Chapter Ten, advocates for children with disabilities were careful not to ask the justices to decide what curriculum the teachers should employ. Instead, they set up a process by which experts, teachers, and parents could work together to structure the lessons or the classroom as they pleased. Plans for effective schools did more than set up a process. They defined how individuals should act within the process and what they should teach.

While Ratner's arguments may not have succeeded in court, the U.S. Congress accepted pleas to encourage schools to adopt such schoolwide reforms as the effective schools model. In 1994, the U.S. Congress changed the direction of ESEA, Title I funds. Under the new regulations, schools with at least 50 percent of the students coming from families that lived in poverty could use the federal monies for some method that would change the entire school. In 1997, the U.S. Congress allocated an additional $145 million per year to help low-performing schools to raise student achievement through some sort of approach that changed the entire atmosphere of the school. With federal money available, developers created many different methods of schoolwide reform. By 1999, researchers listed 24 different brands that had some similarities to the effective schools model, that the federal legislation mentioned by name, and that many school districts adopted (American Institutes for Research 1–9).

The third method recommended by advocates was to argue that the standards set by the U.S. Congress and by state legislatures established the legal basis of a right to an effective education. For example, Paul Weckstein argued that when the U.S. Congress or a state legislature raised academic standards, those agencies had to provide the resources for students to meet the new requirements. Thus, lawyers could challenge the programs and curriculums that did not teach the children the skills identified by the standards. For example, Weckstein noted that in 1988 the U.S Congress added a component to Title I demanding that the schools make substantial progress toward identified outcomes to qualify for federal funds. To avoid problems in compliance, some states defined their instructional objectives as changes in average scores on standardized tests. Although Weckstein complained that such changes did not refer to children acquiring basic skills, he believed this resulted because the states' educational administrators did not act properly. Thus, he recommended that parents should watch over the process. When administrators ignored important aspects of the children's education, the parents should seek legal remedies. He noted that, in such cases, the parents would have to contend that students had a right to an educational program designed to meet the new standards (Weckstein 353–354, 359–360).

How could the proposal to create a national testing program establish the parents' rights to effective schools?

In 1986, Tennessee governor, Lamar Alexander, announced that the National Governors' Association decided to abandon the model of reform exemplified by the NCEE. Instead of specifying what subjects students pursued or how long they should stay in school, the governors wanted to focus on the results of that teaching. According to Chester Finn, this statement was an expression of frustration with the problems the NCEE encountered in regulating the processes of education. He acknowledged, however, that, in order to focus on the schools' achievements, public officials would have to set up clear goals and they would have to approve tests to measure the progress that schools made in achieving the standards (Finn 124–125).

Although state governments controlled public education, the federal government had some methods of evaluating public schools. In 1963, the U.S. commissioner of education had asked Ralph Tyler to develop a national educational assessment program. The result was the National Assessment of Educational Progress (NAEP). By 1986, the NAEP administered tests of reading, writing, science, and mathematics to nationally representative samples of nine-, thirteen-, and seventeen-year-old students. From time to time, the tests included other subject areas, such as history, geography, and civics (Alexander, James, and Glasser 3, 74).

In 1986, the U.S. Department of Education requested that the National Academy of Education set up a panel to review the NAEP. Asserting that the NAEP was the primary source of information on what American students know, the panel made recommendations, such as establishing a governing board that included members from different levels of education to strengthen the test and turn it into a tool for school improvement. The panel suggested that the regular assessments cover the core subjects of reading, literacy, and writing; mathematics and science; and history, geography, and civics. The sample of students should be taken from the grades 4, 8, and 12 because these were the important transition points in schooling. Most important, the panel warned that the tests had to be designed to reflect the educational conditions accurately but in a way that maintained continuity so that researchers could track the changes in educational achievements (Alexander, James, and Glaser 7–11).

A separate panel reviewed these recommendations and agreed that the citizens had a right to know what students accomplished, what schools undertook, and what more had to be done. The panel urged caution, however, in using the NAEP as a tool for educational reform. The review panel wanted a more careful explanation of how the measures could be used to change schools. In this regard, the review warned that school improvement raised complex issues, and hasty actions could cause harm (Alexander, James, and Glaser 47–50).

The review panel's caution proved to be reasonable because there were several technical problems in using the NAEP as a means to reform schools. For example, in 1988, Congress authorized voluntary state assessment trials, but when an independent research service considered whether such comparisons could be a tool for school reform, the researchers found that they could not. The main difficulty was that no one could assume that differences in scores between states reflected differences in the effects of educational policies. Instead, the researchers found that a combination of four demographic factors—number of parents living at home, parents' education, community type, and state poverty rates—explained the variations that appeared in comparisons of achievement test scores. Since the schools could not control these demographic factors, it was unreasonable to attribute the differences in scores to the success of any school policies. Some statisticians proposed ways to adjust the scores to reflect more fairly the effect of such factors as school resources, but these methods were complicated and controversial. As a result, the research service report concluded that federal money should not go to perfecting methods of comparing state achievement scores. A better plan would be to spend the funds helping state governments to improve their schools (Robinson and Brandon 12, 15–17).

On the other hand, supporters of standards and tests, such as James Popham, argued that intelligently constructed large-scale tests could enable parents and citizens to protect their rights to effective schools. Popham had created competency tests for a dozen state governments. He acknowledged that large-scale testing could not be used to judge the effectiveness of certain schools or teachers because factors such as the child's background or social class influenced test scores. But, he thought that large-scale tests could illuminate whether instruction had been successful if the tests focused on a very few high-priority outcomes, if the tests required students to use important knowledge, if teachers knew in advance what the tests would measure, and if the tests' difficulty matched the appropriate level. Constructed with these principles in mind, the tests could be a means for educational policy makers to gradually improve schools, he concluded (Popham 55–65, 76).

Given the disagreements among researchers, it is not surprising that, from 1989 to 1997, members of the U.S. Congress debated the wisdom of establishing educational standards and national tests to measure student achievement. U.S. presidents Bush and Clinton embraced the ideas. But they faced significant opposition. Liberal politicians wanted to spend money on improving the quality of the schools before establishing the standards and the tests. Conservative politicians opposed establishing standards and the tests because they feared that setting national standards would increase federal control over schools. To some extent, state governments began the processes of establishing benchmarks for their schools. Thus, although the federal government stopped pressing for such innovations, the ideas persisted in state governments (Jennings 182–183).

If parents exercised their rights to free choice, would they act in ways that caused schools to improve?

In addition to creating the NCEE to stipulate the reforms needed to improve schools, President Ronald Reagan endorsed the idea that parents should exercise their rights of free choice. He claimed that the resulting competition among different schools would lead to improved education. As a result, during almost every year of his administration, Reagan sent to the U.S. Congress proposed legislation that would offer tuition tax credits to parents paying for private schools or vouchers redeemable at either public or private schools, but Congress rejected all of these proposals (Toch 246–247).

In 1991, two economists, John E. Chubb and Terry M. Moe, claimed that if parents had the freedom to choose where to send their children for schooling, education would improve for all people. Chubb and Moe approved of many of the reforms that Reagan's administration had attempted—for instance, tougher academic requirements, more rigorous curriculums, and co-operative relations among teachers and principals—but they complained that these innovations were inadequate. They claimed that real revolution in education would have taken place if the changes focused on fundamental issues, such as which group did the schools serve. Chubb and Moe decided that the efforts did not succeed because few reformers asked such questions (Chubb and Moe 228).

According to Chubb and Moe, schools operated as democracies. As a result, the parents surrendered their rights to satisfy their desires, and the school administrators exercised a sort of tyranny over them. Parents had the right to elect the members of boards of education of local school districts and state departments of education, but this was the extent of their participation. Once elected, the school officials had the authority to decide what went on in the schools. In a local district, the school board selected the school administrators who could ignore a parent's wishes. Private schools did not expand the parents' options because the parents had only the power to accept or reject what the particular private school in their area provided. On the other hand, Chubb and Moe contended that, in a market system, parents would have the rights and the opportunities to satisfy their individual desires by selecting from a wide array of schools (Chubb and Moe 28–35).

Chubb and Moe urged reformers to think about choice as the panacea for educational problems. They claimed that a public authority, such as a state legislature, could satisfy parents' rights to an effective education for their children by creating a system of schools the public authority could not control. Under these conditions, the schools would be able govern themselves, specify their own goals and methods, select their own student bodies, and make their own personnel decisions. At the same time, the parents would be able to choose among several alternative schools, and they would select the institution that best served their interests. Whether the parents chose to send their children to private or public schools, the parents would cause the schools to become more effective because they had been empowered to exercise their rights. Ineffective schools would close (Chubb and Moe 218, 226).

In making these points, Chubb and Moe expressed the faith of liberal economists. They held the view that, when people acted on the basis of their own self-interest, the rules of the marketplace caused those different actions to result in the greater good of everyone. Some commentators called this the "market ideology."

According to Michael Engel, the market ideology became an important component of educational reform with the publication of *A Nation at Risk.* He defined the market ideology in education to be the view that schools contribute to the economy by developing the human capital or human resources needed to run the factories, operate the stores, and provide the services. In this ideology, Engel contended that three factors were important: (1) Learning should be geared to economic benefits, (2) the assessment of education should be based on the outcomes, and (3) the community could not force the consumers to select any particular schools. The parents had the right to make their own decisions (Engel 27–30).

As noted earlier in this chapter, President Reagan wanted the U.S. Congress to adopt tuition tax credits or vouchers that would allow parents to act as free consumers, but Congress refused. In 1991, the state of Minnesota created a model to offer parents the right to choose the education for their children and to provide teachers the right to create their own institutions. This was the charter school.

In 1988, Ray Budde used the term *charter* to describe an educational system in which school systems granted charter agreements to teachers who wanted to create new curriculums. The idea was that the teachers were going to explore a new educational world, and the charter symbolized or approved of their venture. The idea garnered an important ally when Albert Shanker, president of the American Federation of Teachers (AFT), supported the role charter schools could play in school reform. Shanker had been impressed with the way that an innovative educator had created a teacher-run school in East Harlem in New York City. As a result, in a speech in Minnesota, Shanker expressed his approval for the concept. A state senator heard Shanker's endorsement, led a proposal through the state legislature, and started a wave of reforms. By 1992, there were 64 charter schools in states such as California, Colorado, Georgia, and Massachusetts. Within seven years, over 36 states passed charter school legislation and allowed the establishment of over 2,000 charter schools (Kane and Lauricella 204, 205–206).

In part, the federal government sponsored this growth. In 1994, during the reauthorization of the 1965 Elementary and Secondary Education Act (ESEA), the U.S. Congress appropriated $6 million to support the creation of public charter schools. Both political parties supported the bill, and the national media paid little attention to its passing. Congress gave only a small portion of the $12.7 billion of the ESEA to charter schools in the first appropriations, but the senators and representatives subsequently increased those appropriations for charter school development and research each year. In 1996, the Congress appropriated $18 million. In 1997, Congress appropriated $51 million to charter schools. In 1998, the amount grew $80 million, and in 1999, to $100 million (Leal 58–61).

One reason the charter school movement did not attract public controversy was that the federal appropriations allowed the states to create their own models for charter schools. As a result, each state adopted different laws that allowed for different types of charter schools. In 2001, the most restrictive state was Mississippi. It allowed only six charter schools to exist in the state, and each of them had to have been part of a public school system before they changed their status. On the other hand, the most permissive state was Arizona. In this state, there was no limit to the number of schools that could be formed. Almost anyone or any organization could apply for a charter. Three different types of public bodies could issue charters. These included a local district board, the Arizona Board of Education, and the State Board of Charter Schools. The last board was made up of gubernatorial appointees who served staggered terms. Thus, an anticharter school governor could not appoint a full board of like-minded members. Further, in Arizona, the schools received full funding from the state, and the schools did not need to follow state laws or regulations, nor did they have to abide by collective bargaining arrangements with the unions for teachers or for support personnel (Kane and Lauricella 207; Maranto and Gresham 100–101).

Arizona adopted legislation approving charter schools in 1994. It was so expansive that, by 1999, Arizona had about one-fourth of the charter schools in the nation. These schools enrolled about 34,000 students, which came to about 5 percent of the total public school enrollment. In general, the charter schools in Arizona grew up near population centers. Since they were fully supported by the state, they charged no tuition. Furthermore, the law prohibited them from restricting admission to certain students (Maranto et al. 7).

According to Bryan C. Hassel, the charter schools in Arizona represented what Chubb and Moe requested. They were institutions that the public authority created but that the public authority could not administer. Thus, charter schools in Arizona appeared to offer a way to test whether choice was a panacea (Hassel 84).

It is important to note that if charter schools were to fulfill Chubb and Moe's expectations of fulfilling the rights of parents to effective schools, three conditions had to exist. First, the consumers had to have unfettered opportunities to exercise their right to select among alternatives. Second, the choices had to be real or different choices. Third, the charter schools had to offer more success or they should close from lack of support. Studies of the Arizona schools indicated that the charter school law created some but not all of these conditions. The following paragraphs will explain more fully how this happened.

First, the consumers had to have unfettered choices. In this regard, the Arizona law gave the consumers the opportunity to create and to select charter schools from a wide range of choices. According to Robert Maranto and April Gresham, the Arizona charter schools tended to open wherever there was a demand. Parents and educators who had recently moved to Arizona from outside the state seemed critical of Arizona public schools and wanted an alternative for their children. Thus, in areas settled by newcomers from California, the charter schools flourished. In other parts of the state, Hispanics and Native Americans applied to open charter schools because they thought the public schools ignored their children (Maranto and Gresham 105–106).

Second, the choices had to be real or different choices for the parents to have the ability to exercise their rights. In this case, the charter schools in Arizona did not offer a wide range of different choices. In 1997, most of the charters in Arizona were small. Charter school operators thought this was an advantage because the teachers, children, and parents knew each other well and cooperated effectively. On the other hand, public school officials noted that the small charter schools could not offer the range of resources and curriculum options found in the larger public schools (Maranto and Gresham 108–109).

In regard to real choices, a team of researchers found that different charter schools in Arizona offered distinct curriculum options. For example, one charter school focused on the Montessori Method. Another charter school offered a curriculum based on core knowledge. A third claimed to serve multiple intelligences. But these were not unique opportunities because large public school districts offered these options as well. Further, the researchers found that despite differences among the curriculum orientations of the charter schools, no one of the charter schools offered an important or distinct curriculum innovation. Each charter school could narrow its focus on a particular curriculum orientation, but in so doing, they simply concentrated on things available elsewhere. More important, when researchers compared achievement test scores from students in the public schools to the scores from students in the charter schools, they found that the two groups had similar scores. The researchers did find wide variations among the schools in each category, but they attributed these differences to the types of students that they served. Thus, the researchers drew the conclusion that nothing new was happening in learning or teaching in Arizona charter schools (Stout and Garn 168–170).

Finally, if the free market model was to improve schools, the poorly performing schools had to suffer lack of support and close. This seemed not to happen. Despite the fact that the Arizona charter schools did not seem to offer increased academic achievement, their failures did not lead to their closings. When a pair of researchers tried to determine if the Arizona law led to the elimination of weak schools, they found that it did not. The charter school legislation in Arizona required that oversight agencies would collect and publish information about the conditions of the charter schools. The rationale was that this would enable parents to make intelligent choices and to avoid troubled institutions, but the various agencies responsible for overseeing the charter schools could not perform their roles. As a result, parents could not obtain the information they needed to know about the functioning of a school. Due to the lack of information, neither market forces nor oversight committees closed failing schools (Garn and Stout 153–158).

Other states with more restrictive laws appeared to have similar difficulties in allowing failing charter schools to close. According to national estimates made in December 2000, only 3 percent of the charter schools opened in the United States had closed. Given the fact that the charter schools faced many of the problems of any small business, this was an incredibly low percentage. The few schools that closed did so for four main reasons: financial problems, general mismanagement, failure to carry out an academic plan, and inability to secure a facility. According to Pearl Rock Kane and Christopher J. Lauricella, this low rate of charter school closings reflected two things. The state governments wanted to allow the schools a chance to succeed and the regulating agencies did not want to damage the general popularity of charter schools by attracting attention to poor ones. As a result, though, charter schools appeared to have escaped an important aspect of the market ideology that created them (Kane and Lauricella 212).

Although charter school advocates advertised their schools as means to establish parents' rights to choose effective schools, some teachers thought of the charter schools as methods to protect the rights of teachers. When Albert Shanker spoke in favor of charter schools, he argued for opportunities to allow teachers to exercise their rights to be professionals. In general, the American Federation of Teachers (AFT) and the National Educational Association (NEA) have retained his view, but, in subsequent statements, they have sought to protect the teachers' rights to organize and to participate in school governance. For example, the AFT requests that the charter schools be based on high academic standards. The organization requests that the students in the charter schools and the public schools take the same achievement tests to measure their progress. The AFT policy holds that the teachers be properly trained and certified. The union specifies that the charter schools and the public schools make all information regarding the progress of students on state standards and assessments available to the public. Most important, the AFT wants the teachers to have the right to bargain collectively and be included in the public school district agreement (AFT 1–3).

The NEA offers a similar position supporting innovations in public education such as charter schools, but the union requires that the plans to start these new schools contain safeguards covering the employment conditions of teachers and ensuring the schools will be staffed by licensed educators. Further, the NEA wants the charter schools and the public schools held to the same periodic evaluations (NEA 1).

To some charter school advocates, teachers' unions represent obstacles to teachers and parents who want to exercise their rights. For example, David Harmer argued that the NEA is the largest union of any kind in the country and that it prevents the free association of parents, teachers, and children. He called the NEA a near-monopoly supplier of labor to a government-enforced monopoly consumer. To Harmer, the result is a self-perpetuating cycle. He wrote that NEA collects about $400 per year in dues from each member; the national organization uses the money to elect members of the Democratic Party to public offices; and those Democratic officials defeat proposals that would allow parents to send their children to private schools and thereby foster what he called the monopoly of public schools (Harmer 59–60).

In a similar way, researchers in Arizona found that union members were hostile to charter schools. To the researchers, the reasons appeared obvious. The new schools could cause the teachers to suffer pay cuts, lose retirement benefits, and suffer deterioration in working conditions, but the teachers did not oppose school reform in general. When the researchers asked teachers about the charters, they found the teachers did not oppose other, less drastic reform efforts, such as statewide standards, merit pay for teachers, or site-based management to give individual school buildings control over the hiring and firing of teachers (Hess et al. 176–178).

Perhaps the permissive nature of the Arizona charter school law caused the teachers' union members to dislike the charter school reforms. As noted, the AFT and the NEA approved of charter schools under conditions that would force the charter schools to recognize the rights of the teachers and that would not place public schools at a significant disadvantage. The unions did not approve of the open and free marketplace for education similar to that created by the Arizona law because these threatened to destroy the unions. The task of organizing teachers in hundreds of small schools into a union would be daunting. The obstacles that corporate owners could erect would cripple any recruiting effort. Worse, the public schools, where unions remained strong, operated at a disadvantage since they had to follow state regulations while the charter schools did not.

Despite the fear that charter school operators would hire cheap unskilled teachers, a group of researchers found that most charter schools hired certified teachers who had experience and they paid them well. In the 1996–1997 school year, Gregg Vanourek and his associates collected information from fifty charter schools in nine states. They found in their sample that the average teacher had 5.6 years of experience teaching in a public school, 1.7 years of private school experience, 1.4 years of university teaching experience, and 0.6 years experience in home schooling. About 72 percent of the teachers held certification, and another 17 percent were working toward certification. About 25 percent were members of teachers' unions, and about 40 percent had been union members. About 13 percent of the charter schoolteachers were recent college graduates. About 35 percent said they made more money in the charter school than they had elsewhere, about 28 percent indicated they made the same amount, and about 38 percent said they made less in the charter school (Vanourek et al. 200–202).

Care is needed here. Vanourek's sample did not come from Arizona schools. Thus, it is possible that restrictive laws forced the charter schools he and his colleagues surveyed to hire qualified teachers and to pay them better salaries. On the other hand, it is possible that the schools wanted to succeed and wanted to employ a well-qualified faculty. Nonetheless, charter school enthusiasts want to protect people's rights to start up charter schools and the teachers' unions desire to protect the teachers' rights to organize. Although each side sees the other side as threatening their existence, both sides contend that their rights are at issue.

Part of the free market model for education was that private businesses could organize schools and make a profit. As a result, the charter school laws in Arizona allowed operators to open several different campuses in different parts of the state. This is part of the reason Arizona attracted the most charter schools. In Arizona during the 1997–1998 school year, there were thirty-two companies that conducted multiple campuses. Of these companies with several charter school campuses, one company had twenty campuses; another company had fourteen; and a third had six. The other companies had from four to two campuses. Most important, eight of the seventeen companies that operated three or more campuses in Arizona were for-profit providers (Maranto and Gresham 100–101).

The charter school movement provoked the idea that private corporations could accumulate capital by selling stocks, use those investments to build schools, and make money collecting state funds. In 1998, the largest private manager of charter schools was the Edison Project. Founded by Chris Whittle, the project began with a team of researchers and educators designing a system of schools that reached from the kindergarten to the twelfth grade. Among the members of this design team was John E. Chubb, one of the economists who had extolled the benefits of a market system to improve schools (Chubb 213–214).

According to Chubb, the Edison Project separated the grades in the schools into academies that contained two or three sequential grades. Thus, the schools were small and teachers, students, and parents could work closely together. Second, the design team drew up what Chubb called a rich curriculum covering the important areas of science, mathematics, social sciences, art, and music. To ensure effective instruction, the design team created the objectives for each subject and each level. Third, the Edison schools implemented packages of programs of teaching methods that were well regarded by professionals. For example, in grades K through 5, the Edison schools used *Success for All,* a program designed by Johns Hopkins University. Fourth, Edison schools sought to evaluate the effectiveness of its methods by using a mixture of standardized tests and custom-designed methods. Fifth, the Edison Project included computers as important parts of instruction to the extent that the schools provided each family with a home computer. Sixth, the schools set up a system of professional development to advance the teaching skills of the faculty. Seventh, the Edison Project garnered family support through frequent interaction over email and the use of narrative report cards. Eighth, the project extended the school day and the school year. Finally, the design team hoped that the faculty and administrators in the different Edison campuses would share ideas to improve performance. According to Chubb, the programs that the Edison Project employed cost more than the programs used in most public schools. The profit had to come from the efficiency of the professionals using the programs and from economies of scale (Chubb 214–219).

The Edison Project enjoyed rapid growth. In 1995, the project opened four schools enrolling 3,000 students. By 2000, it grew to about fifty-one schools with 24,000 students. At that time, about two-thirds of the Edison schools existed as part of contracts with local boards of education and about one-third were charter schools (Good and Braden 195–196).

Writing in 1998, Chubb claimed that the Edison Project was succeeding on several measures. First, the schools maintained a system of financial management. On average, the investment for each school cost about $1.5 million. Each building principal had to control the finances of the unit to stay within a set budget, and the Edison Project continued to attract private capital through stock sales. Second, the Edison Project contracted with the Gordon S. Black Corporation to conduct surveys to monitor the satisfaction of the parents, the students, and the faculty. The results were positive. Third, student achievement scores were not clear. Chubb acknowledged that it was difficult to determine if Edison students were advancing more rapidly than their age mates in public schools, yet he indicated that the data indicated that the Edison students appeared to be doing better (Chubb 226–246).

Of all the types of charter schools, the for-profit schools, such as the Edison Project in particular, became the most controversial. A good deal of the criticism was based on particular incidents or abuses. For example, according to Thomas L. Good and Jennifer Braden, one of the ways that the Edison schools sought to make a profit was by excluding students who would pose problems. Arguing that the Edison schools served few students with complicated disabilities, Good and Braden described cases in which the school officials convinced the parents of children with disabilities who sought admission for their children to Edison schools that the public schools would better serve their children (Good and Braden 195–196).

In regard to serving children with disabilities, Chubb asserted that by 1998, the Edison Project implemented programs of responsible inclusion for such students and offered a continuum of services. Although he acknowledged that the U.S. Department of Education investigated an Edison school in Boston and found violations of open admissions policies, he claimed those problems were corrected. In addition, Chubb wrote that Edison schools began programs in English as a second language and bilingual education (Chubb 226).

Listing another difficulty, Good and Braden contended that the Edison Project is supposed to be a management company. In Michigan, the state law requires such companies to aid a group of parents or educators who applied for a charter to start a school but lacked the abilities to run such a business. According to Good and Braden, this was not the way that Edison worked. They complained that one set of researchers found that many charter schools in the state began when the management companies solicited groups to apply for charters that the companies would manage (Good and Braden 196–197).

Deron Boyles cited similar specific abuses to buttress his complaint that for-profit charter schools such as the Edison Project distort the idea of an educational mission. According to Boyles, the Edison Project recruited former federal officials and university professors for large salaries to raise large sums of operating capital and build schools across the country. Boyles noted that the Edison Project did not attract sufficient investors, and the free market did not support it. Boyles asserted that Whittle and his privateer allies, as he called them, made a profit in one case when the total amount their Renaissance School in Boston, Massachusetts, received from tax funds per pupil exceeded the amount the Boston Public Schools received per pupil. According to Boyles, the discrepancy illustrates how the advocates of a market ideology for education violate their own ideas with the result that the people who already enjoy material success gain more wealth (Boyles 143–144).

Boyles saw the for-profit charter schools as contributing to the inordinate influence that private corporations have on public schools. Calling for a more democratic image of schooling that would ostensibly satisfy everyone's rights to be full human beings, Boyles claimed that teachers and students have to recognize that there are multiple ways of knowing. He imagined that for-profit schools would only offer those programs that earned the school prestige and profit. To make this point, he quoted advertisements that promised increased achievement test scores for students who entered the for-profit schools and ultimately better jobs. Although he did not explain how the rich curriculum created by Edison's design team could turn art and music into narrow channels, he asserted that the teachers in the for-profit schools would cater to materialist conceptions of knowledge and of life (Boyles 149, 202).

Critics raised the possibility that charter schools would deny some parents the right to enter the schools. They feared that private schools would become racially segregated. The studies on this point are contradictory. On the one hand, in 1997, the U.S. Department of Education released a national evaluation of charter schools contending that in most states the charter schools attracted students that reflected the racial composition of the state itself. On the other hand, two researchers, Casey D. Cobb and Gene V. Glass, complained that the federal survey was overly general and did not reveal the practices and the results in specific charter schools. Thus, in 1999, they analyzed data from the Arizona Department of Education for the years 1994–1997. They found that although the Arizona charter schools as a group demonstrated the same rate of racial integration as the public schools, the individual charter schools were much more segregated than the individual public schools. Usually, charter schools had about 20 percent more white students than nearby public schools. While some charters catered exclusively to minority students, these schools were typically vocational schools that would not lead to college or they were schools of last resort for students expelled from public schools. Most important, the exclusively minority charter schools accounted for most of the minority representation in the overall average calculations of racial balance (Cobb and Glass 2–4, 19).

Cobb and Glass found that many of the Arizona charter schools appeared to take the best applicants from the available pool. For example, four charter schools near Scottsdale were located in the less affluent and most ethnically mixed neighborhoods. Yet, these four schools enrolled a higher proportion of white students than did the nearby public schools. Further, three charter schools accounted for the majority of black charter students in the state (Cobb and Glass 19).

Two mechanisms may have contributed to the segregation within charter schools. The first is that the parents of the minority students may want to protect their children from the problems of racial integration. For example, in 1992, Amy Stuart Wells and Robert L. Crain noted this possibility when they considered the effects of a free market on education. In that paper, they acknowledged that parents would try to select a school that was best for their children. Wells and Crain did not think this meant that the parents would necessarily select the school that would provide the most academic benefits and the greatest life chances. They acknowledged that black parents might choose to keep their children in poorly performing schools rather than subject their young people to the pain of racism. They claimed this was a rational choice, but it was not a choice that offered the effective education promised by the free educational market. They concluded that the best solution was through some sort of controlled choice program whereby every parent had the choice of several schools but all schools had to be racially balanced (Wells and Crain 80–81).

In 1996, Wells showed that the parents' attitudes influenced the decisions of black students to accept or to remain in racially integrated schools when she published the results of her interviews with black high school students and their parents in St. Louis, Missouri. These students had the chance to participate in an urban/suburban desegregation plan that allowed them to select from 120 white county schools instead of attending a black neighborhood school. Wells divided the students into three groups: those who refused to transfer, those who transferred but returned to the city schools, and those who transferred and remained in the suburban schools. She drew samples for each group from students of middle-income, working-class, and low-income families. According to Wells, the St. Louis plan offered more choice than would be found in any type of voucher system because it offered free transportation, covered the expenses for the receiving school, and required the white schools to increase the black enrollment. She found that students who transferred and stayed had parents who pushed them to transfer, who held strong desires that their children attend prestigious schools, and who believed such schools would help the children to succeed in life. The students' racial attitudes did not seem to affect their decisions. That is, the students in the three groups acknowledged the prejudice in suburban schools. The students who remained saw antiblack prejudice as an obstacle for them to overcome. The transfer students who returned to the city did so for three sets of reasons: They were expelled; they found the prejudice intolerable; or they failed the academic challenges in the suburban schools. The students who stayed in the city thought they could get a good education anywhere, and they enjoyed the comfort of a neighborhood school (Wells 29, 31, 32, 42).

The second mechanism contributing to segregation of charter schools is that the charter schools appear to select their students even when they are forbidden to do so. In 2001, while studying charter schools, Wells and her colleague, Janelle Scott, found that charter schools refined what they called the "art of excluding the unwelcome." They found that charter schools would claim to accept students on a first-come first-served basis, but that the schools sent the information about how to enroll to very few parents. While some charter schools posted flyers in the community, other charter schools depended on word of mouth to spread the enrollment information. As a result, the students who arrived represented an interconnected group. In addition, some charter schools granted priority in registering to certain types of students, such as those who had siblings in the school. Finally, the charters required the parents to attend several meetings and to volunteer to perform services for the school. Wells and Scott found the charter school people thought these meetings and the volunteer work were valuable because they ensured that the students were committed to the school (Wells and Scott 250–251).

The racial and social segregation of charter schools is most important. As described in Chapter Nine, academic achievement follows social class status. That is, wealthier students tend to perform better than economically deprived students. More important, the most effective way to raise the achievement of students from low-income families is through programs that integrate them with students from higher-income families. Although researchers found that such integration functioned within limits, it was more effective than programs of compensatory education designed for the children from low-income families. Worse, if the charter schools that attract minority students are vocational or last chance efforts for students who have been expelled, the schools cannot hope to boost the academic performance of minority youth. As a result, the mechanisms that cause charter schools to be racially or socially uniform threaten the chances of parents exercising their right to the most effective education. This was true even when the parents chose the less effective schools for good reasons, such as protecting the child from racism.

In what ways did standards, tests, and choice represent efforts to satisfy parents' rights to effective educations for their children?

The politicians, business leaders, and educators who wanted to build an effective program of basic education tried to implement their plans by claiming that parents had a right to an effective education for their children. They sought to have parents and educators work together to make such changes as reinforcing a core curriculum of basic subjects, implementing rigorous testing, and extending the school day and year. When these methods failed to produce the desired results, economists argued the easiest way to provide effective basic education to the children was to allow parents to choose the schools they wanted them to attend. During the 1990s, the most popular mechanism was charter schools. Arizona adopted the charter school law that most completely allowed the parents free choice of schools, but studies of the charter schools showed that they did not provide the effective education for all social classes. The charter schools were racially segregated.

Thus, the problem came full circle. The parents had a right to an effective education. Conservative politicians did not want to reform schools by administrative decree. Thus, they sought to give parents the choice to select their schools, but parents did not always select the best schools for their children, and the best schools often rejected the parents in the most need. As a result, the children who received the least effective education were the ones who should have profited most from their parents' satisfying their right to an effective education.

In 2002, the U.S. Supreme Court approved vouchers as another mechanism for school choice. Although vouchers were an old idea, politicians avoided them because the voucher could be used to send children to religious schools. In the case of *Zelman v. Simmons-Harris,* however, the justices decided that children's parents could use government vouchers to pay for tuition in private religious schools. The case involved Ohio's Project Scholarship Program, which provided tuition aid for students in the Cleveland schools to attend the public or private schools of their choice. In the 1999–2000 school year, about 82 percent of the participating private schools had a religious affiliation, and no public school participated. As a result, the program sent about 96 percent of the children to the religious schools. Sixty percent of the students who participated came from families who lived at or below the poverty line (*Zelman v. Simmons-Harris* 2).

The question in this case was whether the state was supporting religious schools in defiance of the clause in the First Amendment of the U.S. Constitution that forbids the states from enacting laws to advance or inhibit religion. The justices argued that since the money went to the religious schools because of the personal choices of the students, the government did not purposely enhance or inhibit religion (*Zelman v. Simmons-Harris* 6–7).

The U.S. Supreme Court issued its decision in June 2002. By August, newspapers reported that a group of Catholic school supporters were rallying a movement, Catholic Families for School Choice, to collect names on petitions in various states. The aim was to pressure state legislatures to recast laws allowing parents to use public school funds to send their children to Catholic schools. According to the founder of the web site, Catholic Online, the U.S. Supreme Court decision has wide potential implication and the work to change state constitutions is under way.

Vouchers may represent another method of enabling parents to satisfy their right to an effective education. But, unless there are strict guidelines for the vouchers' use, it is hard to imagine that vouchers will help those parents who need it the most or that vouchers will protect the teachers' rights to organize to protect their working conditions.

In all, it is important to recall that the reformers who want to improve schools by enhancing parents' rights to exercise free choice considered themselves as advocates who served the interests of a restricted group of people. As a result, they tended not to consider wider social problems or if they did, they followed limited ways of thinking. For example, the ideas of effective schools seemed to discount implementing instruction that catered to students' interests. Instead, advocates who favored some organization of effective schools sought to establish instruction that enabled the students to pass standardized tests. Other suggestions rejected the progressive ideal of democracy in favor of free choice. In this regard, Chubb and Moe concluded that efforts to organize schools democratically led to a form of tyranny of the majority. Although Chubb and Moe contended that the freest model was that of a free market, researchers found that parents did not have the information on which to base their choices. Worse, in some cases, the parents would not choose schools that would provide effective instruction. They chose schools in which the children felt comfortable.

The point is that the reformers who felt that parents had rights to effective educations for their children and those advocates who saw the free market as a means to achieve this goal shared similar assumptions with the special educators and the bilingual educators described in Chapter Ten. Like the special educators, these reformers selected a method by which parents, teachers, and local officials could agree about the ways the schools should run. They did not impose any idea of what constituted a good education. In a manner similar to the bilingual educators, these advocates saw themselves as advancing the interests of particular groups of people, and they tended not to think about wider problems of social harmony.

The reason these similarities exist is that the special educators, the bilingual educators, the advocates of effective schools for basic skills instruction, and the free market advocates share the assumption that schools should affirm the rights of students and parents. Although this assumption appears similar to the progressive notion of meeting students' and society's needs, these advocates imitated the legal and the political tactics of the NAACP and SCLC to the extent that they forgot the wider social concerns the progressives considered.

Summary

From 1981 until 2000, reformers claimed that parents had a right to an effective education for their children, and they used this claim to implement their proposals to improve school effectiveness. In this chapter, four examples illustrate this tendency. First, in 1981, President Ronald Reagan commissioned a blue ribbon committee to determine what the public schools should do to overcome the economic problems facing the country. The resulting document, "A Nation at Risk," claimed that the mediocre performance of schools threatened the economic prosperity of the country. To change the schools, the authors of the report urged parents and citizens to petition for their right to effective schools for the children. The second effort came from lawyers who suggested that parents' groups could imitate the success of the NAACP and sue in federal court to establish their legal right to effective schools. The third effort came from officials who wanted to set goals for national school improvement and to offer measures of various schools' effectiveness. They claimed that citizens had a right to know how the schools worked. By 1990, many politicians and educators gave up on these efforts to improve schools, and they adopted the fourth example. They argued that parents had the right to choose the school their children attended. The hope was that if parents exercised their right of choice, they would select the most effective schools. Market forces would erase the less effective types. Although there were a variety of mechanisms to provide choice, the most popular was the charter schools movement. In 1994, Arizona adopted the most permissive legislation and more charter schools opened in that state than anywhere else. When researchers examined Arizona's charter schools, however, they found they did not offer new innovations and they did not raise educational achievement. Teachers' unions urged that state legislatures adopt charter school reforms in ways that protected the teachers' right to organize. Another serious problem arose when researchers found that models of free choice for parents led to racial and social segregation. The efforts of these reformers were similar to the efforts of special educators and bilingual educators discussed in Chapter Ten. That is, these advocates imitated the tactics of the NAACP and SCLC as well. As a result, their programs suffered from similar oversights. In all these cases, the advocates sought to serve the interests of particular groups and ignored wider aims of education. This distinguished their efforts from those of the progressive educators who worked during the first half of the twentieth century.

CHAPTER TWELVE

AFFIRMING PEOPLE'S RIGHTS TO COMMUNITY THROUGH SCHOOLS, 1981–2000

In 1970, Paulo Freire published the English translation of his book, *Pedagogy of the Oppressed,* describing a method of teaching adults to read and to write that he had developed in Brazil, Bolivia, and Peru. Freire's idea was to imbue literacy with political significance. In his model, peasants came together to talk, to read, and to write about their lives and at the same time to explore ways to improve their living conditions.

Writing from the perspective of a person in South America, Freire divided society into two social classes: the owners who controlled everything and the workers who submitted to the wishes of the owners. In this world, Freire noted that there was a conflict of rights. On the one hand, the workers had the rights to their own lives and their own purposes. Freire called this the right to be human, and he believed it was a legitimate historical and natural right. On the other hand, the owners thought they had the right to control everything they owned including the labor of the workers. The owners justified their rights to increase their possessions on the grounds that they had worked for their riches or took risks to obtain them. Freire argued the owners did not have legitimate rights to control other people because when they exploited the workers, the owners denied their own humanity (Freire 45, 63).

According to Freire, only the workers or the oppressed people could break the existing state of oppression, but they had to do it as a community. The owners could not liberate the workers, and individual workers could not free themselves as individuals, but when the members of the community of workers were in constant dialogue, they could be a sufficient force to liberate the owners and themselves (Freire 28, 42, 53).

Unfortunately, Freire found that the workers did not want to form such communities because they feared freedom. Instead of seeking a more democratic world, the workers identified with the owners to the extent that they considered progress to be changes that would allow them to become the bosses and rule over vast accumulations of things and people. Thus, the problem for Freire was to show the workers that they had taken on the inhuman aspects of the owners (Freire 31–33).

Freire found the answer by asking members of the class of owners to join the oppressed in their struggle for their rights to liberation. Although these former owners were to lead the revolution, they could not act like bosses by believing that they had any special solutions or answers. Instead, they had to have faith that the workers could do it on their own. Freire untangled this apparent contradiction with a saying that he took from Mao Tse-tung about the role of the revolutionary party: "We must teach the masses clearly what we have received from them confusedly." This meant that teachers had to develop solidarity with the peasants or the workers and find ways to reflect back to the workers the views of the world and the options for its transformation that the workers held (Freire 46, 82).

To illustrate how the method might work, Freire described an experience of Patricio Lopes who worked with tenement residents in Santiago. One day, Lopes and the participants in his group sat in what Freire called a "culture circle" and discussed a picture showing a drunken man walking on the street while three young men stood on the corner talking. To everyone's surprise, the residents heard themselves saying that the only productive person in the picture was the drunken man. They claimed that the drunken man worked all day to support his family, but he did not earn enough to care for them. To hide his worries, he drank himself into a pitiful state (Freire 111).

Freire explained that Lopes was not a social worker. He did not want to show the tenement residents the contradictions between alcohol abuse and familial affection. If he had such a narrow aim, his lesson would simply have been to point to the truth of moral axioms about the evils of liquor and the need for temperance. Freire added that a social worker would have missed the important connections the residents revealed to themselves among earning low wages, feeling exploited, and drinking. Having made these connections clear to themselves, Lopes and the tenement residents could seek ways to garner decent wages for honest labor in hopes this would transform some of the limiting contradictions in their lives (Freire 111–112).

The key element in Lopes's experience was the picture of the drunken man on the street. Freire called such pictures "codes." For Freire, a code could be any sort of concrete object, such as a picture, a book, a play, or a tape-recorded conversation, that captured a situation familiar to the participants. The objects could not simply be visual aids. For example, posters or advertisements carried clear messages because they were propaganda. A code could not be overly clear, but a code was not a work of art because art objects were often enigmatic and asked the viewer to bring to the pieces his or her own interpretations. As a code, an enigmatic object would force the participants to guess at what the code conveyed (Freire 106–107).

Freire wanted the codes to reveal people's views of things in the world. As a result, he claimed that the codes had to be organized into what he called "thematic fans." That is, Freire believed that human history was a record of themes. These themes were concrete representations of a complex of ideas, concepts, hopes, and doubts that the people in each epoch held as well as the things that prevented their development. Each of these elements strove for completion. By representing the people's hopes and their frustrations, the codes illustrated what Freire called the "people's limit-situations." By discussing these codes in open, free, and trusting dialogue, people could put words on the things that served or that restrained them. His hope was that the discussions about the codes—called "decoding" or "reflection"—would inspire people to engage in some action to transform the limits the codes revealed. The people would return to the culture circle, construct new codes that typified the conditions the actions had revealed and determine other courses of action (Freire 91–97).

Freire called his process "problem-posing." It differed from the problem-solving techniques found in engineering classes or chemistry laboratories because in those situations the teachers had the correct answers. In problem-posing education, the teachers and the students worked together to understand the situations and to test alternatives for action, but the limit-situations could not be resolved because every action led to new, unanticipated problems (Freire 66–72).

Freire contrasted problem-posing instruction with traditional educational approaches that used textbooks, lectures, and exams. He called the traditional model "banking education" because he believed that teachers deposited information in the students and expected the students to withdraw the information at appropriate times. Freire claimed that, in traditional classes, the teachers did not engage in dialogue to learn with the students. Instead, banking educators dominated the students and taught them how to dominate other people in hopes they would succeed in life. Although Freire contended that most teachers would realize in time that the conventional notion of success denied the larger aim of becoming human, he argued that the humanist educator could not wait for people to realize the contradictions between their desires and their actions. The revolutionary teachers had to adopt methods that led to mutual humanization (Freire 61–62).

Although Freire argued that workers had the right to their own purposes and the right to become more fully human by learning how to transform their limit-situations, he did not describe advocates defending these rights in courts as lawyers in the United States did for African American students or for children with disabilities. Freire accepted the more abrupt methods of resistance, such as strikes, that took place in South America. For example, Freire stated that if the workers formed culture circles and landowners wanted them to return to work under exploitive conditions, the workers had a right to defend themselves and protect the possibility of dialogue. If the landowners used violence to try to restore the previous order, the workers had the right to use the same tactics to prevent the restoration of the oppressive regime. Further, according to Freire, the landowners could not claim that the workers were oppressing them because Freire defined oppression as anything that prevented people from becoming more human. Thus, when the landowners oppressed the workers, the result was violence. Freire did not consider it violence if the workers held a landowner hostage while taking over a farm provided they did this in the course of freeing themselves (Freire 42–43, 50–51).

Freire claimed that teachers had a moral obligation to work with oppressed people to affirm their rights to become fully human. The method of revolution was a sort of awakening that took place through dialogue or what he called "praxis." This was reflection and action upon the world in order to transform it. Since dialogue led to increased critical reflection, the aim of the dialogue was always in the direction of more dialogue. To Freire, the ideal of community was this image of people working together to increase their own freedoms and affirm their rights to their own purposes (Freire 52, 66–67, 76–77, 82–83).

How did educators in the United States apply Freire's ideas to their classrooms?

In a short time, Freire's ideas gained popularity among educators in the United States. Part of the reason this took place was that during the 1960s the federal government and the NAACP conducted campaigns to use the schools to affirm that children from low-income families and African Americans had the rights to a prosperous life. Arguments about the need for racial integration had led to discussions about the lessons that students learned through the social surroundings in the schools. For example, in 1970, the Association of Supervision and Curriculum Development (ASCD) conducted a conference of noted educators to discuss the implications of what became known as the hidden curriculum. During that conference, Philip W. Jackson described what he called the "secondary consequences of school," such as the tendency for students to learn to behave in a certain way or to develop specific attitudes (Jackson 8).

Lawrence Kohlberg described the ways that the moral characters and ideologies of the teachers and administrators translated into a social atmosphere that influenced the children to develop certain moral outlooks (Kohlberg 120). Robert Dreeben used the concept to explain why people in the United States had difficulty acting in positions of authority. He claimed that during their years in schools, students learned to accept direction, not to administer it (Dreeben 102–103).

Another effect of the efforts of the federal government to improve the academic performance of children from low-income families was to stimulate research that caused educators to accept Freire's socialist orientation. In 1976, Samuel Bowles and Herbert Gintis claimed that the failure of programs of compensatory education showed that schools could not reduce economic inequalities. They argued that, although politicians talked about equality in education, the goal of education in a capitalist society was to prepare children to enter adult society. To them, this meant that schools replicated the hierarchal relationships that existed in the economy and prepared children to take different positions in large corporations. Thus, in vocational and general tracks in high schools, students from low-income families learned to follow rules and to work under the close supervision of the teachers. This corresponded to the work they would do in factories or as laborers. On the other hand, students from wealthier families enrolled in college-track programs and learned in a more open atmosphere while still conforming to accepted norms. This prepared them for the roles they would play in management positions. Finally, according to Bowles and Gintis, the grades that students received made the different treatments they received appear appropriate (Bowles and Gintis 101–103, 131–133).

To determine how students received grades, Bowles and Gintis analyzed data from a study of 639 national Merit Scholarship finalists. While all the students had high IQ scores, they did not share good academic records. Trying to account for the variation in grades among these finalists, Bowles and Gintis found that the students' drive to succeed and their willingness to obey teachers' instructions accounted for most academic success. Thus, Bowles and Gintis agreed with Freire that traditional schools used banking education where the teacher was the authority and the students had to accept what the teacher told them if they were going to receive rewards (Bowles and Gintis 40–41).

Discouraged that schools played such a reactionary role, Bowles and Gintis offered five guidelines for revolutionary educators. First, the educators should work to make schools more democratic. Second, when teachers allowed students and parents to have more control in education, their efforts should aim to separate school success from economic success. Third, revolutionary educators had to develop a philosophy of education. Fourth, educators had to create curriculums that liberated people and made them aware of their situations. Fifth, although Bowles and Gintis believed the only reform would come when the economic system was changed, they recommended that socialist educators try to win a series of small practical victories, such as installing open enrollment practices or adequate financial aid for minorities in colleges, rather than wait for a cataclysmic revolution to change everything (Bowles and Gintis 287–288).

The result of assessments such as those by the ASCD and Bowles and Gintis was that educators wrote about the ways the hidden curriculum could contradict the stated aims of education. For example, in 1983, Henry Giroux and David Purpel edited a book of essays on the hidden curriculum. Writing the introduction, Maxine Greene drew heavily on the ideas of Freire. She praised the writers in the volume for resisting what was taken for granted in the classrooms. She noted that most of the contributors believed that the norms of the hidden curriculum followed Freire's description of banking education. According to Greene, the advantage of the essays was that they posed problems. She called the book a mode of pedagogy if the readers engaged with the various authors and considered how to transform schools (Greene, "Introduction" 4–5).

As Greene noted, some of the essays portrayed the traditional schools as engaged in banking education. For example, Michael Apple and Nancy King described the pattern of events in a kindergarten class to illustrate the way the hidden curriculum prepared the students for the work they would do as adults. In this case, as a result of being together for a full year, the teacher and the students learned to concentrate on work, the teacher led these work activities, and they were compulsory. The teacher told the students to persist in those activities even while other students outside their room made distracting noises. Play was reserved for free time. Students had some limited choices, though. After visiting a fire station, they had to draw a picture of something they saw, but they could pick the subject of the drawing. According to Apple and King, the students learned to obey instructions and to persevere in their efforts within institutional settings. Thus, even in early grades, schools prepared children for life in an industrial society (Apple and King 88–95).

In another essay, Giroux joined with Anthony Penna to argue that social studies educators should think about the complex relationships among schools, political institutions, and businesses if they wanted to advance democratic education. Giroux and Penna asserted that social studies teachers should follow Freire and help students think about the way each learning experience related to the larger social-economic reality. To Giroux and Penna, this meant that students had to learn how to change society. Consequently, they listed some reforms that could undermine the authoritarianism in classrooms. Selecting strategies more like those of Bowles and Gintis than Freire, they called for an end of grouping students by abilities and suggested that the students who mastered material faster could help those who learned more slowly in heterogeneous classes. To lessen the power teachers could wield over students, they urged an end of grades and recommended what they called "dialogic grading" whereby students and teachers would participate in small groups to share and evaluate each other's work. Furthermore, they suggested that class periods be arranged more flexibly (Giroux and Penna 114–117).

Other educators sought to find ways that they could directly apply Freire's model in their classes. When educators in the United States adopted problem-posing education, however, they omitted the political action that Freire seemed to think was an essential part of the work. For example, Ira Shor, a professor of English at Staten Island College, New York, tried to use Freire's ideas in his classrooms. In 1987, Shor complained that the educational reforms sought by President Reagan were authoritarian approaches that aggravated the problems in schools. Shor particularly disliked the recommendations found in *A Nation at Risk* that required all students to take certain basic courses, to do more homework, and to take more tests. He believed the result of these reforms was to alienate the students and encourage them to misbehave. In response, the teachers became discouraged. Shor asserted that the answer to these problems was for teachers to adopt the method he called "critical pedagogy" (Shor, "Educating" 8–13).

Shor claimed the idea of critical pedagogy came from Freire. It required teachers to learn several different skills not found in most teacher training programs, such abilities as knowing how to conduct problem-posing discussions with the students, to situate the students' learning in their lives, and to foster changes in the society (Shor, "Educating" 23–26).

Acknowledging that teachers could not simply apply Freire's ideas in their classrooms, Shor recommended that teachers tailor Freire's plans to fit the different circumstances found in industrialized societies. For example, Shor claimed that he began his classes by telling the students that he used a unique approach. He asked each of them to come forward and introduce themselves to the class. For the next class, he asked the students to write a paragraph describing the worst teacher they had or the most dangerous moment they experienced. He recommended that the students use prewriting techniques, such as constructing a mental picture of their subject, making a list of important points, and writing the essay from the list. In demonstrating these techniques in the classroom, Shor stood at the blackboard and wrote the characteristics of the bad teachers the students provided. He claimed that this exercise offered him the opportunity to think about his own teaching, and it offered the opportunity for the students to think about how schools could repress or liberate students (Shor, "Monday" 104–110).

Although Shor offered a series of similar examples that might encourage critical thinking, none of them involved action to change the school or the society. In a similar fashion, other teachers who claimed to follow Freire's model restricted their lessons to classroom discussions. For example, Nina Wallerstein claimed that Freire's model was most appropriate for classes in English as a Second Language (ESL) taken by immigrant or refugee adults who came to the United States with low-social or -economic backgrounds and restricted access to education. When she described her methods, she allowed the possibility that students could engage in social reform activities, but those efforts took place outside class with the students doing it on their own (Wallerstein 33–34).

Noting that the first step in Freire's method was to discover the themes in the peasants' lives, Wallerstein began her classes by asking the students to talk about personal things, such as their families or their work. From such discussions, she gathered enough information to identify issues they should discuss in class. The next step that Wallerstein took was to construct codes. To do this, she took a situation that upset the students and created a short script to illustrate the problem. These scripts were similar to representations of conversations that any language teacher would use except that Wallerstein's scripts focused on issues of oppression. For example, when a student complained about unsafe working conditions in a factory, she created a dialogue of six sentences that took place between two people. In that script, one person noted that a health report from the safety inspector was available and it showed there were no dangers in the factory. The other person asserted that, if that was the case, the report must be incorrect. During the discussion of the script, the students talked about how they could resolve problems of safety on the job. Although the discussion did not go beyond listing the different alternatives, Wallerstein noted that students could take action on their own such as join with other workers to form a union. She made such possibilities appear outside the class and beyond the reach of the teacher (Wallerstein 34–43).

While Shor and Wallerstein claimed that they led their students to become critical analysts of their society, it is hard to see how their lessons differed from those found in many social studies classrooms or language courses found in traditional schools. In traditional schools, students and teachers consider social problems. In traditional schools, students and teachers discuss possible responses to social difficulties, but, as noted, Freire expected problem-posing education to be a form of political activism. If the villagers stopped after discussing the codes, Freire considered such lessons to be empty verbalism. If the villagers blindly resisted the owners, Freire considered such responses to be mindless activism. He believed that the proper mix was in what he called "praxis." This was reflection and action to transform the world (Freire 75–76).

There may be three different reasons why teachers in the United States removed the activism from Freire's model. The first possibility is that Freire did not clearly describe how political demonstrations would play a role in problem-posing education. For example, in Chapter One of his book *Pedagogy of the Oppressed,* Freire explained that teachers had to engage in action with the oppressed. Although Freire praised such revolutionaries as Che Guevara who led workers' insurrections with Fidel Castro, he described the work of teachers and members of literacy teams as observing people, discussing what they saw, and creating codes. Beyond these apparently academic activities, Freire did not tell how the teachers might join with students in social reform.

The second possibility is that Freire changed his thinking about praxis as he became involved in large adult literacy programs. According to Peter Roberts, when Freire began his work in Brazil, he created a new approach to adult literacy. He replaced the term *teacher* with the word *coordinator* and changed the term *students* to *group participants.* He recruited almost 600 young university students who were willing to adopt a new approach to teaching to work as coordinators, but when Freire went to Chile, he had to work with former schoolteachers who were less willing to ignore the traditional forms of instruction they had used in the past. When he left Chile, he worked in Sao Tome, Principe, and Guinea-Bissau. In these efforts, the governments constrained his efforts and he came to rely on textbooks and workbooks rather than the dialogues in culture circles that he began in Brazil. As a result, Freire seemed to fall into several contradictions. He wanted the people to engage in action but he concentrated on teaching literacy skills. He wanted the people to think independently, but his texts listed the correct thoughts (Roberts 75–85).

The third possibility is that, while the advocates of critical pedagogy looked to Freire as a model, they added to his ideas many other theorists' opinions. For example, in 1989, Peter McLaren contrasted critical pedagogy with the dominant curriculum. He claimed that critical pedagogy sought to uncover the relationships between knowledge and power; the traditional model sought to impart knowledge to the students as a technical skill. Thus, he asserted that critical educators asked questions about how schools perpetuate the social relationships found in the wider society. McLaren noted that many theorists contributed to this orientation. He began by pointing out Jonathan Kozol; he moved to Paulo Freire; and he went on to John Dewey (McLaren 180, 186, 192–197).

If critical pedagogy resulted from a blend of such disparate thinkers as Kozol, Dewey, and Freire, the exponents of that view could have acted in any way they wished. For example, when Kozol described the curriculum that schools designed for black children from low-income families should adopt, he listed such subjects as Latin grammar, calculus, and physics (59–61). When Dewey set up a curriculum, he wanted the students to engage in what he called occupations that would help them understand the industrial and economic development of the society. Freire centered the curriculum on decoding the thematic fans in various codes that represented some form of the oppression in society. It is hard to see any curriculum recommendations that this group of educators would agree to follow.

Consequently, for several reasons, educators in the United States turned a potentially radical model of thought, critical pedagogy, into a series of classroom discussions about social issues. Although they claimed that Freire offered them inspiration, they created a model that mirrored the traditional classroom. Thus, the critical pedagogues suffered an ironic fate. Although they wanted to open classrooms beyond the confines of banking education, they constructed limited curriculums that recreated the problems of banking education. This happened because they shared the same perspective that special educators, bilingual educators, and the free market advocates. That is, they saw themselves as serving the interests of a limited group of people. In this case, they thought they could help those students or people they called oppressed to form their own communities and thereby become forces for social reform. Unfortunately, since the critical pedagogues placed the goal of social change as an external result of classroom activities, the lessons appeared separate from doing in the same way that teachers Freire called banking educators presented lessons in accounting to prepare the students for a vocation.

Did some feminists ignore or change Freire's ideas in their efforts to affirm their rights to their voices?

Freire described oppressed people as having been deprived of their voices (Freire 34–35). In writing *Pedagogy of the Oppressed,* Freire followed the then current practice in Portuguese of using the male pronoun to refer to an anonymous person and, by the time his books were published in English, people in the United States considered this to be sexist language. Furthermore, he wrote exclusively about the problems of social class. Since Freire appeared to overlook the plight of women, it was not surprising that some feminists either ignored his work or changed the concepts that he employed to fit their own conceptions of the ways that women should affirm their right to establish community.

Although the idea that men and women think differently had been part of the folklore for many years, Carol Gilligan gave the notion scientific standing in 1982. Writing *In a Different Voice,* Gilligan explained the differences she found in three studies in which people were interviewed about their conceptions of self and morality. The first study involved twenty-five college students who had taken a course on moral and political choice. She asked them questions about what constitutes morality and its relationship to making life choices. In the second study, Gilligan asked similar questions of twenty-nine women who were pregnant and were considering an abortion. The third study compared the responses of matched sets of men and women about morality and about choices in moral dilemmas. She concluded that the women and men used the same words to describe their thoughts, but they had different conceptions of morality and of self-development. While men seemed concerned with notions of rights and justice, the women seemed to focus on responsibilities and caring (Gilligan 2–3, 172–174).

Gilligan believed that men and women could easily misunderstand each other because they had different rationales for their beliefs although the ways in which they thought about morality reinforced each other as well. For example, men's concerns for rights and justice implied that everyone should be treated in the same manner. Women's concerns for care implied that no one should be hurt. Gilligan thought these two notions could merge in showing that inequality hurts both parties in unequal relationships and that violence destroys everyone involved. Thus, Gilligan called for people to realize that there was more than one model of human development. She asserted that, if people attended to the different voices of women, they could see more clearly both the complex dialectic of human development and how separation and relationships aid in human life (Gilligan 173–174).

As Gilligan's work became popular, it attracted considerable criticism. For example, in 1984, Lawrence Walker reviewed thirty-one studies that used Kohlberg's measures of moral development and that examined differences between the sexes in the development of moral reasoning. The total number of subjects in these studies was nearly 3,000 and their ages ranged from five to seventeen. While he found that a few of the studies showed that women thought differently than men did, he concluded that women and men followed remarkably similar patterns of moral reasoning (Walker 1984).

Despite the controversies, Nel Noddings applied to education Gilligan's idea that women had different notions of morality. In 1984, Noddings claimed that philosophers had written about ethics using what she called the voice of the father. This appeared in the language of principles, fairness, and justice. She claimed that ethics could be devised in a feminine manner rooted in receptivity, relatedness, and responsiveness. By bringing the voice of the mother to ethics, Noddings thought that she could accomplish three things. First, she wanted to focus attention not on judgments but on ways of meeting other people. Second, she wanted to preserve the uniqueness of human encounters. And third, by depending on what she called an ethical ideal that brought universality to her ethics, she wanted to emphasize the importance of education (Noddings 1–6).

Noddings believed children could learn the caring attitude because they had experienced the warmth of being cared for at some time in their lives. The desire to rekindle those sentiments offered the motivation for later lessons and provided the motivation to apply them. The problem she faced was to break out of a purely subjective sense of ethics. That is, if she thought that ethical behavior was rooted in caring, Noddings faced the problem of determining how to act in cases where there were no emotional attachments. To solve this problem, she created a model of ethical caring based on what she called the "ethical ideal." This was the view that in all actions people would want to consider themselves as caring individuals (Noddings 6, 49–51).

Although Noddings thought rules, principles, and logical arguments about duties represented the voice of the father, she thought people who wanted to be caring should be able to decide if particular actions were moral or not. Thus, she set up a sort of calculus wherein a person could determine if a decision was grounded in morality on two criteria: the existence of or potential for relation and the possibility for growth in relation. To illustrate how the calculus might work, she offered the case of a woman who became pregnant but was not married. She kept the child because the pregnancy resulted from a caring relationship. The child was a girl. When the woman's daughter was an adult, she became pregnant. The mother could advise an abortion in this case if the pregnancy developed from an unloving relationship and the new mother might reject the unborn child. According to Noddings, both of the contradictory actions were ethical because they were rooted in caring (Noddings 86–90).

For Noddings, education had to foster this ethical ideal in the students. Thus, she constructed everything about the school so the students could develop the image of themselves as caring people and practice skills of caring. This meant that the teacher met the students as a person who cared about them. The caring came out in dialogue that she defined as the opportunity for students and teachers to talk openly and frankly about any subject. The caring came out in the opportunities the students and the teachers had to provide services for other people or animals. Further, the caring came out in the tendency of the teacher to confirm that the students have the potential to be ethical and intellectual beings. Noddings believed it was so important for the teachers to confirm the abilities of the students that she eschewed the practice of individual teachers awarding grades to the students. Instead, she wanted teachers and students to work together to perform well on externally administered objective exams (Noddings 182–195).

Despite Noddings's careful logic, critics complained that educators who focused on the differences between men and women overlooked the struggle for liberation that Freire had made popular. For example, in 1988, Maxine Greene complained that neither Gilligan nor Noddings dealt with the concept of freedom. Greene did not doubt that bonding and caring could be central aspects of the human existence, but she worried that without a concern for human freedom, the ideals of caring could become repressive. Thus, she admonished Gilligan and Noddings to direct their notions of concern and care toward establishing places for freedom (Greene, *Dialectic* 85–86).

Greene was correct in noting a difference between the aims that Freire held and those that Noddings sought. The differences appeared in the ways they viewed the nature and aim of dialogue. For both of these thinkers, dialogue was an important element in building community. On the one hand, Freire defined dialogue as community, and he used it as a tool to achieve liberation. On the other hand, Noddings considered dialogue as a means to affirm the idea that people had of themselves as caring individuals.

As noted earlier, Freire thought that dialogue was always about the world. It resulted when people tried to name the world, and it had to lead to the conquest of the world for the liberation of people. Freire gave dialogue more than an instrumental value. That is, since dialogue was a horizontal relationship of people based on trust that would transform and humanize the world, it was the means to bring about community, and it was the presence of community at the same time. Thus, Freire wrote that dialogue required love for the world and for human beings. It required humility and faith in people to remake the world (Freire 76–81).

On the other hand, Noddings gave dialogue an instrumental value. It was a means to reinforce the ethical ideal. As a result, in life, dialogue offered opportunities to share and to reflect aloud with another person. While Freire wanted dialogue to lead to social change, Noddings wanted it to increase the receptivity in each individual. In schools, Noddings saw dialogue as a means by which the teacher affirmed the reality of the student. Thus, she wanted teachers to listen to whatever was of intellectual interest to the students: sex, God, love, or fear. She added that teachers should respond in sensitive ways, but that the changes this would make were changes in the ideal the children formed for themselves. Noddings hoped the open, sensitive response of the teacher would encourage the students to appreciate the values and beliefs that other people held even while they criticized those opinions (Noddings 121–122, 182–187).

While Noddings ignored the ideas of Freire, another feminist educator changed Freire's ideas to make them fit her concern with personal development. Mary Field Belenky claimed that Freire's model of problem-posing education could help women move through the stages needed to develop their own ways of knowing. In 1986, Belenky and her coauthors interviewed 135 women asking them how they developed their self-concepts. What they found was that women appeared to move through different stages. The first was a stage of silence in which the women seemed to live in a state of isolation. Few of the women lived in such a stage at the time of the interviews and those that did were the youngest women in the study and the most deprived socially, economically, and educationally. Some of the subjects remembered having gone through such a period (Belenky et al. 23).

The second stage was one in which the women took direction from some external authority. In the case of one subject, she moved from living in silence to learning from other people when she had a baby. She went to a clinic and followed the instructions of the experts who helped her. In this stage, the women viewed moral questions as either right or wrong. They could not seem to grasp gradual change or development (Belenky 35, 50).

In the third stage, the women swung to the other extreme and rejected external suggestions. They had decided that the truth was subjective or personal. These women did not see social issues in simple terms of right or wrong, and they became more self-confident. Unfortunately, once these women had decided on something, they could not be dissuaded because they rejected rational methods of proving an idea to be correct or incorrect. Despite the danger of isolation presented by this stage, these women seemed to be concerned about their relationships with other people although the knowledge they valued from these relationships were things about themselves (Belenky 52–53, 74, 84).

Some of the women experienced tensions when they tried to hold a subjectivist view and maintain relationships with other people. As result of these difficulties, they moved into the fourth stage or "procedural knowing." For example, one woman, Naomi, who held her own opinions about art most highly, wanted to graduate from college as an art major. To do so, Naomi had to write essays following the teachers' patterns. The tension between her desire to maintain her own views and her wish to succeed in college led her to adopt a more reasonable approach. In this fourth stage, Naomi decided that intuitions could be misleading and that people can know things they have not experienced (Belenky et al. 87–93).

Belenky and her colleagues found that women who entered the fourth stage of procedural knowing could use two methods. The women who looked as Naomi did for external, impersonal rules or standards to evaluate a work of art employed what Belenky and her colleagues called "separate knowing." Although these women remained suspicious of scientific reason and the opinions of experts, they learned how to evaluate other people's views and to use what appeared useful or true. But when women tried to determine what the artist was trying to say to them, they employed what Belenky and her coauthors called "connected knowing." While these women depended on personal experience, they could take information from another person because they developed the ability to empathize and thereby approximate the other person's experiences (Belenky et al. 100–104, 112–114).

The fifth stage Belenky and her colleagues called "constructed knowledge." In this stage, the women sought to integrate knowledge that they felt intuitively was correct and that they had learned from others. In this view, the women decided that people had constructed their knowledge. As a result, the people who knew something were part of what they knew. For example, a woman expressed constructed knowledge when she noted that scientists derived their information from models that they had built, which were simpler than the real world. The women who operated at this stage often posed questions or problems rather than asserting concrete answers (Belenky et al. 133–139).

To enable women to move through these stages, Belenky and her colleagues turned to Freire for a description of connected teaching. They compared the role of the teacher to that of a midwife helping the students preserve their newborn thoughts, fostering the students' growth, and focusing on the students' knowledge, not their own. As result, most of the instruction took place through dialogue in which the roles of teacher and student merged and changed (Belenky et al. 215–228).

Although Belenky and her colleagues quoted Freire to explain why their model was essential and why it worked, they described the goals of connected teachers to be the therapeutic aims of assisting the students' self-development. They claimed that the women's quest for self and voice transformed their ways of knowing and that within each stage new problems unfolded, but these problems were difficulties in the students' views of themselves. In some sense, the development was a pursuit of freedom. It was an effort to be free from the constraints that the women had within themselves and it was supposed to lead to greater personal development.

Noddings took the contention that women think differently from the way men think and turned it into a model of ethical reasoning and a method of instruction. In this way, she saw herself as an advocate for the voice of the mother. Unfortunately, critics complained that Noddings's model of ethical reasoning left out wider problems of social change. In a similar manner, her educational ideal was focused on the development of personal skills of caring and relationships that seemed to ignore larger issues of social development.

Belenky and her colleagues argued that many women suffered from some form of deprivation that caused them to approach the world inadequately. Belenky and her colleagues recommended that teachers follow a model they identified with Freire to encourage the women to move through the stages of mental development. In making this suggestion, Belenky and her colleagues saw themselves as advocates for women. As a result, they stripped Freire's ideas of dialogue from their Marxist origins and turned the conversations into therapeutic exercises.

The point is that Noddings and Belenky shared a similar assumption with special educators, bilingual educators, and free market advocates. They wanted to affirm the rights of specific groups of people. Since their goals were restricted, they proposed limited conceptions.

Did gay or lesbian educators turn to Freire's model to support homosexual youths?

Although gay or lesbian educators could have used a model of education similar to that of Freire, they tended to ask schools to affirm the rights of the children to develop freely. When the gay or lesbian educators wrote about political activities, they usually referred to those activities that openly gay or lesbian teachers conducted outside schools. Nonetheless, they claimed that having a teacher who was a gay or lesbian activist encouraged the students to be more accepting and tolerant. In this regard, the efforts of Eric Rofes are instructive.

In 1989, Rofes published an article in the *Harvard Educational Review* urging educators to open the classroom closet. He claimed that few educators had taken up the cause of gay and lesbian youths. As a result, these children had low self-esteem and had suicidal feelings. He expressed the hope that the situation was changing for the better (Rofes, "Opening" 444–445).

Rofes praised two educational programs that he claimed met the needs of gay and lesbian youths. These were Project 10 in Los Angeles, a counseling program, and the Harvey Milk School in New York, an alternative high school. In both cases, the programs offered counseling to gay and lesbian youths, specific training to teachers to eliminate harassment of gay and lesbian children, and support for the students. Despite the benefits of the programs, Rofes quoted some policy analysts who believed that these programs did not affirm the gay and lesbian students' rights to an equal education. The analysts suggested that lawyers should pursue litigation that would require schools to enforce the gay and lesbian students' rights to an equal and integrated education. This meant that teachers had to prevent harassment, disciplinary rules had to be equitably enforced, and textbooks had to show tolerance toward homosexuality. Although the analysts made these suggestions in 1986, Rofes noted that by 1989 lawyers had not followed this strategy (Rofes, "Opening" 447–451). In fact, in 1996, Teemu Ruskola argued that courts were unwilling to recognize that gay or lesbian youths existed. The justices took the notion expressed by most people that the children were simply confused or passing through a stage (Ruskola 1–2).

In 1997, Rofes complained that in the years since he wrote his article in the *Harvard Educational Review,* he had seen little progress. No school district opened a Harvey Milk School for gay and lesbian youths, and few districts tried to implement the Project 10 type of counseling programs. He was especially discouraged because no gay or lesbian activists had tried to open a charter school for gay or lesbian youths even though other groups opened charter schools for special or niche populations long neglected by public schools (Rofes, "Foreword" xiii–xiv).

In 1999, Rofes decided he should find out what efforts he had on his students. About twenty years earlier, Rofes taught sixth grade in a progressive independent school in Cambridge, Massachusetts. During the five years that he held the job, he was a gay activist. As a result, he took part in several controversies about gay teachers. News reporters interviewed his students asking about their gay teacher. One group of students authored a book about divorce that became a best-seller, and it contained a chapter entitled "Loving Your Gay Parent" (Rofes, "What" 83–84).

Although Rofes could find only eight of his former students, the members of this select group made him feel that his influence had been positive. The students who had grown to adulthood told him that they learned there was nothing wrong with being gay. Some students claimed their experiences with Rofes enabled them to accept friends and family members who were gay. Another student said she did not think that it made any difference to her that Rofes was gay, although when she had a child, she placed him in the care of a gay caregiver. Since she never worried that the experience would make her son gay, she decided Rofes must have had some influence on her attitudes. Rofes's discussions with his former students convinced him that gay activists were wrong to argue that gay teachers had no influence on their students. He thought the activists should proclaim that openly gay teachers could help the students be more accepting of the differences among people (Rofes, "What" 83–92).

In his article about the effects he had on his students, Rofes noted that advocates of critical pedagogy discuss issues far removed from children's lives. He suggested that these educators should focus on issues related to the schools, such as hiring openly gay or lesbian teachers (Rofes, "What" 91).

Rofes may have wanted advocates of critical pedagogy to concern themselves with gay and lesbian rights, but it would be hard to claim that he followed the ideas of Freire when he was a teacher. Rofes claimed that, when he was a teacher, reporters interviewed his students and quoted them in newspapers or on television shows, but these incidents came from Rofes's public announcement that he was gay. The students were not involved in demonstrations or political efforts. Although the students wrote a book about divorce, this appears to be more in the direction of encouraging personal development than fostering social change.

Thus, Rofes seemed to present a limited notion of education. Although he wanted schools to help liberate children, he saw himself as an advocate of a particular group and he took a limited notion of what constituted liberation. In this way, he shared the assumptions and the difficulties of other advocates who sought to reform schools.

Was there something in Freire's model of pedagogy that led advocates to hold limited notions of education?

As Freire became popular, critics made three important complaints. Sociologists interested in economic development argued that Freire encouraged authoritarianism by advocating Marxist notions of revolution. Ecologically minded critics complained that Freire's model built on Western ways of thinking and, when employed in non-Western cultures, it did not lead to liberation but to cultural imposition. Finally, feminists noted that Freire did not acknowledge the differences that existed between women and men or among the different types of women. Worse, they complained that his views could support a patriarchal view of liberation. Although most of these critics recognized the important contributions that Freire made, they contended that these several problems had to be considered before educators applied the model widely.

In 1974, Peter L. Berger, a sociologist interested in economic development, wrote the results of his extended studies of economic development in Third World countries. When Berger considered problems of education, he focused attention on Freire. He acknowledged that Freire had taught previously illiterate adults of average intelligence to read in about six weeks. According to Berger, the method succeeded because the adults learned to read and to write about topics related to their everyday experience, and their motivation increased when Freire connected literacy to the improvement of their living conditions. According to Berger, the problem in Freire's method was in his effort to enlist higher-class individuals to raise the consciousness of lower-class people (Berger 111–113).

Berger recognized that these ideas came from Marxism wherein intellectuals inspired by the need for revolution were supposed to help the proletariat overcome their false consciousness that kept them bound to oppressive bourgeois thinking. Berger recognized that this notion could apply to Brazil where the university students working with Freire knew more about politics than did the peasants they taught, but he suggested that the peasants knew more about other things, such as farming. Unfortunately, Berger worried that Freire would not allow for this difference in types of knowledge because Freire characterized the peasants as being like animals. Freire claimed the oppressed people were unable to think about the future and could not change their conditions. The danger that Berger saw in the arrogance of consciousness-raising was that the university students would impose their views on the peasants. While such imposition might be essential for the modernization of a country like Brazil, Berger noted that it would be more truthfully called conversion than liberation (Berger 114–118).

To offer a simple example of Freire's authoritarianism, Berger asked about a possible situation where the teacher thought the people should repair the roofs of their homes and helped the peasants select a democratic method of apportioning the work. Given the university students' perspective, this would be a reasonable way to improve the lives of the people, but Berger pointed out that the people might have preferred to attend to their ancestral shrines. Would the university students allow the peasants to hold their own priorities when every rational measure indicated that the ancestral shrines would not improve the peasants' lives but repairing the roofs would reduce disease (Berger 119–120)?

In making his study, Berger was interested in economic development more than education. As a result, he noted that in economic development, officials gambled with the lives of other people, and he feared that Freire's ideas of consciousness-raising could lead the officials to find ways to manipulate the people, ignoring the possibility that the people had rights to their own beliefs. Of course, the officials would claim they were affirming the peasants' rights to their own community while the officials imposed their own values (Berger 131).

The second set of complaints came from ecologically minded educators. Taking views similar to those of Berger, these individuals argued that Freire and the advocates of critical pedagogy held a Western, rational model of thinking, and they applied this culturally specific model as if it was universally valid. For example, in 1987, C. A. Bowers acknowledged that Freire thought that critical reflection was the legitimate basis for human action. This implied that people could have commitments, be responsible for the world in which they live, and change restrictive conditions. The problem that Bowers saw was that Freire considered critical reflection to be the only source of knowledge and authority. As a result, Freire ruled out any other methods by which a community may develop systems of authority. Since everything depended on critical reflection, people could apply their reflections to everything including traditional shared meanings. Thus, they would erode things, such as religious traditions. Bowers noted that such corrosive powers of thinking might act in ways that Freire did not expect if they destroyed the cultural ties and left the people open to manipulation by mass movements (Bowers, *Elements* 128–131).

Bowers criticized Freire for presenting most questions as if there were only two sides. One side favored human liberation, and the other side induced oppression. According to Bowers, Freire's dependence on dichotomies of good and evil led him to overlook the problems that could take place within his own programs. That is, Freire assumed that revolutionaries who developed solidarity with the peasants would always think along with them. They would become selfless persons who pursued the common good, but Bowers complained that critical reflection could lead people astray to the point that they would confuse their pursuit of the common good with their own self-interest (Bowers, *Elements* 129–131).

Finally, Bowers claimed that Freire's model was culturally specific. That is, other cultural groups, such as the Northern Ojibwa, did not think in the manner of Western rationalists. For example, the Ojibwa language did not distinguish between things and people, and they could not liberate themselves by learning to control things. Thus, Bowers concluded that, although Freire implied emancipation was a specific direction, the idea of liberation varied from language group to language group (Bowers, *Elements* 131–135).

The third set of criticisms came from feminists who sought to overcome the tendency in Freire's ideas that could lead to the imposition of a patriarchal view. One such feminist, bell hooks, wrote that she found Freire's work at a time in her life when she was thinking about the impact of racism, sexism, and social class exploitation. As a black woman, hooks identified with the peasants. She found that Freire gave her a language with which to face the oppression. Yet, hooks noted that she was always aware of the ways Freire linked liberation with the experiences of patriarchal manhood. Although she acknowledged this blind spot, she did not want the awareness of this problem to overshadow his contributions. She added that no one should apologize for the sexism in problem-posing methods. Instead, she thought that critical pedagogy invited a critical interrogation of the flaw (hooks 46–49).

Writing in a similar fashion in 1991, Kathleen Weiler noted that Freire's book *Pedagogy of the Oppressed* made many universal and abstract claims that seemed untrue. Yet, she did not want to discard his model of pedagogy. Instead, Weiler contended that the women's movement developed in the 1960s and 1970s through consciousness-raising groups in ways that corresponded to Freire's ideas. She claimed that small groups of women gathered spontaneously during the Civil Rights movement and sought ways to change society to affirm their rights as women. Thus, Weiler concluded that the women's groups engaged in what Freire called "praxis" (Weiler 455–458).

In addition to the debt the women's movement owed Freire, Weiler noted that the movement exposed three ways that Freire's ideas could be enriched. The first way was that teachers could not simply be coequal with students as Freire described. Instead, the authority of a woman as an intellectual had to be affirmed in the process of helping the students become theorists of their own lives. The second way was that feeling or intuition could be added to rationality as a way of knowing or experiencing the world. The third way the movement enriched Freire's ideas was that it showed there was no such category as women's experiences. Instead, Weiler claimed that women of culture and lesbians pointed out a range of complex experiences that different women underwent at different times. Thus, Weiler noted that women's pedagogy agreed with Freire's approach, which recognized the human capacity to feel, to know, and to change, but she concluded that the movement forced cultural pedagogues to recognize the complex nature of the issues that arose from the distinct histories of different women (Weiler 459–460, 462, 463, 467–468).

Summary

In all, the complaints of Berger, Bowers, hooks, and Weiler indicate that Freire suffered from a limited notion of education. As in the cases described in Chapters Ten and Eleven, Freire developed his blind spots because he claimed to be the advocate for a particular group of people. Despite his shortcomings, it should be clear that Freire encouraged critical theorists, feminists, and gay activists to justify their educational reforms on the grounds that they would affirm the students' rights to form communities. Although these groups of educators held to different ideas about the methods of teaching the appropriate curriculum and the most satisfying type of community, in each case educators adapted Freire's ideas to fit their own particular goals.

Some of the advocates of critical pedagogy blended Freire's ideas with the traditional lessons found in any student-centered social studies classroom. The result was that students may have thought about the nature of their society, but the activities appeared to be separate from activities to determine the truth of falsity of those beliefs.

Other educators applied Freire's ideas in college English classes. Although these educators thought they were encouraging critical reflection about the nature of society and education, their classes resembled the more traditional composition courses except the students wrote about controversial subjects.

Some feminists found Freire to be important. They argued that the development of the women's movement followed the pattern of Freire's ideas about consciousness-raising. Other women who wanted to emphasize the feminine perspective in education ignored Freire and eschewed the idea of liberation. Instead, they sought to create an education that reinforced human relationships and caring. Unfortunately, such a curriculum lacked opportunities to learn about wider social issues and mechanisms of social change.

On the other hand, some feminists turned Freire's ideas into a therapeutic model of self-development. These educators took the methods of dialogue that Freire used, but applied them to the acquisition of traditional academic subject matter instead of to social transformation. The result was what the feminists called connected teaching, and it was supposed to help women move through the feminine stages of knowing.

Gay activists should have had several reasons to want to use Freire's methods, but when Rofes wrote about his experiences, he found that an important element of his work was that an openly gay man offered an example to the children. As result, they learned many important lessons about tolerance and the acceptance of different people. Such a view was far removed from the problem-posing that Freire suggested. Worse, increased tolerance among students might signal the end of the harassment of gay and lesbian people, but it might not represent a desire to work for a more equitable distribution of goods and services in the economy.

There may have been flaws within Freire's model that caused educators who praised him to embrace limited views of education. Critics accused Freire of encouraging authoritarianism, and he seemed to view the situations and the possible solutions in simple but vague ways that made intelligent actions impossible. Not surprisingly, educators who followed him most closely seemed to suffer from similar difficulties.

Despite the differences that separated the critical theorists, the feminists, and the advocates of gay and lesbian students, the members of the different groups sought to affirm the students' rights to form communities. Insofar as they saw themselves as advocates of particular groups of students, these groups shared the same perspective of the special educators and bilingual educators who wanted to affirm students' rights to appropriate educations. Despite the good that came from these perspectives, the educators that held them seemed to overlook larger social questions. As a result, these educators differed in many ways from the educators discussed in Chapters Three through Nine who wanted to meet the students' needs in ways that enhanced democracy. Although the educators in this chapter sought social transformation in the direction of liberation, the freedom they had in mind seemed to overlook the idea of social harmony valued by the progressive educators described in the earlier chapters.

CONCLUSION

From the beginning to the end of the twentieth century, ideas of educational reform proliferated as schools spread, attracting more and more teachers and students. After the debates with idealists, the Herbartians set the mode of educational reform. As the twentieth century began, educators tried to use the ideal of democracy to fashion a model of education that would enable children to develop skills and abilities that would be personally rewarding in ways that enhanced society. By the middle of the century, though, educators saw themselves as advocates who struggled to force schools to meet the children's special needs. The change was important because it signaled a new set of approaches to education. At the same time, it opened a new set of difficulties for educators to confront.

At the turn of the twentieth century, educators who called themselves Herbartians complained that educators, such as W. T. Harris, did not understand how children learned. The Herbartians had adopted the ideas of a German philosopher who constructed a model of teaching based on his views of the ways children acquired new insights and became moral persons. Of course, educators like Charles De Garmo and Francis Parker did not follow Herbart's ideas in slavish manners. They wanted teachers to proceed in steps that began with some sort of activities to capture the students' interests, followed by the introduction of new ideas, and concluded with opportunities for the students to associate the new and the old information and to apply the new insights. Since the lessons began with something from daily life, these educators argued that they could show the children how academic subjects were integrated with practical affairs.

Harris claimed that Herbartians misunderstand the capacities of the children and the nature of learning. He argued that academic subjects required a different way of thinking than was found in practical affairs. Further, Harris contended that in order for children to see the way that academic subjects related to each other and illuminated practical affairs, the children had to make a leap from one form of learning to another. Most important, Harris argued that it was at this point of personal integration that students developed interests by recognizing the connection among subjects and activities. Further, he believed that students had to make these connections for themselves. Teachers could not help them.

Although Harris was the U.S. Commissioner of Education and had enjoyed an illustrious career, his voice was of a time gone past. Herbartians expressed the ideas that most educators shared for the next fifty or sixty years when they claimed that school subjects could be tied to students' interests and that such lessons increased the children's moral sensibilities.

From World War I through the Cold War of the 1950s, educators used some variation of the Herbartian perspective; they tried to meet students' needs in ways that advanced the democratic society. Although these educators disagreed about what was the appropriate content of the curriculum and about the ways the teacher should present the material, they shared the assumption that they could discover the students' needs and that they could satisfy them. In this way, they wanted to build a more moral and harmonious society. Unfortunately, the contradiction between individual desires and social needs was not easily resolved. Since they sought to encourage some form of harmony, the progressive educators seemed to impose on the students in different ways.

In the 1960s, educators chose to imitate the tactics of the NAACP and the SCLC. Seeing themselves as advocates for particular types of students, these educators used a variety of legal and political methods to establish the rights of their constituents to appropriate educations. Several of these groups enjoyed success. A surprising range of educators and politicians saw themselves as advocates who had to establish and affirm the rights of some group of students. They ranged from educators who sought to advocate the education of children with disabilities or linguistic differences to critical pedagogues who wanted schools to liberate students. Since these different types of educators saw themselves as advocates for distinct groups of students, they seemed to share the same perspective that schools had to affirm the rights of these groups of students. As a result, they paid less attention to the meaning and aim of a good education.

The educators who worked before 1960 and those who worked after 1960 were alike in that the educators in each period shared a perspective of educational reform. They differed because the perspectives that they shared differed from each other. One group wanted to meet students' needs. The other group wanted to affirm students' rights.

These two perspectives may appear to be similar, but the similarity is more apparent than real. This is best illustrated by noticing that the educators who worked before 1960 faced a different set of problems from those who worked after 1960.

The Herbartians had rejected Harris's idealistic theories because they thought teachers could lead students to recognize relations among academic subjects and practical activities. They believed that teachers could use students' interests to make academic subjects more appealing and relevant. Above all, they thought that well-designed lessons would lead the students to understand and enhance a democratic society. Unfortunately, the educators who followed this path could not easily resist the temptation to train the children to occupy an appropriate place in adult society. For example, educators may have believed that academic studies enhanced the children's abilities to think critically and thereby advanced the democracy, but these educators had difficulty resisting the temptation to introduce vocational training that prepared the children for specific slots in adult society. Once the educators accepted the view that academic studies were related to practical affairs, they could not point to a place where vocational training was excessive.

On the other hand, educators who worked after 1960 had difficulty including a vision of wider social issues in their educational reforms. For example, special educators created a model of curriculum planning that enabled parents, teachers, and specialists to construct an individual educational plan that met the child's specific needs. The problem is that the model of the individual educational plan does not contain any effort to define a good education. According to this model, the best education for the child is whatever the members of the team agree is appropriate. It was possible that the plan could be an intelligently devised set of activities that enable the child to develop his or her abilities while learning to shape his or her desires in ways that enhance social good. This would be a progressive educator's dream. It was also possible that the plan could be the worst collection of drill and repetition exercises aimed at encouraging the child to master basic academic skills. This would be a progressive educator's nightmare. Yet, the model as defined in the Education for All Handicapped Children Act did not distinguish between these possibilities.

The educators who worked in the first half of the century seemed to overlook the need for students to learn to continually reconstruct the society because they defined a good education as one that engendered social harmony. These educators worried about helping everyone fit into the society.

More contemporary educators focused attention differently. They saw themselves as advocates struggling to force schools to protect the individual's rights. In so doing, though, they seemed to ignore wider educational problems. They were worried more that some people were excluded or oppressed than they were worried that everyone worked together in some harmonious fashion.

To some extent, the difference between these two attitudes is the distinction between democracy and pluralism. That is, democracy is a form of living in which everyone shares and from which everyone profits. This is the ideal that dominated educational thinking in the first half of the century. Pluralism is a form of living in which different groups maintain their own styles of life but do not suffer for retaining their own perspectives. This represents a form of living that more contemporary educators share.

As important as the distinctions between democracy and pluralism might be, people can make too much of them. Both perspectives share many important aspects. They are based on ideas of the essential dignity of people, on desires for tolerance and equality, and on some belief that people can improve their situations. Furthermore, a democracy requires that some people think differently from other people. Otherwise, there is no way for new ideas to appear. A pluralistic society requires that every group share some understandings. Otherwise, there is no way the members of different groups can work for the common good. Nonetheless, knowing if a perspective leads to pluralism or democracy may be helpful in avoiding the temptation to follow any idea past the point where it is helpful. As the preceding chapters illustrate, during specific periods of time, educators shared certain of these perspectives. At some point, each of those ideas began to cause problems.

Chapter One explains the public debates that took place between Harris and the Herbartians. These set the stage for the developments in the next chapters because educators repudiated Harris's idealistic conceptions. The importance of this shift is evident in Chapter Two. During campaigns for compulsory education, the practical value of schooling became an important issue. Educators favoring manual training had argued that exercises in wood shop or sewing offered concrete applications of abstract academic skills. In a short time, vocational educators used the same arguments to advance their programs. The transition was important because the vocational educators wanted students to acquire specific skills that manufacturers could use. The educators favoring more general studies could not easily defend their positions. As a result, schools seemed to be advancing the interests of factory owners and exacerbating the distinctions among social classes.

From 1900 to 1930, there were three different efforts to Americanize the immigrants. These are the topics of Chapter Three. The programs extended from the model of liberal progressive reformers, such as Addams and Dewey, to the extreme supporters of the Americanization movement. Although ethnic religious groups saw the liberal progressives as threatening their traditional values, the Americanization movement led to bigotry, enforced enculturation, and deportation. Since the problems did not decline until the U.S. Congress restricted immigration severely, this indicated that educators could not easily find the point at which the need for social harmony began to harm the interests of individuals.

Four innovations that educators hoped would make the schools more democratic are discussed in Chapter Four. These include the model of the comprehensive school, the use of scientific curriculum making, the project method, and the development of textbooks that explained social problems. In each case, the approaches were based on the Herbartian ideal described in Chapter One, and they leaned in the direction of helping the student adapt to society more than they helped the children pursue their own interests.

During the Great Depression, educators sought to change society, but, as Chapter Five describes, the four programs seemed to help students adjust to society more than radically change it. One was the effort to change the social studies. Another was the Civilian Conservation Corps. The third and fourth examples were programs to reform the education of Hispanic Americans and Native Americans in New Mexico. Despite the differences among these programs, they shared the view that students should learn things that related to their lives. The problem was that, in each case, the teachers were to do so by encouraging the students to accept a particular version of the culture.

The Eight-Year Study and the conservative reaction, essentialism, are the subjects of Chapter Six. The PEA's Eight-Year Study was an important effort to show how schools could satisfy children's needs in ways that met social obligations. Ironically, critics in the 1950s complained that such progressive education caused excessive peer pressure and led to social conformity. If this was true of the PEA, the conservatives who opposed the organization encouraged conformity because they wanted all students to pursue academic subjects regardless of the students' interests. These complaints arose because the progressives and their critics, the essentialists, agreed the curriculum should be aimed at benefiting the society.

Chapter Seven describes the ways that educators sought to meet the nation's needs during World War II and the uneasy peace that followed. Some educators wanted the schools to require that all children study academic courses. Vocational educators believed the United States should set up separate types of schools to allow gifted students to develop into productive scientists. A chemist and former president of Harvard University, James Conant, offered a compromise. Since supporters of liberal arts training and the advocates of separate trade schools sought to meet student needs in ways that produced a better society, Conant accepted this assumption as well. Unfortunately, in as much as Conant assumed the perspectives of the competing reformers, his model of the comprehensive high school suffered from the same problems. It did not help children to move from their social classes.

The subject of Chapter Eight includes efforts to develop curriculums in physics, mathematics, biology, chemistry, and social studies that tried to teach students of different abilities to follow the same types of thinking used by scholars in the academic disciplines. Although scholars who designed the new curriculums believed that the subject matters could be designed in some way that the students could become intelligent independent thinkers, they shared those views of the progressive and the traditional educators that placed primary importance on helping children become responsible citizens. As a result, critics complained that the new curriculums imposed a set of values on the children.

With Chapter Nine, the book describes the events that led educators to adopt new assumptions about the proper nature of educational reform. Following campaigns by the NAACP and the SCLC, the federal government passed the U.S. Civil Rights Act of 1964 and the Elementary and Secondary Education Act (ESEA). These laws reinforced each other. The Civil Rights Act gave the federal government the authority to forbid local boards of education to receive federal funds unless they racially desegregated the schools, and ESEA offered educators over $1 billion in federal money to improve the education of children from lower-income families. Although neither of these efforts proved successful, the laws inspired educators to adopt new models for educational reform. Instead of trying to persuade school people to meet students' needs, reformers came to see themselves as advocates who had to engage in legal and political campaigns to force schools to affirm students' rights.

In line with Chapter Nine, Chapter Ten explains how advocates serving children with disabilities and children with linguistic differences imitated the tactics of civil rights organizations. They claimed that public schools denied the rights of the children. They sued in federal courts for redress. They pointed to the resulting legal victories as requiring local school officials to follow a set of procedures that to the advocates constituted equal educational opportunities. Since the participants of these campaigns shared the view that they were advocates of particular students, they did not attend to larger social concerns. They wanted to force schools to affirm the children's rights to an appropriate education.

Chapter Eleven shows that conservative politicians followed the logic of the advocates for children with disabilities and limited English proficiency. In this case, the politicians and educators wanted to affirm the parents' rights to effective educations for their children. As a result, they tried several ways to encourage parents to combine and force school teachers to concentrate on basic academic skills instruction. For example, they tried to publicize the test results of different schools, to create uniform measures of academic excellence, and to provide parents with the freedom to choose schools for their children through such mechanisms as charter schools and vouchers. As in the case of advocates for children with disabilities, these reformers overlooked broader social questions because they pursued narrow ends.

The final chapter discusses the ideas of three different groups of educators who imitated the ideas of Paulo Freire: critical theorists, feminists, and advocates for gay and lesbian youths. Although these reformers differed considerably among themselves, they assumed that they should serve as advocates for a group of students. They should have considered broad social issues because they sought social transformations. Ironically, they tended to offer limited reforms since their focuses were narrow.

A danger of reading such a list of reforms and resulting problems is that it could encourage people to develop pessimistic attitudes. Instead of causing people to surrender to inevitable failure, this list of efforts and limited successes should encourage people to learn more about schools and schooling. The reformers fell into predictable categories and their proposals shared similar difficulties. If people can determine the assumption on which a particular proposal is based, they should be able to minimize the dangers that would result. For this reason, it is important for people to know a great deal about education and to think deeply about the assumptions on which any curriculum rests.

WORKS CITED

Abbott, Edith, and Sophonisba P. Breckinridge. *Truancy and Non-Attendance in the Chicago Schools: A Study of the Social Aspects of the Compulsory Education and Child Labor Legislation in Illinois*. Chicago: University of Chicago Press, 1917.

Addams, Jane. "The Public School and the Immigrant Child." *NEA Journal of Proceedings and Addresses*. Chicago: University of Chicago Press, 1908, 99–102.

———. *Twenty Years at Hull House*. New York: Macmillan, 1912.

Aiken, Wilford M. *The Story of the Eight-Year Study*. New York: Harper and Brothers, 1942.

Alberty, Harold. *Reorganizing the High School Curriculum*. New York: Macmillan, 1947.

Alexander, Lamar, H. Thomas James, and Robert Glasser. *The Nation's Report Card: Improving the Assessment of Student Achievement*. U.S. Department of Education. Washington, DC: GPO, 1987.

American Federation of Teachers (AFT). *Charter School Laws: Do They Measure Up?* A.F.T. Department of Research. August 2002. http://www.aft.org/research/reports/charter/csweb/conclude.htm.

American Historical Association. *Annual Proceedings of the American Historical Association for the Year 1935*. Volume I—1933, 1934, and 1935. Washington, DC: GPO, 1936.

American Institutes for Research. *An Educator's Guide to Schoolwide Reform*. Arlington, VA: Educational Research Service, 1999.

Angus, David L., and Jeffrey Mirel. *The Failed Promise of the American High School, 1890–1995*. New York: Teachers College Press, 1999.

Apple, Michael, and Nancy King. "What Do Schools Teach?" In *The Hidden Curriculum and Moral Education: Deception or Discovery?* edited by Henry Giroux and David Purpel. Berkeley, CA: McCutchan, 1983, 82–99.

Armor, David J. "The Evidence on Busing." *Public Interest* 28 (Summer 1972): 90–126.

Aronson, Julian. "The Pedagogues Sound the Tocsin." *School and Society* 41(1935): 95–97.

Ayers, Leonard P. *Laggards in Our Schools: A Study of Retardation and Elimination in City School Systems*. New York: Russell Sage Foundation, 1909.

Bagley, William Chandler. *Education and Emergent Man*. New York: Thomas Nelson and Sons, 1934.

———. *The Educative Process*. New York: Macmillan, 1905.

———. "An Essentialist's Platform for the Advancement of American Education." *Educational Administration and Supervision* 24.4 (April 1938): 241–256.

Bailey, Stephen K. *Education Interest Groups in the Nation's Capital*. Washington, DC: American Council on Education, 1975.

Bailey, Stephen K., and Edith K. Mosher. *ESEA: The Office of Education Administers a Law*. New York: Syracuse University Press, 1968.

Ballou, Frank W. "Statement Concerning the Report of the Commission on the Investigation of History and the Other Social Studies." *School and Society* 39 (1934): 701–702.

Bancroft, Cecil F. P. "Report of the Committee of Ten." *Educational Review* 8 (1894): 275–285.

Bangura, Abdul Karim, and Martin C. Muo. *United States Congress and Bilingual Education*. New York: Peter Lang, 2001.

Barry, Coleman J., O. S. B. *The Catholic Church and German Americans*. Milwaukee: Bruce Publishing, 1953.

Beale, Howard K. *Are Teachers Free? An Analysis of the Restraints upon the Freedom of Teaching in the American Schools*. New York: Charles Scribner's Sons, 1936.

Beard, Charles. *A Charter for the Social Sciences in the Schools*. New York: Charles Scribner's Sons, 1932.

Belenky, Mary Field, et al. *Women's Ways of Knowing*. New York: Basic Books, 1986.

Berger, Peter L. *Pyramids of Sacrifice: Political Ethics and Social Change*. New York: Basic Books, 1974.

Bestor, Arthur. *Educational Wastelands: The Retreat from Learning in Our Public Schools*. 1953. Urbana: University of Illinois Press, 1985.

Blauch, Lloyd E. *Educational Service for Indians*. Washington, DC: GPO, 1939.

Bloomfield, Meyer. *The Vocational Guidance of Youth*. 1911. New York: Arno Press, 1969.

Board of Education of the Hendrik Hudson Central School District v Rowley. 632 F. 2d 945 U.S. Supreme Court. 1982.

Bobbitt, Franklin. *The Curriculum*. 1918. New York: Arno Press and *The New York Times,* 1971.

———. *Curriculum-Making in Los Angeles*. Chicago: University of Chicago Press, 1922.

———. "Questionable Recommendations of the Commission on the Social Studies." *School and Society* 40 (1934): 201–208.

257

Bode, Boyd. "Editorial Comment." *The Phi Delta Kappan* 17.1 (1934): 1, 7.

———. *Modern Educational Theories*. New York: Random House, 1927.

———. *Progressive Education at the Crossroads*. New York: Newson and Co., 1938.

Bogardus, Emory S. *Essentials of Americanization*. 3rd edition. Los Angeles: University of Southern California Press, 1923.

Bourne, Randolph. *History of a Literary Radical and Other Essays*. Edited by Van Wyck Brooks. New York: B. W. Huebsch, 1920.

Bowers, C. A. *Elements of a Post-Liberal Theory of Education*. New York: Teachers College Press, 1987.

———. *The Progressive Educator: The Radical Years*. New York: Random House, 1969.

Bowles, Samuel, and Herbert Gintis. *Schooling in Capitalist America: Educational Reform and the Contradictions of Economic Life*. New York: Basic Books, 1976.

Boyles, Deron. *American Education and Corporations: The Free Market Goes to School*. New York: Garland Publishing, 1998.

Brain, George B. "The Early Planners." In *Project Head Start,* edited by Edward Zigler and Jeanette Valentine. New York: Macmillan Publishing, 1979, 73–77.

Brinkman, William W. "Educational Literature Review: The Secondary School." *School and Society* 72.1859 (5 August 1950): 84–91.

Bromley, Dorothy Dunbar. "Education for College or for Life?" *Harpers* 182 (1941): 407–416.

Brookings Institution. *The Problem of Indian Administration*. 1928. New York: Johnson Reprint Corp., 1971.

Brubacher, John S. *Modern Philosophies of Education*. New York: McGraw-Hill, 1939.

Brueckner, Leo J. "Language: The Development of Ability in Oral and Written Composition." In *Child Development and Curriculum,* edited by Guy Montrose Whipple. Bloomington, IL: Public School Publishing Company, 1939, 225–240.

Bruner, Jerome S. *The Process of Education*. New York: Random House, 1960.

Buczek, Daniel S. "The Polish-American Parish as an Americanizing Factor." In *Studies in Ethnicity: The East European Experience in America,* edited by Charles A. Ward, Philip Shashko, and Donald E. Pienkos. New York: Columbia University Press, 1980, 153–165.

Bunker, Frank Forest. *Reorganization of the Public School System*. Bulletin No. 8. U.S. Department of the Interior. Washington, DC: GPO, 1916.

Butler, Fred Clayton. *Community Americanization: A Handbook for Workers*. Bulletin No. 76. U.S. Department of the Interior. Washington, DC: GPO, 1920.

———. *State Americanization: The Part of the State in the Education and Assimilation of the Immigrant*. Bulletin No. 77. U.S. Department of the Interior. Washington, DC: GPO, 1920.

Campbell, J. A. "CHEM Study—An Approach to Chemistry Based on Experiments." In *New Curricula,* edited by Robert W. Heath. New York: Harper & Row, 1964, 82–93.

Carbone, Peter F., Jr. *The Social and Educational Thought of Harold Rugg*. Durham, NC: Duke University Press, 1977.

Carter, Launor F. "The Sustaining Effects Study of Compensatory and Elementary Education." *Educational Researcher* 13.7 (August/September 1984): 4–13.

Casanova, Ursala, and M. Beatriz Arias. "Contextualizing Bilingual Education." *Bilingual Education: Politics, Practice, and Research*. Ninety-Second Yearbook of NSSE. Chicago: University of Chicago Press, 1993, 1–35.

Chamberlin, Dean, et al. *Did They Succeed in College? The Follow-Up Study of the Graduates of the Thirty Schools*. New York: Harper and Brothers, 1942.

Channing, Edward, Albert Bushnell Hart, and Frederick Jackson Turner. *Guide to the Study and Reading of American History*. Boston: Ginn and Co., 1912.

Charters, W. W. *Curriculum Construction*. 1923. New York: Arno Press, 1971.

Chilman, Catherine S. *Growing Up Poor*. 1966. Washington, DC: GPO, 1969.

Chubb, John E. "The Performance of Privately Managed Schools: An Early Look at the Edison Project." In *Learning from School Choice,* edited by Paul E. Peterson and Bryan C. Hassel. Washington, DC: Brookings Institution Press, 1998, 213–248.

Chubb, John E., and Terry M. Moe. *Politics, Markets, and America's Schools*. Washington, DC: The Brookings Institution, 1990.

Cicirelli, Victor G. "Head Start: Brief of the Study." In *Britannica Review of American Education,* vol. I, edited by David G. Hays. Chicago: Encyclopedia Britannica, 1969, 233–243.

Class of 1938. *Were We Guinea Pigs?* New York: Henry Holt and Co., 1938.

Clifton, John L. *Ten Famous Educators*. Columbus, OH: R. G. Adams and Co., 1933.

Clowse, Barbara Barksdale. *Brainpower for the Cold War: The Sputnik Crisis and National Defense Act of 1958*. Westport, CT: Greenwood Press, 1981.

Coates, Charles Penny. *History of the Manual Training School of Washington University*. U.S. Bureau of Education Bulletin No. 3. Washington, DC: GPO, 1923.

Cobb, Casey D., and Gene V. Glass. "Ethnic Segregation in Arizona Charter Schools." *Educational Policy Analysis Archives* 7.1 (1999): 1–27. http://epaa.asu.edu/epaa/v7n1/.

Cohen, David K., Thomas F. Pettigrew, and Robert T. Riley. "Race and the Outcomes of Schooling." In *On Equal-*

ity of Educational Opportunity, edited by Frederick Mosteler and Daniel Patrick Moynihan. New York: Random House, 1972, 343–368.

Colachio, David P. *The Education for All Handicapped Children Act: A Historical Study of Public law 94-142.* Diss. Texas A&M University, 1985: UMI 1985. 8605241.

Coleman, James S. "Correspondence: Response to Petti-grew and Green." *Harvard Educational Review* 2 (1976): 217–224.

———. "Evaluation of the Report." In *On Equality of Educational Opportunity,* edited by Frederick Mosteler and Daniel Patrick Moynihan. New York: Random House, 1972, 146–167.

Coleman, James S., et al. *Equality of Opportunity.* Washington, DC: GPO, 1966.

———. *Trends in School Desegregation: 1968–1973.* Washington, DC: Urban Institute, 1975.

Collier, John. *Indians of the Americas: The Long Hope.* New York: New American Library, 1947.

Collings, Ellsworth. *An Experiment with a Project Curriculum.* New York: Macmillan Co., 1925.

Commission on History. "Final Report and Recommendations of the Commission on History to the College Entrance Examination Board." *Social Studies* 27.8 (1936): 546–566.

Commission on the Relation of School and College. *Thirty Schools Tell Their Story.* New York: Harper and Brothers, 1942.

Commission on the Social Studies. *Conclusions and Recommendations of the Commission.* New York: Charles Scribner's Sons, 1934.

Committee on Education and Labor. U.S. House of Representatives. 90th Congress 1st session. *Bilingual Education Programs.* (28 and 29 June 1967). New York: Arno Press, 1978.

———. 98th Congress 2nd session. *Hearing on Bilingual Education.* (28 March 1984). Washington, DC: GPO, 1984.

Committee on the Function of Art in General Education. *The Visual Arts in General Education.* New York: D. Appleton-Century Co., 1940.

Committee on the Function of English in General Education. *Language in General Education.* New York: D. Appleton-Century Co., 1940.

Conant, James Bryant. *The American High School Today: A First Report to Interested Citizens.* New York: McGraw-Hill, 1959.

———. *The Comprehensive High School: A Second Report to Interested Citizens.* New York: McGraw-Hill, 1967.

———. *My Several Lives: Memoirs of a Social Inventor.* New York: Harper & Row, 1970.

———. *Slums and Suburbs.* New York: McGraw-Hill, 1961.

Conference of Americanization as a War Measure. *Ameri-canization as a War Measure.* Bulletin No. 18. U.S. Department of the Interior. Washington, DC: GPO, 1918.

Conference on Teaching Children and Youth Who Are Educationally Disadvantaged. *Programs for the Educationally Disadvantaged.* Washington, DC: GPO, 1962.

Counts, George S. *The Selective Character of American Secondary Education.* Chicago: University of Chicago Press, 1922.

———. *The Social Foundations of Education.* New York: Charles Scribner's Sons, 1934.

Cox, Philip W. L. "Are the Conclusions and Recommendations of the Commission on the Social Studies Startling or Alarming?" *School and Society* 40 (1934): 554–557.

Crain, Robert L., and Rita E. Mahard. "Desegregation and Black Achievement: A Review of the Research." *Law and Contemporary Problems* 42.3 (Summer, 1978): 17–56.

———. *Desegregation Plans That Raise Black Achievement: A Review of the Research.* National Institute of Education. Santa Monica, CA: Rand Corporation, 1982.

———. *The Influence of High School Racial Composition on Black College Attendance and Test Performance.* U.S. Department of Health, Education, and Welfare. Washington, DC: GPO, 1978.

Crain, Robert L., Rita E. Mahard, and Ruth E. Narot. *Making Desegregation Work: How Schools Create Social Climates.* Cambridge, MA: Ballinger Publishing, 1982.

Crain, Robert L., and Carol Sachs Weisman. *Discrimination, Personality, and Achievement: A Survey of Northern Blacks.* New York: Seminar Press, 1972.

Creel, George. *How We Advertised America.* 1920. New York: Arno Press, 1972.

Cremin, Lawrence A. *The Transformation of the Schools: Progressivism in American Education, 1876–1957.* New York: Alfred A. Knopf, 1964.

Cruey, G. Wayne. "The Educational Program of the CCC: Its Provision for Leisure Time and Vocational Pursuits." Masters Thesis. Bowling Green State University, 1938.

Cuban, Larry. "Federal Vocational Education Legislation." In *Work, Youth, and Schooling: Historical Perspectives on Vocationalism in American Education,* edited by Harvey Kantor and David B. Tyack. Stanford, CA: Stanford University Press, 1982, 45–78.

Danoff, Malcom N. *The Evaluation of the ESEA Title VII Spanish/English Bilingual Education Program: Overview of the Findings.* (1978): fiche ERIC Document Number ED 162 524.

Danoff, M. N., and Coles G. J. "AIR Researchers Respond to Nickel's Criticism." *Phi Delta Kappan* 61. 4 (November 1976): 261–262.

Davis, C. O. "Training for Citizenship in the North Central Association of Secondary Schools." *Fourth Yearbook of the National Association of Secondary School Principals*. Menasha, WI: George Banta Publishing, 1920, 45–65.

Davis, Robert B. *The Changing Curriculum: Mathematics*. Washington, DC: Association for Supervision and Curriculum Development, 1967.

De Garmo, Charles. "Introductory Remarks." In *The First Yearbook of the Herbart Society,* edited by Charles McMurry. 1895. New York: Arno Press and *NY Times,* 1969, 3–26.

———. *Herbart and the Herbartians*. New York: Charles Scribner's Sons, 1896.

———. "Present Status of the Doctrine of Interest." In *The Second Yearbook of the National Herbart Society,* edited by Charles McMurry. 1896. New York: Arno Press and *NY Times,* 1969, 141–144.

Demott, Benjamin. "The Math Wars." In *New Curricula,* edited by Robert W. Heath. New York: Harper & Row, 1964, 54–67.

Dewey, John. *Child and Curriculum and School and Society*. 1900. Chicago: University of Chicago Press, 1956.

———. *Democracy and Education: An Introduction to the Philosophy of Education*. 1916. New York: Macmillan, 1966.

———. *Experience and Education*. 1938. New York: Collier Books, 1971.

———. "Interest in Relation to Training of the Will." In *The Second Supplement to the Herbart Yearbook for 1895,* edited by Charles McMurry. New York: Arno Press and *NY Times,* 1969, 5–34.

———. "Interpretation of the Culture-Epoch Theory." In *The Second Yearbook of the National Herbart Society,* edited by Charles McMurry. 1896. New York: Arno Press and *NY Times,* 1969, 89–95.

———. "Learning to Earn: The Place of Vocational Education in a Comprehensive Scheme of Public Education." In *John Dewey: The Middle Works, 1899–1924,* Vol. 10, edited by Jo Ann Boydston. Carbondale, IL: University of Illinois University Press, 1980, 144–150.

———. "Nationalizing Education." National Education Association. *Addresses and Proceedings*. Chicago: University of Chicago Press, 1916, 183–189.

———. *The School and Society and The Child and the Curriculum*. 1902 and 1915. Mineola, NY: Dover Publications, 2001.

———. "Some Dangers in the Present Movement for Industrial Education." In *John Dewey: The Middle Works, 1899–1924*. Vol. 7, edited by Jo Ann Boydston. Carbondale, IL: University of Illinois University Press, 1979, 98–103.

Diederich, Paul E. "The Eight-Year Study: Some Comments." *School and Society* 73 (1951): 41–42.

Dimond, Paul R. "The Constitutional Right to an Education." *Hastings Law Journal* 24 (1973): 1087–1127.

Dolan, Jay P. *The American Catholic Experience: A History from Colonial Times to the Present*. New York: Doubleday and Co., 1985.

Douglas, Paul Howard. *American Apprenticeship and Industrial Education*. 1921. New York: AMS Press, 1968.

Dow, Peter B. *Schoolhouse Politics: Lessons from the Sputnik Era*. Cambridge, MA: Harvard University Press, 1991.

Dreeben, Robert. "Schooling and Authority: Comments on the Unstudied Curriculum." In *The Unstudied Curriculum: Its Impact on Children,* edited by Norman V. Overly. Washington, DC: Association of Supervision and Curriculum Development, 1970, 85–103.

Dunkel, Harold B. *Herbart and Education*. New York: Random House, 1969.

Editor. "Editor's page." *Social Studies* 27.8 (1936): 567.

Editorial. *Educational Review* 9 (1895): 417–423.

Educational Policies Commission (EPC). *Education for All American Youth*. Washington, DC: National Education Association, 1944.

———. *Education for All American Youth: A Further Look*. Washington, DC: National Education Association, 1952.

———. *What the Schools Should Teach in Wartime*. Washington, DC: National Education Association, 1943.

Eisenhower, Dwight D. "Radio and Television Address to the American People on Science and National Security." 7 November. *Public Papers of the Presidents of the United States*. Washington, DC: GPO, 1957, 789–799.

———. "Special Message to the Congress on Education." 27 January. *Public Papers of the Presidents of the United States*. Washington, DC: GPO, 1958, 127–131.

———. "Statement by the President Summarizing Facts in the Development of an Earth Satellite by the United States." 9 October. *Public Papers of the Presidents of the United States*. Washington, DC: GPO, 1957, 733–735.

Eliot, Charles W. "Assumptions of the Committee of Ten." *Educational Review* 30 (1905): 325–343.

———. "Industrial Education as an Essential Factor in Our National Prosperity." *Bulletin No. 5. Proceedings of First Annual Meeting*. New York: National Society for the Promotion of Industrial Education, April 1908, 9–14.

Engel, Michael. *The Struggle for the Control of Public Education: Market Ideology vs. Democratic Values*. Philadelphia: Temple University Press, 2000.

Ensign, Forest Chester. *Compulsory School Attendance and Child Labor*. 1921. New York: Arno Press, 1969.

Evenden, Edward S. *Teacher Education in a Democracy at War*. Washington, DC: American Council on Education, 1942.

Eyler, Janet, Valerie J. Cook, and Leslie E. Ward. "Resegregation: Segregation within Desegregated Schools." In *The Consequences of School Desegregation*, edited by Christine H. Rossell and Willis D. Hawley. Philadelphia: Temple University Press, 1983, 126–162.

Fife, Brain L. *Desegregation in American Schools: Comparative Strategies*. New York: Praeger, 1992.

Finn, Chester E., Jr. "Whose Afraid of the Big Bad Test." In *Debating the Future of American Education: Do We Need National Standards and Assessments?* edited by Diane Ravitch. Washington, DC: Brookings Institution, 1995.

Finney, Ross L. "The Sociological Principle Determining the Elementary Curriculum." *School and Society* 7.169 (23 March 1918): 338–349.

———. "Tentative Report of the Committee of the American Sociological Society on the Teaching of Sociology in the Grade and High Schools of America." *The School Review* (April 1920): 255–262.

Forrest, Suzanne. *The Preservation of the Village: New Mexico's Hispanics and the New Deal*. 1989. Albuquerque: University of New Mexico Press, 1998.

Freire, Paulo. *Pedagogy of the Oppressed*. Translated by Myra Bergman Ramos. New York: Herder and Herder, 1970.

Garcia, Ignacio. *United We Win*. Tuscon: University of Arizona Press, 1989.

Garn, Gregg A., and Robert T. Stout. "Closing Charters: How a Good Theory Failed in Practice." In *School Choice in the Real World: Lessons from Arizona Charter Schools*, edited by Robert Maranto et al. Boulder, CO: Westview Press, 2001, 142–158.

Getz, Lynne Marie. *Schools of Their Own: The Education of Hispanos in New Mexico, 1850–1940*. Albuquerque: University of New Mexico Press, 1997.

Gilligan, Carol. *In a Different Voice: Psychological Theory and Women's Development*. Cambridge, MA: Harvard University Press, 1982.

Ginsburg, Herbert. *The Myth of the Deprived Child: Poor Children's Intellect and Education*. Englewood Cliffs, NJ: Prentice-Hall, 1972.

Giroux, Henry, and Anthony Penna. "Social Education in the Classroom: The Dynamics of the Hidden Curriculum." In *The Hidden Curriculum and Moral Education: Deception or Discovery?* edited by Henry Giroux and David Purpel. Berkeley, CA: McCutchan Publishing, 1983, 100–121.

Glass, Bentley. "Report on AIBS Biological Sciences Curriculum Study." In *New Curricula*, edited by Robert W. Heath. New York: Harper & Row, 1964, 94–119.

———. *Science and Liberal Education*. Baton Rouge: Louisiana State University Press, 1959.

Good, Thomas L., and Jennifer S. Braden. *The Great School Debate: Choice, Vouchers, and Charters*. Mahwah, NJ: Lawrence Erlbaum, 2000.

Grant, Gerald. *The World We Created at Hamilton High*. Cambridge, MA: Harvard University Press, 1988.

Greene, Maxine. *The Dialectic of Freedom*. New York: Teachers College Press, 1988.

———. "Introduction." In *The Hidden Curriculum and Moral Education: Deception or Discovery?* edited by Henry Giroux and David Purpel. Berkeley, CA: McCutchan Publishing, 1983, 1–5.

Greer, Edith S., and Richard M. Harbeck. *What High School Pupils Study: A National Survey of the Scholastic Performance of Pupils of Various Abilities*. Bulletin 10. U.S. Office of Education. Washington, DC: GPO, 1962.

Grobman, Arnold B. *The Changing Classroom: The Role of the Biological Sciences Curriculum Study*. New York: Doubleday & Co., 1969.

Haggerty, M. E. "The Low Visibility of Educational Issues." *School and Society* 41 (1935): 273–283.

Hakuta, Kenji. *Mirror of Language: The Debate on Bilingualism*. New York: Basic Books, 1986.

Hall, G. Stanley. *Adolescence, Its Psychology and Its relations to Physiology, Anthropology, Sociology, Sex, Crime, Religion and Education*. Vol. II. New York, 1908.

———. *Educational Problems*. New York: Appleton and Co., 1911.

Hanus, Paul H. *A Modern School*. New York: Macmillan, 1913.

Harby, Samuel F. *A Study of Education in the Civilian Conservation Corps Camps of the Second Camp Area*. Ann Arbor, MI: Edwards Brothers, 1938.

Harmer, David. *School Choice: Why You Need It—How to Get It*. Washington, DC: Cato Institute, 1994.

Harrington, Michael. *The Other America: Poverty in the United States*. New York: Macmillan, 1962.

Harris, William Torrey. "Five Co-ordinate Groups of Studies." *Educational Review* 11 (1896): 323–334.

———. "Herbart's Doctrine of Interest." *Educational Review* 10 (1895): 71–80.

———. "The Intellectual Value of Tool-Work." *N.E.A. Journal of Proceedings and Addresses*. Topeka, KS: Kansas Publishing, 1889, 92–98.

———. "Professor John Dewey's Doctrine of Interest as Related to Will." *Educational Review* 11 (1896): 486–493.

———. *Psychologic Foundations of Education: An*

Attempt to Show the Genesis of the Higher Faculties of the Mind. New York: Appleton, 1899.

Hartmann, Edward George. *The Movement to Americanize the Immigrant.* New York: Columbia University Press, 1948.

Harvard University. Committee on the Objectives of a General Education in a Free Society. *General Education in a Free Society.* Cambridge, MA: Harvard University Press, 1945.

Hassel, Bryan C. "Charter Schools: A National Innovation, an Arizona Revolution." In *School Choice in the Real World: Lessons from Arizona Charter Schools,* edited by Robert Maranto et al. Boulder, CO: Westview Press, 2001, 39–57.

Hatfield, W. Wilbur. *An Experience Curriculum in English.* New York: Appleton-Century-Croft, 1935.

Hawkins, Layton S., Charles A. Prosser, and John C. Wright. *Development of Vocational Education.* Chicago: American Technical Society, 1951.

Hayden, Robert W. *A History of the New Math Movement in the United States.* Diss. D Iowa State University, 1981, Ann Arbor: UMI. 8209127.

Hershberg, James G. *James B. Conant: Harvard to Hiroshima and the Making of the Nuclear Age.* New York: Alfred Knopf, 1993.

Hess, Frederick, et al. "How Arizona Teachers View School Reform." In *School Choice in the Real World: Lessons from Arizona Charter Schools,* edited by Robert Maranto et al. Boulder, CO: Westview Press, 2001, 173–188.

Higham, John. *Strangers in the Land: Patterns of American Nativism, 1860–1925.* New Brunswick, NJ: Rutgers University Press, 1955.

Hill, Edwin G. *In the Spirit of the Mountain.* Pullman, WA: Washington State University Press, 1990.

Hogan, David John. *Class and Reform: School and Society in Chicago, 1880–1930.* Philadelphia: University of Pennsylvania Press, 1985.

hooks, bell. *Teaching to Transgress: Education as the Practice of Freedom.* New York: Routledge, 1994.

Horn, Ernest. *Distribution of Opportunity for Participation among the Various Pupils in Classroom Recitations.* New York: Teachers College, Columbia University, 1914.

Hosic, James F., and Sara E. Chase. *Brief Guide to the Project Method.* New York: World Book Co., 1926.

Hotchkiss, E. A. *The Project Method in Classroom Work.* Boston: Ginn and Co., 1924.

Humphrey, Hubert H. *War on Poverty.* New York: McGraw-Hill, 1964.

Hutson, Percival W. "Collectivism and Democracy." *School and Society* 40 (1934): 354–355.

International Reading Association. "High Stakes Assessments in Reading: A Position Statement" *ERIC* Microfiche ED435084, 1999.

Jackson, Philip W. "The Consequences of Schooling." In *The Unstudied Curriculum: Its Impact on Children,* edited by Norman V. Overly. Washington, DC: Association of Supervision and Curriculum Development, 1970, 1–15.

Jencks, Christopher, et al. *Inequality: A Reassessment of the Effect of Family and Schooling in America.* New York: Harper & Row, 1972.

Jennings, John F. *Why National Standards and Tests? Politics and the Quest for Better Schools.* Thousand Oaks, CA: Sage Publications, 1998.

Johnson, Helmer G. "Some Comments on the Eight-Year Study." *School and Society* 72 (1950): 337–339.

———. "Here We Go Again." *School and Society* 74 (1951): 41–43.

Johnson, Henry. "Report of the Committee on History Teaching in the Schools." *Annual Report of the American Historical Association for the Year 1921.* Washington, DC: GPO, 1926, 73–74.

Jorgenson, Lloyd P. "The Oregon School Law of 1922: Passage and Sequel." In *Enlightening the Next Generation: Catholics and Their Schools, 1830–1980,* edited by F. Michael Perko, S. J. New York: Garland Publishing, 1988, 26–37.

Kallen, Horace M. *Culture and Democracy in the United States.* 1924. New York: Arno Press, 1970.

Kandel, Isaac Leon. *The Impact of the War upon American Education.* Chapel Hill, NC: University of North Carolina Press, 1948.

Kane, Pearl Rock, and Christopher J. Lauricella. "Assessing the Growth and Potential of Charter Schools." In *Privatizing Education: Can the Marketplace Deliver Choice, Efficiency, Equity, and Social Cohesion,* edited by Henry M. Levin. Boulder, CO: Westview Press, 2001, 203–233.

Kantor, Harvey A. *Learning to Earn: School, Work, and Vocational Reform in California, 1880–1930.* Madison, WI: University of Wisconsin Press, 1988.

Katz, Michael. *A History of Compulsory Education Laws.* Bloomington, IN: Phi Delta Kappa, 1976.

Keller, Franklin J. *The Comprehensive High School.* Westport CT: Greenwood Press, 1955.

———. *The Double-Purpose High School: Closing the Gap between Vocational and Academic Preparation.* New York: Harper & Brothers, 1953.

Kellor, Frances A. *Straight America: A Call to National Service.* New York: Macmillan, 1916.

Keyserling, Leon H. *Progress or Poverty: The U.S. at the Crossroads.* Washington, DC: Conference on Economic Progress, 1964.

Kilpatrick, William Heard. *Foundations of Method: Informal Talks on Teaching.* New York: Macmillan, 1925.

———. *The Project Method: The Use of the Purposeful Act in the Educative Process.* 1918. New York: Teachers College, Columbia University, 1922.

King, Martin Luther, Jr. *Why We Can't Wait*. New York: Signet Books, 1963.

Kirp, David L. *Just Schools: The Idea of Racial Equality in American Education*. Berkeley: University of California Press, 1982.

Kliebard, Herbert. *The Struggle for the American Curriculum, 1893–1958,* 2nd ed. New York: Routledge, 1995.

Kline, Morris. *Why Johnny Can't Add: The Failure of New Math*. New York: St. Martins Press, 1973.

Kluger, Richard. *Simple Justice: The History of Brown v. Board of Education and Black America's Struggle for Equality*. New York: Vintage Books, 1975.

Kohl, Herbert. *36 Children*. Illus. by Robert George Jackson, III. New York: New American Library, 1967.

Kohlberg, Lawrence. "The Moral Atmosphere of the School." In *The Unstudied Curriculum: Its Impact on Children,* edited by Norman V. Overly. Washington, DC: Association of Supervision and Curriculum Development, 1970, 104–127.

Kozol, Jonathon. *Free Schools*. Boston: Houghton Mifflin Co., 1972.

Krug, Edward A. *The Shaping of the American High School, 1880–1920*. Vol. I. Madison, WI: University of Wisconsin Press, 1969.

———. *The Shaping of the American High School, 1920–1941*. Vol. II. Madison, WI: University of Wisconsin Press, 1972.

Lander, Louise, ed. *War on Poverty*. New York: Facts on File, 1967.

Latimer, John Francis. *What's Happened to Our High Schools?* Washington, DC: Public Affairs Press, 1958.

Lau et al. v Nichols et al. 483 F. 2d 791.1974.

Lazerson, Marvin. *Origins of the Urban School: Public Education in Massachusetts, 1870–1915*. Cambridge: Harvard University Press, 1971.

Leal, David L. "Congress and Charter Schools." In *School Choice in the Real World: Lessons from Arizona Charter Schools,* edited by Robert Maranto et al. Boulder, CO: Westview Press, 2001, 58–67.

Leiderman, Gloria F., William Chinn, and Mervyn E. Dunkley. *The Special Curriculum Project: Pilot Program on Mathematics Learning of Culturally Disadvantaged Primary School Children*. No. 2. California: Leland Stanford Junior University, 1966.

Leuchtenburg, William E. *The Perils of Prosperity, 1914–1932*. Chicago: University of Chicago Press, 1958.

Levine, Erwin L., and Elizabeth M. Wexler. *PL 94–142: An Act of Congress*. New York: Macmillan, 1981.

Lewis Mumford Center. *Choosing Segregation: Racial Imbalance in American Public Schools, 1999–2000*. 2001. http://www.albany.edu/mumford/census.

Lippman, Leopold, and I. Ignacy Goldberg. *Right to Education: Anatomy of the Pennsylvania Case and Its Implications for Exceptional Children*. New York: Teachers College Press, 1973.

Lissak, Rivka Shpak. *Pluralism and Progressives: Hull House and the New Immigrants, 1890–1919*. Chicago: University of Chicago Press, 1989.

Mahard, Rita E., and Robert L. Crain. "Research on Minority Achievement in Desegregated Schools." In *The Consequences of School Desegregation,* edited by Christine H. Rossell and Willis D. Hawley. Philadelphia: Temple University Press, 1983, 103–125.

Mahoney, John J. *Americanization in the United States*. Bulletin 31. U.S. Department of the Interior. Washington, DC: GPO, 1923.

Maranto, Robert, et al. "Real World School Choice: Arizona Charter Schools." In *School Choice in the Real World: Lessons from Arizona Charter Schools,* edited by Robert Maranto et al. Boulder, CO: Westview Press, 2001, 1–18.

Maranto, Robert, and April Gresham. "The Wild West of Education Reform: Arizona Charter Schools." In *School Choice in the Real World: Lessons from Arizona Charter Schools,* edited by Robert Maranto et al. Boulder, CO: Westview Press, 2001, 99–114.

Maritain, Jacques. *Education at the Crossroads*. New Haven: Yale University Press, 1943.

Marsh, Paul E., and Ross A. Gortner. *Federal Aid to Science Education: Two Programs*. Syracuse, NY: Syracuse University Press, 1963.

Marshall, Leon C., and Rachel Marshall Goetz. *Curriculum-Making in the Social Studies*. New York: Charles Scribner's Sons, 1936.

Martens, Elise H. *The Needs of Exceptional Children*. Washington, DC: GPO, 1944.

Massachusetts Commission on Industrial and Technical Education. *Report*. Boston: Wright & Potter Printing, 1906.

McClymer, John F. "The Federal Government and the Americanization Movement, 1915–1924." *Prologue* 10.1 (Spring 1978): 23–42.

McLaren, Peter. *Life in Schools: An Introduction to Critical Pedagogy in the Foundations of Education*. New York: Longman, 1989.

McMurry, Charles A. *Elements of General Method*. 1903. New York: Macmillan, 1910.

———. "Interest: Some Objections to It." *Educational Review* 11 (1896): 146–156.

———. *Teaching by Projects: A Basis for Purposeful Study*. New York: Macmillan, 1920.

Medina, Noe, and D. Monty Neill. *Fallout from the Testing Explosion: How 100 Million Standardized Exams Undermine Equity and Excellence in America's Public Schools*. Cambridge, MA: National Center for Fair and Open Testing, 1990.

Melby, Edward O. "A Critique." In *Child Development and Curriculum,* edited by Guy Montrose Whipple. Bloomington, IL: Public School Publishing Company, 1939, 439–442.

Miami Valley Regional Center for Handicapped Children. *Working Together to Develop the IEP*. Dayton, OH: Author, 1981.

Michael, Deanna. "National Defense Education Act." In *Historical Dictionary of American Education,* edited by Richard J. Altenbaugh. Westport, CT: Greenwood Press, 1999, 249–250.

Miller, Frank C. "Introduction." In *The Problem of Indian Administration,* Brookings Institution. 1928. New York: Johnson Reprint Corp., 1971, v–xvi.

Mills v Board of Education of the District of Columbia. 348 F. Supp. 866.1972.

Mock, James R., and Cedric Larson. *Words That Won the War*. Princeton, NJ: Princeton University Press, 1939.

Moran, Rachel F. "The Politics of Discretion: Federal Intervention in Bilingual Education." *California Law Review*. 1988. Lexis-Nexis Academic Universe, 2002.

Nash, Gary, Charlotte Crabtree, and Ross E. Dunn. *History on Trial: Culture Wars and the Teaching of the Past*. New York: Alfred A. Knopf, 1998.

National Advisory Council on the Education of Disadvantaged Children. *America's Educationally Neglected: A Progress Report on Compensatory Education*. Washington, DC: GPO, 1966.

National Commission on Excellence in Education (NCEE). *A Nation at Risk: The Imperative for Educational Reform*. Washington, DC: GPO, 1983.

National Education Association (NEA). *Charter and Nontraditional Public School Options*. NEA 2001–2002 Resolutions. August 2002. http://www.nea.org/resolutions/01/01a-30.html.

———. Commission on the Reorganization of Secondary Education. *Cardinal Principles of Secondary Education*. Bulletin No. 35. Department of the Interior. Washington, DC: GPO, 1918.

———. Commission on the Reorganization of Secondary Education. *Vocational Guidance in Secondary Education*. Bulletin No. 19. Department of the Interior. Washington, DC: GPO, 1918.

———. Committee on Articulation of High School and College. *College Entrance Requirements*. Bulletin No. 7. Department of the Interior. Washington, DC: GPO, 1913.

———. Committee on the Social Studies. *The Social Studies in Secondary Education*. Bulletin No. 28. Department of the Interior. Washington, DC: GPO, 1916.

———. *The Invisible Minority*. Washington, DC: Author, 1966.

———. *Preliminary Statements by the Chairmen of the Committees of the Commission of the National Education Association on the Reorganization of Secondary Education*. Bulletin No. 41. Department of the Interior. Washington, DC: GPO, 1913.

———. Report of a Committee on a Course of Study from Primary School to University, 1876. In George Willis, et al., eds. *The American Curriculum: A Documentary History*. Westport, CT: Praeger, 1994, 73–83.

———. *Report of the Committee of Fifteen on Elementary Education with the Reports of the Subcommittees*. New York: American Book Company, 1895.

———. *Report of the Committee of Ten on Secondary School Studies with the Reports of the Conferences Arranged by the Committee*. New York: American Book Company, 1894.

———. *Wartime Handbook for Education*. Washington, DC: National Education Association, 1943.

National Institute of Education and the War. *Handbook on Education and The War*. Washington, DC: GPO, 1943.

National Society for the Study of Education. *Philosophies of Education* 41st, pt 1. Bloomington, IN: Public School Publishing Co., 1942.

———. *Philosophical Redirection of Educational Research* 71st, pt 1. Chicago: University of Chicago Press, 1972.

———. *Philosophy and Education* 80th, pt 1. Chicago: University of Chicago Press, 1981.

Nickel, K. N. "Experimentation, Extraopolation, Exaggeration: Thy Name Is Research." *Phi Delta Kappan* 61. 4 (November 1976): 260–261.

Noddings, Nel. *Caring: A Feminine Approach to Ethics and Moral Education*. Berkeley, CA: University of California Press, 1984.

Novick, Peter. *That Noble Dream: The Objectivity Question and the American Historical Profession*. Cambridge, U.K.: Cambridge University Press, 1988.

O'Brien, Marjorie A. "An Evaluation of the Civilian Conservation Corps as an Educational Institution." Masters Thesis. Ohio University, 1970.

Office of Education. *Biennial Survey of Education, 1926–1928*. Bulletin No. 16. Department of the Interior. Washington, DC: GPO, 1930.

Ogbu, John U. *The Next Generation: An Ethnography of Education in an Urban Neighborhood*. New York: Academic Press, 1974.

Oregon School Cases: Complete Record. Baltimore, MD: Belvedere Press, 1925.

Orfield, Gary. "The 1964 Civil Rights Act and American Education." In *Legacies of the 1964 Civil Rights Act,* edited by Bernard Grofman. Charlottesville, VA: University Press of Virginia, 2000, 89–128.

———. *The Reconstruction of Southern Education: The Schools and the 1964 U.S. Civil Rights Act*. New York: Wiley-Interscience, 1969.

Orfield, Gary, et al. *Dismantling Desegregation: The Quiet Reversal of Brown v. Board of Education*. New York: The Free Press, 1996.

Oxley, Howard W. *CCC Camp Education: Guidance and*

Recreational Phases. Bulletin No. 38. Department of the Interior. Washington, DC: GPO, 1938.

Parker, Francis W. "Dissent to Report of the Committee of Fifteen." In *The American Curriculum: A Documentary History,* edited by George Willis et al. Westport, CT: Praeger, 1994, 105–106.

———. *Talks on Pedagogics.* 1894. New York: Arno Press and *NY Times,* 1969.

Parker, J. Cecil, Wilmer Menge, and Theodore D. Rice. *The First Five Years of the Michigan Study of the Secondary School Curriculum, 1937–1942.* Lansing, MI: State Board of Education, 1942.

Parman, Donald L. *The Navajos and the New Deal.* New Haven, CT: Yale University Press, 1976.

Perkinson, Henry J. *The Imperfect Panacea: American Faith in Education.* 3rd ed. New York: McGraw-Hill, 1991.

Pettigrew, Thomas, and Robert Green. "School Desegregation in Large Cities." *Harvard Educational Review* 1 (1976): 1–53.

Pettigrew, Thomas, et al. "Busing: A Review of the Evidence." *Public Interest* 30 (Winter 1973): 88–118.

Phelps-Stokes Fund. *The Navajo Indian Problem.* New York: Phelps-Stokes Fund, 1939.

Philosophies and Procedures of SMSG Writing Teams. Stanford, CA: School Mathematics Study Group, 1965.

Philp, Kenneth R. *John Collier's Crusade for Indian Reform, 1920–1954.* Tucson, AZ: University of Arizona Press, 1977.

Pius XI. *Christian Education of Youth.* Washington, DC: National Catholic Welfare Conference, 1936.

Popham, W. James. *The Truth about Testing: An Educator's Call to Action.* Alexandria, VA: Association for Curriculum and Development, 2001.

Pratt, Richard. *Pluralism in Education.* Springfield, IL: Charles C. Thomas, 1979.

President's Panel on Mental Retardation. *A Proposed Program for National Action to Combat Mental Retardation.* Washington, DC: GPO, 1962.

Ratner, Gershon M. "A New Legal Duty for Urban Public Schools: Effective Education in Basic Skills." In *Child, Parent, and State: Law and Policy Reader,* edited by S. Randall Humm et al. Philadelphia: Temple University Press, 1994, 311–350.

Ravitch, Diane. "From History to Social Studies." In *Challenges to the Humanities,* edited by Chester E. Finn, Jr., Diane Ravitch, and P. Holley Roberts. New York: Holmes and Meier, 1985.

———. *Left Back: A Century of Battles over School Reform.* New York: Touchstone Books, 2000.

Redefer, Frederick L. "The Eight-Year Study . . . After Eight Years." *Progressive Education* 28.2 (1950): 33–36.

Reese, William J. "The Philosopher-King of St. Louis." In *Curriculum and Consequence: Hebert M. Kliebard and the Promise of Schooling,* edited by Barry M. Franklin. New York: Teachers College, 2000.

Regents' Inquiry. *Education for American Life: A New Program for the State of New York.* New York: McGraw-Hill Book Co., 1938.

Reports. "The Final Report of the Commission on the Social Studies." *School and Society* 39 (1934): 680–683.

Reynolds, Maynard C., and Jack W. Birch. *Teaching Exceptional Children in All America's Schools: A First Course for Teachers and Principals.* Reston, VA: Council for Exceptional Children, 1977.

Rice, Theodore D., and Roland C. Faunce. *The Michigan Secondary Study.* Lansing, MI: State Board of Education, 1945.

Rickover, H. G. *Education and Freedom.* New York: E.P. Dutton & Co., 1959.

Riessman, Frank. *The Culturally Deprived Child.* New York: Harper, 1962.

Rigdon, Susan. M. *The Culture Façade: Art, Science, and Politics in the Work of Oscar Lewis.* Urbana, IL: University of Illinois Press, 1988.

Riis, Jacob A. *The Children of the Poor.* 1892. New York: Arno Press, 1971.

Robinson, Glen E., and David P. Brandon. *NAEP Test Scores: Should They Be Used to Compare and Rank State Educational Quality?* Arlington, VA: Educational Research Service, 1994.

Robinson, James Harvey. *The New History: Essays Illustrating the Modern Historical Outlook.* 1912. Springfield, MA: Walden Press, 1958.

Roberts, Peter. *Education, Literacy, and Humanization: Exploring the work of Paulo Freire.* Westport, CT: Bergin & Garvey, 2000.

Rofes, Eric. "Foreword." In *School Experiences of Gay and Lesbian Youth: The Invisible Minority,* edited by Mary B. Harris. New York: Haworth Press, 1997, xiii–xviii.

———. "Opening up the Classroom Closet: Responding to the Needs of Gay and Lesbian Youth." *Harvard Educational Review* 59.4 (1989): 444–453.

———. "What Happens When the Kids Grow Up? The Long-Term Impact of an Openly Gay Teacher on Eight Students' Lives." In *Queering Elementary Education: Advancing the Dialogue about Sexualities and Schooling,* edited by William J. Letts IV and James T. Sears. New York: Rowman & Littlefield, 1999.

Ross, Dorothy. *G. Stanley Hall: The Psychologist as Prophet.* Chicago: University of Chicago Press, 1972.

Rossell, Christine H. *The Carrot or the Stick for School Desegregation Policy: Magnet Schools or Forced Busing.* Philadelphia: Temple University Press.

———. "School Desegregation and Community Change."

Law and Contemporary Problems 42.3 (Summer 1978): 131–183.

Rothstein, Richard, and Karen Hawley Miles. *Where's the Money Gone?* Washington, DC: Economic Policy Institute, 1995.

Rugg, Harold. *Changing Governments and Changing Cultures: The World's March toward Democracy.* New York: Ginn and Co., 1932.

———. "Do the Social Studies Prepare Pupils Adequately for Life Activities?" In *The Social Studies in the Elementary and Secondary School,* edited by Guy Montrose Whipple. The Twenty-Second Yearbook of the National Society for the Study of Education. Bloomington, IL: Public School Publishing Co., 1923, 1–27.

———. "Foreword." In *The Social Studies in the Elementary and Secondary School,* edited by Guy Montrose Whipple. The Twenty-Second Yearbook of the National Society for the Study of Education. Bloomington, IL: Public School Publishing Co., 1923, vii–viii.

———. *That Men May Understand.* New York: Doubleday, Doran, Co., 1941.

Ruskola, Teemu. "Minor Disregard: The Legal Construction of the Fantasy that Gay and Lesbian Youth Do Not Exist." *Yale Journal of Law and Feminism* (1986). Lexis-Nexis Academic Universe.

Russell, John Dale. *Vocational Education.* Washington, DC: GPO, 1938.

Salomone, Rosemary C. *Equal Education Under the Law: Legal Rights and Federal Policy.* New York: St. Martins Press, 1986.

Sanders, James W. *The Education of an Urban Minority.* New York: Oxford University Press, 1977.

Schaffter, Dorothy. *The National Science Foundation.* New York: Frederick A. Praeger, 1969.

Scheffler, Israel. *The Language of Education.* Springfield, IL: Charles C. Thomas Publisher, 1960.

Schrag, Peter, and Diane Divoky. *The Myth of the Hyperactive Child.* New York: Pantheon Books, 1975.

Schwab, Joseph J. "Structure of the Disciplines: Meanings and Significances." In *The Structure of Knowledge and the Curriculum,* edited by G. W. Ford and Lawrence Pugno. Chicago: Rand McNally & Co., 1964, 6–30.

Secretary's Committee on Mental Retardation. *Response to the Recommendations of the President's Panel on Mental Retardation.* Washington, DC: U.S. Department on Health, Education, and Welfare, 1963.

Sevilla, Jennifer. "Bilingual Education: The Last Twenty-Five Years." In *Helping At-Risk Students: What Are Educational and Financial Costs,* edited by Patricia Anthony and Stephen L. Jacobson. Newbury Park, CA: Corwin Press, 1992, 38–65.

Shanabruch, Charles. *Chicago's Catholics: The Evolution of an American Identity.* Notre Dame, IN: University of Notre Dame Press, 1981.

Shepard Lorrie A., and Katherine Cutts Dougherty. "Effects of High Stakes Testing on Instruction." *ERIC* Microfiche ED 348382, 1992.

Shor, Ira. "Educating the Educators." In *Freire for the Classroom: A Sourcebook for Liberatory Teaching,* edited by Ira Shor. Portsmouth, NH: Boynton/Cook Publishers, 1987, 7–32.

———. "Monday Morning Fever." In *Freire for the Classroom: A Sourcebook for Liberatory Teaching,* edited by Ira Shor. Portsmouth, NH: Boynton/Cook Publishers, 1987, 104–121.

Shorter, Edward. *The Kennedy Family and the Story of Mental Retardation.* Philadelphia: Temple University Press, 2000.

Shriver, Sargent. "The Origins of Head Start." In *Project Head Start,* edited by Edward Zigler and Jeanette Valentine. New York: Macmillan Publishing, 1979, 49–67.

Smith, Eugene P. "A Look at Mathematics Education Today." *The Mathematics Teacher* 66. 6 (1973): 565–570.

Smith, Eugene R., and Ralph W. Tyler. *Appraising and Recording Student Progress.* New York: Harper and Brothers, 1942.

Snedden, David. "History and Other Social Sciences in the Education of Youths Twelve to Eighteen Years of Age." *School and Society,* 5.115 (10 March 1917): 271–280.

———. "The Problem of Vocational Education." In *Vocational Education: Its Theory, Administration, and Practice,* edited by David Snedden. New York: Houghton Mifflin Co., 1910, 1–82.

———. *Vocational Education.* New York: Macmillan Co., 1920.

Spring, Joel. *The American School: 1642–2000.* 5th ed. Boston: McGraw Hill, 2001.

———. *The Sorting Machine: National Educational Policy Since 1945.* New York: David McKay Co., 1976.

———. *The Sorting Machine Revisited: National Educational Policy Since 1945.* Updated edition. New York: Longman, 1989.

Stein, Colman Brez, Jr. *Sink or Swim: The Politics of Bilingual Education.* New York: Praeger, 1986.

Stevenson, John Alford. *The Project Method of Teaching.* New York: Macmillan Co., 1921.

Stimson, R. W. *The Massachusetts Home-Project Plan of Vocational Agricultural Education.* Bulletin No. 8. U.S. Bureau of Education. Washington, DC: GPO, 1914.

Stout, Robert T., and Gregg A. Garn. "Nothing New: Curricula in Arizona." In *School Choice in the Real World: Lessons from Arizona Charter Schools,* edited by Robert Maranto et al. Boulder, CO: Westview Press, 2001, 159–172.

St. John, Nancy H. *School Desegregation Outcomes for Children*. New York: John Wiley and Sons, 1975.

Subcommittee on Education. *Notes and Working Papers the Concerning Administration of Programs: Title I of Public Law 89-10*. Washington, DC: GPO, 1967.

Sundquist, James. *Making Federalism Work*. Washington, DC: Brookings Institution, 1969.

Talbert, Ernest L. "Opportunities in School and Industry for Children in the Stockyards District." In *Readings in Vocational Guidance,* edited by Meyer Bloomfield. Boston: Ginn and Co., 1915, 396–453.

Tanner, Daniel, and Laurel Tanner. *Curriculum Development: Theory into Practice*. 3rd ed. Englewood Cliffs, NJ: Merrill, 1995.

———. *History of the School Curriculum*. New York: Macmillan, 1990.

Teachers of History at the Phillips Exeter Academy. "Further Dissent." *Social Education*. 1.4 (1937): 258.

tenBroek, Jacobus. *Equal Under the Law*. New York: Collier Books, 1965.

Tenenbaum, Samuel. *William Heard Kilpatrick: Trail Blazer in Education*. New York: Harper and Brothers, 1951.

Thayer, V. T., Caroline B. Zachry, and Ruth Kotinsky. *Reorganizing Secondary Education*. New York: D. Appleton-Century Co., 1939.

Thorndike, Edward L. *Education: A First Book*. 1912. New York: Macmillan Co., 1923.

Thorndike, E. L., and R. S. Woodworth. "The Influence of Improvement in One Mental Function Upon the Efficiency of Other Functions." *Psychological Review* III (1901): 247–261.

Toch, Thomas. *In the Name of Excellence: The Struggle to Reform the Nation's Schools, Why It's Failing, What Should Be Done*. New York: Oxford University Press, 1991.

Troen, Selwyn K. *The Public and the Schools*. Columbia, MO: University of Missouri Press, 1975.

Turnbull, H. Rutherford. "Accountability: An Overview of the Impact of Litigation on Professionals." In *Public Policy and the Education of Exceptional Children,* edited by Frederick J. Weintraub et al. Reston, VA: Council for Exceptional Children, 1976, 362–367.

Tyack, David B. *The One Best System*. Cambridge, MA: Harvard University Press, 1974.

Tyler, Ralph W. *Basic Principles of Curriculum and Instruction*. 1949. Chicago: University of Chicago Press, 1969.

———. "The Tyler Rationale Reconsidered." In *The American Curriculum,* edited by George Willis et al. Westport, CN: Praeger, 1994, 393–400.

Urban, Wayne, and Jennings L. Wagoner. *American Education: A History*. 2nd ed. Boston: McGraw Hill, 1958.

U.S. Commission on Civil Rights. *A Better Chance to Learn: Bilingual Bicultural Education*. N.P.: Clearinghouse Publication, 1975.

———. *Fulfilling the Letter and the Spirit of the Law: Desegregation of the Nation's Public Schools*. Washington, DC: GPO, 1976.

———. *Racial Isolation in the Public Schools*. Vol. I. Washington, DC: GPO, 1967.

———. *Statement on Metropolitan School Desegregation*. Washington, DC: GPO, 1977.

United States Congress. House. Science Policy Research Division. Subcommittee on Science, Research, and Development. *The National Science Foundation: A General Review of Its First 15 Years*. 89th Congress. 1st sess. Washington, DC: GPO, 1965.

———. Cong. Senate. Committee on Labor and Public Welfare. *Hearings*. 85th Congress. 2nd sess. Washington, DC: GPO, January–March 1958.

U.S. Department of Education. *The Nation Responds: Recent Efforts to Improve Education*. Washington, DC: GPO, 1984.

———. *What Works: Research about Teaching and Learning*. Washington, DC: GPO, 1986.

U.S. Department of Health, Education, and Welfare. *Report on the National Defense Education Act: Fiscal Year Ending June 30, 1960*. Washington, DC: GPO, 1961.

U.S. Office of Education. *Life Adjustment Education for Every Youth*. Bulletin 22. Washington, DC: GPO, 1951.

Valentine, Charles A. *Culture and Poverty: Critique and Counter-Proposals*. Chicago: University of Chicago Press, 1968.

Vanoured, Gregg, et al. "Charter Schools as Seen by Students, Teachers, and Parents." In *Learning from School Choice,* edited by Paul Peterson and Bryan C. Hassel. Washington, DC: Brookings Institution Press, 1998, 187–212.

Vinyard, JoEllen McNergney. *For Faith and Fortune: The Education of Catholic Immigrants in Detroit, 1805–1925*. Urbana, IL: University of Illinois Press, 1998.

Wakeham, G. "Education for College or for Life? *School and Society* 54 (1941): 12.

Walker, Lawrence J. "Sex Differences in the Development of Moral Reasoning." *Child Development* 55 (1984): 677–699.

Wallerstein, Nina. "Problem-Posing Education: Freire's Method for Transformation." In *Freire for the Classroom: A Sourcebook for Liberatory Teaching,* edited by Ira Shor. Portsmouth, NH: Boynton/Cook Publishers, 1987, 33–44.

Watras, Joseph. *Politics, Race, and Schools: Racial Integration, 1954–1994*. New York: Garland Publishing, 1997.

Weckstein, Paul. "New Educational Standards and the Right to Quality Education." In *Child, Parent, and*

State: Law and Policy Reader, edited by S. Randall Humm et al. Philadelphia: Temple University Press, 1994, 351–363.

Weiler, Kathleen. "Freire and a Feminist Pedagogy of Difference." *Harvard Educational Review* 61. 4 (1991): 449–474.

Weinberg, Meyer. *Minority Students: A Research Appraisal.* National Institute of Education. Washington, DC: GPO, 1977.

Wells, Amy Stuart. "African-American Students' View of School Choice." In *Who Chooses? Who Loses? Culture, Institutions and the Unequal Effects of School Choice,* edited by Bruce Fuller and Richard F. Elmore with Gary Orfield. New York: Teachers College Press, 1996, 25–49.

Wells, Amy Stuart, and Robert L. Crain. "Do Parents Choose School Quality or School Status? A Sociological Theory of the Free Market Education." In *The Choice Controversy,* edited by Peter W. Cookson, Jr. Newbury Park: CA: Corwin Press, 1992, 65–83.

Wells, Amy Stuart, and Janelle Scott. "Privatization and Charter School Reform." In *Privatizing Education: Can the Marketplace Deliver Choice, Efficiency, Equity, and Social Cohesion?* edited by Henry M. Levin. Boulder, CO: Westview Press, 234–262.

Whipple, Guy Montrose. "Reviews: The Educative Process." *Educational Review* 30 (November 1905): 418–421.

Whyte, William. *The Organization Man.* New York: Doubleday and Co., 1956.

Wilkinson, J. N. "Report of a Discussion of Herbartian Principles for Secondary Schools." *The First Yearbook of the Herbart Society.* 1895. New York: Arno Press, 1969, 105–115.

Willis, George, et al. *The American Curriculum: A Documentary History.* Westport, CT: Praeger, 1994.

Wingo, G. Max. *Philosophies of Education: An Introduction.* Lexington, MA: D.C. Heath and Co., 1974.

Wirth, Arthur G. *John Dewey as Educator, 1894–1904.* New York: Wiley, 1966.

Wittke, Carl. *German-Americans and the World War.* Columbus, OH: Ohio State Archeological and Historical Society, 1936.

Woods, Robert A. *The City Wilderness: A Settlement Study.* 1898. New York: Arno Press, 1970.

Woodward, Calvin M. *The Manual Training School.* 1887. New York: Arno Press, 1969.

———. "The Results of the St. Louis Manual Training School." *N.E.A. Journal of Proceedings and Addresses.* Topeka, KS: Kansas Publishing, 1889, 73–91.

Woolley, Helen Thompson. "Charting Childhood in Cincinnati." In *Readings in Vocational Guidance,* edited by Meyer Bloomfield. Boston: Ginn and Co., 1915, 220–233.

Wooten, William. *SMSG: The Making of a Curriculum.* New Haven, CT: Yale University Press, 1965.

Wraga, William G. *Democracy's High School: The Comprehensive High School and Educational Reform in the United States.* Lanham, MD: University Press of America, 1994.

———. "A Progressive Legacy Squandered: The Cardinal Principles Report Reconsidered." *History of Education Quarterly* 41 (2001): 494–519.

Zelman v Simmons-Harris, US, 122 S.Ct.2460, 153 L. Ed. 2nd 604, 2002.

Zettel, Jeffrey, and Joseph Ballard. "The Education for All Handicapped Children Act of 1975: Its History, Origins, and Concepts." In *Special Education in America: Its Legal and Governmental Foundations,* edited by Joseph Ballard, Bruce A. Ramirez, and Frederick J. Weintraub. Reston, VA: Council for Exceptional Children, 1982, 12–22.

INDEX